Transactions
of the
Royal
Historical
Society

SIXTH SERIES

V

Published by the Press Syndicate of the University of Cambridge
The Pitt Building, Trumpington Street, Cambridge CB2 IRP
40 West 20th Street, New York, NY 10011 –4211, USA
10 Stamford Road, Oakleigh, Melbourne 3166, Australia

First published 1995

A catalogue record for this book is available from the British Library

Library of Congress cataloguing in publication data applied for

ISBN 0 521 55200 1 hardback

SUBSCRIPTIONS. The serial publications of the Royal Historical Society, *Royal Historical Society Transactions* (ISSN 0080-4401), Camden Fifth Series (ISSN 0960-1163) volumes and volumes of the Guides and Handbooks (ISSN 0080-4398) may be purchased together on annual subscription. The 1995 subscription price (which includes postage but not VAT) is £35 (US$56 in the USA, Canada and Mexico) and includes Camden Fifth Series, volumes 5 and 6 (published in July and December) and Transactions Sixth Series, volume 5 (published in December). There is no volume in the Guides and Handbooks series in 1995. Japanese prices (including ASP delivery) are available from Kinokuniya Company Ltd, P.O. Box 55, Chitose, Tokyo 156, Japan. EU subscribers (outside the UK) who are not registered for VAT should add VAT at their country's rate. VAT registered subscribers should provide their VAT registration number.

Subscription orders, which must be accompanied by payment, may be sent to a bookseller, subscription agent or direct to the publisher: Cambridge University Press, The Edinburgh Building, Shaftesbury Road, Cambridge CB2 2RU, UK; or in the USA, Canada and Mexico: Cambridge University Press, 40 West 20th Street, New York, NY 10011-4211, USA. Copies of the publications for subscribers in the USA, Canada and Mexico are sent by air to New York to arrive with minimum delay.

SINGLE VOLUMES AND BACK VOLUMES. A list of Royal Historical Society volumes available from Cambridge University Press may be obtained from the Humanities Marketing Department at the address above.

Printed and bound in Great Britain by Butler & Tanner Ltd, Frome and London

CONTENTS

PAGE

Presidential Address: The Peoples of Britain and Ireland, 1100–1400: II Names, Boundaries and Regnal Solidarities
R. R. Davies   I

'His Special Friend'? The Settlement of Disputes and Political Power in the Kingdom of the French (tenth to mid-twelfth century)
Jane Martindale   21

The Structures of Politics in Early Tudor England
Steven Gunn   59

Liberalism and the Establishment of Collective Security in British Foreign Policy (*The Alexander Prize Essay*)
Joseph Charles Heim   91

Empire and Opportunity in Britain, 1763–1783 (*The Prothero Lecture*)
P. J. Marshall   111

FROM KNIGHTHOOD TO COUNTRY GENTRY, 1050–1400?

Thegns and Knights in Eleventh-Century England: Who was then the Gentleman?
John Gillingham   129

Knights, Esquires and the Origins of Social Gradation in England
Peter Coss   155

From Stenton to McFarlane: Models of Societies of the Twelfth and Thirteenth Centuries
David Crouch   179

Miles in Armis Strenuus: The Knight at War
  Michael Prestwich   201

Institutions and Economic Development in Early Modern
  Central Europe
  Sheilagh C. Ogilvie   221

Report of Council for 1994–1995   251
Officers and Council 1995   269

TRANSACTIONS OF THE
ROYAL HISTORICAL SOCIETY

PRESIDENTIAL ADDRESS

By R. R. Davies

THE PEOPLES OF BRITAIN AND IRELAND
1100–1400
II. NAMES, BOUNDARIES AND REGNAL SOLIDARITIES

READ 18 NOVEMBER 1994

DURING 1301 the propaganda war between the king of England and the Guardians of the kingdom of Scotland reached a climax in a welter of claims and counter-claims submitted to the Pope. Differing historical mythologies were part of the arguments deployed by both parties. The English case was based on a gloss placed on one of the wondrous legends recorded in Geoffrey of Monmouth's *History of the Kings of Britain*.[1] Britain, according to the legend, had been divided by its illustrious eponymous ruler, Brutus, between his three sons, Locrine, Albanact and Camber. Scotland, originally known as Albany, was Albanact's portion; but—and here we come to the gloss placed on the legend—he was to be subordinate to his elder brother and first-born son of Brutus, Locrine, to whom alone the royal dignity was reserved. Such was the ultimate historical basis for Edward I's claim to superior lordship over Scotland. The Scots could not be expected to accept such a tall story lying down. They did not. They countered with their own even taller tale. They insisted that Brutus's three sons were of equal standing, 'so that none of them was subject to another'; they even queried whether Albany had ever been equated with the whole of what we know as Scotland, suggesting instead that it was the part of the original Britain which stretched from the Humber to the Forth, but no

---

[1] *Edward I and the Throne of Scotland 1290–1296. An Edition of the Record Sources for the Great Cause*, ed., E. L. G. Stones and Grant Simpson (Oxford, 1978), II, 298–300; *Anglo-Scottish Relations 1174–1328. Some Selected Documents*, ed. E. L. G. Stones (Oxford, 1970), 194–7.

further north.[2] They then went on the offensive, asserting that a lady called Scota, daughter of Pharaoh of Egypt, had conquered the northern part of Britain (if indeed it was such), expelled the Britons and renamed it Scotland in honour of herself. 'From that time', so they concluded, 'the Scots, as a new people and having a new name, had nothing to do with the Britons'.[3] Just in case the English were incapable of grasping the logic of this irrefutable historical argument the Scottish advocate, Baldred Bisset, spelt it out for them: the Egyptians had a claim to Scotland far superior to that of the English![4]

The merits of these two historical mythologies are not our concern; but the assumptions that inform them deserve our attention. Or rather one assumption in particular. It can perhaps be best expressed in Walter Bower's transcript of the Scottish case presented at the Papal curia in 1301: referring to the triumph of the Scots over the British, he comments, 'the name and memory of the British people (*gens*) was abolished from Albany; instead of the name of Albany the new name of Scotland and its people (*cum sua gente*) was established'.[5] Names are central to the identity of people; to change a people's name is to change its identity; to threaten to abolish its name is to call its very existence into doubt. That is why invoking the name of a people was one of the most potent of rallying calls. 'Nobles of England, most famous Normans by birth', so Bishop Ralph of Orkney is said to have greeted the troops on the eve of the battle of the Standard in 1138, 'it is well to recall what is your name and pedigree as you are about to go into battle'.[6] Whether this famous speech is no more than a literary device is of secondary importance, since the appeal to the name (*nomen*) of a people was clearly regarded as fundamental to its honour. By the same token any threat to the future of a name was tantamount to a proclamation of genocide. Nothing less, so the Welsh believed, was in the mind of Henry I when he launched a campaign against them in 1114: he and his allies, so the native chronicle records 'set their minds upon exterminating all the Britons (= Welsh), so that the name of Britons should never henceforth be called to mind'.[7] The comment was, of course, hysterically exag-

---

[2] *Anglo-Scottish Relations 1174–1328*, 226–7; John of Fordun, *Chronica Gentis Scotorum*, ed. W. F. Skene (Edinburgh, 1871–2), II, 39–40 (Bk. II, c. 6). For the bridge of the Forth as the dividing line between Britain (*Britannia*) and *Scotia* see Walter Bower, *Scotichronicon*, ed. D. E. R. Watt *et al* (Aberdeen, 1987-), VI, 354–7 (XII c. 20).

[3] *Anglo-Scottish Relations 1174–1328*, 226–7.

[4] *Chronicles of the Picts, Chronicles of the Scots* ed. W. F. Skene (Edinburgh 1867), 280.

[5] Walter Bower, *Scotichronicon*, VI. 142 (XI, c. 49). For the editor's comment on these so-called 'Instructions' of 1301 (which he prefers to see as 'Objections' advanced by the Scottish proctors at the papal court) *ibid*, 260–1.

[6] Henry of Huntingdon, *Historia Anglorum*, ed. T. Arnold (Rolls Series, 1879), 262.

[7] *Brut y Tywysogion Peniarth Ms. 20*, ed. T. Jones (Cardiff, 1941), 58–9; *Translation* (Cardiff, 1952), 37.

gerated; but it was a kind of paranoia which was not peculiar to the Welsh. The cool-headed if morbid Henry of Huntingdon explained the Norman conquest of England in terms of God's decision that the English should cease to be a people (*populus*).[8] By the thirteenth century it was foreigners rather than God who were plotting the extermination of the English: Simon de Montfort's supporters put it about that the intention of his enemies was 'to delete the name of the English'.[9]

This obsession with names should occasion no surprise. Nothing touches our individual or collective identity more closely than the name or names with which we are associated. Our very essence seems to rest in them; to lose them is to be threatened with oblivion. It is through names that we order, describe, categorise and label the world. They are truly in J. L. Austin's famous phrase part of the things we do with words. The more abstract they are—be they the names of social classes, peoples or countries—the more willing have men and women been to lay down their lives for them. In terms of ethnic descent (in so far as that can ever be actually determined), let alone in terms of social, economic and gender divisions, most peoples are complex amalgams; but beneath the label of a single name they become, and come to believe themselves to be, a single people. Names in that sense make a people; no people can exist without its name. That is precisely why peoples were so haunted by the prospect of the loss of their name. It was that apocalypse, as we saw, which terrified the Welsh in 1114. Two more centuries' experience of coping with the English only confirmed them in their conviction and terror. When the Welsh leader Sir Gruffudd Llwyd, sent a clandestine letter to Edward Bruce, brother of King Robert I of Scotland, and self-styled king of Ireland, in 1316, it was the same spectre which haunted him: 'the intention of the English', he commented was 'to try to delete our name and memory from the land'.[10] The Scots needed no persuading that the threat was a real one, for later in the century they delivered themselves of the opinion that the English had indeed destroyed the Welsh 'name and nobility' (the twinning is significant) and also those of the Irish, 'so far as they could'.[11]

Names, therefore, were central. The deletion of its name was the greatest threat to a people; the revival of its name to its full pristine glory and resonance was that same people's highest aspiration. The

[8] *Historia Anglorum*, 241.
[9] *The Song of Lewes* ed C. L. Kingsford (Oxford, 1890), ll. 281–2.
[10] J. Beverley Smith, 'Gruffydd Llwyd and the Celtic Alliance, 1315–18', *Bulletin of the Board of Celtic Studies* 26 (1974–6), 478.
[11] 'Papers relating to the captivity and release of David II', ed. E. W. M. Balfour-Melville, *Miscellany of the Scottish History Society*, 9 (1958), 42 quoted in R. Frame, *The Political Development of the British Isles 1100–1400* (Oxford, 1990), 141.

Welsh oscillated between the two polarities. 'According to the prophecies of Merlin', so Gerald of Wales observed of them, 'they confidently hope that both the nation (*natio*) and the name (*nuncupatio*) of the foreigners (i.e. the English) shall be expunged and that the Britons would once more glory in their ancient name (*nomen*) and status in the island'.[12] Given that names had such a remarkable potency, root-and-branch reformers soon recognized that to delete old names was a necessary pre-requisite to creating a new people and thereby a new loyalty. John Mair writing in 1521 had no doubt that the only sure way to resolve the centuries-old enmity between English and Scots was to call both of them Britons. He knew that his suggestion would get short shrift among his fellow Scotsmen, so he prepared his response in advance. 'And what although the name and kingdom of the Scots had disappeared, so too would the name and kingdom of the English no more have a place among men, for in the place of both we should have a king of Britain'.[13] His words were to be echoed by King James VI and I when he advocated that 'the divided name of England and Scotland' be discontinued in order to make way for the new name of 'Great Britain'.[14] Unfortunately for John Mair and King James it requires more than a stroke of a theoretician's or even a monarch's pen for a people to assume a new name; the change must also be effected in the hearts and minds of the people itself. The names of peoples are in a measure political artefacts; but they are also ultimately, more importantly and irreducibly, manifestations of a sense and conviction of collective solidarity.

Names, therefore, are basic to a sense of communal identity; they are redolent of memories and aspirations. Yet there was a problem attached to them. They might appear timeless, literally aboriginal, especially in a society which constructed so much of its history around the concept of an eponymous founder; but they are in fact the product

[12] Giraldus Cambrenis, *Opera*, ed. J. S. Brewer *et al* (Rolls Series 1861–91) VI, 216 (*Descriptio Kambrie*, II, vii). The comment directly echoes one of the Merlinic prophecies recorded by Geoffrey of Monmouth in the 1130s: 'The island will be called by the name (*nomen*) of Brutus and the name (*nuncupatio*) given to it by the foreigners will perish': *Historia Regum Britannie, Bern, Burgerbibliothek, Ms. 568* (Cambridge, 1984) ed. Neil Wright (Cambridge, 1984) 77 (114 (20)). *The Description of England* (for which see below n. 49) made a very similar comment: 'the Welsh go about saying that ... by means of Arthur they will win back the land ... and they will give it back its name. They will call it Britain again'.

[13] John Mair (Major), *History of Great Britain*, ed. and trans. A. Constable (Scottish History Society, 1892), 180. For excellent discussion see Roger A. Mason, 'Kingship, Nobility and Anglo-Scottish Union: John Mair's *History of Greater Britain* (1521)', *Innes Review* 41 (1990), 182–222.

[14] Quoted in J. Wormald, 'The Creation of Britain: Multiple Kingdoms or Core and Colonies?' *ante*, 6th ser., 2 (1992), 178.

of time, circumstance and accident. As such they have no ultimate fixity; they can be modified, transformed or forgotten. Encyclopaedists such as Isidore of Seville recognized that the names of peoples, as of places, came and went; while authors of a pessimistic cast of mind, such as Henry of Huntingdon, found a source for both their historical curiosity and their chronic gloom in comparing the names of places and peoples no longer extant with those now current.[15] But the problem was not merely a general one; it had particular application to the peoples of Britain and Ireland. Already in the ninth century Irish poets were intrigued by the question of why the people of Ireland were called by different names—Scuitt, Gáedil, Féni.[16] In Scotland the issue of the disappearance of named peoples and the shifting labels of countries and peoples was even more obvious and could not be ducked. There was, first of all, the problem of the Picts. For Bede as for 'Nennius' they were most certainly one of the peoples, indeed one of the oldest peoples, of the island of Britain[17]; but they were now no more. That was reason enough to set men thinking about names and peoples. But that was only a beginning. Anyone who considered, or considers, the multiple, changing and often overlapping meanings of the words *Scotia*, *Scotti*, *Alba* and *fir Alban* would soon conclude that names are the most deceiving and least simple of things. When, for example, did the term *Scotti* (which seems originally to have been a common term for the Gaels of both 'Ireland' and 'Scotland') become largely restricted to the inhabitants of Dál Riata? When, likewise, were the terms *Scotia* and *Scotti*, which had once referred to the area and the peoples north of the Forth, extended in common parlance to the country, kingdom and people of a greater Scotland? And to make confusion worse, confounded, when did Alba which had originally meant 'Britain' (though even on that score there was room for disagreement) come to be equated with the unit and peoples which would eventually be called Scotland and Scots, *fir Alban*?[18] The palimpsest of terms in a state of confusing flux is a healthy reminder to us of the shifting, indeed shifty, vocabulary of peoples and units in the early medieval period. The shifts are certainly significant, but if we try to pin them down too exactly or

[15] Isidore of Seville, *Etymologiarum sive originum libri XX*, ed. W. W. Lindsay (Oxford, 1911), IX, ii, 38; Henry of Huntingdon, *Historia Anglorum*, 9.

[16] D. Ó Corráin, 'Nationality and Kingship in pre-Norman Ireland', *Historical Studies* 11 (1978), 6.

[17] *Bede's Ecclesiastical History of the English People*, ed. B. Colgrave and R. A. B. Mynors (Oxford, 1969), 16–19 (i, 1), 230–1 (iii, 6) 560–1 (v. 23); 'Nennius', *British History and the Welsh Annals*, ed. J. Morris (1980), c. 7.

[18] For a recent challenging discussion of these issues, with reference to the views of earlier scholars, see D. Broun, 'The Origin of Scottish Identity', *Nations, Nationalism and Patriotism in the European Past*, ed. C. Bjørn, A. Grant and K. J. Stringer (Copenhagen, 1994), 35–55. I wish to thank Dr. Broun for giving me early sight of this paper.

to order them into a pattern which corresponds neatly with our modern theories and aspirations, we may clarify our own thoughts but at the expense of clouding the essential fluidity of early medieval peoples and their nomenclature.

Of the peoples of these islands it was, significantly, the English who sorted out their nomenclature earliest and did so with a briskness and directness which contrasted with the ambiguities and uncertainties of their neighbours. It marked them out as a people who knew where they were going and how to get there. They faced two problems and solved both with consummate mastery. First, what were they to do about the names of the island and its inhabitants—Britain and Britons—which were now largely under their control. Already in the late tenth century Ealdorman Aethelweard gave a pithy answer to that question which has done good service for a thousand years: 'Britain', he said, 'is now called England, thereby assuming the name of the victors'.[19] That, as they say, is that. All that was needed was to prop the claim up with suitable historiographical underpinning. Henry of Huntingdon obliged in his gloss on Geoffrey of Monmouth's list of the kings of Britain. With the death of Cadwaladr, the last of these kings, 'the Britons lost the name (nomen) and kingdom'.[20] In the next century Roger of Wendover garnished the explanation a little by commenting that the decision was the co-ordinated response of early Anglo-Saxon kings.[21] One can almost hear the smack of firm government at this first recorded, if imaginary, constitutional convention in England's history. Geoffrey of Monmouth, it is true, rather queered the pitch of this early English triumphalism with his account of the global glories of the early Britons; but his story ends with the defeat and utter dejection of the Britons, prophetic hopes notwithstanding; while in the First Variant version of his *History* the triumph of the English is specifically linked to the loss of the name of Britain (nomen Britanniae).[22]

---

[19] *Chronicle of Aethelweard*, ed. A. Campbell (Edinburgh, 1962), 9. Aelfric soon followed suit by commenting how the persecution of St Alban, a Romano-British martyr, extended to 'Angla lande': quoted in P. Wormald, 'Engla Lond: The Making of an Allegiance', *Journal of Historical Sociology* 7 (1994), 13.

[20] Henry of Huntingdon, 'Epistola ad Warinum' in Robert of Torigni, *Chroniques*, ed. L. Deslisle (Rouen, 1872-3), I, 111. The observation soon became commonplace, as in the chronicles of Alfred of Beverley or Gervase of Canterbury. In a similar vein Roger of Howden converted Arthur from 'king of the Britons' to 'king of England': John Gillingham, 'The Context and Purposes of Geoffrey of Monmouth's *History of the Kings of Britain*', *Anglo-Norman Studies* 13 (1991), 103 n. 23.

[21] Roger of Wendover, *Flores Historiarum*, ed. H. O. Coxe, (1841), I, 92-3.

[22] Cf. Geoffrey of Monmouth, *Historia Regum Britannie* ed., N. Wright, I (1984), pp. 134-5 (c. 188) 145-6 (c. 204) and II (1988) 178 (c. 188) and esp. 190 (c. 204). The issue, and many others, are very illuminatingly discussed in R.W. Leckie, jnr., *The Passage of Dominion: Geoffrey of Monmouth and the Periodization of Insular History in the Twelfth Century* (Toronto, 1981), esp. 104-7.

Now that the name of Britain had been deleted, it remained only to address the second question: what was to be the name of the new people which had now so triumphantly taken charge of the island? It was a measure of its genius that it solved the problem not by theorising but by action. Cutting through any sensitivities of nomenclature it had certainly found a solution by the early eighth century at the latest: the English, *Anglici, Angelcynn.* There was, of course, as later generations acknowledged, some explaining to do. Why, as a later text put it, were the peoples called English rather than Saxons? The latter group, after all, was 'the most powerful in the country' and it was the Wessex monarchy's superiority and conquests which were to be the basis of English political unity.[23] There were some suitably ridiculous answers to the question, such as inventing a Queen Angela, daughter of a renowned Saxon leader.[24] Modern historians have emphasized the rôle of conversion, the ambitions of Canterbury and the adoption by the Roman church of the term 'Angli' to describe the Germanic converts of its newly-established province as key factors in the establishment of this anomalous name.[25] But the charming if fictitious explanation put forward by Ranulf Higden has also a great deal to recommend it, because in its innocence it shrewdly recognized the key role of kingship in the making of the English people. About 800, so Ranulf reported, Egbert king of the West Saxons commanded that all the men of the land be called English, *Angli.*[26] It was never that simple, of course; but it is undoubtedly true that from the tenth century, initially though not consistently in charters and thereafter on coins, the monarchs adopted the title king of the English, *rex Anglorum.*[27]. They were kings of a people, a named people.

The assumption of a name, by an individual or a people, is an act of self-identification. In the case of a people it is an acknowledgement that it perceived itself as having a communal identity, a sense of

[23] *Le Livre des Reis de Brittanie et Le Livre de Reis de Engleterre*, ed. J. Glover (Rolls Series, 1865), 41. Geoffrey of Monmouth, with uncharacteristic self-restraint, ducks the problem by commenting blandly: 'Hinc Angli Saxones vocati sunt qui Loegriam possedunt et ab eis Anglia terra postmodum dictum est': *Historia Regum Britannie*, II, 172. (c. 186).

[24] Ranulf Higden, *Polychronicon*, ed. C. Babington and J. R. Lumby (Rolls Series, 1865–86), II, 4.

[25] H. E. J. Cowdrey, 'Bede and the "English" People', *Journal of Religious History*, XI (1981), 501–23; P. Wormald, 'Bede Beowulf and the conversion of the Anglo-Saxon aristocracy', *Bede and Anglo-Saxon England*, ed. R. T. Farrell (British Archaeological Reports no. 46, 1978); *idem*, 'Bede, the Bretwalda and the Origins of the *Gens Anglorum*', *Ideal and Reality in Frankish and Anglo-Saxon Society. Studies presented to J. M. Wallace-Hadrill*, ed. P. Wormald, D. Bullough and R. Collins (Oxford, 1983), 99–129.

[26] Higden, *Polychronicon*, II, 152.

[27] Cf. Susan Reynolds, 'What do we mean by "Anglo-Saxon" and "Anglo-Saxons"?' *Journal of British Studies* 24 (1985), 395–414.

togetherness, *wirgefühl*. This may arise from, or manifest itself in, a belief in common lineage descent, as happened in Ireland to peoples such as the *Uí Néill*. It may also express a sense of fellowship arising from being dwellers of the same district: such, at least etymologically, is the root of the word *Cymry* employed from a least the seventh century to refer to the Britons of Strathclyde-Cumbria as well as to those of the country we know as Wales.[28] A name may also be assumed relationally, since nothing perhaps serves to raise a people's awareness of itself and of its distinctiveness, or superiority, more than living cheek by jowl, often indeed in conflict, with other peoples. What probably made the early English, *Angelcynn*, most aware of themselves as a single people deserving a single name—in spite of their memory that they were composed of different ethnic-groups (Saxons, Angles, Jutes) and in spite of their divided political structures and loyalties—was their awareness of their solidarity *vis-à-vis* the other peoples, more especially the Celtic-speaking peoples, of Britain.

A people may assume a name, though for the medieval period it is very rarely that we know when or under what circumstances it did so. But it may also be given a name by others; the two sets of names sometimes, but by no means always, coincide. Indeed the name that is given by one people to another may be perceived as an act of cultural domination, a deliberate imposition of one's own terminology at the expense of the indigenous name. The thin-skinned Gerald of Wales certainly regarded the English usage of the words 'Wales' and 'Welsh' in that light.[29] They were, he thought, demeaning terms: they derived from a generic Germanic word for anything foreign and had no foundation other than in the perceptions of the invading peoples themselves. Gerald had at least half a good case: the Welsh knew themselves as Britons (or Cymry) and there was no reason, other than the ambition of the victor to appropriate such an evocative term for his own use[30] or, alternatively, to abolish it, why the English could not have used it. Etymologically Gerald's outrage may have been well-founded; but victors rarely pay much heed to the niceties of etymology. It is their categories and names which normally win the day. Contemporaries had no doubt about that: 'when the Saxons conquered

---

[28] Ifor Williams, *The Beginnings of Welsh Poetry*, ed. Rachel Bromwich (Cardiff 1972), 71–2, 86; R. Geraint Gruffydd in *Astudiaethau ar yr Hengerdd*, ed. R. B. Jones and Rachel Bromwich (Cardiff, 1978), 25–44.

[29] Giraldus Cambrensis, *Opera*, VI, 179 (*Descriptio Kambrie*, I, vii). For comment Robert Bartlett, *Gerald of Wales 1146–1223* (Oxford, 1982), 185; but Gerald did not consistently use *Kambria* in preference to *Wallia*.

[30.] For *Britones* used as a synonym for *Angli* see e.g. *The Political Songs of England from the reign of John to Edward III* (Camden Society, 1839), 128, 131. For *Britannia* in the styles of pre- Conquest Kings, E. John, *Orbis Britanniae and other Studies* (Leicester 1966).

this land', as Henry of Huntingdon remarked, 'they established seven kings and they imposed their names (*nomina*) at their whim on the kingdoms'.[31]

Names, I hope you will agree, are important to an understanding of peoples, especially of the self-perception of peoples. But names, it should also be clear, are treacherous. They deliberately set out to manufacture a facade of unity and to establish a mythology of timelessness and unchangeability. In Benedict Anderson's striking phrase, they 'turn chance into destiny'.[32] In reality names change their meanings as the social realities which they seek to describe themselves change. So it is with peoples. One important era of change is that which I have chosen as the chronological focus of these lectures, the eleventh to the fourteenth centuries in the British Isles. During those centuries, as I suggested in last year's address, the identities of the peoples of the British Isles became more clearly etched and simplified and so, accordingly, did their names; those names also acquired many of the connotations which they have retained since. In other words it was a formative period in the definition of the labels of the peoples of the British Isles. Contemporaries recognized as much as the period drew to its close. When Ranulf Higden compiled his Universal Chronicle at Chester in the mid-fourteenth century he dutifully listed the seven peoples who had at one stage or another come to Britain; but of those seven two, he conceded, had disappeared—the Picts and the Danes; one, the Flemings, was no more than the memory of a distant episode in south-west Wales; and as to the Normans they were now 'intermingled throughout the whole island', as he put it, with the English. That left three peoples—English, Scots and Welsh.[33]

Taking a leaf from Higden's book I would like to look briefly at these peoples of mainland Britain and the names they bore—with an occasional glance over my shoulder towards Ireland—and to do so in the light of two interlinked criteria which may have shaped their identities and thereby their names during these formative centuries. The first of those criteria is, to borrow Susan Reynolds' most servicable phrase, that of regnal solidarity.[34] In other words how far was the identity of a people and the label it bore shaped by the growth of a

---

[31] Henry of Huntingdon, *Historia Anglorum*, 8.

[32] Benedict Anderson, *Imagined Communities. Reflections on the Origins and Spread of Nationalism* (revised edition, 1991), 12.

[33] Higden, *Polychronicon*, II, 152–4.

[34] Susan Reynolds, *Kingdoms and Communities in Western Europe 900–1300* (Oxford, 1984), 261. Borrowing this phrase is only a minor indication of the immense debt of stimulus, and reassurance, that I owe to this book. At least if I am barking up the wrong, or non-existent, tree I am in good company.

more powerful, penetrative and well-articulated royal authority which mediated its view of the world and of its subjects through the language of its public documents? What was the relationship, in short, between peoples and kingdoms, nations and states? The second criteria is that of territorial definition or boundaries. Peoples and boundaries are not, of course, necessarily connected. A people is defined by its own collective sense of self-identity and its cultivation of the mythologies and emblems of such identity rather than by a necessary attachment to a particular area of land. Indeed a never-never land in the past and/or the future can often be a more potent force in creating a sense of ethnic cohesion than the mundane realities of a particular terrain in the present. Nevertheless the notion of a homeland, actual or mythical, and of regarding such a homeland as sacred is a potent feature of the ideology of most peoples, ancient and modern. Defining the boundaries of such a homeland may also serve to define membership of a people.

It is with the English, *gens Anglorum*, that we begin, because they were first off the mark. In 1100 they started with both a handicap and a huge headstart. Their handicap was that they had twice suffered the trauma of conquest in the eleventh century. That, as Henry of Huntingdon lugubriously remarked, was evidence enough that God wished to delete them as a people.[35] If so, God did a poor job of it, since the English seem to have recovered much of their poise and confidence well before the centenary of the battle of Hastings was celebrated. If we seek an explanation for the divine failure it rests surely in the fact that the headstart was ultimately far more important than the handicap. It was in fact a double headstart. The English, as we have been seen, had sorted out their identity and name as a single people—*gens Anglorum*, *Angelcynn*—at least three centuries before the disaster of 1066 struck. The ideological underpinnings of the sense of Englishness—what a spokesman at the Council of Constance many centuries later was to call 'the habit of association'[36]—had been successfully cultivated for centuries, and with increasing effectiveness from the tenth century.[37] Such a sense of collective solidarity could be badly dented; it was unlikely to be eradicated. Secondly the Old English monarchy was, in James Campbell's phrase, 'a formidably organized state' where the practice and habits of effective rule under a single king had instilled a

[35] Henry of Huntingdon, *Historia Anglorum*, 214.

[36] C, M. D. Crowder, *Unity, Heresy and Reform 1378–1460. The Conciliar Response to the Great Schism* (1977), 120 (*collectio*). For comment see L. R. Loomis, 'Nationality at the Council of Constance. An Anglo-French dispute', *American Historical Review*, 44 (1939), 508–27; J. P. Genet, 'English Nationalism: Thomas Polton at the Council of Constance', *Nottingham Medieval Studies* 28 (1984), 60–78.

[37] Wormald, 'Engla-lond', as cited in n. 19 above, and the references given there to Wormald's earlier work.

sense of unity, regularity and common experience among its inhabitants or subjects such as no comparable unit of power in contemporary Europe enjoyed.[38] To this was added the fact that England had already acquired a remarkable degree of fixity as a territorial unit, and thereby as a kingdom and a country. It is not without significance in this respect that it is in the late tenth century that the word England, *Engla-Lond*, first appears in the surviving evidence.[39] Edward the Confessor could be accorded the title 'king and defender of the English borders', with the clear assumption that it was known where the borders were.[40] Likewise the message of Domesday Book in this respect—regardless of some fuzziness in the north and, to a lesser extent in the west—is surely that England was already a well-known and well-measured country, in its internal divisions as well as in its external boundaries; it was truly compassable in its parts as well as in its whole.[41] What all this meant in terms of collective identity and sentiment, regnal solidarity and territorial boundaries was perhaps best expressed in the famous state-ment attributed to Earl Byrhtnoth by the poet who commemorated the battle of Maldon: he was ready to die guarding 'this country, the home of Ethelred my lord, people and land'.[42] King, people and country formed the unity that was England and the English people.

The English, therefore, had a formidable headstart; Anglo-Saxon historians are surely right to claim the essential shaping of English identity, and the basic vocabulary of such an identity, as the achievement of their period *par excellence*. The Norman conquest and settlement may have proved a massive setback to that achievement, but it was only a temporary setback. One of the truly exciting achievements of recent English medieval historiography has been to reclaim the twelfth century for the English.[43] The age of Normans and Angevins it might be; but

---

[38] James Campbell, *Essays in Anglo-Saxon History* (1986) esp. chaps. 10–11; *idem, Stubbs and the English State* (The Stenton Lecture, 1987. Reading).

[39] *Oxford English Dictionary, sub verbo*. For a recent comment on the earliest recorded usage of the word, J. A. Burrow, 'The Sinking Island and the Dying Author: R. W. Chambers Fifty Years On', *Essays in Criticism*, 40 (1990), 20 n. 11.

[40] F. Barlow, *Edward the Confessor* (1970), 136, n. 10.

[41] Campbell, *Essays in Anglo-Saxon History*, 220: 'the unity, the regularity, the compassibility of the England the Normans conquered'.

[42] *English Historical Documents I c. 500–1042*, ed. D. Whitelock (2nd edition, 1979), 320.

[43] This has been in particular the achievement of John Gillingham esp. in 'The Beginnings of English Imperialism', *Journal of Historical Sociology* 5 (1992), 392–409; 'The English Invasion of Ireland', *Representing Ireland* ed. B. Bradshaw and others (Cambridge, 1993), 24–42; 'Henry of Huntingdon and the Twelfth-Century Revival of the English Nation'; *Concepts of National Identity in the Middle Ages*, ed. L. Johnson and A. V. Murray (forthcoming). I owe an immense debt to the writings and conversations of John Gillingham. See also James Campbell's pioneering article, 'Some Twelfth-Century Views of the Anglo-Saxon Past', *Essays in Anglo-Saxon History*, 209–29, and Patrick Wormald's comment on the author of *Quadripartitus* (as cited below in n. 46 pp. 139–40).

it was also the era of the assertion, or re-assertion, of English identity. In the first half of the century a remarkable group of historians—notably William of Malmesbury, Henry of Huntingdon, and Geffrei Gaimar—set out to create an interpretation of the past which, in spite of occasional human folly and divine intervention, is triumphantly English and almost teleologically England-centred. Latin or French may be its language, but it is the English which are its focus—*Gesta Regum Anglorum, Historia Anglorum, Estoire des Engleis*. The authors show a fascination with the name of the English: 'they', commented Wace, and through him Lawman, referring to the Saxon invaders, 'called themselves English in order to commemorate their origins and Engle-land the land which was given them'.[44] What is more—as John Gillingham in particular has emphasized—their writings show a disdain toward the non-English peoples of the British Isles as essentially barbarous and uncivilised; it is an attitude which is in marked contrast to the respect shown to Irish and Welsh scholarship and religiosity in earlier centuries.[45] In law, likewise, it is the emphasis on the distinctive Englishness of the law which is one of the noteworthy characteristics of these generations—be it in the cultivation of the *laga Edwardi* and the antiquarian collections of pre-Conquest laws, in *Glanvill's* announcement that what he was expounding was 'the laws and customs of the kingdom of England', in the distinction that was officially drawn in 1201 between 'the law of England' and 'the law of Wales', or in the chronicler's comment that King John 'caused English laws and customs to be instituted in Ireland'.[46] History, law and, one might add the church (*ecclesia anglicana*) were triumphantly English, certainly by 1200 and in many respects much earlier; the kings needed no multiple address clause when they now greeted their subjects in England. England was truly the land of the English.

If we now apply our two criteria—boundaries and regnal solidarity—we might well conclude that both had contributed to the defining and stabilising of the name English. To take boundaries first. By 1157 we can say, with hindsight, that England had achieved its historic bound-

[44] Wace, *Le Roman de Brut*, ed. Ivor Arnold (Paris 1938–40), II. 13,645–8; Lawman, *Brut*, trans. Rosamund Allen (1992), ll. 14672–8.

[45] D. Bethell, 'English Monks and Irish Reform in the 11th. and 12th. centuries', *Historical Studies*, 8, ed. T. Desmond Williams (Dublin, 1971), 111–35; John Gillingham, 'Beginnings', as cited n. 43.

[46] See respectively, Patrick Wormald, 'Quadripartitus', *Law and Government in England and Normandy. Studies presented to Sir James Holt* (Cambridge, 1994), 111–72; *The Treatise on the Laws and Customs of the Realm of England commonly called Glanvill*, ed. G. D. G. Hall (1965), 1 *(leges anglicanas')*; *Rotuli Litterarum Patentium* (Record Commission, 1838) I, i, 86 ('law of England' and 'law of Wales'); Roger of Wendover, *Flores historiarum* ed. H. G. Hewlett (1886–9), II, 56; Paul Brand, 'Ireland and the literature of the early Common Law', *Irish Jurist*, XVI (1981), 95–113 (English law in Ireland).

aries. There might be some tiny uncertainties in the west;[47] but Wales was a separate country, and the extensive English-controlled districts within it were not incorporated into the kingdom of England but rather left in a sort of anomalous limbo known as the march of Wales, *marchia Wallie*. Henry II's recovery of the northern counties of England proved, in the event, to be definitive and was eventually recognized as such.[48] England had taken final shape; those who lived within its boundaries were assumed to be English or they needed to explain themselves. But there was more to England and Englishness than neatly reticulated boundaries on a map; there was also an intimacy with, and an affection for, the country which no amount of cartography can communicate. The *Description of England*, which may have been composed as early as the 1140s, already breathes the pride in the provincial particularities of England which was to be so characteristic of Leland, Camden and their contemporaries four centuries later.[49] England was apparently a country already at ease with itself, whose people—regardless of differences—had no difficulty in recognizing themselves as English.

Nothing brought the recognition of a common Englishness nearer home, literally into one's pocket, than that of being subjects of a single king—using his money, paying his taxes, obeying his officers, observing his laws and so forth. From the tenth century onwards it was this symbiosis between king and people which came to define in practical terms what it meant to be English. In this respect the Norman Conquest represented no hiatus: William the Conqueror assumed the title king of the English, *rex Anglorum*, without batting an eyelid, and (as Patrick Wormald has argued) the expectation that all English freemen over the age of twelve should pledge their loyalty to the king has an unbroken history from at least the early-eleventh to the late fifteenth-century.[50] This was regnal solidarity indeed: to be English was to have sworn allegiance to the king of England. Two episodes may serve to illustrate the perceived link. In 1295 Edward I decreed that Elié d'Aubigné, a

[47] R. R. Davies, *Lordship and Society in the March of Wales 1284–1400* (Oxford, 1978), 17–18. Cf. *Gesta Stephani*, ed. K. R. Potter and R. H. C. Davis (2nd edn. Oxford, 1976), 24 ('per omnes fines Angliae et Walloniae').

[48] G. W. S. Barrow, 'Frontier and Settlement: Which influenced which? England and Scotland, 1100–1300', *Medieval Frontier Societies* ed. Robert Bartlett and Angus Mackay (Oxford, 1989), 3–21; *idem*, 'The Anglo-Scottish Border: Growth and Structure in the Middle Ages', *Grenzen und Grenzregionen* ed. Wolfgang Haubrichs and Reinhard Schneider (Saarbrücken 1994), 197–212.

[49] Lesley Johnson and Alexander Bell, 'The Anglo-Norman Description of England', *Anglo-Norman Anniversary Studies*, ed. Ian Short (Anglo-Norman Text Society 1993), 11–47. I am very grateful to Lesley Johnson for giving me an advance copy of this article. The suggestion of a date as early as c. 1140 is made in Gillingham 'The Context and Purposes' (cited above n. 20), 112.

[50] Wormald, 'Engla-lond' (cited above n. 37), 6–7.

man of Breton stock, should be treated as an Englishman in the courts
of England and be regarded as 'a pure Englishman'.[51] Likewise when
Henry of Lancaster, earl of Derby, took the town of St Jean d'Angély
in 1346 he coolly reported the news that 'its inhabitants swore an oath
to us and became English'.[52] Ethnic identities were now apparently a
matter of a stroke of the political or military pen.

In fact the instant Anglicisation of the citizens of St Jean d'Angély
should warn us not to press arguments from territorial boundaries and
regnal solidarity too far in defining peoples and the names of peoples.
The first caveat relates to territoriality. Those who lived within the
bounds of England might indeed be now normally regarded by definition as English; but such a definition would be far too limiting. The
settler communities in Wales and Ireland certainly regarded themselves
as English in all sorts of ways;[53] so, factitiously, did the good citizens of
St Jean d'Angély after 1346. Secondly, while regnal power had a
transforming effect on collective identities, the two could also be out of
kilter with each other. That was to some degree true of England in the
thirteenth century, when an almost xenophobic sense of Englishness
was deliberately cultivated to thwart the ambitions of what was represented as a royal court dominated by aliens.[54] Thirdly the collective
solidarity that is a people need not ineluctably be tied to a king or a
kingdom. There had been a *gens Anglorum* long before there was a *regnum
Anglorum* or *Anglie*. The link between the two had been extraordinarily
intimate since the tenth century; but when during the turmoil of 1258
the barons referred to 'the nation of the kingdom of England' they
were drawing attention both to the link *and* to the distinction between
nation and kingdom.[55]

Some of these issues might come into clearer focus if we consider,
however briefly and inexpertly, the evolution of the Scots, as a people
and a name, in the high middle ages. The name of the Scots, *Scotti*, is
a very old one, attested long before the *gens Anglorum* puts in its first
appearance; that is the trouble with it. It became an almost endlessly
elastic term, hugely deceptive in its apparent unchangeability and
common usage. What, for example, are we to make of the entry in the

[51] *Rotuli Parliamentorum* (Record Commission), I, 135.
[52] Adam Murimuth, *Continuatio Chronicarum*, etc. ed E. M. Thompson, (Rolls Series, 1889), 373.
[53] Robin Frame, ' "Les Engleys née en Ireland": The English Political Identity in Medieval Ireland', *ante* 6th ser., 3 (1993), 83–105; R. R. Davies in *The British Isles 1100 1500: Comparisons, Contrasts and Connections* ed. R. R. Davies, (Edinburgh, 1988), 13–15.
[54] For general discussion M. T. Clanchy, *England and its Rulers 1066–1272. Foreign Lordship and National Identity* (1983), chap. 10; Michael Prestwich, *English Politics in the Thirteenth Century*, chap. 5.
[55] *Documents of the Baronial Movement of Reform and Rebellion 1258–1267*, ed. R. F. Treharne and I. J. Sanders (Oxford, 1973), 80.

Anglo-Saxon Chronicle for 924 that 'the king of Scots and all the people of the Scots' accepted Edward the Elder as 'father and lord'? 'Scotia' and 'Scots' were Russian-doll words; their chronic terminological instability is an indication that profound changes in identities and perceptions, and thereby language, are taking place. In 1100 *Scotia* referred to the land north of the Forth, and the Scots were the inhabitants of that land, to be contrasted with the men of Lothian, the Britons of Strathclyde/Cumbria and the inhabitants of Galloway. By the early thirteenth century such a restricted usage of the terms *Scotia* and Scots was becoming rather archaic; by 1300 it had virtually disappeared.[56] What changes in the self-identification and self-perception of the Scots do these shifts (if I have represented them correctly) represent?

Let us begin again with the criterion of regnal solidarity. The rôle of the monarchy in transforming, indeed in some respects in creating, the concept of a Scottish people seems to be an undeniably primary one. Large, even extravagant, claims have been made for the early Scottish monarchy of late;[57] but in one respect at least they are justified. It was an unitary and successful monarchy, in marked contrast to the fragmentation and instability of political authority in the Celtic societies of Ireland and Wales. Its king proclaimed himself from his earliest surviving charters to be 'king of the Scots', *rex Scottorum*, and he could refer to his subjects in the singular as 'our people', *gens nostra*.[58] Such statements were as yet programmatic aspirations for the most part in terms of effective and well-articulated royal authority over much of the country that we know as Scotland; but aspiration was converted into reality at a remarkable pace in the two centuries after 1100. By the 1160s the expression 'kingdom of the Scots' or 'kingdom of Scotland' makes its first appearance in recorded documents in a clear territorial sense and by the late twelfth century had become a commonplace.[59] A geographically more ample and king-inspired definition of the Scots as

[56] Note in particular the comments of A. A. M. Duncan, 'The Making of Scotland', *Who are the Scots?* ed. G. Menzies (Edinburgh, 1971), 129–30; and G. W. S. Barrow, *Regesta Regum Scottorum, I. Acts of Malcolm IV* (Edinburgh, 1960), 39–40; *idem*, 'The Scots and the North of England', *The Anarchy of King Stephen's Reign*, ed. Edmund King (Oxford, 1994), 231–53.

[57] Alfred P. Smyth, *Warlords and Holy Men. Scotland A.D. 80–1000* (1984), 175, 237–8.

[58] For the most recent discussion see Joseph Donnelly, 'The Earliest Scottish Charters', *Scottish Historical Review* 68 (1989), 1–22. 'Gens nostra': Eadmer, *Historia Novorum*, ed. M. Rule (Rolls Series, 1884), 236. The legend on Alexander I's seal read 'Deo rectore rex Scottorum', A. A. M. Duncan, *Scotland. The Making of the Kingdom* (Edinburgh, 1975), 553.

[59] G. W. S. Barrow, *The Anglo-Norman Era in Scottish History* (Oxford, 1980), 153–4. For a grant of the late 1230s by 'Michael the Scot of the kingdom of Scotland', *idem* 'Some East Fife Documents of the Twelfth and Thirteenth Centuries' in *The Scottish Tradition. Essays in Honour of Ronald Gordon Cant*, ed. G. W. S. Barrow (Edinburgh, 1974), 30–1.

a people was taking shape. As Geoffrey Barrow has recently expressed it: 'By the twelfth and thirteenth centuries the kingdom of Scotland and its ruling dynasty were themselves determining what made the Scottish nation'. And in the process 'the four or five disparate peoples north of Tweed and Solway' of the early middle ages were forged into the *Scottorum nacio* of the Declaration of Arbroath.[60]

The definition of who constituted the members of this nation would to some degree be determined geographically by the definition of the boundaries of Scotland. In a sense the borders of Scotland were old: that is why Malcolm Canmore refused to meet William Rufus other than 'on the borders of their realm'.[61] In another sense, of course, they were extremely fluid: in the south formally until the Treaty of York finally accepted the Berwick-Solway frontier, in the west until the Treaty of Perth of 1266 ceded the western isles to the king of Scotland with the significant requirement that their inhabitants should henceforth 'be subject to the laws and customs of the kingdom of Scotland';[62] and in the case of the northern isles not until the 1460s. Long before that, however, the boundaries of the kingdom had come to be regarded as historic, defining the kingdom of Scotland and thereby, through the allegiance of its inhabitants, the Scots. It was in that spirit that the Treaty of Birgham in 1290 insisted that Scotland 'was separate and divided from England ... according to its rightful boundaries and marches'[63] and it was in support of such a vision that historians such as John of Fordun created the image of an almost immemorial Scotland which stretched from the Tweed, or even a more southerly river, to the Orkneys.

Regnal solidarity and definition of boundaries substantially made Scotland and the Scots of 1300 or 1329. But the argument should not be taken too far. 'The *gens Scotica*' so it has been asserted of late 'preceded the *regnum Scottorum*'.[64] The two were, or became, lineally and causally related; the two interpenetrated each other and were reshaped to each other's needs; but both could have developed differently and, arguably, independently. The kingship provided a focus for the enlarged and transformed Scottish nation; the boundaries gave it territorial definition. But a people does not exist by royal fiat or boundary markers. It is—if this does not sound sentimental—created and recreated in

[60] The two quotations come, respectively, from G. W. S. Barrow, *Robert Bruce and The Community of the Realm of Scotland* (3rd edition, Edinburgh, 1988), xi and Duncan, *Scotland*, 111.

[61] 'Florence' of Worcester's chronicle in *Scottish Annals from English Chroniclers* ed. A. O. Anderson (1908), 110.

[62] *Acts of the Parliament of Scotland* (Edinburgh, 1844), I, (Alexander III), 78.

[63] *Foedera etc.* ed. T. Rymer (revised edition, 1816–69), I, ii. 735.

[64] Barrow, *Robert Bruce*, xi.

the hearts and minds of men and women. Historians may differ in their emphasis as to when and why the process of the creation of a single Scottish nation can be said to be completed—whether 'land' and 'kingdom' preceded 'nation' in the vocabulary and substance of solidarity, whether the Wars of Independence were a consequence and manifestation of the process or were themselves the furnace in which Scottish nationhood was forged.[65] As so often in historical debate, the polarities of such arguments may simplify what was no doubt, as with so many social and political movements, a complex, even contradictory, process. What is surely striking—be it in the obligation of service in the common or Scottish army, in the iconographical maturity of the minority seal of Alexander III, in the sense of communal desolation at his death expressed in the earliest surviving piece of Scottish poetry, in the remarkable invocation to St Andrew to be 'the leader of the compatriot Scots' engraved on the seal of the Guardians of the kingdom in 1286, or in the remarkable political rhetoric, reaching its magnificent coda in the Declaration of Arbroath, with which the Scottish case was propounded from the 1290s—is the degree to which the growth in the power of the monarchy is matched by the evidence for an active, self-identifying community or solidarity, a single people.[66] Ultimately if a people did not believe itself to be a people it could not act as such: those who sneer cynically at the Declaration of Arbroath as inflated rhetoric might care to remember what the Scottish people, the *Scottorum nacio*, had done during the previous twenty five years, for ten of them even formally without a king of their own.

The wars of those years were wars between two peoples as well as between two polities. So indeed were the wars between the English and the Welsh: that is indeed how they were described.[67] And so we come finally, and significantly for my argument, to the Welsh. The Welsh most certainly considered themselves to be a people and are equally certainly seen as such by external observers. But what constituted their Welshness? If we apply our criterion of territorial boundaries, then certainly by the

---

[65] Note, in particular, A. A. M. Duncan's view on these issues e.g. 'The Making of Scotland' (*ut supra* n. 56), 129–30, 137–8; *The Nation of Scots and the Declaration of Arbroath 1320* (1970), esp. 31–2; 'The making of the kingdom', *Why Scottish History Matters* (Saltire Society, 1991), 12–3.

[66] See, respectively, Barrow, *Anglo-Norman Era*, 161–8 (common or Scottish army); Grant G. Simpson, 'Kingship in Miniature: A Seal of the Minority of Alexander III, 1249–57', *Medieval Scotland. Crown, Lordship, Community. Essays Presented to G. W. S. Barrow*, ed. Alexander Grant and Keith J. Stringer (Edinburgh, 1993), 131–40 (minority seal); Alexander Grant, 'Aspects of National Consciousness in Medieval Scotland' in *Nations, Nationalism* (as cited above. 18), 79–81 (poem on death of Alexander III); Barrow, *Bruce*, 17 (seal of the Guardians); Norman H. Reid, 'Crown and Community under Robert I', *Medieval Scotland*, 203–23 (the language of Scottish propaganda 1296–1329).

[67] *Littere Wallie*, ed. J. G. Edwards (Cardiff, 1940), 1.

twelfth century, and probably much earlier, they had developed a clear image of Wales. It is true that they still had hang-ups about their glorious British past and accordingly dwelt wistfully on their original homeland in north Britain (*yr hen Ogledd*) and continued to expound the boundaries of the Britain which they one day hoped to recover.[68] But in their more realistic moments they had come to terms with the concept of a more restricted homeland—bounded by Offa's Dyke and the rivers Dee and Wye (though memories of a greater Wales extending to the Severn survived) and described as stretching diagonally from Porth Wygr in Anglesey to Portskewet on the Severn estuary, and from the gate of Chester to an unidentified Rhyd Taradyr.[69] When a Welsh princeling declared it his intention in 1198 'to restore to the Welsh their ancient liberty and their ancient proprietary rights and their boundaries' or when a poet exhorted another prince 'to take Wales from end to end' it was this precisely defined country that both had in mind.[70]

Not only was it precisely defined but it was also deeply loved. The poets regarded a circuit of Wales, *cylch Cymru*, as one of their favourite literary exercises; and Welsh literary lore regarded an easy familiarity with the place-names and regions of Wales as a natural expectation in its audience. But it was Gerald of Wales who provided what is perhaps the best-known vignette of the bond between the Welsh and their land in the words that the old man of Pencader is alleged to have spoken to the worldly-wise and much-travelled Henry II: 'the Welsh people (*gens ista, Kambrica*) will never be destroyed except by the anger of God alone ... because on the Day of Judgement no people or nation (*gens, lingua*) other than that of Wales will answer for this little corner of the world before the Supreme Judge'.[71] It is an assertion which has warmed the cockles of many a Welsh heart on St David's Day ever since; but for this more prosaic and academic exercise it has the virtue of identifying how far land and people were already inextricably one. The Welsh were well content with one word for both, *Cymru, Cymry*.

Perhaps they had more need than either the English or the Scots to cling to a territorial identity, however compromised that may have been by alien settlement, as one of the crucial emblems of their individuality as a people, because they did not show up well by the

---

[68] *Trioedd Ynys Prydein. The Welsh Triads*, ed. Rachel Bromwich (2nd edition. Cardiff 1978), cxxiii–cxxvii, 228–37; *Brut y Tywysogion Peniarth Ms. 20 Translation* (as cited above n. 7), 37.

[69] D. Myrddin Lloyd, 'The Poets of the Princes', *A Guide to Welsh Literature*, ed. A. O. H. Jarman and G. R. Hughes (Swansea, 1976), 161–2, 175; *Trioedd* (as cited in n. 68), 228–9.

[70] *Brut* (as in n. 7), 79; *Llawysgrif Hendregadredd*, ed. J. Morris-Jones and T. H. Parry-Williams (Cardiff, 1933), 207. See in general R. R. Davies, *The Age of Conquest. Wales 1063–1415* (Oxford, 1991), 15–20.

[71] *Opera*, VI, 227 (*Descriptio Kambrie*, II, x).

other criterion, that of regnal solidarity. It was not so much that the Welsh, or the Irish for that matter, lacked the vision of a political unity to complement their perception of their ethnic identity. Terms such as *rí Érenn* and *fir Érenn* (king and men of Ireland) appear as early as the ninth century; some Irish historians see great promise in 'the centralising policies of the great twelfth-century "high kings" '; while an occasional Irish king could try to turn dreams into reality by the stroke of a title as did Brian Ó Néil in 1260 when he allegedly styled himself 'king of the kings of Ireland' *(rex regum Hibernie)*.[72] In Wales the auguries for an effective regnal solidarity appeared to be, arguably, even better. The native chronicle could scarcely conceal its glee when the princes of Wales united against the English as they did in 1165 or 1198;[73] but it was the vigorous all-Wales, or at least all-native-Wales, ambitions of the princes of Gwynedd in the thirteenth century which provided the best prospect of an unitary polity. In 1215 Llywelyn ab Iorwerth had secured, in the Latin chronicle's phrase, 'the monarchy of almost the whole of Wales'; but it was his grandson who came closest to entering the promised land when he assumed, or was accorded, the title of prince of Wales in 1258 and had it formally confirmed in a treaty with the English negotiated by the papal legate in 1267.[74]

But it was not to be. Neither Wales nor Ireland attained the regnal solidarity which was so crucial in the making of the English and Scottish peoples. Three reasons at least suggest themselves why this was so. In neither country did effective and sustained unitary political structures develop, or develop soon enough, to provide an institutional corset for the well-developed sense of common ethnicity. In both countries the vastly superior strength of the English monarchy and its command of economic wealth served to destabilize further the native polities and to frustrate any movement towards native political consolidation. Furthermore the establishment of substantial enclaves of English settlers and powers in major parts of both countries from an early date meant that they were countries with at least twin ethnic identities within them. This ethnic duality was henceforth built, and indeed institutionally embedded, into the descriptive fabric of both countries—be it in legal and administrative division between Englishries and Welshries or between those areas *inter Anglicos* and those *inter Hibernicos*, in the fierce mentality of exclusiveness and superiority of communities such as 'the English of the county of Pembroke' or 'the English or Ireland', or in

---

[72] Ó Corráin, 'Nationality' (as cited n. 16 above) 8, 34; F.J. Byrne in *A New History of Ireland. II Medieval Ireland 1169–1534*, ed. A. Cosgrove (Oxford, 1981), 7–13, 37–42; *Close Rolls 1259–61*, 64.

[73] *Brut* (as cited in n. 7) *sub annis*.

[74] 'Cronica de Wallia' ed. T. Jones, *Bulletin of the Board of Celtic Studies* 12 (1946), *sub anno* 1215; in general, Davies, *Age of Conquest*, 236–51, 308–30.

the growing demonisation of 'the pure Irish' (*meri Hibernici*) as 'the wild Irish, our enemies'.[75] Regnal solidarity, therefore, could not, and did not, play the part in defining the Welsh and the Irish as a people which it had done very considerably for the English and the Scots. Yet the Welsh and the Irish retained in a considerable measure their strong sense of being separate and identifiable peoples. That suggests that there may be other variables which we should consider in trying to determine what constituted the identity of a people. Such will be the theme of the remaining two lectures.

It remains to pull together, briefly, the threads of the present lecture. Peoples are artificial creations; they assume a particular shape and definition according to time and circumstance. There is no single formula that adequately covers their relationship with political structures and territorial area. In the process of identification—both self-identification and identification by others—the acquiring of an accepted name and the definition of that name is one important phase. In the case of Britain and Ireland the centuries from the eleventh, or perhaps more correctly the tenth, to the fourteenth were a key period in shaping the nomenclature of the peoples of these islands in a form which, regardless—or indeed because of—its ambiguities and simplifications, was to last long into the future. They were also centuries of importance in bonding peoples to particular political structures and demarcated countries. By the fourteenth century it was clearer than arguably ever before that Britain and Ireland were countries of twin major kingships but of multiple, or perhaps one should say quadruple, peoples. The position of the Scots admitted of no argument. The position of the Welsh and the Irish, and in a different sense the English peoples of Ireland and Wales, within this regnal pattern was much more difficult. It was graphically pinpointed by the growing requirement that Welshmen and Irishmen should secure letters of denizenship in order to enjoy the privileges of Englishness and that Irish immigrants in England be treated as aliens.[76] The structure of the precocious English state which had developed in the middle age was, in the full sense of the word, quintessentially English; it has been part of its problem ever since to come to terms with the perception that Britain and Ireland are the lands of several peoples. Not least of the obstacles to the solution of that problem has been until recently and with some notable exceptions, the studied indifference of historians, past and present, to this fact.

[75] For these distinctions, and for the evidence, Davies, *Lordship and Society* (as cited n. 47), 302–18; *New History of Ireland II*, 241–3, 334–45, 393–6, 528; Robin Frame, 'Les Engleys' (as cited, n. 53); Art Cosgrove, *Late Medieval Ireland 1370 1541* (Dublin 1981), 72–82.
[76] R. A. Griffiths, 'The English Realm and Dominions and the King's subjects in the Later Middle Ages', *Aspects of Late Medieval Government and Society*, ed J. G. Rowe (Toronto, 1986), 83–105.

'HIS SPECIAL FRIEND'? THE SETTLEMENT OF DISPUTES AND POLITICAL POWER IN THE KINGDOM OF THE FRENCH (TENTH TO MID-TWELFTH CENTURY)

By Jane Martindale

READ 4 MARCH 1994

'FAILING help from God and Saint Martin, the canons found it necessary to renew their complaint before the lord Hugh, their abbot and count'.

'For almost six years', the canons of Saint-Martin de Tours had been trying to regain possession of land in the neighbouring diocese of Poitiers.[1] They complained that through 'the cupidity of Frankish men' they had been deprived of two estates; and, because 'they could never get justice for their claim', they were asking their lay-abbot, Hugh, for his advice. Hugh counselled them ' to go again and put their claim to the lord Count Ebles, his special friend' and to Ebles' own faithful men (*iterum ad domnum Ebolum comitem, suum specialem amicum, et praescriptos suos fideles*). Where God and his saint had not come to the canons' aid, co-operation between the two most powerful laymen of these regions broke this judicial deadlock: after intervention by Counts Hugh and Ebles, the viscounts of Thouars recognised that they had unjustly deprived Saint Martin of his property, and the two estates could be returned to the

---

[1] 'Tunc necesse fuit canonicis S. Martini ut excepto Dei & S. Martini adiutorio exinde ad domnum Hugonem abbatem suum & comitem reclamarent ...', cited from *Notitia de evindicatis in Thoarcinsi*, *Ex pancharta Nigra Turon.*, ed. J. Besly, *Histoire des Comtes de Poictou et Ducs de Guyenne* (Paris, 1647) [hereafter *Poictou*], *preuves* 218–20. See E. Mabille, 'La pancarte noire de Saint-Martin de Tours brûlée en 1793', *Mémoires de la Société Archéologique de la Touraine*, XVII (1865), no. cxvi; P. Gasnault, 'Les actes privés de l'abbaye de Saint-Martin de Tours du VIIIe au XIIe sièle', *Bibliothèque de l'Ecole des Chartes*, CXII (1954) [hereafter *BEC*], 24–66 (and 36–7 for this community's '*notices judiciares*'); G. Tessier, 'Les diplômes carolingiens du chartrier de Saint-Martin de Tours' in *Mélanges d'histoire du Moyen Age dédiés à la mémoire de Louis Halphen* (Paris, 1951), [hereafter, *Mélanges Halphen*], 683–91. A more recent edition of this document merely goes back (with some errors) to Besly's publication, M. Garaud, *Essai sur les institutions judiciaires du Poitou sous le gouvernement des comtes indépendants (902–1137)* (Poitiers, 1910) [hereafter Garaud, *Institutions judiciaires*], 169–70.

community of Saint-Martin once they had renounced their possession of
the *villae* of Curçay and Antogné.[2]

The notice which relates the details of this dispute between the
canons of Tours and the viscounts was issued on May 21st in the castle
of Thouars, and confirmed on the 29th at the villa Avrigny in the third
year of the reign of King Raoul (*Rodulfus*—i.e. in the year 926).[3] Because
it is an extended and elaborate account of an important legal dispute—
but also because of the political prominence of the lay-abbot Hugh and
his 'special friend' Count Ebles—this document provides an arresting
introduction to the nature of what Yvonne Bongert called the 'interpenetration of politics and justice' which is the main theme of this paper.[4]
In particular, the 926 notice provides a useful starting-point from which
to reconsider some widely held assumptions about the interaction of
Carolingian royal decline and the working of 'judicial institutions'
within the western Frankish kingdom—or some more restricted region

---

[2] For their return to the canons' possession, see the confirmation issued by King Odo
at Orléans on 2 June 896, *Recueil des actes d'Eudes roi de France (888–898)*, ed. R-H. Bautier,
Chartes et diplômes publiés par les soins de l'Académie des Inscriptions et Belles-Lettres
(Paris, 1967) [hereafter Ch. et dipl.], no. 41 (included in a list of lands previously *subtractas*).
A diploma of Charles 'the Simple' issued at Compiègne, 14 June 910/11 included
'Antoniacus, quin etiam ad eorum vestimenta et Curciacus cum omnibus rebus per-
tinentibus ...'. *Recueil des actes de Charles III le Simple roi de France (893–923)*, ed. P. Lauer,
Ch. et dipl., 2 vols. (1949), I, no. lxii; but cf. no. ci (dated 27 June 921, Herstal) for an
elaborate privilege issued for Saint-Martin de Tours in which these *villae* are not named
among the Saint's lands. By 24 March 931 they were once more confirmed as belonging
to the Saint by King Raoul, *Recueil des actes de Robert Ier et de Raoul, rois de France (922–
936)*, ed. J. Dufour, Ch. et dipl., (1978), no. 15. There is some difficulty over the
identification of these two *villae*, since (i) the canons' possessions included two places
called '*Curciacus*', *Actes de Charles III*, 99, but this is likely to be Curçay, (con. Trois-
Moutiers, dép. Vienne): and the second either (ii) Antogné (canton Châtellerault, Vienne),
or Antoigné (now in dép. Maine-et-Loire, near Montreuil-Bellay), see *Recueil des actes de
Pépin Ier et de Pépin II, rois d'Aquitaine (814–38)*, ed. L. Levillain, Ch. et dipl., (1928), 44 and
index.
[3] *Poictou*, 220: 'Data est autem haec notitia XII. Kal. Iunii in castro Thoarcinsi, et
percorroborata. 4. [thus] Kal. Iunii in villa Auriniaco anno. 3. regnante Rodulfo rege'.
This king's 'election' and consecration occurred at Soissons, 13 July 923, Dufour, ibid.,
introduction, xcviii. That results in the year 926 rather than 925, as given by Garaud,
Les châtelains de Poitou et l'avènement du régime féodal (XIe et XII siècles, Mémoires de la Société
des Antiquaires de l'Ouest, 4th series VIII (1964), 9 n. 22 [hereafter, *Châtelains de Poitou*,
and MSAO]. Cf. also A. Richard, *Histoire des comtes de Poitou*, 2 vols. (Paris, 1903) [hereafter
Richard, *Comtes*], I, 70–1 (with year 926).
[4] Y. Bongert, *Recherches sur les cours laïques du Xe au XIIIe siècle* (Paris, 1949), 143 (referring
favourably to the extension of royal judicial authority during the twelfth century by
means of war, as well 'judicial' activity). Cf. the comment, 'Early medieval court cases
were political', *The Settlement of Disputes in Early Medieval Europe*, ed. W. Davies and P.
Fouracre (Cambridge, 1986), [hereafter Davies and Fouracre, *Disputes*], 233; and also
Fouracre, 'Carolingian justice: the rhetoric of improvement and contexts of abuse', 1–16
(to appear in the 1995 volume of the *Settimane di Studio* of Spoleto). My thanks to Paul
Fouracre for allowing me to see this before publication.

within it. Furthermore, the Saint-Martin notice has an intrinsic regional and political importance, since the topics to be considered in this paper relate primarily to disputes which occurred within the 'territorial principality' built up by Count Ebles and his descendants—the duchy of Aquitaine (or of 'the Aquitanians'). The timespan of the paper will cover the tenth to approximately the first half of the twelfth century.[5]

The need to invoke divine aid, and the long delays which the canons of Saint-Martin experienced before they got human justice, appear to fit a pattern often regarded as characteristic of the late Carolingian and early Capetian eras. The centralisation associated with Carolingian royal government could, it has been argued, no longer be imposed or maintained. According to Jean-François LeMarignier, at this time the dispersal of 'regalian rights' was allied to 'an extreme fragmentation of public power, such as has never previously occurred and, in any case, has never been surpassed in any other period of history': in a seminal and much-quoted study Lemarignier argued that regional 'fragmentation' was demonstrated by 'the dislocation of the *pagus*' which resulted in loss of comital political control. The authority of the traditional territorial court, the *mallus*, was also—according to this interpretation—irreversibly undermined.[6]

[5] The conviction that some, at least, of the current views on the settlement of disputes in post-Carolingian 'France' are in need of modification was prompted by the documentary material associated with the government and political power of the Poitevin dukes of Aquitaine (one of the chief themes of a forthcoming book). As there is no printed edition or catalogue of these rulers' *acta*, charters and notices will be cited from numerous sources; but discussion of the disputes in which members of the Poitevin dynasty were involved is based on an unpublished calendar of their *acta* of these rulers prepared, but not included, in Martindale, 'The Origins of the Duchy of Aquitaine and the Government of the Counts of Poitou (902–1137)' (D. Phil. thesis of the University of Oxford, 1964). This paper coincides with the timespan of Garaud's pioneering work of legal history, but it has a political—rather than a strictly legal—point of departure, and thus needs to consider ducal territories beyond Poitou. The limiting 'date' is the year 1137, for with the marriage of Louis VII to Eleanor, the Poitevins' 'territorial principality' passed for the next twenty-five years into the hands of the Capetian king.

[6] J-F. Lemarignier, 'La dislocation du "*pagus*" et le problème des "*consuetudines*" (Xe–XIe siècles)' in *Mélanges Louis Halphen*, 401–10 (citation, 408–9); and for comparisons between royal control in the tenth and early eleventh centuries, id. *Le gouvernement royal aux premiers temps capétiens (987–1108)* (Paris, 1965), 29–30, 65. Similar views were expressed by Bongert, ibid., 37–9, 291–2); cf. J. P. Poly and E. Bournazel, *La mutation féodale, Xe–XIIe siècles*, (Paris, 1980), 59–103. On the earlier territorial organisation of 'the ordinary court, that is the county court or *mallus*', F-L. Ganshof, 'The impact of Charlemagne on Frankish institutions' in *The Carolingians and the Frankish Monarchy, Studies in Carolingian History* (London, 1971–1st appeared 1965), 147–52 (evidence chiefly taken from sources of prescriptive character); and for the comital role cf. K. F. Werner, '*Missus-Marchio-Comes*: entre l'administration centrale et l'administration locale de l'Empire carolingien', *Histoire comparée d l'administration (IVe–XVIIIe siècles), Beihefte der Francia*, IX (1980), 199–200 [hereafter '*Marchio-missus-comes*']. Cf. also next note. Two important aspects of these developments have had to be omitted from this paper for lack of time and space. They are: the

The classic development of that thesis is to be found in the studies by Georges Duby on southern Burgundy, and more especially on the Mâconnais—the *pagus* where the abbey of Cluny was established in the early tenth century. Duby's investigations also led him to consider that comital control of the *mallus* was lost by the turn of the tenth and eleventh centuries: thus a court whose jurisdiction had originally extended over all regional magnates (the *proceres patriae*) was transformed into a body largely composed of household officials and personal dependants. Superior judicial power within this region of Burgundy came to be dispersed between the heads of wealthy religious communities (like the abbot of Cluny) and local castellans. At this stage of disintegration, in Duby's words, 'the castle is the fundamental element in judicial organisation': it follows, too, that the count is no longer the 'centre of political life', as he had been when he sat in justice in the territory committed to him by Carolingian kings.[7] Moreover councils for 'peace', which made their appearance in the Mâconnais from the late tenth century onward, were in Duby's opinion both 'a cause and a proof of the weakening of comital power'.[8] The working out of these views has lent great authority to the assumption that there was a direct—indeed causal—relationship between political decline and

---

prominence attached to *consuetidines*/'customs' in the post-Carolingian world, and the fate of the 'immunities' which kings bestowed on ecclesiastical communities.

[7] G. Duby, *La société aux XIe et XIIe siècles dans la région mâconnaise* (Paris, 2nd edn. 1971) [hereafter *Mâconnais*], 95–8, 140–5 (quotation, 142), 146–8; and id., 'Recherches sur l'evolution des institutions judiciaires pendant le Xe et le Xie siècle dans le sud de la Bourgogne' in *Hommes et structures du moyen âge, recueil d'articles* (Paris/The Hague, 1973—art. 1st published 1946), 14, 28–31. For the application of those conclusions to a very different *cadre*, J-P. Delumeau, 'L'exercice de la justice dans le comté d'Arezzo (IXe-début XIIIe siècle)', *Mélanges de l'École francaise de Rome*, XC (1978), 563–4; cf. P.J. Geary, 'Vivre en conflit dans une France sans état: typologie des mécanismes de règlement des conflits', *Annales ESC*, XL (no. 4), (1986), esp. 1107–10; and for a recent assessment of the social implications of some of the political and judicial changes postulated by Duby, S. White, *Custom, Kinship and Gifts to Saints*, The Laudatio Parentum *in Western France, 1050–1150* (Chapel Hill, 1988), 180–86. For more traditional 'positivist' accounts of the operations of justice within 'la société féodale', Halphen, 'La justice en France au XIe siècle', *Région angévine'* in *A travers l'histoire du moyen âge* (Paris, 1950—first appeared 1901), 175–202; Ganshof, 'Contribution à l'étude des origines de cours féodales en France', *Revue historique de droit francais et etranger*, 00 (1928), 644–65.

[8] Duby, *Mâconnais*, 140—late tenth to early eleventh century, and for a general review, id., 'Les laïcs et la paix de Dieu' in *Hommes et structures* (1st pub. 1966), 227–40; but cf. H.J.A. Cowdrey, 'The peace and the truce of God in the eleventh century', *Past and Present*, XLVI (1970), 42–67. For a recent collection of studies on many facets of that 'movement', *The Peace of God, Social Violence and Religious Response in France around the Year 1000*, ed. T. Head and R. Landes, (Ithaca, 1992); for a study which has a bearing on the background to this paper, Martindale, 'Peace and war in early eleventh-century Aquitaine' in *The Ideals and Practice of Medieval Knighthood*, ed. C. Harper-Bill and R. Harvey, IV (1992), 147–76 [to be reprinted during 1995 in a volume of collected essays, *Status, Authority and Regional Power: Aquitaine and France, Ninth to Twelfth Centuries*, Variorum Press, no. VI].

judicial weakness; but, even where such views have been questioned, they remain extremely influential and have often provided the framework for discussion of the power exercised in 'territorial principalities'.[9]

To return to the canons of Saint-Martin in the year 926. Their demands for the restitution of Curçay and Antogné may have met with protracted secular resistance, but the account of the dispute gives no hint that, once their *reclamatio* was taken up by the counts, the traditional organisation and administration of justice were in decline. On the contrary, the proceedings which resulted in a settlement in Saint Martin's favour were complicated and time- consuming. Initially, a chosen party of canons travelled from the city of Tours to the castle of Loudun in Poitou and then on to a number of other places, including the city of Poitiers and the *villa Curciacus* itself. At Loudun an oral complaint was made: 'they represented to [the viscount] the misery and straitened circumstances of the brethren ... and he commiserated with them...': they also produced the letter sent by Count Hugh to his 'special friend'. (Unfortunately that letter, if it survived the conclusion of the settlement, was not kept in the canons' archive). At this stage both Count Ebles and Bishop Frotherius of Poitiers were personally drawn into the dispute, and are mentioned prominently in the settlement of the canons' grievances. It is difficult to decide, however, whether the turning-point of the dispute was—as the narrative implies—the recognition that the claimants' 'professions were right and just', or whether—as we may suspect—a settlement was brought about through the pressure brought to bear on the viscounts by two of the most powerful laymen of the Loire region. But no *amateur* of this type of document will be surprised to read that the viscounts and their men (described as both their *compares* and *fideles*) are portrayed as voluntarily renouncing everything 'inspired by the divine clemency and compelled by love of Saint Martin'.[10]

[9] For criticism of the assumption of 'the strength of the state being measured by the frequency of uncompromising judgments in courts, potentially cutting across all local relationships', Davies and Fouracre, *Disputes*, 236; and in general on the prevalence and importance of 'collective judgments' over a long timespan, S. Reynolds, *Kingdoms and Communities in Western Europe, 900–1300* (Oxford, 1984), 23–34; cf. White, '*Pactum ... legem vincit et amor judicium*', the settlement of disputes by compromise in eleventh-century western France', *American Journal of Legal History*, XXII (1978), esp. 281–5, 307–8. Cf; below, 29–31.

[10] 'Dominus ergo Savaricus vicecomes voluntates et professiones illorum rectas et iustas intelligens ...', *Poictou*, ibid. (Garaud's edition here reads *possessiones* for *professiones*, *Institutions judiciaires*, 170). All quotations are my translations from Besly's text of the notice which (with the MS. tradition of the lost Poitevin charters for this religious community) will be discussed at greater length in the study already mentioned in note 5. For the venerable connection between Frankish kings and Saint Martin, J. Fleckenstein, *Die Hofkapelle der deutschen Könige. Grundlegung. I, Die Karolingische Hofkapelle*, Schriften der Monumenta Germaniae Historica [hereafter MGH], (Stuttgart, 1959), 11–16; and for

The formalities which concluded the settlement were elaborate. In the first place, the transfer of the lands to Saint Martin was made by Viscount Savari 'with the staff which he was holding in his hand ...' to the canons' *prepositus Farmannus* 'in place of all the brothers'. Then a 'notice' was drafted and read out publicly before Count Ebles and a body of his men in the castle of Colombiers; finally—and at yet another place—the parchment was subscribed in the customary fashion. The list of subscribers begins: 'the lord Ebles confirmed it first, and requested his faithful men to confirm it. S[ign] of Count Ebles who faithfully completed this '*justiciam*' for love of Saint Martin'. As a written instrument this document seems to have fulfilled a number of different functions. Essentially as a text it provided proof of the settlement of a complaint made by one of the most influential ecclesiastical communities in the west Frankish realm; but, although the document was authenticated according to established convention, the canons' possession of their two estates also depended on what, in a memorable phrase, has been described as '*le jeu de symbole germanique*'.[11] The need for investiture with a 'symbolic object' is mentioned in the text, but additionally the parchment seems to have acquired its own material significance, since indeed, 'the lord Bishop Frotherius by touching it confirmed it with devotion' (*Domnus vero Frotherius eam tangens votive firmavit*—i.e. the *notitia*, now brought to the *villa* Avrigny).[12]

Since the power to pronounce and enforce judgments has often been

---

Saint Martin as personal *patronus* of the members of the 'Robertian' dynasty, *Actes de Robert ier et de Raoul*, no. 40 (Appendix), grant of a. 897 by the Count-abbot Robert (future king and father of the Count-abbot Hugh of this document).

[11] A. de Bouard, *Manuel de diplomatique française et pontificale* II, *L'acte privé* (Paris, 1948), 94–6, 100–01 (100 for the citation). Medieval historians have often primarily studied the use of such symbols as part of a 'system' of 'vassalage', J. LeGoff, 'Le rituel symbolique de la vassalité' in *Pour un autre moyen âge, temps, travail et culture en occident* (Paris, 1977—1st pub. 1976), 349, 365, 414–19; cf. the 'classic' exposition by Ganshof, *Feudalism* (transl. P. Grierson, 3rd Eng. edn. 1964), 125–7 (under 'Investiture'). For a rather different viewpoint relating to the Germanic and Vulgar Roman law background to '*la saisine*', P. Ourliac and J. Gazzaniga, *Histoire du droit privé français de l'an mil au Code Civil* (Paris, 1985), 205–11; and now for a critical analysis of the whole 'construct of feudalism', Reynolds, *Fiefs and Vassals, The Medieval Evidence Reinterpreted* (Oxford, 1994), 1–16 (p. 10).

[12] Frotherius bishop of Poitiers, a. 900–36, *Gallia Christiana* ..., 16 vols., ed. D. de Ste Marthe et al., II (Paris, 1720), cols. 1159–60. The *Diagram* (p. 27) is intended to convey rapidly some impression of the extensive travels of the canons which have not been fully described here. Loudun and Colombiers were both described as fortified (*castrum*) in the *noticia*, but the former was also the seat of a Carolingian *vicaria*—i.e. an administrative subdivision of the *pagus*—(both now dép. Vienne, see Garaud, *Châtelains*, 5, 16, 32; cf. id. 'Les circonscriptions administratives du comté du Poitou et les auxiliaires du comte au Xe siècle', *Le Moyen Age*, LIX (1953), 13–61; and 'La construction des châteaux et les destinées de la "vicaria" et du "vicarius" carolingiens en Poitou, *RHDFE* (1953), 55, n. 4. *Auriniacum* seems identifiable with Avrigny in the same département, but I have been unable to identify *Orbiacum/Orbiciacus*.

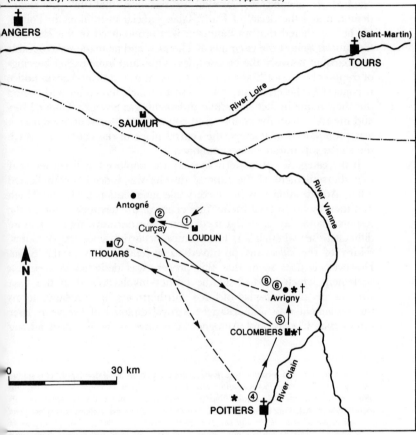

**Map to illustrate the course of dispute between canons of
Saint Martin de Tours and Viscounts of Thouars (926)**
(from J. Besly, Histoire des Comtes de Poictou, Paris 1647, pp218-20)

✝ bishop's see, <u>civitas</u>

▪ castle, fortified site

● other sites (unspecified or <u>villae</u>)

_.._ approximate boundary of archdiocese of Tours
and northern Poitou (dioc. Poitiers)

►① Probable order of canons' journey (dotted line = less certain course:
the sequence is confusing, and the judgement at <u>Poitiers</u> may have occurred earlier)

③ <u>Orbiacum</u> is unidentified

✱ Presence of Count Ebles noted in text

✝ Presence of Bishop of Poitiers

regarded as the most important sign of an effective legal system, this narrative has sometimes been dismissed for its signs that compromise and voluntary renunciation were the means by which settlement was reached. It seemed to Garaud, for instance, that the 926 notice demonstrated the decay of Carolingian judicial institutions in Poitou, for he considered that no judgment was pronounced in this claim by the canons against the viscounts of Thouars; and he made unfavourable comparisons between the proceedings of 926 and some earlier hearings of disputes by Count Ebles in Poitiers. As far as the Saint-Martin notice is concerned, he erred: the document to which the count and bishop put their name in fact states that judgment was given by Count Ebles and his *fideles* 'with the counsel and consent' of all present: moreover it was pronounced in Poitiers, the central place of the county, to which the *mallus* was traditionally summoned.[13]

If the categories of modern analysis are employed, it becomes clear that the settlement of the canons' dispute was indeed a complicated affair. Adjudication was involved; while intervention by Count Hugh and then by his 'special friend' (the count of the territory in which the disputed lands lay) involved mediation. The narrative makes it more difficult to see whether any compromise occurred, since the viscounts' return of the *villae* was portrayed as a renunciation to the Saint. However, it does seem that this process was designed to secure a settlement which satisfied all the parties involved, and in this case without any direct display of force. Furthermore, in cumulative terms this settlement was 'authoritative': a royal diploma of five years later shows that Curçay and Antogné were once more included among

---

[13] The viscounts' renunciation was made 'secundum etiam quod domnus Ebolus suique fideles ex ipsa ratione Pictavis iudicaverant per consilium et consensum in circuitu omnium residentium ...', *Poictou*, ibid (this gathering is not called a *mallus*, but its members were behaving like one); but cf. Garaud, for whom the settlement was '*cet accord ... confirmé par le comte. Il n'y avait pas de jugement*', *Châtelains de Poitou*, 9. n. 22. *Noticiae* of three earlier occasions when Count Ebles presided over legal proceedings have been preserved, and all the disputes were heard and settled in Poitiers, on 4 May 903, 30 March 904, 28 April 925: *Chartes de l'abbaye de Nouaillé de 678 à 1200*, ed. P. de Monsabert, Archives Historiques du Poitou XLIX (1936) [hereafter AHP], nos. 32, 31 (from original, Paris, Bibliothèque Nationale, Collection de Bourgogne vol. 76, no. 4; Poitiers, Archives Départementales de la Vienne, fonds Nouaillé, no. 20); *Chartes et documents pour servir à l'histoire de l'abbaye de Saint-Maixent*, ed. A. Richard, AHP XVI–VII (1886) no. 11 (BN, ms. nouv. acqu. lat., 2386, no. 1) [hereafter all published documents from ecclesiastical archives will be cited under the name of the appropriate house]. Those who 'sat' with the count were described in these documents as *obtimates/optimates* or as comital *vassalli*. For Garaud these gatherings embody 'le type des premiers cours féodales qui ont conservé ... le caractère des plaids carolingiens', *Institutions judiciaires*, 37–41; cf. on Carolingian counts' unfavourable press in judicial matters, Fouracre, 'Carolingian justice', 9.

Saint-Martin's possessions—and being used to provide for the canons' clothes.[14]

Conflict and war are the dominant themes of the early tenth century as portrayed by narrative writers like Flodoard of Reims who traced the activity of kings, princes, and great ecclesiastics between the years 919 and his death in 966. Two years before the settlement of the complaint by the canons of Tours, Hugh's own lands 'between Seine and Loire' had been devastated by Rollo's men from the province of Rouen; in Poitiers during the same year Count Ebles gave protection to monks from Brittany who were fleeing from similar attacks, and brought with them the body of their saint.[15] Troops of 'Hungarians' would soon appear in the western kingdom too—first in Mediterranean Gothia, then in Burgundy and even Aquitaine.[16] And the political setting of the Saint-Martin's dispute was equally sombre. The Carolingian King Charles was captive in Péronne, while the lay-abbot Count Hugh's father (King Robert) had been killed in battle against Charles three years previously.[17]

Against that background the 926 notice—far from confirming the view that political instability was resulting in governmental and judicial breakdown—shows that time and energy continued to be devoted by two of the most powerful laymen of the Loire region to make a secure

[14] Above, n. 2. For the distinctions between methods of settlement of disputes, Davies and Fouracre, *Disputes*, 235–6; S. Roberts, 'The study of disputes: Anthropological perspectives', in *Disputes and Settlements: Law and Human Relations in the West*, ed. J. Bossy (Cambridge, 1983), 1–17; cf. M. Gluckman, *Politics, Law and Ritual in Tribal Society* (Oxford, 1965), esp. 123–215; F. Cheyette, 'Suum cuique tribuere', *French Historical Studies*, VI (1970), 292–3.

[15] *Les Annales de Flodoard*, ed. P. Lauer, Collection de textes pour servir à l'étude et à l'enseignement de l'histoire (Paris, 1905), 24—a. 924, 'Ragenoldus cum suis Nordmannis, quia nondum possessionem intra Gallias acceperat, terram Hugonis inter Ligerim et Sequanam depopulatur'; and cf. 6 -a. 921 (for Hugh's father's attempt to expel those wishing to make a permanent settlement in the Loire region). For the movements of Saint Maixent's body, recalled in the cartulary of the Breton monastery of Redon, Besly, *Poictou*, 217–8; *Cartulaire de l'abbaye de Redon en Bretagne*, ed. A. de Courson, (Paris, 1863), no. 283. In general on that phenomenon, M. Bloch, *Feudal Society*, transl. L. Manyon, (London, 1961), 20–22; but for a more critical attitude towards evidence of this type, L. Musset, *Les invasions, le second assaut contre l'Europe chrétienne (VIIe–XIe siècles)*, Nouvelle Clio, (Paris, 1971), 228–9.

[16] *Annales de Flodoard*, 26, cf. 61, 65–6 (devastation of *Francia* a. 937), 66–7 (same year, region of Reims and movement to the *pagus* of Bourges in Aquitaine), 131 (entry into Aquitaine, a. 951), 137 (Burgundy and Lotharingia/Lorraine, a. 954).

[17] A. Eckel, *Charles le Simple* (Paris, 1899), 130; and 123–4 for the battle near Soissons which preceded the accession of Raoul; cf. P. Lauer, *Robert 1er et Raoul de Bourgogne, rois de France (923–93)* (Paris, 1910), 11–45; *Actes de Robert 1er et de Raoul*, intro. xcvi. For the wider political background, R. McKitterick, *The Frankish Kingdoms under the Carolingians, 751–987* London, 1983), 306–13; *Histoire de France*, I, K. F. Werner, *Les origines* (Paris, 1984), 451–51; M. Sot, 'Hérédité royale et pouvoir sacré avant 987', *Annales E.S.C.* (1988), 705–33.

settlement for the canons of Saint Martin. They were doing this in a pragmatic, but extremely traditional, way in an attempt to find a remedy for the deficiencies of what we know—but perhaps they did not—was 'late' Carolingian administration, on the way out. For when Count Hugh sent the canons of Saint-Martin's to his 'special friend' Ebles he was apparently acknowledging that, in order to regain land in Poitou, the canons must 'plead' in that 'friend's' county, since the chief resources of their powerful lay-abbot and the Saint's burial-church lay elsewhere, in the diocese of Tours and beyond.[18] It was not then, so much the 'dislocation of the *pagus*' which impeded the canons' search for justice, but what might be better described as a 'dislocation between *pagi*'. In the absence of any royal authority capable of despatching *missi* throughout the kingdom, one practical legal solution for the settlement of a case like this was co-operation between secular magnates whose political authority could be used to bridge the boundaries which now divided 'autonomous' regional units and thereby serve, as they saw it, the interests of justice. This was not simply a 'one-off' solution: in the later tenth century, for instance, the monks of Saint-Denis succeeded in regaining land in Normandy after they had made their initial complaint 'in a joint plea of *Normanni* and *Franci*'.[19]

The 'special friend' provided the link between the parties in 926, and the term *amicus* conveyed a range of meanings which would have been well understood in aristocratic circles at this time.[20] Three years before Hugh's despatch of his letter to his 'special friend' Ebles, King Robert (Hugh's own father) and the German King Henry I made a public declaration of their friendship; it seems probable that this would have been concluded in a similar fashion to the agreement between King Charles the Simple and the same German king in the year 921/2.

---

[18] For an earlier example of ecclesiastics from the Touraine being obliged to cross into Poitou (then within the *regnum Aquitanorum*) in order to obtain a settlement about lands held in that county and diocese—admittedly from the regional king, *Recueil des actes de Pépin 1er et de Pépin II, rois d'Aquitaine, (814–48)*, ed. L. Levillain, Ch. et. dipl. (1926), no. XII—9 June 828; and for discussion, cf. J. Nelson, 'Dispute settlement in Carolingian West Francia' in *Disputes*, 48–52, 246–7.

[19] '... communi Francorum Normannorumque placito petierunt reclamantes', *Recueil des actes des Ducs de Normandie*, ed. M. Fauroux, Mémoires de la Société des Antiquaires de Normandie, XXXVI (1961) [hereafter *Ducs de Normandie*], no. 3, 18 March 968. Like the Saint-Martin dispute, this went through a number of stages: first heard at Gisors, before it was moved to Rouen where Count Richard [i.e. Duke Richard I] 'decreed' the return of their *potestas* to the monks. Finally the latter travelled to Berneval, and the land of Saint-Denis was formally returned to them.

[20] The drafter of the 926 *noticia* was careful in his use of terms denoting social and political relationships—*dominus* and *fideles*, the unusual *compares*, as well as *amicus*. Interestingly another judicial document from this *scriptorium* also describes the counts Berengar and the lay-abbot Robert (Hugh's father), as *amici*, *Actes de Robert 1er et de Raoul*, no. 37—13 June 892, (141).

Charles had sworn, 'I will be a friend to my friend according to my knowledge and ability, just as a friend ought by right to behave to his friend.'[21] 'Friendship pacts' have been much discussed by historians of the post-Carolingian German kingdom in recent years, and these pacts were obviously of considerable significance in the political world of the early tenth century; but as yet that significance does not seem to have been widely recognised among historians of the western kingdom. As Karl Schmid observed, a properly defined 'semantic field' has not yet been established as the basis for discussions of tenth- century friendship; nevertheless, it is important to emphasise that the Tours notice being considered here brings out the equality of the two 'friendly' parties, showing that social relationships at this time were not only created through bonds of consanguinity and dependence (which have chiefly attracted historians' attention for these years). 'Friendship', too, might be employed to set in motion or influence legal disputes thrown up in these decades of political conflict.[22]

Both Hugh and Ebles were among the greatest founders of 'territorial principalities' within the former West Frankish kingdom—and well qualified to employ political power in order to pursue judicial ends. As well as being the son and nephew of kings, Hugh was also brother-in-law of the current *rex Francorum Rodulfus* and was himself married to a daughter of King Athelstan of the West Saxons; but, despite the great power which he wielded, with hindsight his political position is more often assessed in terms of his ancestry of the royal Capetian dynasty, and more particularly as father of the Hugh who became king in 987.[23]

[21] K. Schmid, 'Unerforschte Quellen aus Quellenarmer Zeit: Zur *amicitia* zwischen Heinrich I und dem westfränkischen König Robert im Jahre 923', *Francia* XII (1984), 136, 141; and for the text of the oath, 142 and n. 94. Cf. the wording of the vernacular fraternal oaths sworn by the Carolingians Louis and Charles at Strasbourg in Feb. 842, *Nithard, Histoire des fils de Louis le Pieux*, ed. P. Lauer, Les classiques de l'histoire de France au moyen âge, (2nd edn., Paris, 1964), 104–5.; and see next n.

[22] '... so zeigt dies, dass ein bestimmtes Bedeutungsfeld des Begriffs "amicitia" noch nicht richt im Blick ist', contrasting the attention lavished by historians on the meanings of '*Gefolge, Vasallen*', Schmid, ibid., 144 and to 146; G. Althoff, *Verwandte, Freunde und Getreue*, (Darmstadt, 1990), 105–7. But for *amicitia* between men who were not social or political equals, T. Reuter, *Germany in the Early Middle Ages (800–1056)*, (London, 1991), 138–41, 144–50 (Otto I's refusal to conclude such pacts), 259, 290; and in general on the 'networks' created by such alliances, S. Airlie, 'After Empire—recent work on the emergence of post-Carolingian kingdoms', *Early Medieval Europe* II (1993), 156–7.

[23] A comprehensive bibliography on the 'rise of the Capetians' would be out of place in this context, but in general see now especially, McKitterick, *The Frankish Kingdoms under the Carolingians*, 314–36; Werner, *Les origines*, 463–96; J. Dunbabin *France in the Making (843–1180)* (Oxford, 1985), 65–8, 96–7, 103–4, 133–40; E. Hallam, 'The king and the princes in eleventh-century Capetian France', *Bulletin of the Institute of Historical Research*, LIII (1980), 143–56. Cf. the influential study by J. Dhondt, *Etudes sur la naissance des principautés territoriales en France (IX–Xe siécle)* (Bruges, 1948). 81–146; but also Werner, 'Kingdom and principality in twelfth-century France', in *The Medieval Nobility, Studies on the Ruling Classes*

The connections of his 'special friend' Ebles were less illustrious but, as count of Poitiers, Ebles was the son of Ramnulf who—like Hugh's uncle Odo—was included in an annalist's list of 'petty-kings' (*reguli*). They were the political figures who emerged in the aftermath of Carolingian failure to defend the city of Paris against the Northmen, and following the death of the Emperor Charles the Fat. As future 'dukes of Aquitaine' Ebles's descendants also came to assert authority over far more extensive territories in the eleventh and twelfth centuries than their ancestors had done as counts in Poitou under Carolingian rulers.[24]

The significance of the 926 judicial notice may be summarised before proceeding, since it serves as a starting-point for what follows—as well as its essential background. Firstly, the 'judicial process' was set in motion by two powerful laymen, not by the king. Their political authority and the pursuit of legal aims were linked. But—and this is the second point of importance—the subsequent proceedings show that these men employed customary and traditional methods. Hugh respected the territorial jurisdiction of a neighbouring count, while (if we are to believe the text of this notice) Ebles bent all his efforts to ensure that his men would yield to the 'justice' of the canons' claim, and renounce their misappropriation of the Saint's estates. The whole elaborate process indicates respect for traditional methods and practices, but it also suggests that the settlement of disputes in general was regarded as one of the main functions to be performed by a 'territorial prince'. That, at any rate, is the assumption on which the rest of this paper is based.

The overriding aim is now to pursue the connection between judicial activity and the exercise of political power through an investigation of regional disputes and their settlement viewed from the standpoint of the secular ruler. That involves the sorting and classification of the relevant documents according to political criteria; this approach might

---

of France and Germany from the Sixth to the Twelfth Century, ed. and transl. T. Reuter (Amsterdam/New York, 1978), [hereafter 'Kingdom and principality'], 243–90.

[24] 'Odo filius Rodberti usque ad Ligerim fluvium vel Aquitanicam provinciam sibi in usum usurpavit; deinceps Ramnolfus se regem haberi statuit', *Annales Fuldenses*, ed. F. Kurze, MGH, scriptores in usum scholarum (Hanover, 1891), 116 -a. 888; another annalist described this Ramnulf as '*dux maximae partis Aquitaniae*', *Annales Xantenses et Annales Vedastin*, ed. B. de Simson, MGH ... in usum scholarum, (Hanover, 1909), 67- a. 889; Sot, 'Hérédité royale', 713–7. For the expansion of the power of Ebles and his descendants, L. Auzias, *L'Aquitaine carolingienne* (Paris/Toulouse, 1937), 461–518 (a fragmentary part of this posthumous work); Dhondt, ibid. 194–6, 215–26 (in need of considerable revision, however); McKitterick, ibid. 313, 320; Dunbabin, ibid., 58–63; Werner, 'Kingdom and principality' 247–9, 252–3. The history of these counts is followed through on a chronological basis in Richard's standard account, see n. 3.

be regarded as correcting a prevailing trend, since in recent years the framework for discussion of such material has often been provided by the legal interests of religious communities, or by the decline of central control which has appeared to be of paramount importance to modern historians. Another approach has been via the setting of a geographical region.[25] In the first place, it seemed probable that the investigations of areas of known political and territorial expansion could throw light on a number of problems which have often been envisaged by historians of French regions largely in terms of disintegration and decline. Additionally the nature of the proceedings in which 'princes' became involved raises questions which need further airing, since historians (and perhaps especially historians interested in law) have often approached these topics with readymade conceptions about the nature of 'feudal justice', and about jurisdiction in the post-Carolingian world. Should 'concord' and 'judgment' be regarded as complementary, rather than contrasting, methods of reaching a settlement, for instance? This already seems to have been the case in the 926 notice just considered. And how far did judgment involve recourse to methods of proof which could be interpreted as part of a '*zauberpriestlicher Prozess*', or which might seem to betray signs of an irrational outlook on the world?[26]

The material for discussion has been largely drawn from documents issued for the members of the Poitevin dynasty who were Count Ebles's descendants; but comparisons have also been made with material available for rulers of two very different territories of Carolingian origin, the counts of Anjou and Angoulême (again until approximately the mid-twelfth century).[27] Then, because the material may perhaps be

[25] Cf. the account and examples cited above. See also White, 'Feuding and peace-making in the Touraine around the year 1000', *Traditio* XLII (1986), 195–263; id. 'Inheritances and legal arguments in Western France, 1050–1150', *Traditio*, XLIII (1987), 55–103; cf. R. Balzaretti, 'The monastery of Sant' Ambrogio and dispute settlement in early medieval Milan', *Early Medieval Europe*, III (1994), 1–18. For a well-merited attack on the excessively centralising standpoint of many historians, Werner, 'Royaume et *regna*, Le pouvoir en France comme enjeu entre le roi et les grands' in *Pouvoirs et libertés au temps des premiers Capétiens*, ed. E. Magnou-Nortier, (Cholet, 1992), 25–6, 45–52.

[26] For the description of ordeals as 'magico-priestly', R. Van Caenegem, 'Methods of proof in western medieval law', in *Legal History: a European Perspective* (London, 1991— article first publ. 1983), 73; and further below, 47–50 (and nn. 61–8). For analysis of the varying methods employed to secure settlement whether by 'state' or 'local community', Davies and Fouracre, *Disputes*, 235–6—note the comment 'adjudication and mediation are in principle opposites, and can be separated analytically. But they do not represent *historical* oppositions'.

[27] (i). For the *acta* of the Poitevin rulers, see below n. 30. (ii). a) Between the end of the tenth century and c. 1109, between 56–65 documents have been preserved relating to disputes in which the Angevin counts were involved—figures based on a correlation of the calendars and *pièces justificatives* in L. Halphen, *Le comté d'Anjou au XIe sièle* (Paris, 1906) and O. Guillot, *Le comte d'Anjou et son entourage au XIe siècle L'Anjou de 1109 à 1151*, 2 vols., Paris, 1972). The discrepancies can be largely accounted for by the rather different

more familiar to English medieval historians, I have also drawn on the *acta* of the Norman rulers for the years preceding Duke William's conquest of the English kingdom.[28] Unfortunately the scope of this paper did not provide any opportunity to discuss the survival or revival of Roman law in the *pays d'oc*. In Poitou this might still occasionally be known as the 'Law of Laws' in the early tenth century, but it does not seem to have had any impact on methods of court procedure, or on the settlement of disputes.[29] Although time prevents detailed critical discussion of this material, a few preliminary remarks on the distribution or provenance of these regional sources are nevertheless essential, for where 'originals' exist they derive from the archives of litigants and beneficiaries, and were almost invariably the products of ecclesiastical *scriptoria*. The absence—or just possibly the disappearance—of secular archives has fairly obvious implications for the survival of legal or judicial documents; but so does the fact that many important transactions undoubtedly took place without the benefit of writing. (Once more, the 926 notice revealed the importance in a legal context both of symbolic gestures and oral performance). The surviving documents preserving records of the settlement of disputes or the preceding processes were the products of a society for which 'memory' had certainly not been replaced by 'written record'. Perhaps that also helps to account for the

---

criteria employed in these works. b) 45 documents of judicial character are included in the later catalogue compiled by J. Chartrou, *L'Anjou de 1109 à 1151, Foulque de Jérusalem et Geoffroi Plantegênet* (Paris, n. d.). Documents relating to Angevin rule in Normandy under Geoffrey 'le Bel' have not, however, been included. (iii). The *acta* of the counts of Angoulême (to the mid-twelfth century only) will be cited from the appendices to the unpublished thesis by Rowan Watson, 'The Counts of Angoulême from the Ninth to the Mid-thirteenth Century', (PH.D. of the University of East Anglia, 1979), which I am very grateful to be allowed to cite here. Between c. 1003×4 to the mid-twelfth century there are 12 documents of judicial character in which these counts were involved. (Two documents relating to Count Vulgrin's appearance before the Duke of Aquitaine with other secular lords of Oléron in the year 1131 are not included, see below, n. 45).

[28] The edition of Norman ducal *acta* before 1066 (see, above n. 19) indicates the survival of 14 documents of judicial character in which Norman rulers were involved. Cf. the cautious interpretation of the evidence for ducal dispute settlement by D. Bates, *Normandy before 1066* (London, 1982), 160–1; with the more tendentious discussion of 'feudal jurisdiction' by Ch. Haskins, *Norman Institutions* (New York, 1918), 24–7.

[29] '*Legis legum xansit autoritas ...*', Garaud, 'Le droit romain dans les chartes poitevines du XIe au XIe sièles' *Mélanges de droit romain dédiés à Georges Cornil*, 2 vols (Paris, 1926), I, 400–24 (citation, 424). The following are nevertheless of wide general importance, P. Ourliac, 'L'esprit du droit méridional', and 'La "*convenientia*"' in *Etudes d'Histoire du droit médiéval* (Toulouse, 1979), 313–31; 245–55; Cl. Brunel, 'Les juges de la paix en Gévaudan au milieu du XIe siècle', *BEC*, CXIX (1951), 32–41; A. Gouron, 'Les étapes de la pénétration du droit romain au XIIe siècle dans l'ancienne Septimanie', *Annales du Midi*, LXIX (1957), 103–20; id. 'Diffusion des consulats méridionaux et expansion du droit romain au XIIe et XIIIe siècles', *BEC*, CXXXI (1963), 26–76 (and for late twelfth-century penetration of Roman law into Aquitaine, see his diagram II, 53).

absence of documentary material relating to criminal matters.[30]

The sheer size of the principality of Aquitaine eventually put together by Ebles's descendants needs emphasis; and, as historians have long recognised, that was reflected by the titles which were attributed to them. Although the style *dux Aquitanorum/Aquitaniae* was already normal by the late tenth century, the great territorial acquisitions made by these rulers were also expressed in titles far more elaborate than the simple *comes* or *comes Pictavorum* attributed to Ebles and his son. The 'troubadour' Duke William IX (1086–1126) was on one occasion described as 'duke and lord of all Aquitaine by the will of almighty God and by hereditary right of my father and *parentes*'; while this dynasty's rule over Gascony and the Gascons is sometimes distinguished from other titles. The momentous (but short-lived) Poitevin occupations of Toulouse were also marked by the employment of titles drawing attention to this important inheritance—e.g. 'count of the city of Toulouse and simultaneously prince of the Poitevin province'.[31] This extension of the Poitevins' authority to regions where Count Ebles and his immediate successors had never been installed under a Carolingian régime makes it easier to test the hypothesis that, where there was territorial expansion, there was also 'interpenetration of politics and justice'; and, largely for that reason, the investigation which follows will begin with the region which is most remote from the Carolingian county in which the kindred of Ebles were originally settled under the Carolingians. That expansion clearly generated its own problems, however—especially if the ruler were expected to appear in person to

[30] None of the documents of the Poitevin dukes cited below has a secular provenance, although possibly some were preserved in a rudimentary ducal archive—see the Limoges charter cited, in n. 43; cf. Bates, ibid. on the defects of this type of 'record'. A body of c. 420 charters has survived from the centuries of the Poitevin counts' government between 902–1137: of these only 37 are 'dispute documents', very unevenly distributed throughout these centuries. (i) After the four produced during the period of Count Ebles's rule (902–c. 34) only two have been preserved for the next century (i.e. during three generations). On the other hand one of those implies the continuous functioning of a court and comital activity, n. 58 below; and this last does not include the *conventum* referred to below, nn. 73–6. (ii) Between the mid-eleventh century and 1137 31 documents have been preserved referring to pleas heard, ordered, or judged by these rulers: a full calendar cannot be given here. However, it is unlikely that they represent the total judicial activity of those secular rulers. For these points, see above, 23–6 (and especially n. 13); below 44–6.

[31] (i) Bordeaux, Archives Départementales de la Gironde, G. 335: for a partial facsimile, see C. Higounet, *Bordeaux pendant le haut moyen âge, Histoire de Bordeaux*, I, (Bordeaux, 1963), plate V; and *Archives Historiques de la Gironde*, XXX (1890), 1–4 and pl. I. (ii) ed. J-L. Lacurie, *Histoire de l'abbaye de Maillezais* (Fontenay-le-Comte, 1852), 296. For a detailed chronological review of the titles attributed to successive members of the dynasty, W. Kienast, *Der Herzogstitel in Frankreich und Deutschland (9 bis 12 Jahrhundert)* (Munich/Vienna, 1968), 175–241; the summary in *Histoire des institutions françaises au moyen âge* I, 158–62 is skimpy and unreliable.

do justice; but compared with this setting it seemed that a paradigm of judicial and political change based on the *Mâconnais*—a region of little more than 30 kilometres at its greatest width by about 40 kilometres in length—was not appropriate to the very different scale of the county of Poitou, let alone the duchy of Aquitaine, with its long Atlantic coastline, ancient cities and widely varying population.[32]

South of the Garonne the Poitevin counts established their control by stages around the mid-eleventh century and, although this was justified on grounds of 'hereditary right', it had certainly entailed the use of force.[33] The earliest dated record of a dispute settled by the Duke in that region occurs in the year 1084 when the prior of La Réole on the Garonne laid claim 'in the presence of Duke Geoffrey of Aquitaine' to a church which was in the hands of the diocesan bishop. At a time when secular intervention in 'spiritual things' was beginning to be seriously frowned on by ecclesiastics, it is interesting—and a significant comment on ducal power—that a monastic complaint should be made to a layman, even though he was a secular ruler regarded as a friend to religious reform. A second undated plea in which this priory of the abbey of Saint-Benoît-sur Loire became involved found the prior travelling to the castle of Taillecavat 'to Count William, Duke of Gascony' where his plea was heard (and decided in the monks' favour) *coram comite*. In 1103 the prior of La Réole had to make a longer journey to Poitiers to make another complaint to Duke Geoffrey's son, at that time 'residing' in Poitiers; but on this occasion the monks' grievance related to the institution of a new toll, for their priory was sited near an important crossing of the River Garonne. The duke's reaction was to summon a court composed of the greatest laymen of the province (a *curia Vasconie* is how it is described in the surviving post-medieval cartulary); unfortunately no details of the proceedings are preserved, but it did not sit until the ruler had himself reached Gascony, while its decisions were intended to guarantee that the toll was never again

---

[32] To some extent these great territorial contrasts are self-evident, but should also emerge in their historical dimension from references in the following section of the paper to ducal appearances in places as far from Poitiers as Bordeaux, Toulouse, and Lescar. The itineraries of the Poitevin dukes cannot be extensively discussed here; but even under Carolingian rulers, differences of scale '*couvrait des réalités fort différentes*', K. F. Werner, '*Missus-Marchio-Comes*' 223–4. For diagrams conveying the restricted scale of lordships under the count of Mâcon in the late tenth century and comparisons with *châtellenies* established in the same region by the end of the twelfth century, Duby, *Mâconnais*, 510, 517.

[33] Martindale, 'Succession and politics in the romance-speaking world, c. 1000–1140', in *England and Her Neighbours, 1066–1485, Essays in Honour of Pierre Chaplais*, ed. M. Jones and M. Vale (London, 1989), 30–33 and esp. n. 55 (the succession to Gascony and the Bordelais will receive more extended treatment in the work in course of preparation).

levied.[34] On the other hand, a further Gascon case also involving possession of a church was heard (c. 1072×80) by the duke in person who had 'commanded that right' should be done (... *ad Guidonem comitem Guasconiae*); although judgment was given by *milites de curia sua*, who considered that the dispute—between an unnamed layman and Bernard, Bishop of Lescar—should be settled by a judicial duel. That duel was held before 'Count Guy'.[35]

These legal proceedings are known because settlements were made in favour of an ecclesiastical beneficiary—even though normally only the barest outlines are preserved of the actual course of the dispute; but at some stage the Poitevin duke played a decisive part in that process, even if it were only to ensure that a court was convened. (A suggestive comparison can be made with a number of the early disputes in which the ruler of Normandy was involved).[36] The cartulary of Saint-Jean de Sorde yields a case in which ducal justice is portrayed in a rather different light. The monastery at Sorde was sited just below the foothills of the Pyrenees: it became an important staging-post both for pilgrims to Compostela and for armies entering Spain, and the monks considered it prudent to obtain confirmation of their possessions from the Poitevin duke. On this occasion, (in the 1060s) the secular 'ban' had been breached and the furious count ('*comes, repletus ira*') threatened the abbot with confiscation and deposition; and it was the abbot who began a plea with 'Duke Guy of the Aquitanians' spending a long time (apparently eight days in all) engaged in trying to secure '*fedus et conventiones et pactum*'; but—despite assurances and gifts of money to Duke Guy-Geoffrey—his plea was unsuccessful.[37] In another country

---

[34] The earliest complaint was made '*coram Gausfredo duce Aquitanie*', with three bishops present; the 1103 court sat when the count reached Gascony, although he had already ordered the viscount of Bezaume to make public restitution to the monks, *Cartulaire du prieuré conventuel de Saint-Pierre de la Réole en Bazadais du IXe au XIIe siécle*, ed. C. Grellet-Balguerie, Archives Historiques de la Gironde, V (1864), nos. 139; 70; 88. The castle of Taillacavat is canton Montségur, dép. Gironde: the editor dated that document c. 1090: it too concerned secular reluctance to relinquish control of a church.

[35] An earlier plea concerning possession of this church had been heard before the viscount of Dax, 'as Count Guy ought to have held it'. Unfortunately this important suit is known only from an abbreviated notice from the lost cartulary of the church of Lescar, P. de Marca, *Histoire de Béarn* (Paris, 1640), 283–4 (the dates attributed by me are approximately those of Bishop Bernard of Lescar; cf. Richard, *Comtes* I, 294 with a date of c. 1063). Contrast the judicial proceedings for an ecclesiastical dispute over the tenure of a church heard in a council in Bordeaux (c. 1079×80), *Cartulaire de Saint-Jean d'Angély*, ed. G. Musset, Archives Historiques de la Saintonge et de l'Aunis, XXX, XXXIII (1901–03), no. 100—on that occasion '*Guido comes Pictavensis*' sat in judgment with a number of clergy.

[36] Ed. Fauroux, *Ducs de Normandie*, nos. 71, 72, 115, 145, 157—all dated c. 1034–1066.

[37] The monastic viewpoint was that the count/duke had unjustly deprived the community of lands which had formerly been in the possession of a native Gascon ruler, so their abbot '*predavit villas*'—prompting the count's anger and the subsequent proceedings:

and a century later, Richard FitzNigel countered the criticism that to behave like this was to 'sell justice' when he wrote that, 'to some he [the king] does full justice for nothing, in consideration of their past services or out of mere goodness of heart ... but to others (and it is only human nature) he will not give way for either love or money...'[38]

This huge region south of the Gironde—the *duché de Guienne* of later centuries—has too often been omitted from accounts of 'judicial organisation' under the Poitevin dynasty; but even though records of disputes which the dukes heard or directed are numerically few, the settlement of disputes represented an important aspect of the ruler's authority. However, in order to grasp the scope of ducal authority in the regulation of legal affairs in this region, it is essential to branch out a little and to consider the creation here of *sauvetés* (the Latin term *salvitas* is generally used in documentary sources of this date). Although historians have differed in their interpretation of the significance of these enclaves, there can be no doubt that these had legal as well as economic importance for any religious community fortunate enough to obtain such a grant. The lavishly endowed monastic foundation of La Sauve-Majeure (founded c. 1076 in the Entre-Deux-Mers region) was surrounded by its own *sauveté*; furthermore Duke Guy-Geoffrey's concession that the abbot of the house should have access to the duke wherever and whenever he wanted may also have had judicial overtones. In any case, all territorial grants were based on the duke's own assertion that he and his predecessors held all *comitale ius et iusticiam*, and that they bestowed on the monks those 'rights [which] were described as *libertas*'.[39] Duke William IX permitted the monks of Sainte-Foi de Conques to create a similar enclave in the Médoc[40]; and when (in

---

'*Unde rogemus Dominum ut reddat nobis dominium illum*', *Le cartulaire de l'abbaye de Saint-Jean de Sorde*, ed. P. Raymond, (Pau, 1873), no. 40. Cf. no. 58 for a further complicated dispute in which Guy-Geoffrey's son, Duke William IX, apparently used his 'ban' to ensure the return of monastic possessions (?); and for ducal confirmations, nos. 81 (c. 1120),—made when the ruler was on his way to Spain '*et omnem Xristianitatem exaltare voluisset ...*'; 6 (c. 1128).

[38] *Dialogus de Scaccario*, ed. C. Johnson, Medieval Classics (Edinburgh and London, 1950), 120. Such methods might be considered as appropriate for territorial princes as for kings?

[39] The early charters of this house have never been adequately published: the details supplied here are taken from Bordeaux, Bibliothèque Municipale, Ms. 769 (1st cartulary of La Sauve-Majeure) pp. 10–14, ed. 'The Counts of Poitou and the origins of the duchy of Aquitaine' appendix II nos. 10–15. For the wide-ranging terms of the exemption covered by the *sauveté*: '*securi sint, sive milites, sive rustici, sive mercatores; omnesque homines praeter fures publicatos [thus] et qui latrones vocantur ...*' [Means of ejecting 'thieves' are given ...] These regulations throw much light on problems of jurisdiction and law enforcement in the late eleventh century (together with certain similarities to Carolingian grants of immunity).

[40] *Mansirot* (Marestangh, dép. Gironde) was given by two brothers and then confirmed by the duke at the request of the bishop of Pamplona, '*et quicquid deinceps ab aliquo*

August 1115) this same duke made important concessions to the monks of Lézat in the Toulousain, he guaranteed that inhabitants and visitors should be free from judicial pursuit on the land before the comital '*château de Narbonne*' (a fortified site of great antiquity at the edge of the city of Toulouse). The counts of the Saint-Gilles dynasty who supplanted the Poitevins after their brief period of rule in Toulouse described this area as a '*selvitas*'. It seems important, too, in this context that the establishment of the Poitevin count's rule had been associated with the 'reformation of peace' in the city.[41]

An association between territorial expansion, the doing of justice and settlement of specific disputes is also characteristic of lands north of the Gironde; although for those regions also the material is sparse, and it is by no means clear what activated ducal intervention, or whether this was always occasioned by complaints brought to the ruler's notice (as was so with the cases brought by the monks of La Réole). The Limousin, over which the Poitevin counts had extended some political control by the early decades of the tenth century, presents modern historians with a number of puzzles. Soon after Ebles acquired his father's county of Poitou in 902, a man named Aldebert (who may almost certainly be identified as the viscount of Limoges) appeared at a judicial hearing of the *mallus* in the city of Poitiers (in the year 903); but it is not entirely clear whether he came under that court's jurisdiction because of the Poitevin count's political authority, or because Aldebert was accused of misappropriating monastic land in Poitou.[42] By the late tenth century, however, when the Poitevin ruler played an important role in the

---

in terra mea ad ipsam beatae Fidis salvetatem datum fuerit ingenue concedo, done securitatem semper et ingenuitatem per totam terram meam coram principibus patriae rebus omnibus que ad ipsam prenominatam salvetatem pertinent', *Cartulaire de l'abbaye de Conques en Rouergue*, ed. G. Desjardins (Paris, 1879), no. 481—undated; cf. introd. xcvi–vii—(probably c. 1107×8).

[41] *Cartulaire de l'abbaye de Lézat*, ed. P. Ourliac and A-M. Magnou, Collection de documents inédits sur l'histoire de France, 2 vols. (1984, 87), II, no. 1343: 'damus et firmamus iure perpetuo illam plateam et totum illum locum qui videtur esse ante portam castri Narbonensis ... tali convenientia, ut super ipsos qui ab alienis regionibus ad eundem locum causa manendi venerint seu habitaverint ullus princeps vel ullus vicarius seu aliquis ex nostra familia principatum vel dominationem seu justicias non requirant.' (The editors give references to the *sauveté*, 212; and cf. introd.) Cf. ibid. no. 1342 for the same ruler's visit to Toulouse '*ob reformandum ... pacem*' (probably in the year 1114). For an exemplary study of a cluster of '*sauvetés*' found outside the influence of Poitevin political authority, Ourliac, 'Les sauvetés de Comminges, études et documents' sur les villages fondés par les Hospitaliers dans la région des côteaux commingeois' in *Études d'histoire du droit médiéval*, 31–111.

[42] For the reference cf. n. 13 above; see also R. de Lasteyrie, *Étude sur les comtes et vicomtes de Limoges antérieurs à l'an 1000*, (Paris, 1874), 57–66 and *pièces justifs.*, nos VI (dated 904 rather than 903, however), and VII—grant made to the cathedral of Saint-Etienne de Limoges in May 914 'pro remedio anime ... Aldeberti vicecomite patri meo necnon et matri mee nomine Adaltrude'.

election of the bishop of Limoges, he was regarded as *custos* of the bishopric; and surviving letters envisaged the possibility of the secular ruler's intervention in disputes on behalf of the canons or bishop. Some conception of what may have been involved is revealed in a charter of the later eleventh century (dated 1073), which preserves the record of a violent crisis in the relations between bishop and viscount of Limoges, but no details of court or procedure. All that is noted is that, because he had set fire both to the city and the bishop's see, Viscount Adémar of Limoges paid compensation to the bishop and did penance. This settlement—for surely it was a settlement—was made 'with the knowledge and confirmation of my lord Duke William of the Aquitanians who demanded his own charter...'[43]

Another region which was annexed at an early date to the Poitevin rulers' territories was the Saintonge. The city of Saintes and its surrounding district lost both count and bishop under the impact of maritime attacks by Northmen; and no Poitevin comital intervention in judicial affairs can be traced in this city until after the year 1062 and the expulsion of an Angevin faction which had been established there for some years. Here the Poitevin dukes' *prepositus* had wide powers, although once again this is known only through the medium of disputes involving at least once religious community—normally in the plaintiff's role. 'We made our plea by order of the Poitevin count in the presence of his *prepositus* (*iussu comitis Pictaviensis placitavimus coram preposito suo*)', reads the narrative of a claim brought against a layman by the nuns of the wealthy and aristocratic convent of Notre-Dame de Saintes. On a later occasion (1133) nuns of the same house brought a plea against two laymen who had violently dispossessed them of 'tithes'; and this was settled by a 'right judgment' in the comital court of Count William the Poitevin (*rectum iudicium ... in curia comitis Willelmi Pictavensis*). That body was apparently sitting in the city, as it did on other occasions.[44]

---

[43] ... 'sciente atque annuente domino meo Guillelmo duce Aquitanorum quia proprium exigit cartam ...' [but the 'record' of this survives only in transcripts of the ecclesiastical cartulary], *Sancti Stephani Lemovicensis Cartularium*, ed. J. Font-Réaulx, Bulletins de la Société archéologique et historique du Limousin, LXVIII–IX (1919–20), no. lxxx; cf. the regulations relating to the protection of the canons' and bishop's possessions, and the agreement of the *comes Pictaviensis* not to make simoniacal appointments or to alienate the possessions of the see, ibid. no. clxxxi (datable c. 1038–52).

[44] *Cartulaire de Notre-Dame de Saintes*, ed. T. Grasilier, Cartulaires inédits de la Saintonge (Niort, 1871), no. 267 (the bishop sat with the *prepositus*), which I would date c. 1119×22; no. 122—the restoration took place in the court '*non post multos dies*', which perhaps suggests tenure at fairly regular intervals; a similar reference at no. 266 (c. 1119×34) also shows another layman appearing '*coram preposito comitis Pictaviensis*'. Cf. no. 13 (c. 1066×79?)—an earlier plea (*placitum*) in which a layman claimed that he had been obliged to endow the convent '*non sua sponte*', and was 'commanded' by Abbess Lethburgis to come to the disputed church, where the claim was settled in the nuns' favour '*coram comite Pictavensium Guidone et coram episcopo Xanctonice sedis*'.

The Poitevin ruler also sat in justice in this region outside the city of Saintes. In the year 1131, for instance, the four chief castellans of the Ile d'Oléron were summoned to appear before Duke William 'the Toulousain' on St John the Baptist's Day at the important abbey of Saint-Jean d'Angély. The purpose was to settle a claim brought against them by the monks of la Trinité de Vendôme concerning the lands attached to their priory of Saint-Georges on the island: judgment was pronounced in favour of the monks.[45] The dukes were also involved in other disputes in both the Aunis and Saintonge, but pleas concerning land and possessions in this region were also held elsewhere.[46]

All the disputes mentioned so far relate to territories where the Poitevin counts acquired political power at some stage during the tenth or eleventh century, so that it cannot be argued that there was direct continuity from the era of Carolingian government (except possibly in the Aunis). By contrast, Poitou was a region where the dynasty had been established under Carolingian kings; and the city of Poitiers attracted litigants, as it had formerly done in the ninth century and under Count Ebles. A dispute might be heard and settled (as one was in the year 1081) 'in the hall in Poitiers': a litigant might voice a complaint 'in the count's chamber in Poitiers in the sight of two hundred people': whereas by the later eleventh century references could simply be made to hearings *in curia* ...[47] Here Duke Guy-Geoffrey probably listened to a complaint (*querimonia*) brought by his own *prepositus* relating to rights of jurisdiction claimed by the monks of his own recently founded Cluniac monastery of Montierneuf—'which I settled after both I and my barons had discussed this ... which I ordered to be written in this charter ...' (c. 1082×86). His son, too, in the year 1098 summoned the Viscount of Aunay (*'conventus a comite'*) to appear

---

[45] The count of Angouulême, the viscount of Thouars, Gifard of Didonne and Gumbard de Mornay were named as co-lords. The surviving original charter is a notification by the duke of the decision reached by his *curia*, Blois, Archives Départementales du Loir-et-Cher, 21. H. 173 (no. 2); *Le cartulaire saintongeais de l'abbaye de la Trinité de Vendôme*, ed. C. Métais, AHSA XXII (1893), no. 55 (this, with other documents of the house, was uncritically edited); cf. A. Debord, *La société laïque dans les pays de la Charente, Xe–XIIe sièles* (Paris, 1984), 174, n. 33.

[46] In particular, in the year 1068 a complaint was brought against the ducal *prepositus*, *Seniorulus* of Saintes, by the monks of Vendôme, heard before *Guidonem Aquitanorum ducem* and two others and settled *apud castrum Surgeriis* (i.e. Surgères, dép. Charente-Maritime); while the undated notice of a dispute between a man called Peter *Tronellus* and the Abbot of Maillezais was judged by Duke William and the bishop of Poitiers (*adiudicavimus*), at Fontenay (dép. Vendée), Besly, *Poictou*, 464—the court's decision to award the church to the abbey is recorded in an apparently lost charter drawn up in the bishop's name, with the signa of both bishop and duke (c. 1130×7).

[47] *Chartes ... Saint-Maixent*, nos. 150, 163 (an unsuccessful claim against the count himself brought by the abbot of the house); cf. *Cartulaire de l'abbaye de Saint-Cyprien de Poitiers*, ed. L. Rédet, AHP III (1874), no. 322 (a. 1073×86). And cf. below 47–8.

before him in Poitiers to answer for the damage caused by the viscount's men on monastic land.[48] Indeed, justice has almost certainly been done continuously at the same place in Poitiers for almost a thousand years; for the palace of the Angevins was still serving as a court when I was a student in Poitiers, and their great hall was built over the palace of Queen Eleanor's ancestors who in their turn built on the site inherited from the Carolingians.[49]

In Poitou, as in the other counties or territories within this dynasty's principality, disputes were also heard outside the urban centre. Surviving accounts refer to litigants also coming to churches, or to fortified sites (as the canons of Saint-Martin had done), either expressly summoned by the count, or in hopes of his arrival. This may not seem unusual to historians acquainted with contemporary legal proceedings in the Anglo-Norman realm, but in view of some of the conclusions which have been advanced about the decline of comital authority and the fragmentation of 'judicial institutions' during this period in the French kingdom, it needs to be emphasised. The Poitevin count's control over judicial proceedings is particularly well illustrated by the course of a Marmoutier lawsuit which was initiated (and judgment given) in the comital court in Poitiers; but then, when the outcome provoked a further oral complaint, the count himself sent the dispute for further hearing at the comital castle of Talmont.[50]

The distribution and range of locations where princes' disputes were heard or settled demonstrates that there was a connection between the extension of political power and the exercise of judicial functions; and

[48] Reference to the raising of the complaint by the duke's *prepositus*, and the duke's own presence, 'tam ego, quam barones mei in in conspectu meo ventilantes ... Hec autem stabilivi et in manu filii mei, abbatisque eiusdem loci Guidonis baronum meorum firmanda tradidi ...' suggests very strongly that this was heard and settled in Poitiers, *Recueil des documents rélatifs à l'abbaye de Montierneuf de Poitiers*, ed. F. Villard, AHP LIX (1973) nos. 16; 27—the viscount 'hoc placitum confirmavi in manu comitis et episcopi Pictaven[sis]'. Cf. ibid. nos. 81 for a judgment pronounced by the apostolic legate Giles of Tusculum in Poitiers in the presence of the *prepositus* of Poitiers; 79 for a *controversia* and *calumpnia* between the abbot of this Poitevin burial church and ducal *officiarii* in the Saintonge, settled in 1129 by the duke's own 'definition' at an unknown place.
[49] On the modern monument, see H. Le Roux, *Poitiers de A à Z*, (Poitiers, 1976), 219–22, '*Palais de justice*'; for a historical and archeological treatment, D. Claude, *Topographie und Verfassung der Städte Bourges und Poitiers bis in das 11 Jahrhundert* (Lübeck/Hambourg, 1960), 99, 126; R. Favreau, 'Le palais de Poitiers au moyen âge', *Bulletins de la Société des Antiquaires de l'Ouest*, 4th ser. XI (1971–2), 35–65.
[50] '... quatinus rem in respectum mitteret donec comes veniret ad Talemundum & causam audiret ...', *Cartulaires du Bas-Poitou*, ed P. Marchegay (Les Roches-Baritaud, 1877), 93–4 (from the original notice now in the Archives Départementales de la Vendée at La Roche-sur-Yon). Significantly that claim by the monks to control of the *terra Angulorum* had been the subject of at least one previous legal process involving a layman who considered that his consent had not been obtained to the original grants, *ibid*, 91–2. Cf. also below, n. 60 for a very similar case, also relating to Marmoutier's possessions.

this does not accord with the model of virtually simultaneous political and legal disintegration in the late- and post-Carolingian western kingdom.[51] Admittedly, by the standards of later bureaucratic governments the evidence is pitifully thin, and in this paper it has been impossible to deal with the problem of either competing or subordinate jurisdictions; but throughout these centuries ecclesiastics brought their legal disputes to the secular ruler's court—even though such proceedings would be harshly judged before the end of the eleventh century.[52] Nevertheless, in this context useful comparisons can be made with regions outside Aquitaine which lend support to the argument being advanced. There is an interesting correlation between the recurring struggles for political control of the county of Maine and the comital settlement of disputes in that region. In the mid-eleventh century, for instance, a plea between two monastic houses could only be settled by 'public and legal judgment' after 'William Count of Normandy obtained the county of Maine' (c. 1063×66)[53]; the later change of political régime in Maine is marked by five disputes heard in the city of Le Mans by Count Fulk of Anjou and his son Geoffrey between 1109 and the mid-1140s.[54]

The examples assembled here do not support a case for supposing that in these regions 'the castle is the *fundamental* element in *judicial*

[51] Above, nn. 6–9. On the significance of the study of rulers' itineraries as a tool for the understanding of their political activity and government, C-R. Brühl, *Fodrum, Gistum, Servitium Regis* 2 vols. (Cologne, 1968), I, 2–6 and throughout; T. Reuter, *Germany in the Early Middle Ages* (London, 1991), 86–8, 208–12.

[52] Garaud, *Institutions judiciaires*, 43–5, 77–82 (commenting on problems of competence and jurisdiction); cf. G. Mollat, 'La restitution des églises privées au patrimoine ecclésiastique en France du IXe au XIe siècle', *RHDFE*, (1949), esp. 411–23. The extent to which in practice ecclesiastical ideas of *libertas* encroached on these long-established regional patterns will be discussed elsewhere.

[53] See two contemporary versions of a dispute between the abbeys of Marmoutier and Saint-Pierre de la Couture which could apparently only be heard after the establishment of Norman control in the county of Maine (1063, but before the conquest of England). The first complaint was made in the city of Le Mans but later transferred to Domfront, where it was eventually concluded both by 'the aforesaid count and the whole curia', Fauroux, *Ducs de Normandie*, no. 159; the relative informality and formlessness of arrangements for ducal settlement of disputes before 1066 is noted by D. Bates, *Normandy before 1066* 81–2, 160.

[54] A dispute between a layman and the canons of Saint-Vincent du Mans was settled in the city before Count Fulk and Bishop Hildebert (undated, c. 1109×24), Chartrou, *L'Anjou de 1109 à 1151*, catal. no. 64. On the day when he took the cross in the city (24 May 1128), a *concordia* was arranged by the same count (later confirmed in the city of Tours), ibid. no 87—ed. in full, 367–72. Cf. also no. 131 (15 Aug. 1141)—claim made by the canons of Saint-Julien to revenues and exercise of rights over parts of the city's fortifications; and nos. 138 (9 Aug. 1142); 173 (1146). Angevin political expansion along the Loire can to some extent also be traced through the comital tenure of pleas in places formerly outside Angevin control (e.g. Tours, or the important town and fortified site of Saumur), but that topic cannot be further developed here.

organisation' [my italics]. The rural landscape was certainly studded with fortified sites—a development which (as can be seen from the 926 notice) was already well under way in Poitou in the early decades of the tenth century; but cities were still central to the exercise of secular political power. It follows that in Aquitaine a wide range of legal proceedings was still focused on urban sites like Poitiers, Bordeaux, Saintes, or Limoges, even while the nature of cities and urban settlements was being transformed economically (and probably also socially) between the late ninth and twelfth centuries. During the rule of the 'independent' dukes in Aquitaine most peace councils (in the late tenth and early eleventh century) were held in cities, and the term '*civitas*' could be used without any qualification to denote the centre from which the counts of Poitou wielded their power.[55] However, in general it is the absence of any uniform pattern which is interesting, even if some variations can be accounted for in terms of regional difference in organisation. The Poitevin dukes were apparently prepared to introduce *sauvetés* into the Bordelais and Toulousain, but there are no traces of these 'institutions' further north. This is perhaps a salutary reminder that, although modern historians may consider that uniformity is strength, that was not always necessarily so.

The disputes which have been considered here were the products of a society in which legal proceedings were not automatically expected to be preserved by 'the written word', nor had 'memory' (in Michael Clanchy's happy and memnonic phrase) given away to 'written record'. Some implications of this will emerge from a broad discussion of proof and judgment as these make their appearance in the documents which do survive; but the prevalence of 'orality' must have influenced both the numbers of the disputes which were actually the subject of record, and the character of what has been transmitted to historians today.[56] In particular, for the period of time being discussed, almost no recorded disputes have been preserved in which both litigants were laymen (or women): a lacuna which must have affected the issues covered in the

---

[55] Martindale, 'Peace and war in early eleventh-century Aquitaine', map facing 149, 161–3.

[56] The greatly increased interest among medieval historians in the interaction between orality and literacy can only be touched on here but, in addition to many suggestive remarks in the papers ed. by Davies and Fouracre, in the context of the present paper, see H. Grundmann, '*Litteratus-illiteratus* Der Wandel eines Bildungsnorm vom Altertum zum Mittelalter', *Archiv für Kulturgeschichte*, XL (1958), 1–65; P. Wormald, 'The uses of literacy in Anglo-Saxon England and its neighbours', ante 5th ser. XXVII (1977), 95–114; A. Murray, *Reason and Society in the Middle Ages* (Oxford, 1978), 292–302; M. Clanchy, *From Memory to Written Record, England 1066–1307* (2nd edn, Oxford, 1993); R. McKitterick, *The Carolingians and the Written Word* (Cambridge, 1989); and the studies collected in, id. (ed), *The Uses of Literacy in Early Mediaeval Europe* (Cambridge, 1990).

surviving documents. Some notion of what we, as historians, have lost in this area can be glimpsed from an unusually informative Poitevin charter of about the year 1032. This states that Count William (i.e. William 'le Gros') came to the castle of Melle, 'with his judges and *prepositi* and many nobles, [and] determined just judgments about many matters'. One oral complaint about exactions made by comital officials' is, however, the only 'matter' about which any detail is given; moreover this was noted, not so much because the exactions oppressed the local population, as because they affected the rights of the rich abbey of Saint-Maixent. The Count asked if there were any man of 'greater age' who knew the 'ancient customs' and could comment on the charge. A 'subjudge (*subjudex*)' 'testified that his father had been a judge for more than seventy (?) years, and that after his father's death he had a similar job for as many years ...': he was then required to proclaim the customs at the altar on relics (i.e. he appears to have required to make an oath twice): unfortunately although he proclaimed the customs, they were not listed in writing. It's a sobering—and to an early medievalist, a depressing—thought that without this document there would be no knowledge at all of the continued operation of a court at Melle over many decades, or of the existence of its official 'judges'. Although the timespan envisaged seems suspect (since it would take us back to c. the year 890), the setting in which this court was held is of considerable significance, for Melle had been the centre of a *vicaria* and a viscounty, as well as being a strongly fortified site from before the early eleventh century.[58] Comital presence and comital intervention here in the early eleventh century suggest again that territorial 'dislocation of the pagus' had not taken the same course in Poitou as had been postulated for some other regions of this former Carolingian, and now Capetian, kingdom.[59]

[57] A rare surviving notice of adjudication made in the Limousin between two lay parties in the year 898 'apud vicum qui vocatur Briva in mallo publico in manu domni Ademari et Gauzfredi vicecomitum' seems to have turned on the misappropriation of an alod, rather than on any identifiable point of law relating to possession or inheritance, E. Baluze, *Historia Tutellensis Libri Tres* (Paris, 1717), cols. 348–50. Subsequently, secular custom and law in documentary sources can for the most part only be glimpsed through the impact which those had on the often conflicting claims and rights of ecclesiastical communities—e.g. in the Marmoutier case (n. 50 above), according to which 'noluit Morinus filius Frogerii suus homo devenire [i.e. of a new lord of the castle of Talmont] nisi placitum tenere inter eum & monachis Sancti Martini de elemosina ...' The monks were only interested in their own possession, although land had been granted to the monks which Morinus regarded as encroaching on his inheritance.

[58] *Chartes ... Saint-Maixent*, no. 91, from which this compressed account is taken; cf. Cowdrey, 'The peace and the truce of God', 58–9. On Melle, Garaud, 'Les circonscriptions administratives', 13, 38, 49, 51–3, commenting on the continued co-existence of fortified and unfortified *vicariae*.

[59] Above, nn. 6–7; cf. Debord, *La société laïque dans les pays de la Charente*, 94–8, 105–7,

Some of the documents already considered show that, by the later eleventh century, litigants would be summoned to appear at the Poitevin duke's court—witness the two monastic parties to a long-running dispute who Duke Guy-Geoffrey 'made to come to Talmont to his presence to do right about this matter'; but it seems unlikely that these rulers lacked the authority to make such a command at an earlier date. Most disputes appear to have begun with an oral complaint which, although it was not judicialised, may in fact have been less impromptu and spontaneous than is suggested by monastic scribes. The proceedings (where described in any detail) give the impression that they were intended to test the initial credibility of the parties in a low-key start.[60] The following example illustrates this second point. At a plea heard in Poitiers on 4 September 1078 'before duke Guy-Geoffrey ... in the round-house of the bishop' the claimant (the abbot of Sainte-Croix de Talmont) was asked to produce either a document or witness(es), in order to make good his claim to churches at Olonne (on the Poitevin coast) which the abbey of la Trinité de Vendôme claimed by right. His reply was that he could have produced a charter, but it had been taken to Brittany by a previous abbot (he made no reference to witnesses); but this ingenious piece of evasion did not help his cause. At that stage the *grammaticus* Theobald rose and stated that he had already heard judgment pronounced on the issue against Sainte-Croix (there is no comment on whether this was a question of 'right' or 'fact'); and Theobald was prepared to swear that the present Duke's brother had made that pronouncement. Duke Guy-Geoffrey waived the proffered oath, and therefore dismissed the claim by the Abbot of Sainte-Croix. '*Sic fuit in plena curia definitum et diiudicatum*', the notice records; and on this second hearing of the complaint he duke ordered a charter to be drawn up, which was liberally provided with many names of those who attended the court.[61]

---

173. A comparison could perhaps be made with English territorial courts with a local 'catchment area' and regional officials, but which were nevertheless open to royal intervention, see for pre-Conquest examples, P. Wormald, 'Disputes in Anglo-Saxon England' in Davies and Fouracre, *Disputes*, 162–3; and id., 'Domesday lawsuits: a provisional list' in *England in the Eleventh Century*, ed. C. Hicks, Harlaxton Medieval Studies, II (1992), 61–102 (esp. 62, 74–7 and Tables).

[60] '... ille [William IX] ... abbatem Sancte Crucis ad hoc rectum faciendum, Talamontis coram se venire fecit'. When both parties were assembled 'ab utrisque partibus causae narratae fuissent' ..., *Cartuls ... du Bas-Poitou*, 101–4 (dispute between the monks of Ste-Croix de Talmont and of Marmoutier, c. 1098). Cf. for other instances of the exercise of ducal authority, above, 36–9 below, 47, 51–3); but, because there is almost no uniformity in the form of the documents being analysed and little in their language, it is virtually impossible to discover whether there was uniformity of procedure.

[61] Besly, *Poictou*, 359–61; *Cartulaire saintongeais*, no. 33. The earlier plea had been held in the castle of Talmont, although no date was given. Cf. another plea relating to the abbey of la Trinité de Vendôme (Oct. 1068) which was settled in the monks' favour by the

In Aquitaine few of the disputes which came before these princely courts, or were delegated by the Duke to be settled by others, were apparently decided by 'irrational methods' of proof. An oath might be required, but (as has just been seen) on other occasions oral statements would be accepted without such sacral backing; and a settlement might be reached by a process of mediation and negotiation between the parties, or by judgment delivered by the duke, a number of picked individuals, or by consensus 'in full court' (as again can be seen from the Vendôme-Sainte-Croix dispute just cited). Whether there was the same range in methods of proof and settlement applied in lay disputes, it is almost impossible to tell. In Poitevin territory a 'judgment of God', the 'duel', seems only to have been ordered in cases where violence had been used by one of the parties—inevitably the secular party in these disputes—or if one of the litigants had refused an opportunity to reach a compromise or a negotiated settlement. To order the outcome of a dispute to be judged by battle seems to have provided another means of testing a litigant's certainty about the validity of his claim, for in this region withdrawal from this 'judgment' (—*quod non fecit legem*) seems to have entailed loss of the suit (i.e. forfeiture of disputed land or rights).[62]

One of the most interesting of the cases where battle was ordered was clearly a *cause célèbre* in its day: again this concerned land near the Poitevin coast. The monks of Saint-Maixent claimed that, '*mala invasione et violentia*', the nearby castellan Ebles of Châtelaillon had removed from their possession this valuable tract of saltmarsh which had been held without disturbance since the times of 'Frankish kings'; and they made their complaint before Duke Guy-Geoffrey. Without any public hearing the Duke ordered its return to the monks and, when his order was not obeyed by the lord of Châtelaillon, 'he would not put up with that treatment (*noluit amplius pati*)', and arbitrarily returned the land. (And

---

production of their foundation charter guaranteeing them freedom '*ab omni consuetudine consulari*' (except in time of war), Besly, *Poictou*, 347–8; *Cartulaire saintongeais*, no. 23.

[62] The elaboration of the proceedings involved can be seen from the *clamor* brought to Duke Guy-Geoffrey's notice by the abbot of Saint-Maixent in 1081, (above n. 47). The defendant was Robert *de Bonolio* whom the duke's steward (*dapifer*) judged should prove his case in Poitiers, according to the *legem duorum hominum* (Saint-Maixent had been dispossessed, according to the abbot). On the appointed day, Robert did not appear: he was summoned before the count for that failure, distrained, and obliged to relinquish the land on oath. From the year 1130 there is a case with a similar outcome: after duel (*bellum*) was ordered *in curia comitis*, the layman withdrew on the 'battlefield', *Chartes ... Saint-Maixent*, no. 290. The Marmoutier notice (above, nn. 50, 60–1) also suggests that duel would be evaded or avoided wherever possible and, although the precise details are unclear, the dispute was eventually settled by compromise after '*habuit consilium cum eis*'. Cf. Halphen, 'La justice en France' 185–6, for a layman who refused to engage in a duel after 'judgment' (*judicium*) had been pronounced by the bishop of Angers and the count.

what degree of force or pressure was concealed by that bland statement?)
What happened next is of exceptional interest. The monks' narrative
portrays the Duke worried because 'it might seem that he had returned
the land unjustly to the monks'; this seems to imply that there were
doubts about a decision which, however intrinsically 'just', had been
reached without public hearing or discussion. As a result of those
scruples, far more cumbrous judicial proceedings were initiated, including two separate surveys being made of the disputed land in the
presence of the local inhabitants and Ebles 'with his knights' (*cum suis
militibus*)'. In the last resort, however, a duel was ordered—and that
was apparently the duke's decision.[63] The monks' account emphasizes
the honourable reception their party got at the Duke's castle of Surgères
(where the duel was to take place), for their champion was prepared to
fight on their behalf 'just as the Count and his court had judged, and
the ancient charter laid down, and good judges affirmed'. Lord Ebles,
on the other hand behaved 'as though he did not want or dare to
begin the duel'; when it came to the contest he said that in fact his
champion (*pugnator*) had not got the right kind of shoes for fighting.
Perhaps fortunately the monks did not record Ebles's reply to one of
the monks (called Jamo) 'who took off his shoes and freely offered them
to Ebles's champion'. No duel took place—Ebles lost his complaint by
default and the monks got their marsh back.[64]

These surviving accounts of disputes do not seem to show that, in
Van Caenegem's words, 'people resorted to [irrational methods of
proof] readily the moment the initially selected rational proof turned
out to be too difficult'. Admittedly these accounts include almost no
disputes involving the laity alone, and virtually no criminal cases either;
indeed, those written documents which have been preserved suggest
that 'rational' methods of proof were employed in disputes until limits
of socially tolerable behaviour had been exceeded.[65] Any appeal to

[63] *Chartes ... Saint-Maixent*, no. 164—the monastic community was required to mark out
the boundaries of what was claimed: possibly such a public occasion at the disputed site
could have had the ulterior motive of encouraging the parties to reach a compromise.
The layman Morinus on the other hand refused to fight a duel, '*nisi terra percalcaretur*', for
reference see previous note.

[64] The monks' account rather self-righteously recorded that they were prepared to fight
'sicut comes et curia sua iudicaverat, vel sicut antiqua carta monstrabat', ibid. The final
outcome was not happy for the monks, all the same: at the duke's death in 1006 Ebles
once more seized possession of the marsh and, because Guy-Geoffrey's successor was
only a boy, they could not obtain justice.

[65] This seems to be borne out by the settlement of one of the Marmoutier disputes 'per
duelli probationem' because 'deberent ostendere quia mariscus de quo *tanta fiebat contentio*
[my italics], in eodem dono sancto Martino ac sancto Iohanni fuerit datus'. That decision
was reached by the Duke and his officials; and cf. the example of battle between the
ducal *prepositus* and the monastic community of Nouaillé, above, n. 60; below, n. 86. The
situation was probably somewhat different in Gascony, Ourliac, 'Le duel judiciaire dans

numbers is likely to be unreliable, nevertheless relatively few disputes were settled by 'judgment of God' in either Poitevin ruled territories, or in lands governed by the counts of Anjou. None of the recorded disputes in which the dukes of Normandy were involved before the year 1066 was settled by duel or any other form of the 'judgment of God'.[66]

Whatever the rhetoric of religious belief with which the 'judgment of God' was surrounded, the impression which is left after reading the documents associated with the settlement of specific disputes, is that as a judicial proof duel, the *lex duorum hominum*, was predominantly invoked as an inducement to come to terms, and used as a deterrent. This may be almost impossible to prove historically, but by analogy with Gluckman's famous thesis, this was not 'peace in the feud', but 'settlement in the judgment of God'.[67] If that were to be an acceptable working hypothesis, then it would make it easier for modern historians to understand how the threat of violence, adjudication, and a desire for concord could co-exist and not be regarded as incompatible during the centuries under discussion. But even if it is acknowledged that a mixture of procedural *genres* was in fact widely employed for the settlement of disputes, a number of anachronistic historical assessments of these mixed methods may have to be discarded. The introduction

---

le sud-ouest', in *Études d'histoire du droit*, 253–8. For Van Caenegem's assessment of the situation, 'Methods of proof in Western Mediaeval Law', 73; Bongert, *Recherches sur les cours laïques*, 228–261, (esp. 232–3); P. Hyams, 'Trial by ordeal: the key to proof in the early Common Law, in *On the Laws and Customs of England, Essays in honour of S. E. Thorne*, ed. M. S. Arnold, (Chapel Hill, 1981), esp. 112–26; R. Bartlett, *Trial by Fire and Water, The Medieval Judicial Ordeal* (Oxford, 1986), 103–26.

[66] The circumstances surrounding the duel held before Duke-Guy-Geoffrey in Gascony (above, 37) are unknown; but of the eight known disputes north of the Gironde which were ordered to be decided by this method of proof in a comital court, only two were actually so settled (the Marmoutier dispute with Sainte-Croix-de-Talmont, and the 1104 dispute between the duke's own *prepositus* and the monks of Nouaillé, see previous n. and below n. 86). In suits of this nature, and at this level, the unilateral ordeal does not seem to have been employed; although William 'the Great' had offered to send a serf to that ordeal on one occasion, below, 52. In Anjou disputes coming before the count were occasionally 'proved' by the unilateral ordeal, however, see Halphen, *Comté d'Anjou*, catal. no. 235 = Guillot, *Comté d'Anjou*, II, no. 318 (c. 1068×77); Chartrou *L'Anjou de 1109 à 1151*, catal. no. 56 (a. 1123). The absence of examples for Normandy derives from Fauroux's catalogue, but for an example of the *iudicium ferri caldi* to decide a dispute over maternity, P. LeCacheux, 'Une charte de Jumièges concernant l'épreuve par le fer chaud', *Société de l'Histoire de Normandie*, Mélanges, XI (1927), 205–16—set in motion by King William and Queen Mathilda (before c. 1079?).

[67] M. Gluckman, 'The Peace in the feud' in *Custom and Conflict in Africa* (Oxford, 1970), 1–26. The duel, however, would not have such wide social ramifications within a community as feud/vendetta. For an open acknowledgement of the deterrent effect of the threat of duel, see an Angevin example mentioning that the parties 'caventes discrimen pugne, infra terminum fecimus concordiam', Halphen 'La justice en France', 190 n. 6, 191.

to this paper shows that this flexibility was already characteristic of the settlement of one important dispute in the early tenth century, but this was no new development because negotiation and 'concord' were regarded as desirable even by Carolingian kings, who recommended the appointment of counts and other officials ... 'who will make an effort to get litigants to reach agreement—within the limits of justice'.[68] That attitude was perpetuated—or at any rate still prevalent—in the early twelfth century, as can be glimpsed in these regions from a dispute in which the Poitevin duke intervened because it 'had been continuing bitterly for so long that it was decided that it should at length be settled by duel'; but, as a result of ducal negotiation, peace was restored through compromise.[69] That was not incompatible with Duke William's position in 1136, and did not detract from his political authority.

Before the mid-twelfth century in these regions few disputes of exclusively secular character were apparently recorded in writing or, if they were ever written down, they have not survived. It is surely as unthinkable that historians should be expected to believe that between the tenth and early twelfth centuries no legal disputes between laymen should have been settled in court, as to suppose that the legal institutions of Aquitaine and the other regions under discussion were not concerned with 'criminal' cases, because the outcome and penalties of theft and other offences were not recorded either.[70] That pattern is not restricted to regions under Poitevin rule either, for apparently the earliest 'documentary record' of litigation between laymen under the Angevin counts dates only from the time of Count Fulk of Anjou (dated c. 1109×25 by its editor). In an exceptionally interesting charter, the count describes how after 'huge dispute (magna contentio)' he renounced the exactions

---

[68] 'Constituite comites et ministros rei publicae qui ... placita teneant ... ut ... et plus litigantes ad concordiam salva iustitia revocare studeant'—the contrast is with officials who think about the money to be got from doing justice, and who do not attempt to make between disputing litigants, Capitularia Regum Francorum, MGH, Legum sectio II, ed. A. Boretius and V. Krause (1883), II, 436 (dated 858); my thanks to Janet Nelson for drawing my attention to this important passage. L'accord aimable has often in the past been interpreted by historians as a sign of the defectiveness of 'judicial institutions', e.g. by Halphen, ibid., 189.

[69] It concerned the revenues of an oven in the city of Poitiers which had led to confrontation between the canons of the chapter of Saint-Hilaire and a comital official called Brictio. As a result of comital negotiation in the year 1136 the canons permitted the official to hold the oven as casamentum, Documents pour l'histoire de Saint- Hilaire de Poitiers, ed. L. Rédet, 2 vols., MSAO, 1st ser XIV–XV (1847, 52), I, no. 117; cf. above, n. 65.

[70] The chronicler Adémar writing before the year 1034 reveals ducal or comital involvement in cases involving mutilation, witchcraft, and treachery towards a lord, which also preserve some traces of the survival of blood-feud, Adémar de Chabannes, Chronique, ed. J. Chavanon, Collection de textes pour servir à l'étude et à l'enseignement de l'histoire, (Paris, 1897) 147, 150, 186, 191–2, 200—all of which will be considered in the study already mentioned.

which he claimed on the land which his man Andefredus son of Guy held as fee (which '*ad dictum feodum pertinebat*'). After he had put himself on 'the truth of my men of that land', Andefredus came to the count with seventy-seven lawworthy men to support his claim, but (and the words are put into the count's mouth in the charter) 'I chose twelve men ... and made them swear before me on relics, that they would not conceal the truth, for love or for hate ...' The oath being successfully completed in Andefredus' favour, the Count gave way 'peacefully' ... 'because I did not wish to dispute with my man', and made his sons confirm the settlement, ordering it to be written and sealed.[71] By comparison, the earliest record of a dispute between laymen involving the counts of Angoulême dates only from 1157, but directly concerns customs of secular inheritance, and the terms on which an entry-fine should be paid.[72]

For Aquitaine the situation is very different. By contrast, the only surviving secular dispute settlement for the years between the tenth century and 1137 comes from about a century before the Angevin comital charter just mentioned. It is the extraordinary narrative known as the 'Agreement between Count William of the Aquitanians and Hugh leader of a thousand (*Chiliarch*)'. The problem of whether this should in practice be classified as a documentary source has meant that it has often been treated with circumspection by early mediaeval historians, and the last word has not yet been said about it—and certainly was not be the last editor of the Latin text.[73] But, despite its great formal differences from other documents being considered here, it certainly employs the language of dispute and settlement (*placitum* and *placitare, convenientiae, finis ...*) and the main narrative thread is concerned with Hugh's grievances. Both reported and direct speech give it considerable vigour, although that does not mean that the *Conventum* is therefore necessarily strictually factual, let alone 'sincere'.

[71] The rights over which Andefredus was allowed to retain jurisdiction were 'sanguinem et latronem et duellum et omnia alia [note that these are never given a generic description] ... preter exercitum meum et equitacionem et talliatam meam'—Chartrou, *L'Anjou, pièces justificatives*, no. 42, 374–5 (for the background to, and appearance of, the sworn inquest in Anjou under Count Fulk, ibid, 136–9, 153–7); cf. Bongert, ibid. 263–7 (later examples, however). Further discussion needs to be devoted to the vocabulary used in this charter which deals with legal and fiscal, as well as political, 'rights' and obligations.

[72] It was terminated by a *concordia* brought about by the good offices of 'friends' of the two parties, although Count William *Taillaferrus* had first ordered a duel (*pugna*) to be held to settle the disagreement over the sum owed as *acaptamentum*, R. Watson, 'The Counts of Angoulême', catalogue no. 161 (unpublished charter).

[73] Martindale, '*Conventum inter Guillelmum comitem et Hugonem Chiliarchum*', *English Historical Review*, LXXXIV (1969), 528–48. Since the present paper was delivered in early 1994, a more extended study of the *Conventum* has been prepared, 'Conflict and settlement in the *Conventum inter Willelmum comitem Aquitanorum et Hugonem Chiliarchum*: Postscript to the edition of 1969', to appear in the Variorum volume cited above, n. 8 (no. VIII).

'Why don't you come to an agreement with Bernard? You are so much
mine that if I told you to take a peasant for your lord, you would have
to do it ...' 'And if all the world were mine I would not give you even
as much as I could hold on the tip of my finger ...' are two of the
speeches put into the mouth of Count William of the Aquitinians. The
rhetorical purpose of the narrative seems to have been to prove the
justice of the assertion that 'it seemed to Hugh and his men that
the Count was treating him badly (*male tractaret*)', but its underlying
aim may have been to increase the plausibility of Hugh's chief complaint against the Count—and indeed to improve his bargaining
position for lands or damages.[74]

The predominantly oral nature of the procedure described may
explain why there are no similar survivals for the early eleventh century.
'He said these things in the presence of all', the argument was made
'just as it was declared in this settlement' ('*sicut finis locuta fuit*'), are
merely two indications of the atmosphere of orality which prevails; and
yet the legal connotations and character of this narrative cannot really
be doubted. At one stage for, instance, the Count proposes the use of
an ordeal to test his own good faith. Unfortunately, as with the dispute
notices considered earlier, few references enable us to relate different
issues to any specific points of custom or law. The norms to which
Hugh appeals are based on standards governing social and political
relations within his own region, but appear largely self-interested: a
lord should make an advantageous marriage for his *fidelis* and help him
to increase his resources (in land and fortified places), but especially
should not stand in the way of his obtaining the *honor* which had been
in his kin's possession. At one point Hugh seems almost to enunciate a
legal principle when he asserts that 'the castle which you are demanding
of me used to belong to my relatives (*consanguineos meos*), and I have
better right (*rectum habeo melius*) than those who were holding it'; but no
more detailed definitions of 'inheritance right' follow beyond that very
general declaration.[75] Despite references to conflict and on one occasion
to open *guerra*, the authority of the Poitevin count emerges clearly from
this narrative; while his superiority is indicated even through such a
casual reference as 'the count went out from the city, he required Hugh
to come to him ...' His authority was expressed through comital orders
given to his man, to accompany him on a military expedition, or to a
plea (*rogavit, mandavit ... ad curtem comiti*); but at the conclusion of the
narrative after expressing fears that he will be doublecrossed once

---

[74] The text contains 18 references to *conventum* as agreement as opposed to one to
convenientia, 544; and 8 to *placitum* in some form. For noteworthy examples of direct
speech, 544, 547; cf. for the general reflection on the count's treatment of Hugh, 546.

[75] Ibid, 547–8; 541–2. All these points will be considered at length and with comparative
material and bibliography, in the publication already mentioned.

more, Hugh is told by the Count, 'We shall not do that' ... 'I shall make [an agreement] for you, I and my son, without evil intent (*sine malo ingenio*).' Hugh had to accept that assurance, and his oath of fealty preceded the grant by the Poitevin count and his son 'of the honor of Joscelin his uncle, just as that man was holding it a year before he died'. As in the notice with which this paper began, friendship is invoked, but so in this case is anger.[76]

The chief arguments of this paper have been based on the conviction that in the late Carolingian and Capetian kingdom of the French a secular prince's position required him to do justice. Its purpose has been to explore some of the problems posed by the documents which were produced in connection with the settlement of disputes in a selected group of 'principalities' and counties where—for whatever reasons—royal intervention scarcely seems to have occurred on a regular basis before the twelfth century. The suspicion that the material surviving represents only a small proportion of the disputes which in practice came before these secular rulers means that firm conclusions are difficult to make with conviction, but some still need to be advanced. These relate, firstly, to the Carolingian background to the discussion, secondly to developments which followed the political elimination of Carolingian kings, and in the third place to the problem of royal intervention before the mid-twelfth century. Finally, the political setting within which counts and 'princes' exercised their authority judicially can perhaps be most convincingly conveyed by considering some of the dynastic implications of that aspect of their authority.

In the first instance, it needs to be recognised that, although Carolingian 'centralisation' gave the appearance of uniform efficiency throughout huge regions like *Aquitania* or elsewhere, that rests on evidence which is to a considerable extent of prescriptive character, deriving from *capitularia* and other commands issued from the centre to localities which differed widely in their responses to such commands. Where evidence survives—as it does for Poitou during the tenth century—for the actual holding of the *mallus* under control, then that reflects adherence to the established order under which the counts' predecessors had been established. By contrast, the part played by dukes of the Poitevin dynasty in judicial proceedings as they extended their power territorially is only known from a small group of documents; but, although these are not backed up by any pronouncements on the theoretical foundations of their power, each process and settlement

---

[76] *Ibid.*, 545, 546, 548. For Hugh's actions prompted either for *amor* or *amicicia* of the count, 542, 546; however, the count's *ira* is also invoked, 543–4. Cf. the similarity of the language of a *clamor* brought before the count of Angoulême a century later: 'Ipse vero comes, valde iratus pro tanta iniuria, vocavit eum ad iudicium ...', Calendar no. 140 (1120/40), Watson, 'The Counts of Angoulême', 330.

represented a real exercise of authority, in the Saintonge, Limousin, Gascony or—however briefly—in the county of Toulouse. This facet of the many problems relating to the settlement of disputes in the earlier Middle Ages has been pursued at some length in this paper largely because of its recent neglect by historians interested in the investigation of conflict and legal disputes in the post-Carolingian world.

It is understandable that many studies of law and government in the medieval French kingdom, while acknowledging great regional variations in custom and procedure evolved during these centuries, should nevertheless look forward to the re-emergence of royal direction and control of judicial affairs, even if that would be some centuries in the future. However that teleological approach is misleading if it is supposed that the withdrawal of royal authority left a vacuum: that was certainly not the case with territories ruled by the Poitevin dynasty between the early tenth century and the first decades of the twelfth. It seems significant that it was military needs rather than matters of justice which apparently prompted the earliest Capetian royal appearances in the region. King Philip I's well-known appearance in Poitiers during 1076 to ask for military aid against the Norman duke is represented by two royal diplomas, for instance; but the same king used his royal authority to negotiate peace when war was declared between the duke of Aquitaine and the count of Anjou ('*quod Philippus rex concordavit*').[77] The only indication of any royal judicial intervention comes from Abbot Suger's circumstantial account of the confrontation between many parties outside the city of Clermont in the Auvergne: the duke of Aquitaine claimed jurisdiction over the count when the king (Louis VI) appeared at the head of an army to offer protection to its bishop. It seems significant that this intervention should initially have taken place between armed contenders.[78]

The political significance of dispute settlement during these centuries meant that it also had a dynastic and family dimension. Although by the second half of the eleventh century most secular rulers had professional or 'curial' officials at their disposal (*prepositi, milites de curia* and household officials such as seneschals) who were authorised to

---

[77] On the first event, see the passage and comments of Werner, 'Kingdom and principality', 245, 277; *Actes de Philippe Ier, roi de France (1059–1108)*, ed. M. Prou, Ch, et Dipl. (1908), nos. LXXXIII–IV (Poitiers, 9 and 14 Oct. 1076). For the second occasion, *La Chronique de Saint-Maixent, 751–1140*, ed. J. Verdon, Les classiques de l'histoire de France au moyen âge, (1979), 178; cf. A. Fliche, *Le règne de Philippe Ier, roi de France (1060–1108)*, (Paris, 1912), 272–3, 539.

[78] But there can be no doubt that this was intended to be settled by legal proceedings since the king 'diem inter eos [i.e. the bishop of Clermont and the count of Auvergne], presente duce Aquitanie, agendis Aurelianis, quod huc usque renuerant, statuit ...' The problems connected with this expedition (1126?) cannot be discussed here, *Suger, Vie de Louis VI le Gros*, ed. H. Waquet, Classiques ... (2nd edn, 1964), 235–40.

hear disputes and pronounce judgment, it was sometimes considered preferable to employ another member of the ruler's kin.[79] Although the reasons for this procedure are not explained, it presumable normally occurred when the ruler was absent from his own territories or occupied with other business; and this dynastic dimension to the doing of justice can be illustrated both when a woman appears at some stage of the proceedings, or if particular mention is made of a ruler's prospective heir. (This involves rather more than the widespread practice of ensuring that grants or concessions should be ratified or subscribed by close relatives and members of a family). One Angevin example is particularly suggestive: it records an agreement made between the abbey of Marmoutier and the lord of Rillé after the dispute was first heard in a court presided over by Countess Aremburgis, wife of Count Fulk.[80] The significance of such disputes being settled before a member of the ruling dynasty can be well illustrated by comparison with the situation of the formidable Countess Adela of Blois, who ordered a plea to be held at Blois to settle a dispute between a layman who had caused them 'great injury', and the monks of Marmoutier. (She allegedly referred back to the protection afforded by previous rulers of this principality, Count Theobald, and 'her husband Count Stephen').[81] Despite the emergence of a number of powerfully active women married to the Poitevin dukes from the late tenth century onwards, none of the surviving dispute documents show any signs of their intervention in judicial matters. But in any case such variations in practice need to be set in the context of a world in which the wife of a consecrated ruler (like the Empress Mathilda of Germany) might preside over courts assembled to settle disputes in territories under her husband's control.[82]

For a woman to sit in justice was, nevertheless, exceptional. Sons, however—and more particularly those who were potential political

---

[79] The household and curial officials of the Poitevin dukes will be discussed elsewhere.

[80] The count summoned the parties: 'certum locum certumque terminum posuerunt ... Venit utraque pars ad castellum comitis Balgiacum et se ibi comiti et comitisse presentaverunt; sed quia comes quibusdam suis negotiis tunc occupatus erat cause ille tractande non affuit, sed comitisse vice suum et locum committens ut ipsa cum suis baronibus causam iuxte definiret impetravit ... precepit comitissa baronibus suis ut facerent inde iudicium ...', Chartrou, *L'Anjou de 1109 à* catal. no. 72—(dated 1109×26, ed. in part only).

[81] '... donec ad aures dulcissimae domine nostrae Adelae, blesensis comitisse, incliti regis Anglorum Willelmi filiae ...', *Marmoutier Cartulaire Blésois*, ed. Ch. Métais, (Blois/Chartres, 1891), no. cxviii, a. 1104. Further examples of Adela's intervention in dispute process could be cited.

[82] The authority attributed to Duke William IX's wife as claimant to the county of Toulouse needs further investigation, however; and I hope to return to this topic in a more general fashion. Cf. M. Chibnall, *The Empress Matilda* (Oxford, 1991), 33–4 (for Italian examples); and for the contrast with the position of queen-consort as intercessor or parties drawn into disputes, 23–4.

successors to their fathers—are found associated in settlements or disputes from quite an early date (e.g. in the *Conventum* between Hugh of Lusignan and the '*comes Aquitanorum*').[83] 'Learning the judicial ropes' as an aspect of a 'princely' education seems to have been overlooked by historians, although it might be considered as necessary as the military and equestrian training which is always held to have dominated the upbringing of the secular aristocracy during these centuries. Indeed, three instances of very different provenance which seem to illustrate various facets of this training provide a suitable way to bring this paper to a close.

The first illustrates exceptionally well the connection between the exercise of political power and the doing of justice. It is contained in a letter in which Count Geoffrey 'le Bel' of Anjou notifies Henry 'my firstborn son' that a dispute has been settled between the monastery of la Trinité de Vendôme and the monks of Saint-Julien de Tours, concluded 'in Angers ... in my presence and in [an] audience of many laymen and clerics'. The main aim of the letter was to inform Henry (the future King Henry II of England) of this decision, since 'I believe—God willing—that you will succeed to the government of my land'. It was important for the young son of the count and the Empress Mathilda that he should recognise the importance of justice and judgment for the *regimen* of princely territories (that is the term used in the letter). If the date of about 1144 is correct, then the young Henry had perhaps scarcely entered his teens, but he certainly was not more than fourteen years old.[84]

An early version of the *Roman d'Alexandre* casts an interesting light on this question. A passage from the fragmentary lines attributed to Alberic sets the scene of the young Alexander's precocious childhood with a description of the future conqueror walking and running when he was only a year old. Almost immediately, it seems, he was given many expert masters; and, 'well instructed in every art', those masters taught him languages and letters as a little boy, as well as the techniques of fighting with shield and sword. 'The third [master taught him] the law and how to take part in a plea; to distinguish right from wrong'. The essentially legal 'word field' of this early fragment is conveyed more

---

[83] This elaborate series of complaints was concluded after the count offered: 'Relinque mihi omnes querelas de retro quas requirebas, et iura mihi fidelitatem et filio meo ...', *Conventum*, 548; cf. A. Lewis, 'Anticipatory association of the heir in early Capetian France', *American Historical Review*, LXXXIII, (1968), 906–27.

[84] The monks of Tours renounced any further claim *ordine judiciario, Recueil des actes de Henri II concernant les provinces françaises et les affaires de France*, ed. L. Delisle and E. Berger, Ch. et dipl., 3 vols. (1909–27), I, no. iv, 8–10; cf. Chartrou, *L'Anjou*, catal. no. 152. A prince like the count of Anjou also wished to ensure that his son and prospective successor should understand his duty to protect churches founded by their ancestors, Chibnall, *ibid*, 145.

immediately in the original language than in this translation and, because the little Alexander was from birth discernible as '*fil de baron*', the use of the passage seems permissible in the setting of 'princely' as well as royal or imperial education:

> '*Li terz ley leyre et playt cabir*
> *E. l dreyt del tort a discernir*'.[85]

With the last example of all there can be a return to the Poitevin dynasty, and to the charters with which this paper began. No compromise or concord could be reached in a bitter dispute brought by the monks of Nouaillé against a recently appointed comital *prepositus* who, they claimed, had deprived them of the mills of Chasseignes. Indeed the charter implies that the monks found it difficult to get justice because of the Duke's personal affection for this official, and they sought the intervention of—Hugh of Lusignan. The suit was heard by the Duke and his *milites de curia* in Poitiers in the year 1104; but the court judged that the dispute needed to be settled by a duel, which was to be fought on an island in the rivers which circled the city. On this occasion the champions both arrived fully equipped and on the appointed day. Among those who were gathered to watch the outcome of the fight was 'the son of Count William with his tutor (*pedagogus*)'. The boy's education for the complexities of dispute settlement was beginning young: he was five years old.[86]

---

[85] *The Medieval French Roman d'Alexandre*, ed. E. Armstrong, III, *Version of Alexandre de Paris, Variants and Notes to Branch* I, ed. A. Foulet (Princeton, 1949), 41 (ll. 98–9); and cf. the absence of such a precise reference in the *Alexandre Décasyllabique*, ibid. 106 (ll. 212–16 of MS.L); 163 (ll. 341–8 of the G text of Branch I). Note also the different implications of '*De jugement surmonter jugeors/Bastir agait por prendre robeors*', I, 4–5 (Arsenal MS, ll. 56–7). I should like to thank Dr. Ruth Harvey for her help in this matter.

[86] *Chartes ... Nouaillé*, no. 187; (cf. no. 180—which is a plea relating to the same land held between the years c. 1086—1091 before 'Willelmum ducem Aquitanorum et Petrum episcopum et obtimates'). This seems to me to be a plausible explanation of the child's presence, although the motive for recording this may have been that the monks of Nouaillé hoped to impress on the child's mind the victory gained by their contestant. This was in any case a rather more down-to-earth form of education than the letter preserved for the future king Henry II, or even the fictional Alexander's tutorials.

THE STRUCTURES OF POLITICS IN EARLY TUDOR ENGLAND

By Steven Gunn

READ 29 APRIL 1994 AT THE UNIVERSITY OF GLASGOW

SOMETHING of the atmosphere of trench warfare, with its immobility and its desperation, has overcome the historiography of early Tudor politics. The most spectacular impasse concerns the fall of Anne Boleyn. Three scholars have recently set out and defended against one another divergent explanations of her fall.[1] Professor Ives and Professor Warnicke can agree that Dr Bernard is wrong: Anne cannot possibly have been destroyed by a masterful and jealous king who may reasonably have believed her guilty of multiple adultery as charged. Dr Bernard and Professor Ives can agree that Professor Warnicke is wrong: Anne's fall cannot be attributed to her miscarriage of a deformed foetus, awakening the king's fears of witchcraft and its sixteenth-century stablemates, sodomy and incest. Professor Warnicke and Dr Bernard can agree that Professor Ives is wrong: Anne cannot have been ousted by a factional plot at court, coordinated by Thomas Cromwell and cynically using fabricated charges of adultery to hustle the king into destroying the queen and her partisans at a single blow.

This debate is symptomatic of a wider polarisation amongst historians of Henry VIII's reign. On one side stand the champions of a strong king, for whom the rhythms of politics and government were determined by Henry's informed choice of ministers and policies. On the other stand the advocates of faction, for whom the king's choice of policies and executants was determined by the victory of one pressure-group at

---

[1] E. W. Ives, *Anne Boleyn* (Oxford, 1986) [hereafter Ives, *Anne Boleyn*], 335–418; R. M. Warnicke, *The Rise and Fall of Anne Boleyn* (Cambridge, 1989) [hereafter Warnicke, *Rise and Fall*], 191–233; G. W. Bernard, 'The fall of Anne Boleyn', *English Historical Review* [hereafter *EHR*], CVI (1991) [hereafter Bernard, 'Fall'], 584–610; E. W. Ives, 'The fall of Anne Boleyn reconsidered', *ibid.*, CVII (1992), 651–64; G. W. Bernard, 'The fall of Anne Boleyn: a rejoinder', *ibid.*, CVII (1992) [hereafter Bernard, 'Rejoinder'], 665–74; R. M. Warnicke, 'The fall of Anne Boleyn revisited', *ibid.*, CVIII (1993) [hereafter Warnicke, 'Fall revisited'], 653–65. For the subsidiary debate on Anne's religion, see G. W. Bernard, 'Anne Boleyn's religion', *Historical Journal* [hereafter *HJ*], XXXVI (1993), 1–20; E. W. Ives, 'Anne Boleyn and the early reformation in England: the contemporary evidence', ibid., XXXVII (1994), 389–400. I am very grateful to Simon Adams, George Bernard and Cliff Davies for their comments on this paper, though they are by no means responsible for the opinions it expresses.

court over another. Understandably, there are extremists and moderates
in either camp, and individual scholars vary in their emphases: thus
Bernard and Warnicke disagree strongly about the motivation for the
king's decisive action against his second wife. Essentially, however, there
is a bipolar division between the king's men and the factionalists. In
the Anne Boleyn debate, and indeed in general, these historians use
almost entirely the same evidence, though predictably they place
different weight on various parts of the common corpus.[2] What primarily
accounts for the divergence of conclusions is the wide variation in the
assumptions scholars bring to their analysis, a point perhaps illustrated
by Professor Warnicke's publication of two articles on the fall of Anne
Boleyn within three years, the first expounding a view very like that of
Professor Ives, and the second her current theory.[3]

Where do these assumptions about the nature of early Tudor politics
come from? Sometimes they rely on parallels with modern politics or
business, aiming to capture the timeless nature of the arts of influence
or management; but such comparisons can cut both ways. For David
Starkey, 'factions, "wet" and "dry", "right" and "left", struggle for
control of the Conservative and Labour parties, and so for control of
our two-party state', while 'to transfer from Tudor Whitehall to the
modern White House requires little more than a change of clothes!'
For Peter Gwyn, on the other hand, the relationship between Henry
and Wolsey best resembles that between the chairman of a large
company and his managing director: though the MD may control day-
to-day business, the chairman is very much in charge.[4] Chronologically
closer parallels are often drawn with Elizabethan England, especially
as depicted in Sir John Neale's seminal lecture of 1948, 'The Elizabethan
political scene'.[5] But these too have their dangers, since recent historians
are far from agreed about the nature of the Elizabethan political system:
Simon Adams has argued that Neale and others much exaggerated the

[2] As another recent writer on the politics of Henry VIII's reign has put it, in a
footnote discussing the difference between his understanding of the subject and Professor
Warnicke's, 'We often use the same evidence but reach contradictory conclusions.' J. S.
Block, *Factional Politics and the English Reformation 1520–1540* (Woodbridge, 1993) [hereafter
Block, *Factional Politics*], 7n.

[3] R. M. Warnicke, 'The fall of Anne Boleyn: a reassessment', *History*, LXX (1985)
[hereafter Warnicke, 'Reassessment'], 1–15: idem, 'Sexual heresy at the court of Henry
VIII', *HJ*, XXX (1987), 247–68.

[4] D. R. Starkey, *The Reign of Henry VIII: Personalities and Politics* (1985) [hereafter Starkey,
Reign of Henry VIII], 9, 30; P. Gwyn, *The King's Cardinal: The Rise and Fall of Thomas Wolsey*
(1990) [hereafter Gwyn, *King's Cardinal*], 210–11.

[5] E. W. Ives, *Faction in Tudor England*, second edition (1986) [hereafter Ives, *Faction*], 25;
idem, 'The fall of Wolsey' [hereafter Ives, 'Fall of Wolsey'], in *Cardinal Wolsey: Church,
State and Art*, eds. S. J. Gunn and P. G. Lindley (Cambridge, 1991) [hereafter *Cardinal
Wolsey*], 302.

degree of factional division amongst Elizabeth's courtiers and councillors, but Susan Doran has suggested that Dr Adams has swung too
far in the opposite direction.[6] Comparisons with other early-modern
regimes have their uses too, but may reflect little more than historiographical fashion and are dependent on the regimes one chooses.
The stock of Louis XIII of France and Philip IV of Spain as effective
personal monarchs unswayed by faction may well be rising, but that of
the Emperor Charles V and Tsar Ivan the Terrible seems simultaneously
to be on the wane.[7] The comparative handholds are more slippery
than they may appear, and the danger of circularity of argument is
evident.

There is also a more fundamental circularity to many of the arguments deployed in these debates. The interpretation of any one episode
in Henry's reign is tied to the author's interpretation of a number of
other episodes in the same reign, if only as a final reinforcement to an
argument already laid out.[8] Thus a 'strong king' picture or a factional
picture of the politics of the reign is created as a mosaic of pieces, each
of which reflects back the light reflected by all the others. The ultimate
source of the light, however, is the author's general conception of the
nature of Henrician politics. Most of these interpretations, moreover,
are competing narratives. As with the fall of Anne Boleyn, they
concentrate on explaining changes of queen, executions of councillors,
deviations in royal policy or the course of individual careers. The
authors' analyses of the nature of the political system then draw on
these narratives. All too often, however, the gaps in the narrative have
to be filled by assuming the existence of an otherwise invisible process
to explain a visible outcome, rather like Marxist invocation of the class
struggle. This results in such sentences as 'After 29 January, many
secret meetings among the conspirators must have taken place.'[9] When
used with care, these are all perfectly legitimate strategies in historical
argument, but their implications must be borne in mind if we are to
go beyond the current state of debate. What we need is either new
evidence or new assumptions, and ideas for both may arise if we try to

---

[6] S. L. Adams, 'Eliza enthroned? The court and its politics', in *The Reign of Elizabeth
I*, ed. C. A. Haigh (1984) [hereafter *Reign of Elizabeth*], 55–77; S. Doran, 'Religion and
politics at the court of Elizabeth I: the Habsburg marriage negotiations of 1559–1567 ',
EHR, CIV (1989), 908–26.

[7] Bernard, 'Rejoinder', 673–4; A.L. Moote, *Louis XIII, The Just* (Berkeley, CA, 1989);
R. A. Stradling, *Philip IV and the Government of Spain, 1621–1655* (Cambridge, 1988); M.
Rodríguez-Salgado, *The Changing Face of Empire: Charles V, Philip II and Habsburg Authority,
1551–1559* (Cambridge, 1988); N. S. Kollmann, 'The grand prince in Muscovite politics:
the problem of genre in sources on Ivan's minority', *Russian History*, XIV (1987), 293–313.

[8] Bernard, 'Rejoinder', 672–3; Ives, 'Fall of Wolsey', 289–90.

[9] Warnicke, 'Reassessment', 2.

analyse the political system more carefully before we try to write political narrative, rather than vice versa.

Two means to do so are hinted at in my title. The proper context for an understanding of the political life of Henry VIII's reign is a study of the reigns adjacent to it, of the early Tudor period as a whole. This is important not least because so many of the leading politicians at either end of Henry's reign enjoyed prominent careers under his father or his son. Yet detailed and sustained consideration has not yet been given to the impact of the change of rulers on such men's careers, or to the impact of such careers on the continuity of politics and government. Indeed, comparatively little has yet been written on the central politics of Henry VII's reign from any perspective. The continuities and discontinuities of the 1540s have commanded more attention, but there is still much to be gained from looking at Henrician politics in the light of Edwardian and Marian developments. Only when we understand better what was normal in early Tudor politics, and what were the processes of long-term change at work within them, can we properly assess the importance of individual kings, ministers, institutions or ideas.

To speak of the structures of politics, meanwhile, is to remind ourselves of the pervasive influence of Sir Lewis Namier's work on English political history. At first sight, we historians of the early sixteenth century might as well surrender to Namierism, for we are surrounded. In the periods following our own, the Namierites of the eighteenth century grasp hands across the civil war and interregnum with the neo-Namierite revisionists of the early Stuart era.[10] Simultaneously, the great enterprise of mapping the later medieval political landscape by the reconstitution of noble affinities rolls onwards along lines inspired by K. B. McFarlane. McFarlane himself drew the connection between Namier's work and his own.[11] Everywhere the analysis of politics as the struggle for power of identifiable groups bent on little more than mutual advancement seems to hold sway. Yet McFarlane's successors are now debating how to reintroduce political principle to their understanding of the fifteenth century; and, as those who teach the early Stuart period know from all too many first paragraphs of student essays, there are now not only revisionists but also post-revisionists.[12] We too might try to refine the way we use the Namierite legacy.

[10] J. C. D. Clark, *Revolution and Rebellion: State and Society in England in the Seventeenth and Eighteenth Centuries* (Cambridge, 1986).

[11] K. B. McFarlane, 'Parliament and "bastard feudalism" ', in his *England in the Fifteenth Century: Collected Essays* (1981), 19.

[12] M. A. Hicks, 'Idealism in late medieval English politics', in his *Richard III and His Rivals: Magnates and their Motives in the Wars of the Roses* (1991), 41–59; C. Carpenter, *Locality and Polity: A Study of Warwickshire Landed Society, 1401–1499* (Cambridge, 1992) [hereafter

Structure, of course, has taken on many connotations since Namier's day. Tudor politics were shaped by the structures of gender which gave women circumscribed, though real, roles in political life, and the structures of ideas and education which might make people think in adversarial, perhaps even paranoid, terms.[13] There were also structures of language which equipped people to think about politics and government in certain ways, or hindered them from doing so.[14] But what I want to concentrate on today are the social and ideological structures of politics, the structures discussed (or dismissed) in Namier's paradigm.

What sources enable us to recover such structures? There are broadly six classes, each with their own advantages and drawbacks. Two, near-contemporary narratives and ambassadors' reports, generally tend to favour the advocates of faction. One, the archive of state papers, usually runs for the king's men. The others, material generated by trials and investigations, the contemporary literature of satire, panegyric and religious polemic, and records concerning the private affairs of the protagonists, are more ambiguous in their implications.

Narratives written by contemporaries, enjoying hindsight and shaping their material to some grand theme, often tend to the factional explanation. Thus Cavendish sought the origins of the decline and fall of his master Wolsey in the 'secrett grudge' borne by 'the great lordes of the Councell ... because that they could not rewle in the Comenwell (for hyme) as they wold'. They lit on Anne Boleyn as the 'mean to bryng hyme owt of the kynges highe fauour and them in to more auctorytie', and then 'there was Imagyned & Invented among them dyuers Imagynacions and subtill devysis howe this matter shold be brought abought'.[15] From the other side of the religious divide, John Foxe was an equally ardent conspiracy theorist, not least because of his awkward need to glorify Henry VIII for breaking with the pope while lamenting the persecution of the godly and preservation of popish rites so often carried out in his name. Hence perhaps Foxe's enunciation

Carpenter, *Locality and Polity*], 3–9; E. Powell, 'After "After McFarlane": the poverty of patronage and the case for constitutional history', in *Trade, Devotion and Governance: Papers in Later Medieval History*, eds. D.J. Clayton, R. G. Davies, P. McNiven (Stroud, 1994), 1–16; R. Cust, A. Hughes, 'Introduction: after revisionism', in *Conflict in Early Stuart England: Studies in Religion and Politics 1603–1642*, eds. R. Cust and A. Hughes (1989) [hereafter Cust and Hughes, 'After revisionism'], 1–46.

[13] B.J. Harris, 'Women and politics in early Tudor England', *HJ*, XXXIII (1990) [hereafter Harris, 'Women and politics'], 259–81; Cust and Hughes, 'After revisionism', 17; L. B. Smith, *Treason in Tudor England: Politics and Paranoia* (1986) [hereafter Smith, *Treason*], 40–117.

[14] T. F. Mayer, *Thomas Starkey and the Commonweal: Humanist Politics and Religion in the Reign of Henry VIII* (Cambridge, 1989), 18–26, 112–26.

[15] G. Cavendish, *The Life and Death of Cardinal Wolsey*, ed. R. S. Sylvester (Early English Text Society CCXLIII, 1959), 35.

of one of the proof texts of the factional explanation: 'King Henry, according as his counsel was about him, so was he led'.[16] It is an irony of recent scholarship that the revisionist historians of the reformation, eager to disown Foxe's overall picture of the process, have enthusiastically adopted his model of politics to explain the advent of religious change. Yet Foxe also reflected a genuine contemporary perception, as the protestant polemic of the 1540s and the correspondence of the embattled English reformers with their Swiss brethren suggest.[17] Cavendish may equally reflect the view from Wolsey's household. But that such accounts are not all they might seem is suggested by the case of Polydore Vergil, as spitefully critical of Wolsey as Cavendish was admiring. His narrative of the cardinal's decline and fall never invokes faction, since Wolsey, 'like an untamed horse, ... unable to stay quiet' had in his view destroyed himself by his initial advocacy of the king's divorce and his subsequent failure to obtain it.[18]

Ostensibly more independent political reporting is provided by the letters of foreign ambassadors at the English court. These provide striking and directly contemporary accounts of factional conflict. Anne Boleyn's suspicion that Wolsey is not furthering her marriage to the king, reported the Spanish ambassador Iñigo de Mendoza on 4 February 1529, 'has been the cause of her forming an alliance with her father, and with the two Dukes of Norfolk and Suffolk, to try and see whether they can conjointly ruin the Cardinal'.[19] 'Wolsey is in the greatest trouble ever' wrote his French equivalent, Guillaume du Bellay, on 22 May, 'the dukes of Suffolk and Norfolk and the others are convincing the king of England that he has not advanced the marriage as much as he could have done had he wished'.[20] 'The affairs of the cardinal ... are going from bad to worse' wrote the new imperial envoy Eustace Chapuys on 1 September, the failure of the divorce having given an opportunity to 'those who have been watching out for a long time for such an occasion or a similar one to avenge themselves for ancient

---

[16] D. R. Starkey, 'Intimacy and innovation: the rise of the privy chamber, 1485–1547', in *The English Court from the Wars of the Roses to the Civil War*, ed. D. R. Starkey (1987) [hereafter Starkey, 'Intimacy and innovation'], 101–2; G. Redworth, *In Defence of the Church Catholic: The Life of Stephen Gardiner* (Oxford, 1990) [hereafter Redworth, *Gardiner*], 3, 89.

[17] S. E. Brigden, *London and the Reformation* (Oxford, 1989) [hereafter Brigden, *London*], 325–77 ; Redworth, *Gardiner*, 232 and *passim*.

[18] *The Anglica Historia of Polydore Vergil A.D. 1485–1537*, ed. D. Hay (Camden Society, 3rd series, LXXIV, 1950), 325–33.

[19] *Calendar of State Papers, Spanish*, eds. G. A. Bergenroth, P. de Gayangos, M. A. S. Hume and G. Mattingly (15 vols., 1862–1954) [hereafter *CSPS*, all references to document numbers], III, ii, 621.

[20] *Correspondance du Cardinal Jean du Bellay*, ed. R. Scheurer (2 vols., Société de l'Histoire de France, Paris, 1969–73) [hereafter *Correspondance Du Bellay*], I, 22.

enmities and have the administration of this kingdom in their hands'.[21] Similarly, on 1 June 1540 Marillac the French ambassador reported that 'things have come to the point where either the party of the said Cromwell must succumb, or that of the bishop of Winchester and his adherents'; nine days later Cromwell was in the Tower.[22] These men knew faction when they saw it—they were after all involved in the politics of their own courts.[23] English ambassadors, one might add, equally wrote home of those factional struggles abroad as though they were perfectly normal: 'the Cowrte everye where is the Cowrte; that is to saye, a place where is usidde goode shouldering and liftinge at eche other' observed Dr Nicholas Wotton from France, where he found the court 'sumwhat bandidde and divydidde', in August 1546.[24] The case for the ubiquity and dominance of faction seems beyond dispute.

Yet even many of the historians who have used these reports to write Henrician political history more or less in the factional mode have had their doubts about the ambassadors' reliability, and those eager to discount faction are predictably more critical still.[25] Warnicke points out that ambassadors rarely spoke English and were often deliberately fed information for consumption by the governments they represented, either in Henry's interest or in that of the individual informant. She argues that Chapuys was seriously inconsistent in his analysis of political alignments, and that his comments on Anne Boleyn are irrevocably coloured by his conviction that she was the evil temptress who had destroyed Henry's marriage to Catherine.[26] Gwyn suggests that in 1527–9, as Wolsey directed a pro-French foreign policy, Mendoza was indulging in wishful thinking to the effect that every councillor bar Wolsey was working for a return to the alliance with the emperor, and Du Bellay was passing on to the French the picture Wolsey wanted them to receive, that of an embattled cardinal maintaining the French alliance against all the odds and therefore in need of frequent and generous concessions in negotiation.[27]

[21] Public Record Office [hereafter PRO], PRO31/18/2/1, fo. 390v (*CSPS* V, 132).

[22] *Correspondance politique de MM. de Castillon et de Marillac*, ed. J. Kaulek (Paris, 1888), 187–8.

[23] *Ambassades en Angleterre de Jean du Bellay*, eds. V.-L. Bourrilly, P. de Vaissière (Archives de l'Histoire Religieuse de la France, Paris, 1905) [hereafter *Ambassades Du Bellay*], 257–8, 373–5; *Correspondance Du Bellay*, 38, 107.

[24] R. J. Knecht, *Francis I* (Cambridge, 1982), 410–11; *State Papers, King Henry the Eighth* (11 vols., 1830–52) [hereafter *State Papers*], XI, 278.

[25] G. R. Elton, 'Thomas Cromwell's decline and fall', in his *Studies in Tudor and Stuart Politics and Government* (4 vols. to date, Cambridge, 1974–92), 219n; J.- P. Moreau, *Rome ou L'Angleterre? Les réactions politiques des catholiques anglais au moment du schisme (1529–1553)* (Paris, 1984), 109n; Ives, *Anne Boleyn*, 74–5.

[26] Warnicke, *Rise and Fall*, 1–3, 66, 88, 97, 114, 126, 135, 142, 145–6, 174, 181, 184, 200.

[27] Gwyn, *King's Cardinal*, 575–8; the outstanding example is found in *Ambassades Du Bellay*, 359–65. For apparently similar behaviour in 1515 and the early 1520s, see *Calendar*

One can add to these criticisms. For all his intellectual accomplishments and social skills, Chapuys seems to have been rather depressed about the degree of his influence amongst the English: he told another of the emperor's men in September 1544 'that he had known the English for the past fifteen or sixteen years, and that they will do nothing for me and little for him'.[28] Ambassadors disagreed with one another. In 1530 the Milanese ambassador wrote off the view that Wolsey's fall resulted from the 'envy and fear of his rivals'—apparently that we have seen expressed by the French and Spanish envoys—as the 'trivial opinion of the multitude'.[29] Ambassadors also provided information which seemed not to fit their overall interpretation of events, or at least historians' rationalised version of it. Thus Mendoza, who reported the gathering plot against Wolsey in February 1529, had already written in January that Henry had told him that he was dissatisfied with Wolsey's conduct of the divorce.[30] Ambassadors were prone to sententious and ill-informed generalisation about such matters as 'the accusations prevalent in great courts, where favour does not always remain stable'.[31] They used terminology at crucial points which was presumably clear to the recipients of their letters but is no longer so. When Jean du Bellay wrote of the duke of Suffolk's embassy to France in 1529 'C'estoyt de la menee de Anne Boleyn que le duc de Suffolk estoyt allé vers vous', did he mean 'it was as a member of the Anne Boleyn camp that the duke of Suffolk came to see you', or that 'it was by Anne Boleyn's stratagem'? The second implies far less about Suffolk's commitment to Anne, and makes it easier to disregard this explanation of the choice of Suffolk in favour of the wide range of evidence that he was sent because of his military reputation. The second also seems to fit better Du Bellay's use of the term 'menee' in a letter of 1537.[32] But secure interpretation of such fleeting comments is elusive.

A final problem with ambassadors' reports impedes our under-

---

of State Papers, Venetian, eds. R. Brown, C. Bentinck and H. Brown (9 vols., 1864–98) [hereafter CSPV, all references to document numbers], II, 635, and G. Walker, John Skelton and the Politics of the 1520s (Cambridge, 1988) [hereafter Walker, Skelton], 166–7.

[28] Ives, Anne Boleyn, 73; Archives Générales du Royaume, Brussels, EA 1630³, unnumbered letter of Sebastian Bourgeois to Mary of Hungary, 26 September 1544.

[29] Warnicke, Rise and Fall, 88.

[30] CSPS, III, ii, 614.

[31] CSPV, II, 875.

[32] Ives, 'Fall of Wolsey', p. 305; S. J. Gunn, Charles Brandon, duke of Suffolk c. 1484–1545 (Oxford, 1988) [hereafter Gunn, Charles Brandon], 107–9; Letters and Papers, Foreign and Domestic, of the Reign of Henry VIII, eds. J. S. Brewer, J. Gairdner and R. H. Brodie (22 vols. in 35, 1862–1932) [hereafter LP, all references to document numbers], IV, iii, 5523, 5535, 5541, 5547, 5579, 5584; CSPS, V, 16; CSPV IV, 464; D. L. Potter, War and Government in the French Provinces: Picardy 1470–1560 (Cambridge, 1993), 74, cf. 258.

standing of longer-term trends in early Tudor politics. England was only gradually sucked into the developing European network of permanent embassies from the 1510s.[33] In Henry VII's reign ambassadors' reports are scarce and can rarely be compared with each other as, for instance, the runs of French, Venetian and Spanish reports can be for Mary's reign. Before Henry VII's time they are scarcer still. Which of the various political crises of Henry VIII's reign is the Venetian diplomatic diarist Marin Sanudo describing here? 'News from England that King Henry was in trouble [and] had ordered the arrest of one of his chamber attendants.'[34] None: he is writing of the arrest of Lord William Courtenay, Elizabeth of York's brother-in-law and one of Henry VII's closest noble courtiers, in 1502. We must beware the optical illusion of political change produced by changes in the diplomatic evidence.

The third category of evidence used in these debates is that drawn from the records of government. This tends to reinforce the non-factional picture, of a strong king served by councillors and courtiers who generally cooperated with one another. First, it demonstrates an involvement in the work of government and a grasp on the issues involved which fit very ill with any notion of a Henry VIII so ill-informed or weak-minded as to be readily manipulable. In the areas of policy that interested the king, notably foreign policy, religion, treason and the divorce, even in the revision of the statutes of the order of the Garter, there is plenty of evidence that he considered and annotated papers, and that he shaped the policy his ministers executed by correspondence when he was unable to do so in face-to-face discussion.[35] His involvement in foreign policy and religious policy is particularly significant, since these were areas of much lower activity under Henry VII, with whom Henry is often contrasted to demonstrate his inattention to the business of government.[36] Though Henry VII's work-rate may have been exaggerated, he did give painstaking attention to matters of finance and the fiscal and political control of his leading subjects; but for much of his reign the demands on his time of meetings with ambassadors or work on diplomatic correspondence were much smaller

[33] G. Mattingly, *Renaissance Diplomacy* (Harmondsworth, 1965 edn), 146–53.

[34] *CSPV*, I, 822; S.J. Gunn, 'The courtiers of Henry VII', *EHR*, CVIII (1993) [hereafter Gunn, 'Courtiers'], 34, 47.

[35] J.J. Scarisbrick, *Henry VIII* (Harmondsworth, 1971 edn), 522–43; G. Nicholson, 'The act of appeals and the English reformation' in *Law and Government under the Tudors: Essays presented to Sir Geoffrey Elton*, eds. C. Cross, D. M. Loades and J.J. Scarisbrick (Cambridge, 1988), 21; G. Redworth, 'A study in the formulation of policy: the genesis and evolution of the act of six articles', *Journal of Ecclesiastical History*, XXXVII (1986) [hereafter Redworth, 'Six articles'], 45–7, 61–6; *State Papers*, I, 115–49, 174n, 891–2; S.J. Gunn, 'Wolsey's foreign policy and the domestic crisis of 1527–8', in *Cardinal Wolsey*, 157–60; PRO, E163/12/7.

[36] Starkey, *Reign of Henry VIII*, 60.

than those on Henry VIII, and he seems not to have shared his son's
theological preoccupations. Any fair comparison is further hindered by
the loss of the papers of most of Henry VII's ministers, with the
exception of some items from Bray's archive. Henry VII never seems
to have entrusted the same degree of overall coordination of policy to
a single minister that his son did to Wolsey or Cromwell; beyond that
it is hard to go.

The second lesson of the state paper material is equally significant.
This is the impression that most of the time ministers, councillors,
courtiers and noblemen worked together as best they could to serve
the king. Close examination of the correspondence concerning the
attempt to levy the Amicable Grant in 1525, for instance, has convinced
George Bernard that the dukes of Norfolk and Suffolk and Archbishop
Warham were working hard, at Wolsey's coordination, to try to raise
an unpopular levy for the king, rather than stirring up opposition to
the demand or exploiting its difficulties to plot against the cardinal.
Similarly, Peter Gwyn has used Norfolk's correspondence with Wolsey
to suggest that they were engaged in a not unstrained but fundamentally
cooperative relationship, rather than an all-out factional contest.[37]

The problem, of course, is just what such correspondence conceals.
The need for secrecy and mistrust was a stock element in all sixteenth-
century political advice, and, at least for Machiavelli, dissimulation was
the key to success.[38] Contemporaries were aware of the problem. The
duchess of Suffolk assured Cecil, imprisoned in the Tower in 1549, that
she did not suffer from 'the common infection of feigned friendship'.[39]
Thomas Alvard reported to his worried colleague in Wolsey's service
Thomas Cromwell in September 1529 that 'my lord of Suffolke, my
Lord of Rochford, maister Tuke, and Master Stevyns [Gardiner] did
as gently [be]have theymselfs, with as moche observaunce and humy-
[lyte to] my Lords Grace as ever I sawe theym do at any [time] tofor.
What they bere in ther harts' he added ominously, 'I knowe n[ot]'.[40]
Assurances of profound gratitude and undying loyalty came cheaply to
many early Tudor politicians, even when they might seem socially
demeaning: Henry, second earl of Essex, third count of Eu, sixth Lord
Bourchier, pledged himself to 'master Cromwell' in January 1532 'suche

[37] G. W. Bernard, *War, Taxation and Rebellion in Early Tudor England: Henry VIII, Wolsey, and the Amicable Grant of 1525* (Brighton, 1986) [hereafter Bernard, *War, Taxation and Rebellion*], 76–107; Gwyn, *King's Cardinal*, 565–70.

[38] Smith, *Treason*, 42–55; N. Machiavelli, *The Prince* (Harmondsworth, 1961 edn), 99–102.

[39] Harris, 'Women and politics', 279.

[40] *Original Letters illustrative of English History*, ed. H. Ellis [hereafter *Original Letters*], 1st series (2nd edn, 3 vols., 1825), I, 309–10 (*LP*, IV, iii, 5953).

as I am, I am yours durynge my lyffe'.[41] So presumably even Wolsey took with a pinch of salt letters such as that from Sir Richard Wingfield in 1523, assuring him that his kindness to Sir Richard's brother Sir Robert bound both of them to the cardinal's service, and their descendants after them. It was an especially extravagant promise as Sir Robert had no children.[42]

The atmosphere suggested by such correspondence, then, is a helpful guide to the nature of relations amongst the political elite, and the results of their effective cooperation in war, taxation, and other areas of governmental activity show that they must have been able to work together. Duty and self-interest combined to make all determined to be seen to serve the king, if needs be by careful cooperation with the minister of the moment. But that did not exclude the possibility that some might think the best way to render the king service was to remove, or reduce the influence of, some wrong-headed colleague. Just as the narrative and ambassadorial evidence does not clinch the argument for the advocates of faction, neither does the state paper material substantiate all the claims of the king's men.

This is especially the case on the rare occasions when the correspondence of king or minister contains discussions of political divisions or manoeuvres. Thus in 1514–15 Charles Brandon wrote letters to Wolsey which clearly represented the two of them as engaged in partisan competition with the Howards, as many external observers felt them to be.[43] Wolsey and Cromwell, it is true, did not mention the machinations of their enemies in their appeals for the royal mercy, beyond Cromwell's brief 'Myn accusors your Grace knowyth; God forgyve them'; even this may have referred only to Rich and Throckmorton who gave specific evidence of his crimes.[44] Brandon was different. He pleaded it as a point in his favour in 1515, when all the council save Wolsey reportedly asked for his execution or imprisonment as punishment for marrying the king's sister, that 'ther was newar non of thym in trobbyl bout I was glad to helpe thym to me pour and [tha]t your grace knowes byst'; in an earlier letter in the same sequence he claimed that 'I ne[ver went?] abowth to hert non mane'. Both these suggest a system of politics in which some of his colleagues were less benevolent than he claimed to be. His concluding assertion that 'I know your grace of scheth natur [tha]t et cannot ly in thyr power to caus you to dysstru me for ther malles' has a distinctly hopeful air,

---

[41] PRO, SP1/69, fo. 56 (*LP*, V, 728).
[42] PRO, SP1/28, fo. 245 (*LP*, III, ii, 3378).
[43] Gunn, *Charles Brandon*, 27, 33, 35–6; see especially *LP*, I, ii, 3376.
[44] *State Papers*, I, 347–8; *LP*, XV, 776, 824; *Original Letters*, 2nd series (4 vols., 1827), II, 163.

though the hope may have been of a self-fulfilling sort.[45] Once the idea had been planted in Henry's mind that it was a malicious desire to manipulate him into destroying his friend that motivated any advice to the effect that his honour demanded a terrible punishment for Brandon, the errant duke was on his way to being saved.

The evidence supplied by trials and investigations also hints at some of the tensions in Henrician politics. If half the grumbling at Cromwell and the 'knaves and heretycks and smatterers off lernyng' who assisted in the Boleyn marriage and the break with Rome confessed to by the 'Exeter conspirators' really took place, then the marquess of Exeter, Lord Montague, Sir Edward Neville and the rest were seriously alienated from the king's chief minister, to say the least.[46] Though the evidence may be less reliable, it seems that Buckingham too grumbled, about the king, about the surviving ministers of Henry VII, about the jumped-up young courtiers raking in the king's rewards and above all about Wolsey; on the other hand, it seems that he could not get anyone else of note to listen to his grumbling.[47] Investigations of careless talk also suggest how explicit contemporaries could be in discussing politics. In August 1539 one of Bishop Tunstall of Durham's chaplains excitedly told the bishop's registrar 'that therle of Hampton, Sir William Kyngston, and Sir Antony Browne were all ioyned togyther, and would have had my lord of Duresme to have had rule and chef saying under the kyngs hyghnes'. The chaplain and the registrar agreed that this would be a good thing, but they recognised that Tunstall, knowing 'by his book thinconstancy of prynces' would not let himself be pushed forward.[48]

Literary evidence also cuts both ways. Greg Walker's careful criticism of John Skelton's satires on Wolsey has reduced their credibility as an account of the cardinal's political position, and shown that it is unlikely that they were commissioned by the Howards as weapons in a factional contest.[49] Yet Skelton's caricature of a rantingly dictatorial minister, hoodwinking, manipulating and even bewitching the king, has a curious counterpart in contemporary panegyric on Wolsey, which glorifies him for all the government's central policies and then slips in vague and slightly apologetic references to the way in which he 'bears the weight of the whole commonwealth on his shoulders (under the most

[45] British Library [hereafter BL], Cotton Manuscript Vespasian FXIII, fo. 153 (*LP*, II, i, 367); Cotton Manuscript Caligula DVI, fo. 184v (*LP*, II, i, 80).

[46] *LP*, XIII, ii, 765, 772, 800, 802, 804, 827, 876, 960.

[47] B.J. Harris, *Edward Stafford, Third duke of Buckingham, 1478–1521* (Stanford, CA, 1986) [hereafter Harris, *Buckingham*], 170–2, 176.

[48] C. Sturge, *Cuthbert Tunstall* (1938) [hereafter Sturge, *Tunstall*], 371.

[49] Walker, *Skelton*, 5–34, 124–87.

unconquered king)'.[50] Wolsey's position, as a chief minister quite without parallel in the previous reign, took some explaining whichever polemical stance one wished to adopt. Walker's more recent examination of court drama suggests that plays were used to present partisan political views at Henry VIII's court, as they were at Elizabeth's.[51] If the plays he studies were aimed in part at the king, they provide evidence that Henry was thought to be in charge of affairs but open to persuasion: a bridge between the factional and 'strong king' positions to which we shall return.

The last class of evidence available, and to my mind the most promising and the least exploited, is what one might call the biographical, the evidence of the personal affairs and interrelationships of the political actors. This is of particular importance in analysing a political system in which the boundaries of public and private activity were so blurred. Landholding was the basis of social power and the qualification for local office, the household was a fundamental political and even administrative unit, and personal recommendation was the sole route to promotion.[52] There was a sense in which everything might carry a political charge: the display of heraldry on buildings, possessions and servants, Anne Boleyn's conduct of the game of courtly love, Sir Edward Neville's singing 'meryly' in the marchioness of Exeter's garden about how 'this world wold amend on day', even the presence of the motto 'spes mea &c' in the windows of the countess of Salisbury's house.[53] Yet there was also a sense in which these were all the innocent activities they seemed to be: as the countess pointed out, 'spes mea &c' had been written on her windows long before there was any hope that her son Reginald Pole might return from exile to set the world to rights. Biographical evidence, then, demands careful reading, but its rewards are potentially great.

At its simplest, it may provide signs of how credible the attribution of a particular political or religious position to an individual really is. Statements of political creed such as Edmund Dudley's *Tree of Commonwealth* are rare, but remain under-used by historians. Library lists, such as that of Edmund's grandson John Dudley, Viscount Lisle, in 1550–51, can at least prompt reflection: were Lisle's Testament in French covered in black velvet, exposition of the Creed in French, and 'Frenche

---

[50] R. Whittinton, *Libellus Epygrammaton* (London, 1519), sig. Bv v.

[51] G. Walker, *Plays of Persuasion: Drama and Politics at the Court of Henry VIII* (Cambridge, 1991); M. Axton, *The Queen's Two Bodies: Drama and the Elizabethan Succession* (1977).

[52] D. R. Starkey, 'The age of the household: politics, society and the arts c. 1350–c. 1550', in *The Later Middle Ages*, ed. S. Medcalf (1981), 225–90; Harris, 'Women and politics', 260–5, 280–1; Ives, *Faction*, 6–7.

[53] Ives, *Anne Boleyn*, 84–7, 365–8 (though for qualifications see Warnicke, 'Fall revisited', 654–9); PRO, SP1/138, fos. 224r., 243v. (*LP*, XIII, ii, 804 (iii), 818); *LP*, XIII, ii, 765, 772.

boke of Christ and the Pope' the relics of an attachment to reform in the Dudley household dating back to the 1530s, when French evangelical texts and their authors circulated in the orbit of Anne Boleyn?[54] Wills, for all the difficulties raised by their formulae, and probate inventories likewise have their uses in recreating an individual's physical and mental environment.[55]

More helpful still are sources which suggest how individuals interacted: whom they talked to, whom they trusted, with whom they were in dispute and from whom they held themselves apart. Wills, marriage agreements, property settlements using enfeoffments to uses, records of suretyship and evidence of litigation and violent dispute have been for a generation among the fundamental materials of fifteenth-century political historians, especially those studying local politics. There is disagreement over just how much weight one should place on such associations, and therefore over their reliability in the reconstruction of clearly-defined and competing political networks.[56] But it remains a safe assumption that no-one would entrust the formal ownership of his landed livelihood in an enfeoffment, or the provision for his soul and his family after his death, to another whom he regarded as his mortal enemy: a form of dissimulation against which even Machiavelli might caution. Despite the issue, perhaps wider than we realise, of bonds promising to sureties that they would be fully recompensed by the principal for any liabilities they had to meet, we can also assume that one generally stood surety for those one trusted or cared about.[57] If in Henry VII's reign any did enter bonds on behalf of others in carefree fashion, they would have been brought to their senses by the brisk way in which Henry and his agents set about collecting such debts.[58] To stand surety could be to count the cost of friendship.

[54] T. W. Baldwin, *William Shakspere's Small Latine & Lesse Greeke* (2 vols., Urbana, Ill., 1944), I, 255; Ives, *Anne Boleyn*, 316–26; for supporting evidence see M. Dowling, *Humanism in the age of Henry VIII* (1986) [hereafter Dowling, *Humanism*], 146 and D. Hoak, *The King's Council in the Reign of Edward VI* (Cambridge, 1976) [hereafter Hoak, *King's Council*], 243.

[55] S. J. Gunn, 'Chivalry and the politics of the early Tudor court', in *Chivalry in the Renaissance*, ed. S. Anglo (Woodbridge, 1990) [hereafter Gunn, 'Chivalry and politics'], 110, 119.

[56] M. A. Hicks, 'Bastard feudalism: society and politics in fifteenth-century England', in his *Richard III and His Rivals: Magnates and the Motives in the Wars of the Roses* (1991), 21–8.

[57] PRO, E210/10759; SP1/143, fo. 53 (*LP*, XIV, i, 263, though the calendar does not mention the bond); A. Cameron, 'Sir Henry Willoughby of Wollaton', *Transactions of the Thoroton Society*, LXXIV (1970) [hereafter Cameron, 'Willoughby'], 17.

[58] Such as the £6,300 forfeited by thirteen sureties for Sir Robert Curson's performance as keeper of Hammes Castle: between June 1503 and June 1506, at least eight of them made arrangements to pay £500 or £600 each to the king: *Calendar of the Close Rolls, Henry VII* (2 vols., 1953–63) [hereafter *CCR Henry VII*, all references to document numbers], I, 1060; BL, Additional Manuscript [hereafter Add. MS] 21480, fos. 42v., 92r., 117v.; Lansdowne Manuscript 127, fos. 4r., 18r., 21v.

Vaguer in their implications, but more stimulating to the historical imagination, are the records of sociability. Because at the highest levels of early Tudor society hospitality tended to be exercised to one's social inferiors rather than one's equals, surviving household accounts for the great peers such as Buckingham and Norfolk tell us more about their cultivation of influence among the gentry and yeomanry than they do about politics at court. But social occasions in and around London seem to have been more often used to entertain other courtiers and councillors.[59] Finally there are the records of christenings, weddings and funerals, eloquent of friendships and obligations even when, like those symbolised by the grand marriage alliance between the houses of Seymour and Dudley in June 1550, they turned out to be more hoped-for than real.[60]

Any examination of such records seems to question some elements of the factional interpretation but to confirm others. Thomas, Lord Wriothesley fits awkwardly into his Foxean straitjacket, as a persecutor under Henry and a dedicated opponent of reform under Edward, when it is remembered that he asked that John Hooper, about to be the central figure in the Edwardian round of the vestiarian controversy, preach his funeral sermon; among the beneficiaries of his will, made in 1550, were not only the conservative allies of his brief ascendancy in Edward's council, Sir Richard Southwell, Sir Edmund Peckham and the earl of Arundel, but also his apparent nemesis John Dudley earl of Warwick and Dudley's supporter Sir William Herbert.[61] On the other hand, the sureties recruited by Catherine, duchess of Suffolk, to guarantee to the crown her payments for her son's wardship in February 1546 form a parade of leading reformist courtiers.[62] By assembling large bodies of such material it may be possible to delineate an individual's social, and hence his or her conceivable political, position. But all too often such information comes in scraps whose implications are hard to fathom. Professor Ives would perhaps argue that the countess of Worcester, one of the chief witnesses against Anne Boleyn, was one of the leading mourners at the obsequies of Catherine of Aragon because of her involvement with the conservative circles at court, on whose behalf she would speak out against Queen Anne; Dr Bernard might counter that she may well have been keeping eyes on the old queen's

---

[59] F. M. Heal, *Hospitality in Early Modern England* (Oxford, 1990), 54–90; Harris, *Buckingham*, 92; S. E. Vokes, 'The early career of Thomas, Lord Howard, earl of Surrey and third duke of Norfolk, 1474–c. 1525' (Ph.D. thesis, University of Hull, 1988), 312–15.

[60] W. K. Jordan, *Edward VI: The Threshold of Power* (1970) [hereafter Jordan, *Threshold of Power*], 73.

[61] A. L. Rowse, 'Thomas Wriothesley, first earl of Southampton', *Huntington Library Quarterly*, XXVIII (1965), 126, 128; Hoak, *King's Council*, 239–58; *History of Parliament: The Commons 1509–1558*, ed. S. T. Bindoff (3 vols., 1982) [hereafter *HP*], II, 342.

[62] Gunn, *Charles Brandon*, 198.

interment for Cromwell if she were, as he suspects she may possibly have been, the minister's mistress.[63]

Other varieties of such evidence produce a more nuanced picture. Analysis of voting patterns in the chapters of the order of the Garter shows that knights consistently nominated their friends and associates for election, but that they also proposed those whom one might take to be their enemies. Wriothesley's behaviour at the chapter of 3 May 1546, eight weeks before he racked Anne Ascue, looks especially odd for a man engaged in ongoing factional struggle: he nominated Sir Thomas Seymour, Sir William Herbert and Sir William Paget, all leading members of the reformist regime that would push him out of office early the next year.[64]

Household accounts are potentially even more informative, since they enable us to judge the degree of social contact between the host and different categories of guests, and also to chart changes in such patterns over time. Those of Bishop Thomas Goodrich of Ely, a consistent favourer of reform, lend substance to the idea of a fairly coherent social, religious and political circle linked to Anne Boleyn. Goodrich's hospitality was not exclusively extended to those connected with the queen. On 20 April 1534 Sir Nicholas Carew, already one of Chapuys' contacts and a sympathiser with Queen Catherine and Princess Mary, joined Sir Francis Bryan, Sir Francis Weston and other 'gyntell men of the cortt' at the bishop's dinner-table. But the roll-call of his most frequent visitors is that of Anne's associates: Dr William Buttes dined four times between 20 April and 9 June, Sir Edward Baynton the queen's vice-chamberlain and John skip her almoner twice, Sir Thomas Wyatt, Anne's uncle Sir Edward Boleyn and the London reformist preacher Dr Edward Crome once each. In Baynton's case at least, the favours were mutual: he had sent Goodrich a present of congers within days of his nomination to the bishopric. And in Buttes' case, the attachment was sustained: in 1542 Goodrich was paying him an annual fee, and sent him a New Year's gift worth £10.[65]

The kitchen accounts of Edward Seymour, earl of Hertford give a similar impression of a social circle not rigidly exclusive in its religious or political affiliations, but none the less displaying certain significant inclinations. Various councillors and courtiers traditionally identified with either side of the political divide dined up to a dozen times each at Hertford's table in 1538-9: Norfolk, Gardiner, Wallop, Carew, Neville

[63] LP, X, 284; Ives, Anne Boleyn, 380-2; Bernard, 'Fall', 598.

[64] Gunn, 'Chivalry and politics', 113-16; The Register of the Most Noble Order of the Garter, ed. J. Anstis (2 vols., 1724), I, 435; D. Wilson, A Tudor Tapestry: Men, Women and Society in Reformation England (1972), 220-3.

[65] Cambridge University Library, Ely Diocesan Records, D/5/8, fos. 4v.-21r., unfoliated entries at end; D/5/9; Ives, Anne Boleyn, 303-4, 311, 373.

and Browne amongst the 'old', Cromwell, Audley, Baynton, Buttes, Meautis and Page amongst the 'new'. More controversial guests included Bishop Hugh Latimer and Dr Edward Crome; Crome dined again seven times in 1540–1, when one of the court's protestant doctors, Dr Huick, made ten appearances.[66] Most significant of all are the statistics which point forward to Hertford's political associations in the last years of the reign. In 1538–9 Sir Anthony Denny dined with him only half as often as the earl of Surrey, who would end as Hertford's bitter rival; but Sir John Dudley, whose career so long ran in parallel with Seymour's own, came fourteen times, William Parr, the future earl of Essex and marquess of Northampton, thirty-six, and Parr's brother-in-law William Herbert, the future earl of Pembroke, fifty-one.[67]

Evidence of litigation and other kinds of conflict over private interests is also revealing, whether it concerns the leading figures of the court and council themselves or their dependants. Thus the troubles between the Howard and Brandon affinities in the 1530s help make sense of the awkward relationship between the two dukes in the wake of their cooperation around the time of Wolsey's fall, as does the contest between them for the earl marshalcy.[68] Yet by 1544, Norfolk could appeal for Suffolk's help on the basis of 'all th'oulde love and acquay-[n]taince that of longe co[n]tynuau[n]ce hathe bene bytwene us', and already in 1536 he had urged that 'the better we agre, the better the kyng shalbe s[er]ved'.[69] The two men were never close, but they could rarely afford to confront one another for long, especially since Henry, like a good late-medieval king, strongly encouraged Suffolk's 'zele to norisshe kyndenes and love bytwene my saide lorde of Norff[olk] and you'.[70] In poisoning the relations between great men such diputes could affect the wider political scene, as most obviously did Somerset's quarrels with Warwick in 1548–9.[71] Yet their significance is often evident only with hindsight, and they certainly did not run along neat factional fault-lines. In their land disputes of the 1530s, Arthur Viscount Lisle tried to use the support of Thomas Cromwell to fend off the attacks of Edward Seymour; but by late 1538, as their second dispute petered out, Lisle was feeding information to Seymour about Cromwell's alarming affinities with the Calais protestants.[72]

[66] Longleat House, Miscellaneous volumes 18–19 (I am grateful for permission to cite these); Starkey, *Reign of Henry VIII*, 113, 118, 121, 137; Brigden, *London*, 307, 327, 330–2.
[67] Longleat House, Miscellaneous volume 18.
[68] Gunn, *Charles Brandon*, 112–13, 115–17, 121–7, 165.
[69] PRO, SP1/191, fo. 46 (*LP*, XIX, ii, 36); SP1/115, fo. 175 (*LP*, XII, i, 318).
[70] PRO, SP1/75, fo. 245v. (*LP*, VI, 415).
[71] W. K. Jordan, *Edward VI: The Young King* (1968), 500–2.
[72] M. L. Bush, 'The Lisle– Seymour land disputes: a study of power and influence in the 1530s', *HJ*, IX (1966), 255–74; A.J. Slavin, 'Cromwell, Cranmer and Lord Lisle: a

Discussion of political alignments in private correspondence may demand caution, yet there is still value in such material when it suggests that perceptions of clearcut division were not confined merely to the newsmongering ambassadors and the 'trivial opinion of the multitude'. In 1526, for instance, Lord Henry Percy warned his brother-in-law, Henry earl of Cumberland, that his father the fifth earl of Northumberland had tried to put Cumberland out of favour with Wolsey. Northumberland, he wrote, 'showyd my Lordes grace that ther was no trust in yow, and desyeryd hys grace to put no conffydens in yow, for ye wer all with my Lord of Norffolk.'[73] Whether this does or does not reflect the realities of Norfolk's relationship with the cardinal, it is still important for what it tells us of others' perceptions of that relationship. If enough people thought that Norfolk was the leader of a pro-imperial party in competition with Wolsey, he could virtually have had such leadership thrust upon him whether he liked it or not.

Most striking are the occasions on which a commentator's fate depended upon accurate identification of political alignments. George Emerson, advising Sir Robert Plumpton how to defeat Sir Richard Empson's attempts to deprive him of his estates, told him to avoid 'Mr Bray, Mr Mordaunt, and such other as are belonging to Mr Bray' as arbitrators, thus excluding the influence of the tight-knit Duchy of Lancaster connection with whom Empson was so bound up. Meanwhile Plumpton could count on his 'good friends' Bishop Fox, Sir Thomas Lovell, Sir Richard Guildford and Richard Weston of the privy chamber, none of them, so far as we can now see, very closely linked with Bray.[74] Four decades later, under investigation for treason, Henry Howard earl of Surrey needed to identify his friends and enemies more urgently still. He asked that only Wriothesley, Gardiner, Sir Anthony Browne and Lord Russell be appointed to examine him.[75] Each of the first three was, to a greater or lesser extent, a known conservative in court politics. Russell he may have seen as an honest broker, but one who had, conveniently, also fallen out with Seymour.[76]

On the other hand, there are many signs that contemporaries were unaware of the allegiances or inclinations historians now seem able to uncover, or at least thought that they did not matter. People did seem to know which leading bishops to contact if they were worried about

study in the politics of reform', *Albion*, IX (1977) [hereafter Slavin, 'Cromwell, Cranmer and Lord Lisle'], 320–30.
[73] *Clifford Letters of the Sixteenth Century*, ed. A. G. Dickens (Surtees Society CLXXII, 1962), 106.
[74] *Plumpton Correspondence*, ed. T. Stapleton (Camden Society IV, 1839) [hereafter *Plumpton Correspondence*], cxiii, 177–8.
[75] *LP*, XXI, ii, 541.
[76] D. Willen, *John Russell, first earl of Bedford: One of the King's Men* (1981) [hereafter Willen, *Russell*], 52–6.

heresy: Gardiner, Stokesley, Sampson and Tunstall.[77] But can Lord Lisle and the Calais conservatives have known that Dr Crome and Bishop Latimer graced the Hertford household when they decided to invoke the earl's help against their local protestant rivals? Did John Hales, the Edwardian protestant social reformer and servant of Cromwell and Sir Ralph Sadler, think of Sir Anthony Browne as we think of him, one of 'the core of the conservative party', when he sent him his 'Oration in commendation of the laws' in the hope Browne would present it to the king?[78] Or did Thomas Lord Vaux, a peer of such conservatism in religion that he stayed away from parliament entirely between 1536 and 1554 and lost his place as a JP over the same period, know what he was doing when he granted an advowson in 1540 to Dr Thomas Wendy, yet another of the king's godly protestant medical men?[79] Such instances expose the dangers inherent in Namierite reconstitution of political groupings which would not have been recognisable to contemporaries.

When all these types of evidence are put together, it seems to me that four types of political structure emerge. The first and most basic appears to have no name, perhaps precisely because it was so generalised. It consisted of a small group bound to each other by close ties, very often those of kinship, working together in matters of patronage, royal service and local politics. The Breretons, the Savages and indeed the Boleyns are well-investigated examples.[80] As the Savages suggest, such groups were nothing new under Henry VIII, and small-scale combinations of courtiers can readily be found in Henry VII's reign and before. Their usual basis in kinship gave them considerable potential for linking together different elements of the political system. Brothers or other close relations in orders could climb the ladder of ecclesiastical promotion in parallel with their lay relatives. At the top, bishops and archbishops such as James Stanley and Thomas Savage could form part of a grand family enterprise, much as George Neville

---

[77] Redworth, *Gardiner*, 176–207; Block, *Factional Politics*, 149–50; Slavin, 'Cromwell, Cranmer and Lord Lisle', 325, 332.

[78] *HP*, II, 276; Starkey, *Reign of Henry VIII*, 118, 144.

[79] Lincolnshire Archives Office [hereafter LAO], Bishop's Register [hereafter Reg.] 26, fo. 236v.; H. Miller, *Henry VIII and the English Nobility* (Oxford, 1986) [hereafter Miller, *English Nobility*], 44, 125, 204: Dowling, *Humanism*, 68.

[80] E. W. Ives, 'Court and county palatine in the reign of Henry VIII: the case of William Brereton of Malpas', *Transactions of the Historic Society of Lancashire and Cheshire*, CXXIII (1972), 1–38; *Letters and Accounts of William Brereton of Malpas*, ed. idem (Record Society of Lancashire and Cheshire CXVI, 1976); idem, 'Crime, sanctuary and royal authority under Henry VIII: the exemplary sufferings of the Savage family', in *On the Laws and Customs of England: Essays in Honor of Samuel E. Thorne*, ed. M. S. Arnold, S. A. Scully and T. D. White (Chapel Hill, NC, 1981) [hereafter Ives, 'Savage family'], 304–11; Warnicke, *Rise and Fall*, 104–7, 135–40, 147–8, 158–62.

or Lionel Woodville had done.[81] Less often noticed are such careerist clerics as Christopher Litton, brother of Henry VII's under-treasurer of the Exchequer and keeper of the great wardrobe Sir Robert Litton, Richard Wyatt, brother of his keeper of the jewelhouse Sir Henry Wyatt, and Richard Dudley, cousin of Edmund. Richard Wyatt served very regularly as a feoffee and surety for Sir Henry, and Richard Dudley tried to perform a yet more vital service for Edmund, offering Thomas, Lord Darcy, £200 in the hope that he would persuade Henry VIII to spare Edmund's life.[82] In return, the laymen used their influence to advance the clerics' careers: Richard Wyatt was presented to one living by Sir Henry while still a fellow of the King's Hall, Cambridge, and later gained at least two from Henry VII; Sir Robert Litton presented Christopher to three rectories within twenty-two months in 1502–4; and Richard Dudley garnered three crown livings and three other canonries and prebends in a year and a half at the height of Edmund's career.[83]

Meanwhile further siblings might be available to take the role in county government and politics and the round of gentry sociability denied to the members of the dynasty more active at court. Henry VII's lord treasurer, John, Lord Dynham, managed to have one brother as a royal chaplain and archdeacon while two others were busy in Devon and Buckinghamshire.[84] Among such stay-at-home brothers, Sir Robert and Sir Gregory Lovell, brothers of Sir Thomas, and perhaps George Guildford, brother of Henry VIII's Lord Warden of the Cinque Ports Sir Edward and comptroller of the household Sir Henry, seem to have been more effective than the rather lacklustre Sir Henry Seymour.[85] The bonds of kinship made such groupings both durable

[81] M. M. Condon, 'Ruling elites in the reign of Henry VII', in Patronage, Pedigree and Power in Later Medieval England, ed. C. D. Ross (Gloucester, 1979), 113; Ives, 'Savage family', 304–11; C. D. Ross, Edward IV (1974), 96, 319–20.

[82] Descriptive Catalogue of Ancient Deeds in the Public Record Office (6 vols., 1890–1915) [hereafter CAD, all references to document numbers], III, C3170, D1308, VI, C7345; CCR Henry VII, II, 720, 737, 953, 984; Feet of Fines for Essex, IV, ed. P. H. Reaney and M. Fitch (Colchester, 1964), 108, 125; Herts Genealogist and Antiquary, I (1895), 82; BL, Additional Charter 5674; Add. MS 21480, fo. 8ov.; PRO, E36/215, fo. 298v.; C1/303/62.

[83] Richard Wyatt: Norfolk and Norwich Record Office [hereafter NNRO], Reg. 12, fo. 183r.; Canterbury Sede Vacante Institutions (Kent Archaeological Society records branch VIII, 1924), 57; A. B. Emden, A Biographical Register of the University of Cambridge to 1500 (Cambridge, 1963), 661–2; Victoria County History [hereafter VCH] Lancashire (8 vols., 1906–14), IV, 62; Christopher Lytton: LAO, Reg. 23, fo. 183r.; NNRO, Reg. 13B, fo. 20r.; Guildhall Library, MS 9531/8, fo. 73v.; Richard Dudley: Calendar of Patent Rolls, Henry VII (2 vols., 1914–16) [hereafter CPR Henry VII], II, 534, 539, 586; A. B. Emden, A Biographical Register of the University of Oxford to A.D. 1500 (3 vols., Oxford, 1957–9) I, 598–9.

[84] R. P. Chope, 'The last of the Dynhams', Transactions of the Devonshire Association, L (1918), 474–5.

[85] HP, III, 290–1; Select Cases in the Council of Henry VII, eds. C. G. Bayne, W. H. Dunham (Selden Society LXXV, 1958), cxlii–iii; LP, II, ii, 3748, III, ii, 2288, 2352, 2956 (28), 3504.

THE STRUCTURES OF POLITICS IN EARLY TUDOR ENGLAND 79

and recognisable, and could draw them into long-lasting antipathy to one another. The contest between the Guildfords and the Neville Lords Bergavenny apparently linked the politics of the court and council to those of Kent from the last years of Henry VII, through events in 1521–2 connected with the fall of Bergavenny's father-in-law Buckingham, to 1534, when Norfolk used the struggle as a moral example in advising Sir William Musgrave against confrontation with Lord Dacre: 'Luk how the howse of Burgeyne', he warned, 'had subv[er]tyd the howss of Guylldford'.[86]

As such clashes revealed, the ambitions of families or individuals on the wider stage of local politics and government could not be realised without some larger but necessarily looser political unit, an affinity. The affinities of early Tudor noblemen varied with their wealth, competence and political prominence, but those studied in detail so far suggest that the cultivation of some sort of following amongst the gentry and yeomanry of the area where a peer's landed patrimony was concentrated remained important to the death of Henry VIII and well beyond. Kinship, household service, military service and administrative office on a lord's estates, or as his deputies under the crown, were all important in the constitution of early Tudor affinities, as they had been in those of the fifteenth century.[87] Such links, consolidated by a lord's efforts to encourage the coherence and effectiveness of his following by arranging marriages and arbitrating disputes, could it seems perpetuate affinities beyond the death of their creator, as Hastings' former followers in the Midlands held together under Henry VII and the

---

3583, App. 45*, IV, i, 214, 547, ii, 4276; I hope to discuss the Lovell brothers in a forthcoming book.

[86] P. Clark, *English Provincial Society from the Reformation to the Revolution: Religion, Politics and Society in Kent, 1500–1640* (Hassocks, 1977), 14–16; A. Cameron, 'The giving of livery and retaining in Henry's VII's reign', *Renaissance and Modern Studies*, XVIII (1974), 31–4; *Select Cases in the Council of Henry VII*, xxix–xxx, cxlii–iii, 138–49; BL, Lansdowne MS 127, fo. 11r.; J. Gairdner and I. S. Leadham, 'A supposed conspiracy against Henry VII', *Transactions of the Royal Historical Society*, n.s. XVIII (1904), 179–80; PRO, E101/414/16, fo. 256r.; *HP*, II, 263; PRO, SP1/88, fo. 88v. (*LP*, VII, 1647).

[87] C. Rawcliffe and S. Flower, 'English noblemen and their advisers: consultation and collaboration in the later middle ages', *Journal of British Studies*, XXV (1986), 157–77; M. E. James, 'A Tudor magnate and the Tudor state: Henry fifth earl of Northumberland', in his *Society, Politics and Culture: Studies in Early Modern England* (Cambridge, 1986) [hereafter James, *Society, Politics and Culture*], 50–5, 68–77; R. W. Hoyle, 'The first earl of Cumberland: a reputation reassessed', *Northern History*, XXII (1986), 63–72; Gunn, *Charles Brandon*, 24–5, 45–53, 83–8, 127–30, 154–9, 204–6, 210–19; idem, 'Henry Bourchier, earl of Essex (1472–1540)', in *The Tudor Nobility*, ed. G. W. Bernard (Manchester, 1992) [hereafter *Tudor Nobility*], 151–2, 159–65; R. B. Smith, *Land and Politics in the England of Henry VIII: The West Riding of Yorkshire 1530–1546* (Oxford, 1970), 137–9; G. W. Bernard, *The Power of the Early Tudor Nobility: a study of the fourth and fifth earls of Shrewsbury* (Brighton, 1985), 157–62; B. Coward, *The Stanleys, Lords Stanley and earls of Derby 1385–1672: The Origins, Wealth and Power of a Landowning Family* (Chetham Society, 3rd series XXX, 1983), 84–97, 117–22.

Wentworth-Wingfield alignment in Suffolk survived the departure of Charles Brandon.[88] At the same time new men were themselves building up affinities—Sir Thomas Lovell's licensed retinue of 1508 numbered 1,365 men including eight esquires and at least thirteen gentlemen— and new varieties of affinity or clientele were emerging, such as the military followings established by Seymour and Dudley in the 1540s, or the nationwide networks of clients, agents and friends run from the bloated ministerial households of a Wolsey, a Cromwell or a Cecil.[89]

At court we might identify a third variety of political unit, consisting of a small group of leading councillors or courtiers who seem consistently to have cooperated with one another, though in a less permanent or exclusive way than in our first type. Such links seem to have been particularly common amongst the ministers of Henry VII, which may help to account for the comparative stability at the heart of his regime. Thus Giles, Lord Daubeney named his 'singuler goode lord[es] and frend[es]' Bishop Richard Fox, John earl of Oxford and Sir Thomas Lovell as overseers of his will in 1508, 'for the singuler trust and confidence that I have and longe have had in theym'.[90] Eleven months later, Oxford named 'myn olde frende' Lovell as the first of his executors, and when Lovell died fifteen years later, rooms in his house at Enfield were still known as 'my Lorde of Oxforth cha[m]b[er]' and 'my Lorde of Oxfordis closet'.[91] At Henry VIII's court, the relationships between Sir William Fitzwilliam and Sir Thomas Heneage or Sir William Paget and Sir William Petre were perhaps similar.[92] Throughout, the personalities of those involved must have been crucial: in Henry VIII's reign, apparently affable individuals such as Russell and Brandon seem to have formed many and sometimes mutually incompatible working friendships, while their more anxious, prickly or insufferable colleagues—Gardiner and Surrey are prime examples—

[88] Cameron, 'Willoughby', 16–17; D. N. J. MacCulloch, *Suffolk and the Tudors: Politics and Religion in an English County 1500–1600* (Oxford, 1986), 72–3, 93–5.

[89] *Report on the Manuscripts of his Grace the Duke of Rutland*, IV (Historical Manuscripts Commission XXIV, 1908), 559–66; S. L. Adams, 'The Dudley clientèle, 1553–1563', in *Tudor Nobility*, 138; J. A. Guy, 'Wolsey and the Tudor polity', in *Cardinal Wolsey*, 70; M. L. Robertson, ' "The art of the possible": Thomas Cromwell's management of West Country government', *HJ*, XXXII (1989), 799; A. G. R. Smith, *Servant of the Cecils: The Life of Sir Michael Hickes, 1543–1612* (1977), 29–50.

[90] PRO, PROB11/16/16.

[91] W. H. St John Hope, 'The last testament and inventory of John de Veer, thirteenth earl of Oxford', *Archaeologia*, LXVI (1914–15), 313, 318; PRO, PROB2/199, mm. 2, 3.

[92] *Testamenta Vetusta*, ed. N. H. Nicolas (2 vols., 1826), II, 709; *LP*, XIII, i, 795; PRO, E192/2; F. G. Emmison, *Tudor Secretary: Sir William Petre at Court and at Home* (1961), 52, 54, 56, 60–1; S. R. Gammon, *Statesman and Schemer: William, First Lord Paget—Tudor Minister* (Newton Abbot, 1973) [hereafter Gammon, *Paget*], 97, 122, 204, 212, 224.

ploughed a lonelier furrough.[93] At a somewhat lower level, such bonds might manifest themselves as departmental loyalties, as amongst Henry VII's law officers or in the Elizabethan Exchequer.[94]

Fourthly, there do seem at times to have been wider groups than these in operation at court, what we might fairly call factions. Ironically, they are made harder to identify by the very way in which they stand at the centre of the current historiographical debate. The factionalists assume their existence, often without sufficient evidential warrant, whereas the king's men generally pay them only destructive attention, failing to ask whether any paler reality stands behind the 'monolithic factional blocs' whose influence they deny.[95] As we have seen, near-contemporary narrators, ambassadors and some participants wrote as though they felt comparatively large political groupings sometimes took coherent action at the early Tudor court, and some evidence of the biographical type supports the notion that such groups may have had an identifiable existence. They were moulded by different forces, usually either by shared loyalty or hostility to an individual, or by a shared ideology, as in the confrontations reported with such immediacy by Richard Scudamore to Sir Philip Hoby in late 1549 and early 1550 between the 'most parte of the Counsell that favoreth goddes worde' and 'the old sort', 'the byrdes' that 'purposed to haue made a popys fflyght'.[96] Like their predecessors—the household interest under Henry VI for instance—they were potentially brittle and internally divided, they manifested themselves most clearly only when challenged along appropriate lines, and they might dissolve rapidly once the issues uniting them changed or the spirit of *sauve qui peut* took hold. But it seems to me hard to deny their existence entirely.

One can recreate the political system from the point of view of an individual by situating him in groups of each of these types. Edmund Dudley, for instance, to judge from admittedly sketchy evidence, formed part of a small group of close relations by blood and marriage and other dependants, prominent in his private affairs and the work of government alike: his brother-in-law Andrew Windsor, Windsor's stepfather Sir Robert Litton, Dudley's cousin Richard, John Camby,

[93] Willen, *Russell*, 32–5, 41–3; Gunn, *Charles Brandon*, 227; Redworth, *Gardiner*, 77, 181, 209–13, 239; S. E. Brigden, 'Henry Howard, earl of Surrey, and the "conjured league"', *HJ*, XXXVII (1994) [hereafter Brigden, 'Surrey'], 509–10, 520–2, 526–7.
[94] *CPR Henry VII*, II, 188; *CCR Henry VII*, II, 501, 521, 927; PRO, E101/414/6, fos. 13v, 37v; J. D. Alsop, 'Government, finance and the community of the exchequer', in *Reign of Elizabeth*, 111–12.
[95] Walker, *Skelton*, 29.
[96] 'The letters of Richard Scudamore to Sir Philip Hoby, September 1549–March 555', ed. S. E. Brigden, in *Camden Miscellany XXX* (Camden Society, 4th series XXXIX, 990), 97, 114.

keeper of the Poultry Compter prison, and perhaps others.[97] In local affairs he led an affinity best displayed by the rollcall of those accused of raising troops for him in 1509, most of whom can be linked to him using other sources, but which seems to have extended to such families of Wiltshire gentry as the Longs, the Wrottesleys (one of whom married his daughter) and the Beauchamps, Lords St Amand.[98] At court and on the council there are hints that he may have been close to John Ernley, Henry VII's last attorney-general, to Hugh Denis, the groom of the stool, and perhaps to Christopher Bainbridge, master of the rolls and then bishop of Durham and archbishop of York; but, significantly, not to any of the older-established great men of Henry's court and council.[99] On the widest, factional, plane as it related to personalities, he was probably a client of Bray's, but evidently not a special friend of Lady Margaret Beaufort.[100] Where he stood on the great issues of Henry VII's last years, the rallying-points of ideological faction, we can only infer from his actions and the views he expressed in the *Tree of Commonwealth*: presumably for the judicial and fiscal offensives against the abuses of merchants, nobles and gentry, for the peaceful alliance with the house of Burgundy and, with some reservations, for the assertion of royal tutelage over the church.[101] Only in 1509, isolated with Empson and a few others, did he find himself in demonstrably clear confrontation with others at court, and in this, as in so many of the crises of Henry VIII's reign, we have to guess at the political alignments mainly from the outcome.[102]

To understand the system as a whole, two further factors must be taken into account. One is the role of the monarch, and that I shall leave until last. The other is the way in which various allegiances or inclinations were capable of cross-cutting the group loyalties we have discussed, and thus affecting the stance of an individual on any

[97] *CPR Henry VII*, II, 396, 542, 594; *CCR Henry VII*, II, 143, 283, 617, 629, 762, 972; *CAD*, I, A1492; BL, Add. MS 21480, fos. 98v., 120v.; J. C. Wedgwood, *History of Parliament: Biographies of Members of the Commons House, 1439–1509* (1936) [hereafter Wedgwood, *Commons*], 565–6; Cheshire Record Office [hereafter CRO], DCH/B/43, 44; J. P. Cooper, 'Henry VII's last years reconsidered', *HJ*, II (1959), 120–1.

[98] S. J. Gunn, 'The accession of Henry VIII', *Historical Research*, LXIV (1991) [hereafter Gunn, 'Accession'], 285–6; Wedgwood, *Commons*, 55, 286–7, 975; *CPR Henry VII*, II, 589.

[99] *CCR Henry VII*, II, 616, 617, 663, 726, 759, 762, 972; CRO, DCH/B/44; Wedgwood, *Commons*, 286–7; BL, Add. MS 21480, fo. 125v.; *CPR Henry VII*, II, 591; University of Durham, Department of Palaeography, Priory Register V, fo. 102.

[100] E. Dudley, *The Tree of Commonwealth*, ed. D. M. Brodie (Cambridge, 1948) [hereafter Dudley, *Tree of Commonwealth*], 3; *CAD*, III, A3987; M. R. Horowitz, 'Richard Empson, minister of Henry VII', *Bulletin of the Institute of Historical Research*, LV (1982), 39, 41; M. K. Jones, M. Underwood, *The King's Mother: Lady Margaret Beaufort, Countess of Richmond and Derby* (Cambridge, 1992), 222.

[101] Dudley, *Tree of Commonwealth*, passim.

[102] Gunn, 'Accession', 283–6.

particular issue and complicating his political position as a whole. Personal ambition could readily disrupt even family coherence, as the Stafford brothers in the 1500s or the Seymour brothers in the 1540s showed.[103] Subtler interference came from the varieties of educational and professional identity present amongst the political elite. The habitués of the inns of court, of doctors' commons, of the theology schools and of the tiltyard and tennis-court brought to political debate very different attitudes to the function and development of government, and often conscious or subconscious hostilities to those of other backgrounds or outlooks. Thomas duke of Norfolk, on hearing of the outbreak of rebellion in 1536, burst out that he would not 'sit still lyk a man of law' while others went to fight for the king.[104] The commonlawyer chancellor Sir Thomas Audley reportedly told Exeter, when the jousting marquess offered to fight those who accused him of treason, 'according to the old law', that that law was absurd.[105] Lay civil lawyers such as Paget and Sir Thomas Smith found themselves denounced from both ends of the theological spectrum for their studied lukewarmness in pursuit of a religion of social and political stability.[106] Bishop Nykke, faced with prosecution for praemunire by attorney-general Hobart, denounced him as 'an enemy of God and his churche'.[107] And we may catch an anticipation of the crudely impatient spirit of some aristocratic interventions in parliamentary debates on religion from the 1530s to the 1550s at the funeral of Bishop Ruthal in 1523. One duke, five earls and 'the substance of all other lord[es] and knyght[es] beyng at that tyme resident in the court' were there. Dr Rowland Phillips, one of the most acclaimed preachers of the day, 'a great devyn and a renomed clerk ... made ther a noble sermon and a clerckely, but it was over long for hit was nere to xii of the cloke or he hadde doon, and supposed ther to have taryed longer yff he had not be desyred to abrege his cause'. The ensuing 'great and ... sumptuous feast' at Durham House was presumably more acceptable to the lordly palates.[108] Gardiner's inability to cooperate with Norfolk at one end of the religious spectrum, Dudley's with Cranmer at the other, were symptomatic of more widespread rifts.[109]

[103] Harris, *Buckingham*, 52–4; Gunn, 'Courtiers', 34–5; G. W. Bernard, 'The downfall of Sir Thomas Seymour', in *Tudor Nobility*, 212–40.
[104] PRO, SP1/104, fo. 81r. (*LP*, XI, 601).
[105] *The Lisle Letters*, ed. M. St C. Byrne (6 vols., 1981), VI, 118n.
[106] M. Dewar, *Sir Thomas Smith: A Tudor Intellectual in Office* (1964), 5, 39–44; Gammon, *Paget*, 119, 206.
[107] PRO, SC1/44/83.
[108] BL, Add. MS 45131, fo. 150r.; Brigden, *London*, 72.
[109] Redworth, *Gardiner*, 41, 108–9, 210; D. M. Loades, 'Thomas Cranmer and John Dudley: an uneasy alliance, 1549–53', in *Thomas Cranmer: Churchman and Scholar*, ed. P. Ayris, D. Selwyn (Woodbridge, 1993), 157–72.

Generational differences were also important, especially where religion was concerned. Surrey's deviation from his father's faith is the best-known example.[110] Equally noteworthy is the attachment of many of the older generation to Henry VII's brand of royal religion rather than his son's. The crusading enthusiasm of the old king and his court, and their involvement with the Observants at Richmond and the Bridgettines at Syon, marked the lives of Lords Darcy and Hussey from Henry's death to the moment in 1534 they agreed that they would be 'non heretyke' but would 'die Cristen men'.[111] From 1529, religion was the great breaker and shaper of political alignments. It generated enmities at court of understandable passion. It broke even the unity imposed by service in the king's wars, as conservative councillors were accused of deliberately displacing one of Hertford's protestant nominees in command of a garrison in France.[112] But even religious commitment could be cross-cut by other interests, particularly by strong feelings about foreign policy.[113] Meanwhile for those lords unsure of themselves in the whirlpool of religious debate, and torn in two directions by the religious polarisation of those who called upon their good lordship, ambiguity probably seemed the best policy.[114]

Given the highly complex way in which these factors interacted, it is no wonder that even the advocates of faction stress its fluidity.[115] Yet the heart of their debate with the king's men concerns not the nature of faction, but its effect upon the king. Henry VII and Henry VIII were both active personal monarchs, but both also took counsel as they were expected to do. How far they could be influenced beyond mere advice is hard to tell. Councillors and courtiers exercised some control over the information reaching the king, as discussions in surviving correspondence about whether or not to pass on certain news or letters to Henry VIII suggest.[116] By their contribution to discussion at court, they could also affect the interpretation placed on such information: Hertford asked Suffolk in 1544 to 'helpe to redub with your goode

[110] Brigden, 'Surrey', 513–20.

[111] A. Goodman, 'Henry VII and christian renewal', in *Religion and Humanism*, ed. K. Robbins (Studies in Church History XVII, 1981), 115–25; *CSPS*, I, 552, 577; C. Tyerman, *England and the Crusades, 1095–1588* (1988), 318–19, 343–4, 350–2, 358; *Plumpton Correspondence*, 268–9; M. E. James, 'Obedience and dissent in Henrician England: the Lincolnshire rebellion, 1536' in James, *Society, Politics and Culture*, 243–4; PRO, SP1/118, fo. 123r.-v. (*LP*, XII, i, 899).

[112] Redworth, *Gardiner*, 238.

[113] Redworth, *Gardiner*, 108–9.

[114] Gunn, *Charles Brandon*, 159–64, 198–201, 214.

[115] Ives, *Faction*, 18; Ives, 'Fall of Wolsey', 312.

[116] *Letters of Richard Fox, 1486–1527*, ed. P. S. Allen, H. M. Allen (Oxford, 1929), 44; *LP*, XVIII, i, 741.

worde' if he heard any of his conduct criticised.[117] More crudely, some contemporaries thought that propositions might be 'put into the kyngs had'.[118] At times the council offered collective advice to the king, and at times the privy chamber did so too: Sir Thomas Seymour recalled that six or seven of the privy chamber spoke up for his nominee as treasurer of the ordnance on the 1544 campaign, when the name was presented for Henry's approval.[119] Yet only in his last months was Henry so incapacitated as to be potentially a prisoner of those who controlled access to his private apartments, and it is ironically concerning the events of those few months and the shaping of the settlement for the next reign that Professor Ives has recently argued for the king's personal control.[120]

One useful approach to the interaction between the king and those around him may be to examine it at a number of levels. We might consider five. The small change of politics lay in the quest for patronage. There is no doubt that this was frantic even before the late Elizabethan contraction of opportunity and inflation of the number of aspirants.[121] The expansion of the royal demesne from the 1470s to the 1530s, the dispersal of monastic land and the general increase in the power of central government all intensified the pressure on the king from eager petitioners. This helps to explain the royal insouciance that facilitated Brereton's or Compton's empire-building on the basis of innumerable small grants, as it does Henry VII's reckless and politically disruptive intrusions of courtiers into the politics of the Midlands early in his reign.[122] It explains too Wolsey's concern over the role of privy chamber men as patronage-brokers, and the ability of Hugh Denis in Henry VII's last decade to spend significant sums on the land market: presumably they were made up of large numbers of payments from hopeful or grateful supplicants, such as the 66s 8d paid to him by Sir Richard Carew in 1507–8.[123]

At this level political processes were complicated by the existence of sources of advancement and influence apart from the king. Heads of governmental departments, senior royal ministers and other members

---

[117] *Report on the Manuscripts of the Most Honourable the Marquess of Bath*, IV (Historical Manuscripts Commission LVIII, 1968), 103.

[118] Sturge, *Tunstall*, 370.

[119] *LP*, XIX, ii, 423.

[120] E. W. Ives, 'Henry VIII's will—a forensic conundrum', *HJ*, XXXV (1992), 779–804.

[121] W. C. MacCaffrey, 'Place and patronage in Elizabethan politics', in *Elizabethan Government and Society: essays presented to Sir John Neale*, ed. S. T. Bindoff, J. Hurstfield, C. H. Williams (1961), 95–126.

[122] Ives, 'Court and county palatine', 11–15; Bernard, 'The rise of Sir William Compton, early Tudor courtier', *EHR*, XCVI (1981), 758–62; Carpenter, *Locality and Polity*, 560–96.

[123] Starkey, 'Intimacy and innovation', 107; Gunn, 'Courtiers', 45; Surrey Record Office, 281/2/1, fo. 6r.

of the royal family exercised considerable powers of appointment to office, or at least a recognised voice in the king's appointments. Other sources of patronage remained partially independent of royal control, notably those of the great temporal lords and of the church, offering stewardships, leases, and livings for clerical household or estate administrators or relatives in orders. Thus Cromwell's struggle to engross ecclesiastical patronage in support of his favoured preachers was only the greatest example of an older and wider competition.[124] In the play of influence matters could be still more complex than in questions of patronage. One sympathises with the borough chamberlains who found they had to pay 3s 4d to Lord Daubeney's butler to ask Lord Daubeney to ask Archbishop Morton to 'deign to deal amicably and charitably with the mayor and citizens of Canterbury'.[125] This was a system of politics only partially centralised and homogenised, one of structures not of a structure, just as the links between county politics and those at court remained tangled and inconsistent to the death of Elizabeth and beyond.[126]

At the second level of politics, on the other hand, the king was indisputably central. This was in the making of policy, where the evidence for any involvement by mere courtiers becomes far thinner, and even material concerning Wolsey and Cromwell suggests a working partnership between a well-informed king and ministers capable of proposing but not disposing. Only if Henry were incapable of distinguishing between minor leases in Wales and major affairs of state can one apply all the evidence for the influence of those around him in the distribution of patronage to this second question; and while Wolsey and Cromwell, and to a lesser extent others, enjoyed some leeway to modify policy in its implementation, this ran the risk that any discovery by Henry which he might interpret as a betrayal of his interests—as with Wolsey and the divorce or Cromwell and religious policy—might prove fatal.

This apparently straightforward relationship, however, must be qualified by adding in the third level of politics, the contest of large-scale faction. In the year or so before the fall of each minister there was more sign of strain in his dealings with the king than at any earlier point, but there was also more open criticism by others at court and more discussion of plots by ambassadors and others. The most hardened unbeliever in conspiracies might find it hard to explain away Lord Lisle's instruction to Sir Anthony Browne in May 1539, 'I beseech you,

[124] Block, *Factional Politics*, 68–83, 97–106; J. A. F. Thomson, *The Early Tudor Church and Society, 1485–1529* (1993), 75–7.
[125] Canterbury Record Office, FA7, fo. 138r.
[126] A. Wall, 'Patterns of politics in England, 1558–1628', *HJ*, XXXI (1988), 947–63.

keep this letter close, for if it should come to my lord privy seal's knowledge or ear I were half undone'.[127] These manoeuvres both fed off and aimed to steer the king's own visible changes of inclination. Thus Gardiner encouraged Sampson 'not to fear to help things forward; for the Kings Highnes was very good Lord in them', just as the Boleyns in the wake of Wolsey's fall found the need to imitate him in 'one of the great means the cardinal of York had to maintain his credit, knowing the nature of his master, [which] was to praise his opinions highly'.[128] As Eric Ives has shown, charges against Wolsey were presented to Henry by a number of lords in July 1529, months before his final disgrace; yet as Hall recounts, they did so because they 'perceiued that the kings fauor was from the Cardinal sore minished'.[129] Glyn Redworth and Susan Brigden have shown that Gardiner's part in Cromwell's fall took its cue from the king, but that the opportunity to attack heresy both before and, more intensively, after the minister's dismissal, was not lost on the bishop and his conservative allies.[130] This dependence on constant interaction with the king helps to explain the apparently ramshackle nature of so much factional plotting. Why else, if Cromwell really did 'think up and plan' the fall of Anne Boleyn as he later told Chapuys, did his friend Wyatt have to come within range of the axe only to escape?[131] Why, if Paget and Hertford had been planning for the future from the fall of the Howards and perhaps long before, did they seal the understanding that bolstered the protectorate only 'in the gallery at Westminster, before the breath was out of the body of the King that dead is'?[132]

Individuals and groups did contrive to influence the king for their personal advancement and the implementation of their chosen policies, and that long before the reformation. But did they plot the bloody destruction of their rivals? Here we must link the third level of politics to the fourth and fifth. The fourth was rebellion, open war against the king or queen. In practice it was the recourse of desperate or dedicated men such as the earl of Lincoln in 1487 or Sir Thomas Wyatt in 1554, yet it was for planning such resistance or threatening the throne in equally heinous ways that most of the victims of early Tudor politics died or were disgraced. To gain a proper perspective on their fate, we must recall the timing of these incidents. They clustered in the two great crises of early Tudor monarchy. First there was the dynastic crisis

---

[127] Redworth, 'Six articles', 53.
[128] J. Strype, *Ecclesiastical Memorials* (3 Vols, 1721) [hereafter Strype, *Ecclesiastical Memorials*], ii, 257; *Correspondance Du Bellay*, 104–5.
[129] Ives, 'Fall of Wolsey', 295–300.
[130] Redworth, *Gardiner*, 106–29; Brigden, *London*, 308–24.
[131] Ives, *Anne Boleyn*, 357, 372–3, 416.
[132] Strype, *Ecclesiastical Memorials*, II, ii, 430.

of Henry VII's reign, with its high points in the mid-1490s and in the
king's last seven queasy years. Then there was the interlinked crisis of
reformation and succession in the 1530s and 1540s.

In both these periods, though more obviously in the 1490s than later,
there were genuine conspirators against the Tudors.[133] Yet with treason
in the air, some people seem to have taken the opportunity to accuse
others falsely. John Whyte was studying at the university of Paris when
Henry VII commanded him to return to face treason charges, but after
more than six months in the Tower he cleared himself and emerged to
sue his accuser.[134] William Whitefelde of Northampton allegedly hatched
a plan in about 1505 to destroy William Cutlerd, serjeant-at-law, by
finding a letter in Cutlerd's hand and then searching for someone with
identical handwriting: 'then he wolde haue forgid a lett[er] in [th]e
wiche lett[er] he wold haue put in treason ayenst [th]e kyng and this
same lett[er] shold haue byn caste in to the kyngis chamber and then
master Will[ia]m cutler to haue stonde at his own Joberdey'.[135] Similar
incidents occurred in the 1530s.[136] So plotters at court may have done
the same. Yet treason was more than a rubber-stamp to endorse
factional victory.

In both periods many were investigated for treason and never
charged, and some were tried and acquitted. There was concern, as in
the case of Lord De La Warre in 1538, that prosecution with weak
evidence would impair the king's honour.[137] And there was debate over
which posed the greater danger, false accusation or belated revelation
of genuine treason. Pole and Lupset in Thomas Starkey's *Dialogue*
concluded that English practice was misguided in 'admyttyng such
lyght suspycyon to be accusyd', but in a famous conversation held at
Calais between 1504 and 1506, Sir Sampson Norton regretted that
Henry VII did not give 'hys true knyghtes ... credens in suche thynges
as they should shew for hys surtie, for grett hurt may come by that
mene'.[138]

Malicious accusations aimed to feed off the violence of Henry VII's
insistence on the destruction of those who plotted against him, a

---

[133] I. Arthurson, *The Perkin Warbeck Conspiracy 1491–1499* (Stroud, 1994).

[134] PRO, C1/373/31.

[135] *The Records of the Borough of Northampton*, ed. C. A. Markham, J. C. Cox (2 vols, 1898),
I, 354. For similar examples, see *The Tudor Constitution, Documents and Commentary*, ed. G. R.
Elton (2nd edition, Cambridge, 1982), 61–2; Gunn, *Charles Brandon*, 40.

[136] G. R. Elton, *Policy and Police: The Enforcement of the Reformation in the age of Thomas
Cromwell* (Cambridge, 1972), 110–12, 333–4, 350–64, 375–80.

[137] *LP*, XIII, ii, 968.

[138] T. Starkey, *A Dialogue between Pole and Lupset*, ed. T. F. Mayer (Camden Society, 4th
series, XXXVII, 1989), 81–2; *Letters and Papers illustrative of the reigns of Richard III and Henry
VII*, ed. J. Gairdner (2 vols., Rolls series XXIV, 1861–3) [hereafter *Richard III and Henry
VII*], I, 235.

violence that surprised the Flemish ambassador who wrote to Margaret
of Austria in 1508 'Madam, I should never have thought he had the
thing so much at heart'.[139] He must have done if he turned down, as
it seems he did, the offer of £200 or £300 from Edmund Ferrers'
mother to save her son's life in 1502.[140] Yet some at least felt he was
too ready to discount genuine information for fear that it sprang from
'envy, yll wille and malis'.[141] Like his son, he had to walk a difficult
path between bloody over-reaction to every suspicion of treachery and
a fatal insouciance over genuine threats to his throne or to the Tudor
succession. Henry VIII's combination of fury and self-pity whenever
he felt himself betrayed was if anything more devastating than his
father's grim determination, but he too seems to have learnt to manage
accusation and counter-accusation more deftly by his last years, if some
of Foxe's stories are to be believed.[142] There may have been fabricated
charges of treason at court, but the unpredictable combination of
anxiety and scepticism displayed by both kings may well have been
enough to destroy their victims without any help from plotting rivals,
not least because of the penalties awaiting those who knew about
another's treason and failed to disclose it.

What complicates the king's role is the way in which treason trials
blended the third and fourth with the fifth and last level of politics, the
wider dialogue between the monarch and the political nation. For
Henry VIII, to rid himself of a minister who was starting to outlive his
usefulness as a 'lightning conductor', taking the criticism for policies
agreed between himself and the king, was conveniently to clean the
slate of past difficulties and to re-invent himself as a model ruler, one
taking the counsel of his natural counsellors the nobility.[143] Echoes of
such escapology might be read into Henry VII's curbing of the Stanleys
in 1495 and his removal of Sir James Hobart, an aggressor against the
liberties of the church, from the attorney-generalship in 1507.[144] Here
we should remember that complaint at court—the factional strife of
our third level of politics—was one of the best indicators to the king of
the standing of his ministers and his policies with the wider political
nation: criticism could bring down a rival without elaborately fabricated
accusations of capital crime.

In 1538, Thomas duke of Norfolk wrote to Thomas Cromwell,

[139] *Richard III and Henry VII*, I, 363–4.
[140] BL, Add. MS 21480, fo. 181v.
[141] *Richard III and Henry VII*, I, 234.
[142] L. B. Smith, *Henry VIII: The Mask of Royalty* (1971), 28–37, 88–90; Redworth, *Gardiner*, 200–2, 233–4.
[143] For the coinage of 'lightning conductor' in this context, see Walker, *Skelton*, 174; Bernard, *War, Taxation and Rebellion*, 62.
[144] Carpenter, *Locality and Polity*, 583–8; Gunn, 'Courtiers', 47.

complaining that he was short of money and plate because he had spent too much on monastic land: 'a man' he lamented, 'can not have his cake and eate his cake'.[145] You may well feel the same about this paper; I have tried to reconcile the irreconcilable, and I have not even said what I think caused the fall of Anne Boleyn. Yet a number of the historians on either side of this debate have admitted that the evidence can be read to support either their opinion or the opposite, that 'the truth may well have been a mixture of the two', or that 'no single model of political activity will apply to all cases'.[146] The conclusion that involves least special pleading to discount one type of evidence or another, and least invocation of unprovably cunning and malevolent conspiracies, is that for which I have argued here, one that seems close to those recently reached from different angles by Greg Walker and Glyn Redworth. There were strong kings in early Tudor England, making policy, directing councillors who worked effectively with one another and destroying those they judged to have betrayed them; there were also political groups of varying types working to influence those policies and advance one another's careers, at times at the expense of their competitors. In early Tudor England as in comparable personal monarchies, the interactions between the king and his servants reflected initiatives taken by each in response to those of the other. As our sources rarely take us into the king's council, more rarely into his privy chamber and never into his head, it may be only right to be a little unsure about the ultimate balance between the king and his factions. Perhaps we can have our cake and eat it after all.

[145] PRO, SP1/130, fo. 43r. (*LP*, XIII, i. 504).
[146] Gwyn, *King's Cardinal*, 581, 595–6; Ives, 'Fall of Wolsey', 303; Starkey, 'Intimacy and innovation', 117; Walker, *Plays of Persuasion*, 229.

LIBERALISM AND THE ESTABLISHMENT OF COLLECTIVE SECURITY IN BRITISH FOREIGN POLICY

The Alexander Prize Essay

By Joseph Charles Heim

READ 27 MAY 1994

PERHAPS no phrase is so evocative of inter-war British foreign policy as is 'collective security.' Yet surprisingly, despite this obvious centrality—what political figure did not at one time or another express his views regarding collective security?—there remains a missing dimension regarding our understanding of the part collective security played in British foreign policy during the critical decades of the nineteen-twenties and nineteen-thirties.

Numerous works of scholarship on the British influence in the design of the League of Nations now exist; it is possible to trace quite clearly this British imprint and its making, from the Bryce Group to the Political Intelligence Department to the final pattern that emerged within British governing circles.[1] Then, too, there is a considerable amount of study devoted to the nineteen-thirties when collective security formed a conspicuous element of the prevailing diplomatic orthodoxy. Simply put, both the design and operation of collective security in inter-war British foreign policy have been thoroughly treated; what needs further study is what lies between these two concerns, the political theory of creation and the political action of crisis diplomacy, namely how collective security became established as the fundamental principle of inter-war British foreign policy.

The answer to this, in turn, opens into another, no less important historical issue: the fate of the Liberal party and its leadership. This, of course, is not a new concern.[2] What is novel—and the subject of what

---

[1] E. Goldstein, *Winning the Peace: British Diplomatic Strategy. Peace Planning, and the Paris Peace Conference 1916–1920* (Oxford, 1920); P. Yearwood, ' "On the Safe and Right Lines:" the Lloyd George government and the origins of the League of Nations, 1916–1918,' *Historical Journal*, xxxii (1989), 131–155.

[2] M. Freeden, *Liberalism divided* (Oxford, 1986); P. F. Clarke, *Liberals and Social Democrats* (Cambridge, 1978); M. Bentley, *The Liberal mind* (Cambridge, 1977); T. Wilson, *The downfall of the Liberal party* (London, 1966); G. Bernstein, 'Yorkshire Liberalism during the first world war,' *Historical Journal*, xxxii (1989), 107–129.

follows—is that it should be linked with the establishment of collective security in British foreign policy. A careful study of the leading figures of Liberalism, men such as Asquith and Grey, reveals that, following their departure from government in December 1916, they did not at all enter into a course of opposition; far from it, they consciously sought to avoid this—'we should leave it alone and not embarrass it' Grey remarked to Lord Crewe concerning the Lloyd George government in early 1917[3]—and instead, in a manner most unusual in British politics, sought to establish themselves in a non-adversarial position *above* politics from which they could establish new principles of political conduct.

Liberal disenchantment with contemporary politics antedated December 1916; the assumption of power by Lloyd George and his associates should not be seen as the result of a coup—as John Turner makes clear in his study of British politics during the world war, the would be plotters were themselves disorganized and divided[4]—but rather as a culmination of war-time pressure that eroded the practice and legitimacy of traditional parliamentary government. The formation of the first Coalition government in May 1915, the inability of the Cabinet to exert meaningful control over the military high command in the wake of repeated disasters, and finally the crisis over con-scription—these shattered that confident certainty that had been a hallmark of the Liberal world view.

Not wishing to undermine a national unity considered essential to the war effort or surrender to the demons of despair, the Asquithian Liberal leadership cast about for a part to play in the new political order. It was 'lack of administrative talent' on the part of the new government[5]—the Liberals, after all, had a near monopoly of high office for a decade previously—that first conditioned the approach of the Asquithian Liberals to the Lloyd George regime. The latter was seen, in Grey's words, as being badly in need of 'help'[6]—indeed, Asquith himself said as much during the famous Maurice Debate of early 1918[7].

The Asquithian Liberals saw themselves as the persons most endowed with the ability to provide this needed intellectual assistance and guidance. But, equally, they convinced themselves that they could best accomplish this task if they avoided the machinations and internecine manoeuvering associated with office: Crewe cautioned Asquith not to

[3] Grey to Crewe, 2 February 1917, Crewe Papers, Cambridge University Library (CUL), MS C/17.
[4] J. Turner, *British politics and the great war* (1992), 124–151.
[5] Notes by Edwin Montagu, 9 December 1916, Montagu Papers, Trinity College Cambridge, MS AS 1/10.
[6] Grey to Murray, 21 January 1918, Murray papers, Bodleian Library, MS 139 fo. 10
[7] *Hansard's Parliamentary Debates*, 5th ser., cxxv. 2347–2349, 9 May 1918.

enter government, warning that the 'higgledy-piggledy' of 'irresponsible heads of department' would distract him from larger issues[8], while in a similar vein Grey expressed his relief to Gilbert Murray that thanks to his freedom from ministerial worry, he was 'able to see with sense values and perspectives changed by the greatest catastrophe in human affairs that has occurred within historical memory.'[9]

In this same letter, Grey related that although he truly wished to 'be of help' in political life and did not at all wish to withdraw from public affairs, he confessed he was at a loss as to explaining his position with reference to standard opinion that categorised British politicians according to whether or not they were counted as supporters of the government. Seeming historical parallels—Foxites, Grenvillities, Peelites—were rendered inappropriate for the Asquithians desired not power but influence, and they did not seek to create an opposition policy as much as a change in the way policy was conceived.

It was, however, not self-examination and searching alone that propelled the Asquithian Liberals onto a new course concerning their part in the British politics of the future. Larger events were no less important, both in sharply limiting their choices and paradoxically, opening a new field of endeavor to which they were inescapably drawn by talent and temperament.

The Coupon Election of 1918 effectively marked the end of the Asquithian Liberals as a viable popular political party. The party had been routed, not only by the patriotic fervor aroused by the Lloyd George government, but also by its own inability to mount a modern political campaign in a world where the 1918 electoral reforms nearly doubled the number of voters. Interestingly, this sense that the Asquithians, with their intellectual-aristocratic approach to politics that was reflective of the Edwardian era, were ill-adapted to an age of mass politics, was found even within the ranks of the Asquithians. In a revealing letter written nearly a year after the debacle of the Coupon Election, one leading Liberal parliamentarian remarked that in retrospect, it was now clear that Asquith and the party leadership had indeed long abandoned hopes of office and had devoted their efforts to the establishment of foreign policy principles.[10]

That the Asquithian leadership was possessed of a rare ability in the area of foreign affairs was not open to doubt; indeed, the diary of Maurice Hankey, then secretary to the Cabinet, recounts a powerful and most unusual indication of this: fearing that the looming electoral

[8] Crewe to Asquith, 31 May 1917, Asquith Papers, Bodl. Lib., MS 18 fos. 8–9.
[9] Grey to Murray, 21 January 1918, Murray papers, Bodl. Lib., MS 139 fo. 10.
[10] Acland to Maclean, 17 November 1919, Maclean papers, Bodl. Lib., MS c. 465 fo. 12.

defeat of the Asquithians would deprive the country of valuable statesmanship in foreign policy, King George V himself urged members of the Cabinet to ensure that voices like Lord Grey's would always find an audience within their councils.[11]

Yet more than royal solicitousness was needed if the Asquithians were to proceed towards establishing a more lasting and organized presence in the shaping of foreign policy. This impetus was soon provided by the Paris Peace Conference. In two ways, this fateful conference served as the catalyst that served to bring forth a renewal of public activity on the part of the Asquithians.

The Asquithians were not the only individuals to view the Versailles Peace Treaty as an instance of principle abandoned—indeed, as the eloquent contemporary accounts of both Harold Nicolson and John Maynard Keynes suggest, such a sentiment was prevalent throughout the British elite.[12] They were, however, among the first to detect what they believed was a shift away from principle in British foreign policy; a letter sent to Lloyd George in January 1920 sought to call to the prime minister's attention numerous departures from British war aims.[13]

Unusual among the signatories of this letter was Lord Robert Cecil. An addition to the ranks of the Asquithians, Cecil was a scion of old Tory stock whose service to Conservatism passed through many stations since his start as private secretary to his father, three times prime minister during Victoria's later years. Despite having resigned from the government over the issue of church disestablishment in Wales, Cecil continued to have influence, and during the Paris Peace Conference his expertise concerning international organizations—his 1916 memorandum was perhaps the first governmental effort to address the structure and obligations of a new international organization[14]—was put to use in the drafting of the Covenant of the League of Nations.

This strong attachment to the League of Nations is revealing in another sense: it sheds light on Cecil's affinity with the Asquithianism when that was most associated with public support of the League.

Cecil was increasingly drawn into the Asquithian orbit—in his view, Grey stood for not only the League of Nations, but the restoration of principle in public life at a time when that was, he believed, the

---

[11] Diary entry of M. Hankey, 23 November 1918, Hankey Papers, Churchill College. Cambridge, MS 1/5 fo. 55.

[12] H. Nicolson, *Peacemaking 1919* (1933); J. M. Keynes, *The economic consequences of the peace* (1920).

[13] A printed copy of this letter is Bryce Papers, Bodl. Lib., MS UB 59. Also see Asquith to Bryce, 21 May 1919, Bryce papers, Bodl. Lib., MS UB 1.

[14] Lord Robert Cecil, cabinet memorandum, *Proposals for diminishing the occasion of future wars*, October 1916, Cecil of Chelwood papers, British Library, Additional MS 51102.

fundamental task facing the established order.[15] Later, he would insist that Grey's behest was the reason why he continued to directly serve the government.[16] Given this, it is not at all surprising that Asquith noted that 'Lord Robert Cecil ... is one of us.'[17]

Yet, for the Asquithians, Versailles stood for more than betrayal of principle; it also came to mean the disregarding of the traditional canons of reserve and detachment in the making of foreign policy. Increasingly, politicians crafted foreign policy according to what was presumed to be public opinion. In this view, public opinion was now seen as something in need of courting, an element essential to the government's ability to make its authority felt. Correspondingly, the influence of the Foreign Office was severely diminished and its impact on the outcome of the proceedings in Paris was altogether negligible.[18] Diplomacy by conference, the innovation born of the Paris Peace Conference, inevitably carried in its train not only the loss of Foreign Office influence, but the reduction of its representational powers as well.[19]

Painful as this was for someone like Grey who during his tenure as Foreign Secretary upheld the prerogatives of the Foreign Office even if he did not always accept the advice it proffered, the true Asquithian worry was much larger and more threatening—this newer, more populist perspective in foreign policy making with its emphasis on 'short-sighted' measures designed to boost the government's political position at home led to a failure of vision, an ignorance of larger foreign policy issues that would have dire effects on the country's security.[20] For the Asquithians, this need of the country's translated into a role and duty for themselves; indeed, Grey admitted as much during one of his little noticed trips to the Cabinet office in Whitehall, telling Hankey that the absence of long term perspective in contemporary British diplomacy required elder statesmen like himself to once again attempt to chart the broad course of British foreign policy.[21]

Further, the possibility of being useful in such a manner was made

[15] Cecil to Salisbury, 18 May 1921, CC, BL, Add. MS 51085 fos. 92–97; Lord Robert Cecil, *memorandum on the political situation*, ASQ, Bodl. Lib., MS 34 fos. 9–11.
[16] Viscount Cecil of Chelwood, *All the Way* (1949), 136–137.
[17] Asquith, 'Notes of 5 July 1921,' Asquith papers, Bodl. Lib., MS 34 fos. 22–23.
[18] H. Nicolson, *Peacemaking 1919* (1934); Z. Steiner and M. Dockrill, 'The Foreign Office t the Paris Peace Conference in 1919,' *International History Review*, ii (1982), 55–86; A.J. Sharp, 'The Foreign Office in eclipse 1919–1922,' *History*, lxi (1976), 198–218.
[19] Hardinge to Curzon, 10 June 1920, Hardinge papers, Cambridge University library CUL), MS 45. fo. 38.
[20] Grey to Hardinge, 28 September 1920, Hardinge papers, CUL, MS 43 fos. 19–20.
[21] Grey to Hankey, 8 November 1922, Hankey papers, Churchill College, Cambridge, IS 4/14 fo. 4. Also see Grey to Maclean, 25 August 1924, Maclean papers, Bodl. Lib., IS 467 fo. 114.

more likely because international relations was still seen as an area set apart from the run-of-mill domestic politics, an area where experience was believed deserving of privileged access. As Harold Nicolson remarked in his insightful commentary on this period, diplomacy was in 'a state of transition' from aristocratic to popular control.[22]

The Asquithians, then, were not a displaced and forgotten party, nor were they but a coterie of the embittered and disgruntled. They were instead men possessed of a rare talent—understanding of the workings of international affairs—at a time when that was greatly in demand and the post-war world remained in a state of crisis. Of this larger, world situation, too, they were well aware: one need only refer to Grey's speeches in the House of Lords on the 'dangerous drifting of Europe,' follow Crewe's analogy comparing contemporary Europe with times of religious upheaval in the sixteenth century or detect the anguish in Cecil's letter to his brother when he wrote 'Even if things simply do not improve we are in for great difficulties. Another war must in all human probability destroy all of us ... The war shattered the prestige of the European governing class ... Is it too much to say that the future of European civilisation is still far from secure?'[23]

The Asquithian Liberals had found a place in the Britain of mass politics that arrived during the world war: they were going to be the enlightened aristocratic teachers who set the new mass democracy on the right course in foreign policy before they departed the stage of history.

This self-identification was further reinforced by Liberal history and political culture. The correspondence of the Asquithians during this period reveals a fascination with the Whigs in decline. Ironically, the Asquithians saw their Whig forbearers in exactly the same light Lord Salisbury, their formidable opponent, did: a political group without hope of political power in their own right, they were nevertheless possessed of such a degree of intellectual superiority that they were fully capable of shaping the principles of policy even if they themselves could not direct it.[24]

At times, this intellectual affinity took explicit form; thus, Lord Robert Cecil believed that as 'the Labour Party have organized themselves as a separate party,'[25] the 'Liberal Party was cast for the

[22] H. Nicolson, *Curzon: The last phase 1919–1924* (1934), 384–387.

[23] *Hansard*, 5th ser., (Lords), li, 27 June 1922, col. 43 (Grey); *Hansard*, 5th ser., (Lords), li, 10 June 1922, cols. 18–19 (Crewe); Cecil to Salisbury, 18 May 1921, Cecil of Chelwood papers, BL, Add. MS 51085 fo. 93.

[24] Lord Salisbury, 'Disintegration,' *Quarterly Review*, clvi, (October 1883), 578.

[25] Cecil to H. Gladstone, 10 April 1924, Cecil of Chelwood papers, BL, Add. MS 51164 fo.36.

role of Whigs.'[26] Like the Whigs, he thought the Liberals would eventually settle in the Conservative Party,[27] but in the interim they provided the commitment to moral standards and the wisdom that was needed in shaping foreign policy.[28] As a result of Whig reasoning thus applied, Cecil was willing to attach himself to Grey: Grey stood for the establishment of principle in foreign policy[29] and 'experience in foreign affairs when foreign affairs must be our chief preoccupation.'[30] In this same vein, Keynes could claim he had always thought Asquith 'the perfect Whig' since Asquith in his later years stood for intellect and principle above party politics.[31]

'Guardians of principle' was the role the Whigs played in their later days;[32] but this was not the only legitimation of the part the Asquithians had assumed—they also found strong confirmation in that most venerable of sources, William Gladstone, the creator of modern Liberalism, and more often than not, the direct inspiration for many Asquithians entering public life.

'Knowledge is the treasure of the few,' but would only enrich the community if used for moral ends.[33] For Gladstone the elite had a special duty to ensure the larger society progressed by remaining committed to principle.[34] War was brought about by a falling away from this commitment, which was hastened by 'loss of moral equilibrium, especially amongst that part of the body politic which ought to supply stability and guidance both for itself and the rest.'[35] Gladstone thus provided a charge for those with superior knowledge: ensure the governing class of the day followed a foreign policy based on principle and the knowledge they themselves would convey. If they neglected this duty, war—with all its attendant calamity—would result.

Gladstone believed influence in foreign policy was not dependent on the attainment of power. He himself was always more concerned with principles rather than issues; and thought that insight in foreign affairs

[26] Cecil to H. Gladstone, 22 April 1924, Cecil of Chelwood papers, BL, Add. MS 51164 fo.39.

[27] Cecil to Geoffrey Dawson, 8 December 1923, Dawson papers, Bodl. Lib., MS 70 fo. 60.

[28] Cecil to G. Dawson, 11 December 1923, Dawson papers, Bodl. Lib., MS 70 fos. 68–69.

[29] Cecil to Salisbury, 18 May 1921, Cecil of Chelwood papers, BL, Add MS 51085 fos. 92–97.

[30] Cecil to Asquith, 11 May 1922, Cecil of Chelwood papers, BL, Add. MS 51073.

[31] J. M. Keynes *Essays in Biography* (1953), 47.

[32] D. A. Hamer, *Liberal Politics in the age of Gladstone and Rosebery*, (Oxford, 1972), 51.

[33] W. E. Gladstone, 'The paths of honour and shame,' *The Nineteenth Century*, xiii (1878), 591–592.

[34] W. E. Gladstone, *ibid.*, 592.

[35] W. E. Gladstone, *ibid.*, 592.

came when the statesman put himself 'above the liberty and license of partisanship.'[36] Surely, this suggested Gladstone would have approved the actions of the Asquithians. For Gladstone, a career in public life was tantamount to a vocation in political education.

If Gladstone served to hearken the Asquithians to their new role, John Stuart Mill, another guiding light of Liberalism, offered consolation should the Asquithians not achieve success in their new endeavor. Mill's writings were a paean to the virtues of superior intellect—he believed it was clear the community benefited if it allowed the gifted to have not only full freedom,[37] but the ability to shape society.[38] Important for the Asquithians was Mill's insistence new principles of policy were established by those outside of government—'[there is] ... advantage to disjoining the office of control and criticism from the active conduct of affairs'[39]—and in the end, Mill offered the reminder that 'the initiative of all wise and noble things ... comes from individuals ... the strong men of genius ... All he can claim is freedom to point the way.'[40] Nor was all this merely background or formative influence: the Liberal Summer School concluded in 1923 with an address by Ramsay Muir on the theme that 'democracy ... will bring ruin if it means the jealousy of the exceptional man.'[41]

Personal experience as well as intellectual predilection further encouraged the Asquithians in their assumption of the part of tutor of diplomacy. Most had been at Oxford or Cambridge when the idea that commitment to intellect as the basis of public life was firmly established.[42] Likewise, the episode of the imperialist Liberal League demonstrated that even early in their careers Asquith and Grey had sought to influence foreign policy solely on grounds of principle, without any consideration of political support.[43] The fleeting attempts by Cecil to promote a government under Grey in 1921[44] ought to be understood in this context as well. The purpose was not so much to create a centre

[36] W. E. Gladstone, *The Eastern Crisis: a letter to the Duke of Westminster* (1897), 2.

[37] J. S. Mill, *On Liberty*, Collected Works (CW), xviii, (Toronto 1969–1983), 266–268; *Principles of political economy*, CW, x, (Toronto, 1969–1983), 107–112.

[38] J. S. Mill, *Political essays*, CW, x, (Toronto, 1969–1983), 123–124, 320–330; *Considerations on representative government*, CW xix, (Toronto, 1969–1983), 448–450.

[39] J. S. Mill, *Considerations on representative government*, CW, xix, (Toronto, 1969–1983), 448–449.

[40] J. S. Mill, *On Liberty*, CW, xviii, (Toronto, 1969–1983), 369.

[41] *Nation and Athenaeum*, (11 August 1923), 597.

[42] J. P. Roach, 'Victorian universities and the national intelligentsia,' *Victorian Studies*, ii (1959), 144–146.

[43] H. C. G. Matthew, *The Liberal Imperialists: the ideas and politics of a post-Gladstonian elite*, (Oxford, 1972), 287–289.

[44] M. Bentley, 'Liberal politics and the Grey conspiracy of 1921,' *H.J.*, xx (1977), 461–478.

party, though that might have been a consequence, so much as to restore principle as the basis of public life by forming a government of 'honest and straightforward men who will not govern according to party interests.'[45] Cecil, in fact, was quite clear concerning what would have been the charge of a Grey government: in a deteriorating foreign situation, Britain would be best served by a government committed to the establishment of new and more appropriate principles of foreign policy.[46]

Cecil and Grey, therefore, were teachers, men of experience working to lay the foundation of a new diplomacy; indeed, on a number of occasions they defined themselves in exactly such terms. Not too surprisingly, this tone or style of discourse was soon echoed by their admirers—witness the liberal *Nation and Athenaeum*'s endorsement of Cecil's efforts: 'There is a formlessness in England. Lord Robert Cecil ... find him great audiences and a discipleship anxious to learn from a mind that can teach.'[47]

In a larger sense what was occurring was that a number of British political figures, some of whom were at least ostensibly the official heads of a political party were behaving in a manner most unusual for party leaders. Further, this was widely recognised—evidence that the Asquithians were attempting to act as an aristocratic-intellectual elite above politics comes not only from them, but equally, from the reactions of their opponents.

Among the more noteworthy, Liberals like Wedgewood-Benn and C. P. Scott, men who feared that the Liberal Party was controlled by a Whig element unconcerned with popular politics and eager to turn the party away from a progressive programme.[48] These concerns were by no means unfounded and one response by Liberals of this outlook was to challenge not only the new role of the Asquithians but their worthiness to champion the principles they sought to establish:

'... the new Liberalism ... It has its prophets, its competent and aspiring guides, but will the people follow ... Lord Grey and Asquith were members of the Imperialist wing of the Party ... the Makers of the secret agreement with France can hardly be accepted as the champions of open diplomacy.'[49]

[45] Grey to Cecil, 12 April 1921, (not sent), Cecil of Chelwood papers, BL, Add. MS 51073.
[46] Lord Robert Cecil, *memorandum on the political situation*, Asquith papers, Bodl. Lib., MS 34 fos. 9–11; an additional copy is found in Maclean papers, Bodl. Lib., MS c. 466 fos. 50–52.
[47] *Nation and Athenaeum*, (10 June 1922) 369–370.
[48] *The political diaries of C. P. Scott*, ed. T. Wilson (1977), 432.
[49] *Nation and Athenaeum* (29 April 1922), 143.

More deference was accorded by the Labour Party. Clynes and Thomas had signed the Asquithian letter sent to Lloyd George in January 1920 while MacDonald was inhibited from doing so only by his personal aversion to some of the leading Asquithians. Conservatives, too, were aware of the different part being played by the Asquithians within the post- war British political system; in a contemporary book on current affairs, Lord Birkenhead perceptively noted that Liberalism had become a dying creed, kept alive only as a vehicle for a few aristocrats to exert their prestige.[50] Birkenhead's book exhibited all the sarcasm the public readily expected of its author, but nevertheless, it should not be overlooked that behind the caustic tone there was an understanding of exactly what people like Lord Grey were intending to do.

In short, there has been a great deal of misunderstanding regarding the post-war conduct of figures like Asquith and Grey. They did indeed believe they were abandoning political life, if what was meant by that was the exercise of the power of government; but they did not conceive of themselves as having given up public life. This seeming contradiction was reconciled by their belief that they formed a unique group of expertise and commitment to principle which intended to forge a new basis of British foreign policy.

At the end of the war Grey was only fifty-seven years of age, by no means too elderly for public life, especially in the light of the fact that Balfour, his successor at the Foreign Office, was then seventy-one. One would have been surprised to find that a man supposedly 'uninterested in political life'[51] gave a number of public speeches each month, served as the president of the League of Nations Union, and made regular visits to press for particular policies. In addition, there were his duties in the House of Lords where he served as the head of the Liberal peers. And there were also his numerous speeches delivered there, each one distinguished, each on a different theme, from the nature of diplomacy to reparations to European security.

Surprisingly, Grey's post-war status as an active voice in British foreign policy has been overlooked. After all, on at least three occasions, he was again considered for the position of Foreign Secretary. The Marquess of Salisbury thought him one of the most influential people in the post-war period,[52] and Austen Chamberlain, while Foreign Secretary, was once convinced that the majority of public opinion would back his policy because 'Lord Grey made two nights ago [a speech] in which he defines my policy and hope in terms which I

[50] Lord Birkenhead, *Contemporary Personalities* (1924), 100.
[51] G. Trevelyan, *Grey of Fallodon* (1937), 337; K. Robbins, *Grey of Fallodon* (1971), 345–372.
[52] *Hansard*, 5th ser., (Lords), lii, 13 December 1922, cols. 407–409 (Salisbury).

unreservedly accept.'[53] and yet again, thought Grey's approval so significant that he told the ambassador in Paris, 'you will see Grey has blessed my policy.'[54] No contemporary doubted the immense prestige Grey possessed in foreign policy matters.

Nor did Grey's most intimate friends diverge from this view. Gilbert Murray believed that his having helped fashion a new outlook in international relations as significant as any of his pre-war accomplishments.[55] To his friends, Grey was anything but under-active, and when he gave up the Liberal leadership in the House of Lords, he wrote, 'it may possibly increase my public activity outside.'[56] When Asquith was preparing to assume his seat in the Lords, Grey took care to remind him that he could count on his active support there, and he would be 'by your side.'[57] Far from being overwhelmed with fatalism, Grey urged that such an attitude must be resisted.[58] He was most distinctly not a withdrawn and brooding recluse but a man deeply committed to his principles, determined to see them put into effect. That he would be successful, not only he, but many others, had no doubts.

The same ignorance enveloped Asquith. Yet, far from falling into apathy and moroseness, he had written of his 'great faith in the self-recuperative capacity of the world.'[59] Like Grey, he, too, was a man who had found a new purpose, one above political partisanship. He thought himself part of a movement which would make war only a faint memory like duelling, and he saw himself as a crusader in something akin to Wilberforce's crusade against the slave trade.[60]

Nor was Lord Robert Cecil's missionary zeal doubted when he said that putting international relations on a new footing was a Christian duty. In the end, the problems for these men were not those of political adjustment but moral renewal:

'... rivalry was allowed to run riot ... in international affairs the apotheosis of nationalism ... The better plan would be to take ... nations and try to induce them to freely combine ... In other words go back to Christian morality and apply it ... Morality, you say, not politics. In a sense, yes.'[61]

[53] A. Chamberlain to D'Abernon, 2 April 1925, Crewe papers, CUL, MS C/8.
[54] A. Chamberlain to Crewe, 27 June 1925, Crewe papers, CUL, MS C/8.
[55] G. Murray, 'Notes on Lord Grey,' 30 August 1935, Murray papers, Bodl. Lib., MS 139 fos. 107–111.
[56] Grey to Murray, 22 August 1924, Murray papers, Bodl. Lib. MS 139 fo. 60.
[57] Grey to Asquith, 28 January 1925, Asquith papers, Bodl. Lib., MS 35 fos. 1–4.
[58] Lord Grey of Fallodon, *Wordsworth's Prelude*, (1923), 6.
[59] Asquith to Cecil, 19 October 1922, Cecil of Chelwood papers, BL, Add. MS 51073.
[60] Asquith, notes for an Oxford lecture, Asquith papers, Bodl. Lib., MS 63 fos. 81–135.
[61] Cecil to Salisbury, 18 May 1921, Cecil of Chelwood papers, BL Add. MS 51085 fos. 92–97.

The Asquithians, then, were of this stripe. They were not fatalists. Perhaps they best fit the   description once provided by Lord Acton, who once remarked that times of crisis invariably produced leaders who believed that virtue and self-sacrifice on their part was the path to national regeneration.[62]

Kenneth Morgan has called the Asquithians and their allies a court party.[63] Like a court party, they cared little for what was happening in the country. But the label does not fit comfortably; for unlike a court party, the Asquithians had no real desire to again hold the reins of government. They preferred to shape power, rather than actually wield it.

The Asquithians saw themselves as Whigs. Like these forefathers—although this time in the realm of diplomacy rather than domestic affairs, diplomacy continuing to be an aristocratic preserve in style if not always substance well into the inter-war period[64]—they were confronted by a rising popular demand to be admitted into the corridors of power. Like their forefathers, too, these new Whigs decided not to resist this movement, but to educate it into the new truths and verities.

This was not mere congratulatory self-justification; Grey, for one, was well aware of the obstacles posed by an inflamed nationalism, but he believed this could be overcome not only through the exercise of enlightened leadership,[65] but also through the establishment of new institutions—the Royal Institute of International Affairs and the League of Nations Union were but two examples—that would propagate the principles of a new diplomacy throughout the more important segments of British society.[66]

The first lesson these post-war Whigs sought to teach was that what was now needed was not an immediate or wholesale democratising of the institutions of diplomacy, but the replacement of a nationalist by an internationalist dimension in the making of foreign policy.[67] Following this, the causes of war were thought not to lie with one particular state or government, but rather in an unstable or unordered international system. What was evil was an international condition that encouraged

---

[62] Lord Acton, *The History of Freedom and Other Essays* (1907), 53.

[63] K. Morgan, *Consensus and Disunity: The Lloyd George Coalition 1918–1922* (Oxford, 1978), 195.

[64] H. Nicolson, *Curzon: the last phase 1919–1924*, (1934); Z. Steiner and M. Dockrill, 'The Foreign Office Reforms 1919–1921,' *H.J.*, xvii (1974), 131–156.

[65] Lord Grey of Fallodon, 'Some Thoughts on the Public Life,' *The fifth Earl Grey lecture* (1923).

[66] Lord Grey of Fallodon, 'Dedicatory speech on occasion of Chatham House being given to the Royal Institute,' *Journal of the British Institute of International Affairs (JBIIA)*, ii (1923), 222–232.

[67] G. Murray, *The League of Nations and the democratic idea* (1918), 12, 28; Lord Eustace Percy, *The responsibilities of the League* (1919), 47.

uncertainty and fear, especially as 'fear of attack by another state was the cause of war.'[68]

The first world war highlighted the inadequacy of traditional means of international order; in this light, A. F. Pollard told the Liberal Summer School that the balance of power system—where powers freely combine to check or restrain one another—was no longer possible given the absence of any sustainable equilibrium. Concurrently, in the great war states had sought to re-establish a balance, but the destruction of any opposing power. If the balance of power had been viable, it would have provided a settlement of the war in 1916.[69]

Lord Grey himself, in a speech on this subject in the Lords, questioned the alternative of an international order based on a pattern of competing, exclusive alliances:

'... I do not believe ... separate alliances between any two powers, or even a special group of Powers in Europe, will provide security ... They create a counterpoise to themselves which eventually leads to war.'[70]

Far from aiding the cause of peace, alliance damaged it: 'Any attempt to impose peace by partial combinations is bound to end in war.'[71]

Against this, the post-war Whigs offered the historical Whig formula writ large: anarchy and conflict were to be eliminated through the creation of an international constitutional machinery that would guarantee both arbitration and conciliation. This was nothing less than the 'social contract' of classical liberal theory applied on a larger scale; indeed, Grey directly linked the establishment of the League of Nations with previous constitutional evolution in Western history.[72]

The Hobbesian strand of liberal thought was clearly present in this aspect of post-war Whig reasoning. Lord Bryce applauded the League because it instituted 'permanent safeguards' against chaos; like the Leviathan, the League as outlined by Bryce was to have preponderant strength so as to either compel states to enter into a conference to settle their disputes, or failing that, the ability to bring effective sanctions against those who refused to adhere to international norms.[73] Similar also to the Leviathan of Hobbes was the belief that the establishment of the new international constitutional order required states to give up

---

[68] Lord Bryce, *Essays and addresses in war-time* (1918), 112; Lord Robert Cecil, 'The League of Nations and the rehabilitation of Europe,' in *Essays in Liberalism: the papers of the 1922 Liberal Summer School* (1922), 1–18.

[69] A. F. Pollard, 'The Balance of Power,' in *Essays in Liberalism* (London, 1922), 23.

[70] *Hansard*, 5th ser., (Lords), liii, 20 April 1923, cols. 805–806 (Grey).

[71] Lord Robert Cecil, 'Speech at Sunderland,' *The Times*, 31 March 1925.

[72] Viscount Grey, *The League of Nations* (1918), 8–11.

[73] *Hansard*, 5th ser., (Lords), xli, 22 July 1920, col. 440.

many of the rights they previously enjoyed in the international state of
nature, most especially, the right to undertake war: 'We must give up
some part of our own freedom. We must be prepared to allow a
Congress of Powers to settle questions we should prefer to treat as
domestic.'[74]

But in return for this 'surrender of sovereignty' a state was amply
compensated. Henceforth, its leaders could rest secure in the knowledge
that a superior authority possessed the strength and ability to compel
any state to resolve its grievances through an international process of
arbitration.[75]

At its core, this post-war Whig system derived from the consent of
the powers to enter into a general constitutional order as represented
by the League of Nations; in this light, it is significant that the Bryce
group originally used the word 'union' in its description of its proposed
international organization.[76] Of course, this 'consent' was manifested
in the international realm not so much by individuals of various
countries developing allegiance to a new international entity—although
here both Cecil and Grey welcomed what Asquith claimed was an
inevitable consequence of the League of Nations, namely, a growing
sense of 'corporate responsibility of the international polity' on the part
of all European statesmen[77]—but by the powers placing themselves
under some sort of treaty of general guarantee. Here, then, is what
explains the very deep attachment of the post-war Whigs to such
demonstrations of this principle as the strengthening of the guarantee
features of the Covenant of the League of Nations—Cecil's Draft
Treaty of Mutual Assistance (DTMA)—or the establishing of mutual
guarantees, most notably with regard to Britain and France, as a step
towards this larger goal. The post-war Whigs had, therefore, found the
specific policies that embodied their desired principles of international
order.

Still, they had quite a distance to travel before such policies were
accepted by the British governments of the period. The early post-war
period in British foreign policy can perhaps be viewed as the growth
in influence of such individuals as Lord Grey of Fallodon, and the
eventual establishment in British diplomacy of their preferred principles.

But this was, of course, by no means fore-ordained. In the aftermath
of the war, the Coalition government was moved by strong isolationist

[74] G. Murray, *The League of Nations and the democratic idea* (1918), 20.
[75] Lord Robert Cecil, Committee of Imperial Defence (CID) memorandum, *On the treaty of mutual assistance*, Cecil of Chelwood papers, BL, Add. MS 3–23.
[76] Private memorandum, *Proposals for the avoidance of war*, by the Bryce group, 24 February 1915, p. 8; Bryce papers, Bodl. Lib., MS UB 58.
[77] Asquith's notes, n.d., Asquith papers, Bodl. Lib., MS 63 fos. 192–193; also see Grey's remarks in *Hansard*, 5th ser., (Lords), liii, 20 April 1923, cols. 798–813.

currents. European financial recovery was expected to be slow, but consistent, and there appeared no pressing security reasons that might warrant a British military commitment to the Continent.[78] The anxiety of the French, even after the promised Anglo-American guarantee was not realised, was little understood, and it elicited either exasperation— witness Lord Balfour's 'France will never be contented with anything the British are prepared to give'[79]—or genuine puzzlement as the following eloquent words of Lord Birkenhead illustrate:

'... A man naturally does not, at the conclusion of a glorious victory, envisage closely all conceivably possible preventive necessities in relation to those by whose side he fought a great war and side by side with whom he has attained a glorious victory.'[80]

Differences with France over European security—combined with a reluctance to move beyond ambiguity concerning British obligations to the League of Nations—characterised the foreign policy of not only the Coalition government, but equally, its successor that took office under Bonar Law. Numerous summits only served to reveal the full extent of the divergence between the former allies reached its height during the Ruhr crisis which saw France occupy vital areas of German industry, officially in retaliation for German reparations policy but, as the remarks of the French prime minister made during a meeting with his British counterpart indicate, the French action equally demonstrated France's ability to severely disrupt the European order that Britain wished to continue: France could not tolerate a European reconstruction that restored Germany so long as she had no security guarantee against future aggression from that nation.[81]

It was this difference the post-war Whigs sought to bridge, and through that, develop a new consensus not only in Britain, but amongst all the major European powers, that saw advantage in a League of Nations system predicated upon mutual obligation and guarantees. The path to success in this endeavor began not so much with eliciting empathy for France's security dilemma, though the importance of that was always understood,[82] but by emphasizing the new importance of France to British defence:

[78] B. Bond, *British Military Policy between the two world wars* (Oxford, 1980); M. Howard, *The Continental Commitment* (1972).

[79] Lord Balfour, cabinet memorandum, 15 September 1922, Cecil of Chelwood papers, BL, Add. MS 51071-A fos. 81–82.

[80] *Hansard*, 5th ser., (Lords) liii, 21 March 1923, cols. 474–475.

[81] See S. Baldwin, 'Note of a conversation with Poincare,' 19 September 1923, Baldwin papers, CUL, MS 108 fos. 3–37; and Tyrell to Baldwin, 13 September 1923, Baldwin papers, CUL, MS 128 fos. 48–49.

[82] Cecil to Heaton-Ellis, April 1922, Cecil of Chelwood papers, BL, Add. MS 51075 os. 116–118.

'We were brought up to regard this country as an island. It is not an island in the sense of a generation ago ... There will never be a splendid isolation for us again ... A wholly new thing has been introduced by the development of aircraft ... Air squadrons can come here ... the amount of damage which can be done from the air is already very great, and likely to increase ... We have therefore, to regard this question of aircraft as a new feature in the question of home defence, raising a question with which we never had to deal before, and which cannot be met by the old axiom of the supremacy of the Navy alone ... The Channel is little more of an obstacle than a river used to in the old days ... we really are more or less part of the Continent.'[83]

The conclusion was considered obvious: 'under modern conditions, our security depends on France to a degree that it has never done before.'[84] Indeed, ties with France were more important than even those with the Dominions.[85]

Further, the granting of a special security guarantee to France was not at odds with the more general pattern of mutual obligation found within the Covenant of the League. Cecil, while the cabinet minister charged with League matters dealt specifically with the issue in a memorandum to the Committee of Imperial Defence (CID), outlining why the establishment of a League framework for security did not diminish the ability of Britain to extend a special guarantee to France: 'Such special treaties would be quite different from alliances of the old sort. They would mainly be a special application of the general guarantee.'[86]

A guarantee to France was seen not as undermining or distracting attention from the League, but buttressing of it in that France could then afford to make some of the initial concessions required to make an even greater and more embracing security system—'a strengthened Covenant' in Grey's words—best expressed in Cecil's proposed Draft Treaty of Mutual Assistance (DTMA).[87]

The movement of British opinion in the direction of greater support for both France and the League of Nations stands as testimony of the

[83] *Hansard*, 5th ser., (Lords), liii, 21 March 1923, cols. 502–503 (Grey); *Hansard*, 5th ser., (Lords), liii, 13 February 1923, cols. 20–25 (Grey).

[84] *Hansard*, 5th ser., (Lords), liii, 21 March 1923, col. 502.

[85] Lord Grey of Fallodon, 'The Dominions and foreign policy,' *JBIIA*, ii (1924), 308–310.

[86] Lord Robert Cecil, CID memorandum, *On a League of Nations plan for the reduction of armaments*, 20 December 1922, Cecil of Chelwood papers, BL, Add. MS 51103 fos. 1–2.

[87] *Hansard*, 5th ser., (Lords), liii, 13 February 1923, cols. 30–31 (Grey); Lord Robert Cecil, CID memorandum, *On the treaty of mutual assistance*, 6 June 1923, Cecil of Chelwood papers, BL, Add. MS fos. 3–23.

success of the efforts of Grey, Cecil and their associates. More importantly, the change was reflected at Westminster—particularly within the
ranks of the government's supporters; to take but one example, the
debate on Air Strengths in the Lords on 21 March 1923 took a surprising
turn and witnessed a number of Tory lords taking Grey's side and
pressing their own government for a change in policy. Nor was this an
isolated instance; later in the year, Lord Salisbury admitted that he had
greatly 'underestimated' the appeal of the policy being advanced by his
brother and Grey and at the same time, he noted that many younger
Conservatives were now identifying with 'the league policy.'[88]

This steady progress, however, was disrupted by the assumption of
power by a Labour minority government in early 1924. Some key
figures in the new government, Henderson in particular, shared the
views of Grey and Cecil unreservedly;[89] unfortunately for them and for
those like Grey who thought they would exercise influence over the
new government, personal rivalry led the prime minister, MacDonald,
to resort to the unusual step of keeping the portfolio of Foreign
Secretary in his own hands. MacDonald's own foreign policy views
were inchoate and riddled with contradiction—his pamphlet, *Pact or
Protocol*, for example, commenced with his stated opposition to any
form of international sanctions, but concluded with his acceptance of
sanctions as 'they were as harmless as a drug to soothe nerves.'[90]
Hankey, the cabinet secretary, thought MacDonald shared the isolationist sentiments of his two predecessors, but unlike them, he seemed
to offer no reasons as to why he held such views.[91] The resulting
ambiguity could indeed be frustrating as Cecil found when the Labour
government apparently abandoned its support of his DTMA:

'... the policy of the Government appears to be exceedingly ambiguous ... Parmoor announced that they sent a reply turning down the
Treaty ... while MacDonald in the House of Commons was expressing his agreement with Asquith who recited the principles on which
the Treaty was based...'[92]

In any case, the 1924 Labour government was too short-lived to
have any lasting effect upon the course of British foreign policy. The
return of a dominant Conservative majority government in the autumn
of 1924 again raised the question of Britain's commitment to France

---

[88] Salisbury to Cecil, 9 October 1923, Cecil of Chelwood papers, BL, Add. MS 51085
fos. 100–101.
[89] A. Henderson, *Labour and foreign affairs* (1922), 9.
[90] R. MacDonald, *Pact or Protocol*, (1925), 5.
[91] Hankey to Smuts, 22 May 1924, Hankey papers, Churchill College, Cambridge, MS
/16 fo. 139.
[92] Cecil to Murray, 15 July 1924, Murray papers, Bodl. Lib., MS 186 fo. 110.

and the League. The new Foreign Secretary, Sir Austen Chamberlain, was enamoured of Grey whose public stature as an elder statesman was then at its height. The consequences of this admiration were soon felt: not only did he retain Lord Crewe, Grey's close Liberal associate, as the ambassador to France, but by his own admission, he soon adopted Grey's view that an exclusive alliance with France was insufficient and that any guarantee would only be truly effective within a larger framework.[93] The receptivity of Germany—Chancellor Streseman sig-nalled his country's willingness to enter into such an arrangement in early 1925—provided the spark needed; shortly after, Chamberlain launched the diplomatic initiative that would culminate with the Locarno Pact.

Throughout the course of negotiations, Chamberlain was ably sup-ported by such postwar Whigs as Cecil, Crewe and Grey. From the Cabinet rooms to the House of Lords to the embassy in Paris, even inside the Foreign Office—Crowe, the permanent under-secretary, used many of Grey's points in his memorandum to the prime minister that outlined the advantages of a general security system over an exclusive alliance with France[94]—their influence was felt.

Nevertheless, their opponents did not surrender the field without a battle. Although a minority in the Cabinet, they were undoubtedly vocal. Churchill was the most reasoned of Chamberlain's opponents; interestingly, he sought to refute the underlying basis of his diplomatic initiatives, namely, Grey's contention that the strategic realities con-fronting Britain had irremediably changed:

'It is argued that we could never endure the possession of the Channel ports by a victorious Germany ... We dwelt, however, fore centuries when those same Channel ports were in the possession of the greatest European military power, when that power—France—was almost unceasingly hostile to us. It is said that new weapons aggravate the danger. But that depends on who has the best and most powerful weapons. If, in addition to sea supremacy, we had air supremacy, we might maintain ourselves as we did in the days of Napoleon for indefinite periods, even when all the Channel ports and all the Low Countries were in the hands of a vast hostile military power. It should never be admitted in this argument that England, cannot, if worse comes to worst, stand alone. I decline to accept as

[93] Interestingly, Grey remarked that at this point in time, 'any exclusive alliance' was 'a lamentable failure,' Grey to Murray, 1 February 1925, Murray papers, Bodl. Lib., MS 139 fo. 65.
[94] Crowe to Baldwin, 14 March 1925, Baldwin papers, CUL, MS 115 fos. 63–65.

an axiom that our fate is involved in that of France.'[95]

Yet, on this occasion, Churchill's argument, replete with its echoes of past glory, failed to convince—Cecil himself later recalled this to Churchill, and could not help to remark that 'I suppose fundamentally you, as a historian, are more interested in the fruits of victory and less in the hope of permanent peace.'[96] Crucial figures in the cabinet such as Hoare, the Air Secretary and Worthington-Evans, the Secretary of State for War, adopted a line of thinking close to Grey's: in the event of an hostile power established, Worthington-Evans wrote, 'within easy reach of the eastern shores of the North Sea and the English Channel, we would find ourselves under a constant threat of aggression'—in these circumstances, a military guarantee for France was 'a matter of British security.'[97]

After this, with the question of British continental commitment now settled, agreement was rapidly reached regarding the desirability of a general system of guarantee over an exclusive alliance with France. Echoing Grey, Hoare urged the cabinet to understand that

'... the danger to European peace seems to me to come not from the possibility of German aggression but from the division of Europe into two camps ... an Anglo-French Pact will deepen the trenches between these two camps...'[98]

Further, any lingering doubts were dispelled when the military chiefs added their support.

'The General Staff fully realise that there can be no real military security in Europe until Germany herself subscribes to a general policy of non-aggression. They do not, therefore, regard a military pact with France and Belgium as an end in itself; it can be no more than a temporary expedient designed to give security until such time it can be reinforced by mutual pact of non-aggression entered into by Germany and her neighbours, or until it can be developed into a larger alliance including Germany herself.'[99]

Victory was thus achieved within the Cabinet; on 20 March 1925 the government committed itself to a treaty of mutual guarantee in Western Europe. Further, it also recognised that this new treaty—called the Locarno Pact—was itself under the auspices of the League; indeed,

[95] W. Churchill, 'French and Belgian security,' 24 February 1925, Public Record Office, Cabinet papers (CP) 118 (25).
[96] Cecil to Churchill, 8 January 1929, Cecil of Chelwood papers, BL, Add. MS. 51073.
[97] PRO, CP (116) 25, February 1925.
[98] S. Hoare, 'French and Belgian security,' PRO CP (121) 25.
[99] PRO CP 116 (25).

it was this very subordination that allowed the Secretary of State for the Dominions to claim that the Dominion governments (which were signatories to the Covenant) were also bound by the provisions of Locarno:

'... all the agreements initialled at Locarno conform strictly to the Covenant ... [and] ... are placed under the guardianship of the League, [and] that the League is the ultimate authority in regard to the issues which may be raised.'[100]

The post-war Whigs could not but see this as a high point in the achievement of their goals.[101] Not only had they influenced a change in British foreign policy, but, at last, they saw a policy of collective security firmly established, one where the major powers had truly committed themselves to guaranteeing a system of international order that abandoned the idea of blocs and alliances.

[100] Telegram, Secretary of state Dominions affairs to Governors-General, 19 November 1925, Baldwin papers, CUL, MS 111 fos. 202–226.
[101] G. Murray, 'Address to American Foreign Policy Association', 1926, Murray papers, Bodl. Lib., MS 109 fos. 149–158; Viscount Cecil, *All the Way* (1949), 167–168.

EMPIRE AND OPPORTUNITY IN BRITAIN, 1763–75

The Prothero Lecture

By P.J. Marshall

READ 6 JULY 1994

AT the Peace of Paris in 1763 Britain reaped the rewards of a successful war overseas. Great gains were made in North America, the West Indies and West Africa. Two years later Robert Clive signed the treaty of Allahabad by which the Mughal emperor transferred the *diwani* and with it effective possession of the huge province of Bengal to the East India Company. No one could doubt the scale of what had been acquired in so short a time in terms of land, people or resources. How these vast gains could be turned to account, by whom and with what consequences, aroused eager anticipation, a well as serious misgivings, as the British state and many private individuals tried to exploit the opportunities opened up by British military prowess. In so doing they revealed much about the strengths and weaknesses of British overseas expansion in the eighteenth century.

Over the next twelve years weakness was to be at least as apparent as strength. By 1775 Britain was about to embark on and to lose a new war for North America, this time against her own colonial subjects, while the East India Company was only slowly recovering from a crippling financial crisis. Many individuals had launched projects to profit from imperial assets, often of a highly speculative kind; only a few had succeeded. Yet the fruits of war had not gone to waste. Britain's drive to world-wide dominance would survive defeat in North America, and many individuals showed that they had learnt how to take the opportunities offered by an expanding empire.

Land and people were the most obvious assets acquired in 1763 and 1765. The British reading public were left in no doubt of the extent of their new domains. 'Our colonies were preserved, secured, and extended', a popular geography told its readers, 'so far, as to render it difficult to ascertain the precise bounds of our empire in North America, to the northern and western sides: for to the northward it would seem that we might extend our claims quite to the pole itself ... To the westward our boundaries reach to nations unknown even to the native Indians of Canada. If we might hazard a conjecture, it is nearly equal to the extent of all Europe'.[1] On the basis of maps such as those contained in James Rennell's *Bengal Atlas* of 1780, Edmund Burke could tell the House of Commons that the area of Bengal and its subordinate provinces amounted to 161,978 square miles, 'considerably larger than the whole kingdom of France'.[2]

Early estimates of the population of Bengal varied from ten to twenty million. By contrast, the 1763 peace was known to have brought relatively few new subjects to the British empire in America: some French in the Ceded Islands of the West Indies, a very few Spanish in East Florida, about 75,000 French, it was supposed, in Quebec and perhaps some 100,000 Indians. But the new conquests had brought opportunities for a huge redeployment of the population of the empire and for bringing new peoples into British America. The circulation of material like Franklin's *Observations on the Increase of Mankind* drew attention to the extraordinary fecundity of the colonial American population. The board of trade reported in 1763 that 'many of your Majesty's ancient colonies appeared to be overstock'd with inhabitants, occasioned partly by an extremely increasing population in some of those colonies, whose boundaries had become too narrow for their numbers', but chiefly, the board thought, from the inequitable distribution of land within the colonies. The board envisaged that the land newly acquired in America would be developed 'by the industry of emigrants from Europe'.[3] So-called 'foreign protestants' were a source of manpower for British America very much favoured by British policymakers. Germans, Swiss and Huguenots were believed to be readily available and to make admirable settlers. It was axiomatic that migration from Britain itself should be discouraged. Those who were to be settled on new lands should either come from the 'ancient colonies' or from continental Europe. The reality, as Professor Bailyn has shown with such authority, is that the availability of new lands helped to stimulate to ever increasing heights a great flow of migrants from the British Isles, especially from Ulster and Scotland, but later from certain English regions as well.[4] It was fully recognised that the development of the new West Indian islands would require large imports of slaves, which a British slave trade strengthened by acquisitions in West Africa would have no difficulty in providing.

Thus there was no shortage of people available to take up land,

[1] W. Guthrie, *A New Geographical, Historical, and Commercial Grammar and Present State of the Several Kingdoms of the World* (1770), 563.

[2] *The Writings and Speeches of Edmund Burke*, V, *India: Madras and Bengal 1774–85*, ed. P.J. Marshall (Oxford, 1981), 389.

[3] Report of 8 June 1763, *Documents Relating to the Constitutional History of Canada, 1759–91*, ed. A. Shortt and A. G. Doughty, 2 vols (Ottawa, 1918), I.137.

[4] *Voyagers to the West: Emigration from Britain to America on the Eve of the Revolution* (1987).

whether they were moving on from Pennsylvania or the New England colonies or were emigrants from Britain, Europe or Africa. Official priorities were that they should if possible be directed to new acquisitions along the coasts of North America, that is to the Floridas and to territory added to Georgia and Nova Scotia. It was also recognised that much land had become available for effective settlement within the existing colonies, once military victory had finally ended the insecurity caused by the threat of French and Indian attacks. Huge areas in northern New York, along the northern and western edges of New England and in the back country of South Carolina and Georgia had become prime areas for settlement. On the other hand, it was official policy to try to restrain for the time being purchases of land and movement of people into the great areas to the west of the Appalachians. Private promoters and potential settlers had their own priorities and preferences, which did not usually differ very markedly from official ones, although pressures of all kinds quickly developed against the policy of reserving western lands.

The East India Company's new province of Bengal was reputed to be 'one of the richest, most populous and best cultivated kingdoms of the world'.[5] Its population was believed to be abundant and highly skilled as cultivators of the soil and artisans. In the early years of British rule it was assumed that there was no conceivable need to transfer people, beyond a standing garrison of some 3000 European soldiers, skills or capital from any part of the empire to this immensely valuable asset.

Great additions to the economic resources of the empire were eagerly anticipated. The projections of the board of trade were along established lines: more West Indian products; fish, timber, naval stores and fur from Quebec and the other new colonies to the north; indigo, silk and cotton from the Floridas and the territory added to Georgia.[6] Private promoters were more inventive. Concessions were solicited for gold and silver in New York, copper around Lake Superior and for coal on Cape Breton Island.[7] Every kind of exotic crop was predicted for East Florida in particular.

The East India Company promised that the acquisition of the *diwani* would mean a much greater flow of Bengal goods to Britain. The directors instructed their servants at Calcutta 'to increase the investment of your presidency to the utmost extent you can'. They recognised,

[5] Alexander Dow, *History of Hindostan*, 3 vols (1768–72), III, lxviii.

[6] *Documents*, ed. Shortt and Doughty, I, 135–8.

[7] *Acts of the Privy Council of England: Colonial Series* [hereafter *A.P.C.*], ed. J. A. Murray and A. W. Fitzroy, 6 vols (1908–12), IV. 549, 659–61, V. 18–20, 129–37, VI. 362–4; Privy Council Minute, 19 June 1772, Public Record Office [hereafter P.R.O.], C.O. 323/27, fos. 157–75; Treasury Minute, 28 Oct 1766, C.O. 5/67, fos. 97–8.

however, that, although the demand for the staple of the Bengal trade, cotton piece goods, was buoyant both in Britain and in the re-export markets, it was not 'unlimited'. The servants were told that they must do their utmost to develop exports of raw silk, a commodity that could be regarded as being 'a national benefit', and to increase the trade between Bengal and China, to enable the Company's servants stationed at Canton to pay for much greater shipments of tea, another 'national concern'.[8]

If the potential of the great new acquisitions seemed clear, realising this potential was another matter. This was a problem that very much concerned the ministers of the crown. The crown's landed estate in America had been colossally increased and in an indirect sense the crown had acquired an estate in the East Indies as well.

The record of the crown's management of its American lands over a very long period was hardly an encouraging one. Virtually no direct income was derived from them. In the proprietory or corporate colonies the right to dispose of lands or to receive anything at all for them had been alienated. In royal colonies land was granted by the governors, subject to conditions laid down in their instructions. Quit rents were in theory payable on land granted in the name of the crown. They were of some value in Virginia, brought in small sums in Jamaica, New York and the Carolinas, but virtually nothing anywhere else.[9] In the past, a direct income from land had been a lesser priority than the crown's desire to see the colonies 'improved' by settling the maximum number of people with adequate holdings of land. Governors' instructions therefore contained provisions limiting the size of individual holdings and stipulating that land grants should be brought into cultivation within a set time. Official policy was extremely hostile to what was called land jobbing, that is to allowing individuals to acquire large blocks of land which they left uncultivated, waiting for the price to rise in the future. By these criteria royal land policy was also believed to have been a resounding failure for many years. Ministers were told of 'the insatiable desire, every man in this country have, for patents of great tracts of land; from most of which, they have very little prospect of profit in their own time, but hope to get estates for their posterity'. Much land remained unimproved as a result, and settlement was very

---

[8] *Fort William-India House Correspondence*, 21 vols (New Delhi, 1949-85), IV. 207-8, V. 80-1, 136.

[9] 'Explanation of the several branches of H.M.'s revenue arising in the plantations', Bodleian, MS North b. 6, fos. 297-303; Estimate of Quit Rents, W. L. Clements Library [hereafter W.L.C.], Charles Townshend MSS 8/13/32; Board of Trade Report [1766-7], P.R.O., C.O. 5/216, fos. 1-5.

unevenly spread.[10] The administration of land by the governors of New York was reported, to be especially scandalous. Grants of 200,000 acres and even of a million acres were said to be made without survey or any proper record.[11]

Yet the alternative of direct government management of settlement had proved to be even worse. From 1750 to 1752 the crown had shipped out foreign protestants to Nova Scotia at its own expense, but the cost was regarded as prohibitive. When the board of trade was asked by the secretary of state to consider 'the most frugal and reasonable method of settling the new colonies with useful and industrious inhabitants',[12] it could devise no alternative to the established practice of laying out lands 'into small townships and granting them to persons of substance who enter into proper engagements for their settlement'.[13] Grants would be made in Britain, by the privy council on the advice of the board of trade, as well as by the governors in America. Advertisements were put in the *London Gazette* and other places, inviting applications from those willing to settle up to 20,000 acres in East Florida 'within a limited time and at their own expence with a proper number of useful and industrious protestants', either from the old colonies or from Europe.[14] Potential British purchasers deluged the privy council with requests for land, not only in East Florida, but in West Florida, Nova Scotia and New York as well.

Quit rents were set for the new lands, but virtually nothing was ever received from them. The governor of Nova Scotia reported that 5 million acres had been alienated by 1774, for which he should be receiving an income in quit rents of £5000 a year; he had in fact been able to collect £150.[15] The question of an income from American lands was, however, acquiring a new urgency. Attempts to defray the escalating cost of the army in America through parliamentary taxation had come to grief in 1765. The following year Lord Shelburne began to turn his mind towards 'an American fund to support the exigencies of government'. The collection of quit rents was to be properly enforced and future land grants must be made in such a way as to ensure 'real benefit'.[16] That meant that land should be sold. Encouraged by a galaxy of land speculators, Shelburne was turning his eyes towards selling lands to the west of the existing colonial boundaries. Over the next few

[10] Loudoun to Halifax, 26 Dec. 1756, Huntington Library, Loudoun MSS, L.O. 2416.
[11] C. Colden to Captain Cunningham, 6 Dec. 1756, *ibid*, L.O. 2318.
[12] *Journals of the Commissioners of Trade and Plantations 1759-63* (1935), 401.
[13] *A.P.C.*, VI, 358.
[14] e.g. *London Gazette*, 22-6 Nov. 1763.
[15] B. W. Bond, *The Quit Rent System in the American Colonies* (New Haven, 1919), 371 and n.
[16] P. D. G. Thomas, *British Politics and the Stamp Act Crisis* (Oxford, 1975), 298.

years many projects were pushed in front of ministers. The closest that the crown ever came to making anything material from them was the deal with the Grand Ohio Company, who were to acquire a huge grant for new colonies for a payment of £10,460. This venture came to nothing, but plans for a royal income for land sales were again revived in 1774. All existing modes of disposing of land by free grant were to be replaced by sale at auction and quit rents were to be enforced.[17] By 1774 it was, however, far too late for any such policy to be effectively implemented.

If the crown got virtually nothing directly out of American lands, how did private British purchasers fare? The extent of private British interest in American lands after 1763 is very well documented and has been the subject of important studies, notably by Bernard Bailyn.[18] At least fifty persons of great prestige in British public life were listed as investors in the Grand Ohio Company.[19] 77 names of 'land and sea officers, merchants and others' were submitted by the Earl of Egmont as willing to take up rents under his scheme to settle the Island of St John (later Prince Edward Island).[20] The privy council authorised 227 grants for land in East Florida alone to an impressive list of service officers, merchants, gentry, peers and M.P.s.[21] Major British political figures whose names were not in any way connected with American land seem to have been the exception. In addition to the much publicised schemes for large grants, there was a mass of individual transactions. Every colonial governor seems to have invested in land. Francis Bernard, governor of Massachusetts, explained that he could save little from his salary and fees and that 'land is likely to be all that I shall get in America'. He was interested in settlements on the coast of Maine, in Nova Scotia and on the Massachusetts-New York border.[22] William Tryon, while governor of New York, obtained large grants in Vermont and the Mohawk valley.[23] Some of the army officers who went to America during the Seven Years War acquired land then. Those who served in the colonies after the war apparently did so in very large numbers. 'One begins to suspect', John Shy has written, 'that only unusual sloth or ineptness kept an officer from getting a

---

[17] *Royal Instructions to British Colonial Governors 1660–1776*, ed. L. W. Labaree, 2 vols (New York, 1967), II. 533–7.
[18] *Voyagers to the West.*
[19] C. Alvord, *The Mississippi Valley in British Politics*, 2 vols (Cleveland, 1917), II. 98.
[20] *The Memorial of John Earl of Egmont*, [1764], 30–2.
[21] C. L. Mowat, *East Florida as a British Province* (Berkeley, 1943), 58.
[22] Letter to R. Jackson, 20 Oct. 1764, Houghton Library, Sparks MS 4/3, p. 259; W. C. Lane, 'Sir Francis Bernard and his Grant of Mount Desert', *Publications of the Colonial Society of Massachusetts*, XXIV (1920–2), 197–254.
[23] P. D. Nelson, *William Tryon and the Course of Empire* (Chapel Hill, 1990), 103–11.

sizable grant somewhere in America'.[24] It is not surprising that on a visit to Britain in 1766, the Indian trader George Croghan should have reported that 'one half of England is now land mad and every body there has thir eys fixt on this cuntry'.[25]

Yet having one's eyes fixed on America is not at all the same thing as committing one's substance there. Very many of those whose names appear on the lists for various land schemes cannot be regarded as in any sense serious investors. All that they were offering were their names. Anyone with political influence would find themselves courted by colonial American projectors. Grey Cooper, secretary to the treasury, a department that would play a crucial role in deciding on the Ohio project, was told by Benjamin Franklin that, as he had 'those fine children, and are likely to have many more', he should 'take this opportunity of making a considerable addition to their future fortune'. Franklin would put him down for 40,000 acres for which Cooper, for his part, was clearly risking no money at all.[26] Many others, when it came to putting down money, simply withdrew. Of 227 applications received by the privy council for East Florida, only 121 were actually proceeded with and only 16 were ever settled.[27]

There were, however, a few serious investors who committed serious money, most of which was lost. Peter Hasenclever bought lands in New York and New Jersey in 1763 and sent out 300 Germans to establish iron works. In 1767 he claimed that he and the London merchants who backed him had put up £60,000 so far and were hoping to extend their operations into Canada. His affairs ended up in a mass of litigation.[28] Lord Egmont sank £12,000 in East Florida.[29] It has been estimated that those proprietors who actually ventured on the settlement of Prince Edward Island had laid out £40,000 by 1775 on which there can have been no significant return.[30] On a smaller scale, Francis Bernard is unlikely to have got anything back on the £1500 that he has spent on the settlement in Maine before he left America.[31]

Some of the choices for investment, such as most of the projects in Florida, were certainly based on unreal expectations, even if merchants

---

[24] *Toward Lexington* (Princeton, 1965), 357.

[25] *The Papers of Sir William Johnson*, 14 vols (New York, 1921–65), V. 129.

[26] *The Papers of Benjamin Franklin*, ed. L. W. Labaree, et al. (New Haven, 1959–), XVI, 176.

[27] Mowat, *East Florida*, 58–61.

[28] Letter to C. Townshend, 5 Nov. 1765, W.L.C., Charles Townshend MSS, 8/22/8; letter of associates to Gen. Graeme, 8 Nov. 1766 and to Shelburne, 28 Jan. 1767, P.R.O., C.O. 5/67, fos. 100, 181; *Dictionary of American Biography*, VIII. 379–80.

[29] Bailyn, *Voyagers to the West*, 470n.

[30] J. M. Bumsted, *Land Settlement and Politics in Eighteenth-century Prince Edward Island* (Kingston, 1987) 64.

[31] Lane, 'Bernard and Mount Desert', 235.

of great experience and sophistication, like Richard Oswald, put large sums into them. Money could, however, be made out of American land under certain conditions. The exemplary study of Admiral Sir Peter Warren's estate by Julian Gwyn shows how this could be done. Warren's investments in New York prospered because, in the first place, they were effectively managed on the spot by the De Lancey family into which he had married. Secondly, he aimed at capital gains rather than income. Rental returns on American estates were very low, but with the rising demand for land the value of an estate could be expected to increase greatly if it was held for long enough. Warren bought land in the Mohawk valley when it was still a very insecure area; his heirs reaped the benefit of enhanced values after the 1763 peace.[32] The adage that American land was an investment for one's children seems to have been amply justified. Land could be got cheap, but developing it by settling people on it, especially by bringing them from Britain or Europe, was very expensive. It was better to hold the land undeveloped and wait for the great surge of population to push up its value or for other people's investment eventually to improve the land around it. That was the land jobbing which official policy was committed to stamping out, clearly without success. The scramble for American land after 1763 was largely a scramble of would-be land jobbers, willing to do little more than put their names to pieces of paper, rather than of land developers. The crown neither derived an income from American land nor could it impose the pattern of settlement that it favoured.

The development of the West Indian Ceded Islands was an altogether more serious business. Conditions varied from island to island. About half of Grenada had been settled by the French. Because this was an old established French colony, the British accepted that the property rights of the French inhabitants should be recognised. There were also French settlements of St Vincent and Dominica. Since they were thought to have been made contrary to agreements with Britain, French lands were in theory forfeit, but were to be leased back to their occupants by the crown. The whole of Tobago and unsettled lands on the rest of the islands were deemed to belong to the crown.

Evidently unimpressed with the way colonial lands had been disposed of by the board of trade and the privy council, the treasury, under the formidable aegis of George Grenville, laid down the rules for the Ceded Islands. The treasury insisted from the outset that the land should be sold, not granted, and imposed a minimum selling price of £5 an acre for cleared land and £1 for uncleared to be disposed of at auctions, which were to be conducted by a commission appointed by the treasury.

[32] *The Enterprising Admiral* (Montreal, 1974).

Payments could be made by instalments. Quit rents must also be paid.[33]

From the outset in 1764 the commission reported brisk sales. The arch-speculator, Sir George Colebrooke, recalled that 'the madness of the people to become purchasers' meant that 'the money sunk in the Ceded Islands was prodigious'.[34] The commission's secretary later recounted how at the auctions 'the gentlemen attending the sales as purchasers bid in opposition to each other, and in numerous instances, bid up the sales far above what any body could have had an idea that they were worth.' According to him, between 1764 and 1774 the commission sold 174,108 acres for the crown for a total of £620,668.[35] The treasury would seem to have been triumphantly vindicated, but David Murdoch's research tells a rather different story. He calculates that the crown should have received some £700,000, but in fact only £138,851 was ever realised in Britain. Purchasers apparently defaulted massively even on their first instalments, let alone on their later ones.[36]

As they were entitled to do, French settlers in Grenada sold much of their land direct to British purchasers. Sales started immediately after the signing of the peace. According to a memorandum later drawn up by 'The British Proprietors' on the island, extensive purchases by potential planters, backed, it was claimed, by profuse credit from British merchants and from foreign sources too, meant that only one-tenth of the island's property remained in French hands after a few years. The governor later reported that those who bought from the French 'had seldom any capital of their own but speculated on credit; the money was advanced by the London merchants on mortgage of the estates and on condition of having all the produce consigned to them'.[37] A figure that strains credulity of over £12 million was quoted for funds laid out on land purchases and clearing and stocking plantations on Grenada.[38]

Within ten years substantial progress had been made in developing plantation agriculture in all four islands and the Ceded Islands had become a valuable part of the British Caribbean economy. Exports from Grenada by the mid 1770s were worth more than those from any other British colony except for Jamaica. Who had gained from the development of the islands is less clear. The crown had made substantial

[33] P.R.O., T 1/436, fos. 17–51; *House of Commons Sessional Papers of the Eighteenth Century*, ed. S. Lambert, 145 vols (Wilmington, 1975), LXXI. 60–6; *A.P.C.*, IV. 580–609.
[34] *Retrospection or Reminiscences Addressed to my Son*, 2 vols (1898), I. 82.
[35] *Sessional Papers*, LXXI. 221, 223.
[36] 'Land Policy in the Eighteenth-century British Empire: The Sale of Crown Lands in the Ceded Islands 1763–83', *Historical Journal*, XXVII (1984), 549–74.
[37] Cited by E. M. Johnston, 'Grenada, 1775–9', *Macartney of Lisanoure 1737–1806: Essays in Biography*, ed. Peter Roebuck (Belfast, 1983), 111–12.
[38] 'Private Information on the Present State of the Island of Grenada', W.L.C., Shelburne MSS, 78, fo. 281.

gains on paper, a large part of which it had been unable to realise. Lord Mansfield's judgment in Campbell *versus* Hall also prevented the Crown from collecting the $4\frac{1}{2}$ per cent export duties on Ceded Island produce. Some of the original purchases of land had done so in order to speculate in them. Sir George Colebrooke admitted in retrospect that he had formed a syndicate with 'a view merely of speculating in these lands and of reselling them at a future period'. There are indications that the syndicate did well.[39] Colebrooke's operations apparently involved an outlay of £50,000 as a part of a very ambitious scheme for buying up French lands for a nominal £200,000 organised by one Lauchlin Macleane, about whom more will be heard.[40] If speculators made profits on reselling their lands, the early years of the Ceded Islands seem to have been difficult times for those who bought land actually to bring it under cultivation. The enormous level of defaults on purchase payments strengthens this impression. The Grenada planters claimed that they had generally not made profits on their outlays in the early years and that many had actually been ruined.[41] There is abundant evidence of distress after the drying up of credit with the collapse of the Scottish banks in 1772. There was said then to be a 'great want of money' in the Ceded Islands, which was threatening to bring cultivation to a halt.[42]

Given the buoyant demand for sugar in Britain, new West Indian land was a sound investment in principle in the 1760s. Most purchasers in the Ceded Islands seem already to have been engaged in Caribbean sugar production; so it is unlikely that they squandered their money in the way that Colebrooke claimed to have remembered. However, they probably underestimated the difficulty and cost of getting largely undeveloped islands into production and therefore over-burdened themselves with loans with which to buy land at an unrealistic price.

By contrast with the meagre or non-existent quit rents to the crown or low rents to his landlord, if he had one, paid by the American farmer, the Bengal peasant had up to one-third or even more of the yield of his land extracted from him in taxation. This was the famous 'revenue' of Bengal. After 1765 the surplus of this revenue was at the disposal of the East India Company. Robert Clive anticipated that, with deductions for the cost of defending and governing Bengal, there would still be an annual surplus of £1,695,000, which would finance

---

[39] *Retrospection*, I. 82; letter of J. Nelson to G. Grenville, 10 Sept. 1768, British Library Add. MS 57826, fo. 194.

[40] J. N. M. Maclean, *Reward is Secondary* (1963), 81–7.

[41] W. L. C., Shelburne MSS, 78, fo. 281.

[42] Evidence of Oliver Nugent, 22 Jan. 1773, *Parliamentary History of England from the Norman Conquest in 1066 to the year 1803*, ed. W. Cobbett, 36 vols (1806–20), XVII. 687; Petition of Merchant Venturers of Bristol, 20 Jan. 1773, *Journals of the House of Commons*, XXXIV. 55.

both the Company's Indian and its Chinese cargoes and would still 'leave a considerable ballance in your treasury besides'.[43] Even more optimistic estimates of the Bengal surplus circulated widely.

The dilemma from ministers' points of view, as with the new accessions in North America and the West Indies, was whether to be content with the growth in the public revenue which could be presumed to follow from an increased volume in trade (in the case of Bengal from customs and from duties on tea) or whether to seek direct contributions as well. To enforce contributions from the East India Company would raise complex issues about the legal right to the Bengal revenues and the privileges which the Company enjoyed under its charter. Pitt decided to put the matter to the test and establish the public's right to a share in the wealth of Bengal, when he formed his new ministry as earl of Chatham in 1766. 'India', he wrote, 'possesses my heart and fixes my thoughts'. He hoped 'to do the nation justice, and to fix the ease and pre-eminence of England for ages' or, as he put it in another letter, to ensure a 'mighty national benefit'.[44] Very complex negotiations eventually led to a compromise with the Company, embodied in an act of 1767. The Company was bound to pay £400,000 a year to the state. In 1769 the agreement was renewed with the proviso that the Company would be excused payment if its dividend fell below a certain level. This happened in 1773. By that time the exchequer had received £2 million over five years. Asia had paid better than America by a wide margin, but Chatham had hardly got his 'mighty national benefit', and by 1773 the state was actually having to support the Company. By the East India loan act the exchequer waived its claim for the £400,000 a year so long as a loan made to the Company of £1,400,000 remained unpaid.[45]

Private individuals also cast covetous eyes on the revenue of Bengal. Robert Clive devised a means of getting direct access to the taxation raised from the peasants of Bengal for his personal use when he accepted in 1757 a *jagir* or assignment on the revenue from the Mughal emperor. This guaranteed him an income the equivalent of £27,000, in a sense an Indian estate for which he had no responsibilities whatsoever. One or two others tried to get similar grants. Not surprisingly, the East India Company took action to prevent the alienation of their revenues into private hands and fought a long-running campaign against Clive to try to limit or terminate the *jagir*.

The 2500 or so individuals in Britain who held East India stock at

[43] *Fort William-India House Correspondence*, IV. 337–8.
[44] Letters to C. Townshend, 2, 6 Jan. 1767, W.L.C., Charles Townshend MSS, 296/3/35 and 36; letter to Grafton [9 Feb. 1767], *Correspondence of William Pitt, Earl of Chatham*, ed. W. S. Taylor and J. H. Pringle, 4 vols (1838–40), III. 199–200.
[45] 13 Geo. III, c. 64.

any time during this period were also beneficiaries from the revenues of Bengal. The level of the dividend they received and the capital value of their stock depended in large measure on the anticipated flow of wealth from Bengal. Great expectations after the granting of the *diwani* kept up the price of stock and the rate at which dividends were paid for three years, from 1766 to 1769. During that time some major speculative coups were brought off, especially by those with inside knowledge from India, the very high volume of share transactions suggests that small investors were also making their profits.[46] When adverse news from India started a slide in share prices in 1769, some very large sums were lost, most spectacularly by Lauchlin Macleane, who left debts of at least £90,000 to be met by those who had joined in a syndicate with him.[47]

It was easier to turn promises about resources to be added to the empire by conquest into actual flows of trade from Asia than it was from America. The European demand for Indian textiles and Chinese tea took only part of a huge existing output, most of which was intended for Asian consumption. Extra purchasing power from the *diwani* revenues, backed in Bengal by coercion, could secure greater quantities for the Company and increase exports almost immediately. In America, except for commodities like fish, timber or furs, land had to be settled and cleared, labour brought in and equipment installed.

The East India Company responded quickly to its new opportunities. The prime cost of cargoes shipped by the Company from India and China grew from £911,039 in 1764 to a high point of £1,841,838 in 1770.[48] This success was, however, a temporary one. Figures for sales declined over the next five years. By the early 1770s the Company in London was finding it more and more difficult to dispose profitably of the increased cargoes it was receiving from Asia. Bengal cotton cloth and raw silk were regarded as over-priced and tea was so heavily burdened with government duties that the Company could not compete effectively with smuggled tea. Major reductions in tea duties did not come until 1784. The diversification of the European sector of Bengal's economy by private British enterprise towards new export commodities

[46] L. S. Sutherland, *East India Company in Eighteenth-century Politics* (Oxford, 1952) pp. 141–5; Huw Bowen, 'Lord Clive and the Speculation in East India Company Stock 1766', *Historical Journal*, XXX (1987), 905–20 and 'Investment in Empire in the later Eighteenth Century: East India Stockholding 1750–91', *Economic History Review*, 2nd ser., XLII (1989), 186–206.

[47] L. S. Sutherland and J. A. Woods, 'The East India Speculations of William Burke', Lucy Sutherland, *Politics and Finance in the Eighteenth Century*, ed. Aubrey Newman (1984), 330.

[48] Report of the Court of Directors, 1784, appx. 22C, *Sessional Papers*, XL 206.

like indigo only began to take effect even later. The great political revolution brought about in India after the battle of Plassey was only slowly turned to full commercial advantage.

By far the quickest and most substantial commercial returns from the new acquisitions in the western world came from the Ceded Islands. By 1770 Grenada had become a major exporter of sugar. By then St Vincent was also exporting sugar on a significant scale as were Dominica and Tobago from the mid 1770s. The Ceded Islands also added welcome variety to British West Indian exports: Grenada, St Vincent and Dominica all produced coffee and cacao; indigo was grown on Grenada.[49] By contrast, the volume of trade between Britain and the new North American colonies of Quebec and the Floridas was small up to the outbreak of the Revolution.[50]

Any increase in trade of course led to increased customs receipts and thus provided some compensation for the crown's failure to make any major direct additions to its revenue from the new conquests. On the other hand, new conquests entailed expenditure on the costs of administration and above all of defence. These proved to be onerous and attempts to make local communities take up any large part of them were conspicuously unsuccessful. British government expenditure in North America for 1764–75 has been estimated at £5 million (of which nearly £3,500,000 went on the greatly increased peacetime military establishment).[51] The size of the British army stationed in the West Indies was very much larger after 1763 than it had been before the Seven Years War. Two regiments were normally kept in the Ceded Islands. The peacetime deployment of warships in the North American and West Indian stations was also more extensive than before the war. The government and defence of its new conquests imposed very heavy costs on the East India Company. From 1761 to 1771 the Company's military spending in Bengal amounted to £8 million, while its civil government cost £2 million in the same period.[52] The great surpluses of the Bengal revenue, to be sent home as a kind of tribute so confidently predicted by Clive, were never to materialise. In years of heavy spending caused by wars in India, there was in fact no surplus at all.

Public spending created private opportunities. A great expansion of

---

[49] R. B. Sheridan, *Sugar and Slavery: An Economic History of the British West Indies, 1623–1775* (Barbados 1974), 457–9, 492.

[50] J. F. Shepherd and G. M. Walton, *Shipping, Maritime Trade and the Economic Development of Colonial America* (Cambridge, 1972), 47, 94.

[51] Julian Gwyn, 'British Government Spending in the North American Colonies', *Journal of Imperial and Commonwealth History*, VIII (1980), 77.

[52] 3rd Report of Secret Committee, 1773, *Reports from Committees of the House of Commons*, 12 vols (1803–06), IV. 61.

employment overseas was a direct and enduring consequence of victory in the Seven Years War. New civil and military offices overseas attracted at least as much competition as new land in America.

Professor Price has shown how relatively small was the range of civil posts in the American colonies which were open to aspirants in the United Kingdom. He calculates that colonial appointments amounted to no more than 3 per cent or 4 per cent of the total of British public offices in the 1760s.[53] In proprietory colonies the crown had no patronage at all. In royal colonies there was only a scattering of offices which were filled by nomination from London. Most were filled locally by the governor or to an increasing degree by the assembly. The structure of offices in the new colonies created in 1763 was very much on the lines of existing royal colonies: there was an increase but not a spectacular one in a British-staffed colonial bureaucracy in America. The level of competition for such posts as were available was, however, very intense. Governor Bernard commented in 1761 that 'reversionary promises of office in America are now very much solicited'.[54] As the army in North America was reduced at the end of the war, officers scrambled for any civil appointments that might be going.

The major increase in opportunities for employment in America was for naval and military rather than for civil officers. The decision to maintain a sizeable garrison of royal troops in North America and the West Indies after the Seven Years War—sixteen regiments on the mainland and eight in the islands in 1765—offered a significant increase in the number of British army officers who could be kept on full pay in peacetime. After the Seven Years War the reductions of regiments raised for the war were less drastic than after previous wars. New imperial commitments meant a larger peacetime army and better career prospects for many officers. Fewer had to go on half-pay.[55] Those whose regiments were posted to the West Indies generally felt that they had drawn a rather short straw: they had been consigned to islands with a lethal disease environment where careers stagnated; but even the West Indies was presumably better than being on half-pay. Service in North America, on the other hand, seems to have been popular. Many officers bought land and married into colonial families. Even after the loss of the Thirteen Colonies, a large part of the British army was to remain in America, divided between the West Indies and Canada.

India did not become a major peacetime posting for the British army

[53] 'Who Cared about the Colonies?', *Strangers within the Realm: Cultural Margins of the First British Empire*, ed. Bernard Bailyn and Philip Morgan (Chapel Hill, 1991), 397.

[54] *The Barrington-Bernard Correspondence*, ed. A. E. Channing and A. C. Coolidge (Cambridge Mass., 1912), 41.

[55] J. A. Houlding, *Fit for Service: The Training of the British Army 1715–93* (Oxford, 1981), 111.

until after the War of the American Revolution. In 1763 the regiments sent to India during the Seven Years War were recalled. A number of the officers who had been serving with them chose, however, to stay in India and join the rapidly expanding army of the East India Company. John Carnac, for instance, 'heartily tired of being seventeen years a subaltern in his Majesty's service without the least prospect of bettering myself',[56] embarked on a new career which was to bring him much honour in desperate fighting in northern India, and the rank of general, although money never stuck to him and he was to live out his life in India. When it began to augment its army the Company recruited some experienced royal officers like Carnac, but it also began to train up its own service, enlisting very young men as cadets. A large officer corps came into being. For the Bengal army it had risen from 114 in 1763 to 735 in 1772; consisting by then of a brigadier, 29 other field officers, 93 captains and 109 on staff appointments in addition to subalterns and cadets.[57] Some of the senior Company officers became very rich indeed out of the distributions of presents by Indian rulers and opportunities for privileged trade; Richard Smith with his reputed £200,000 was the most notorious.[58] For the great majority, however, the East India Company's service was acquiring the character that it and its successor the Indian army were to maintain for so long. It was a welcome alternative to the British army, especially for the less well-off. Entry was by patronage, not purchase, with promotion by seniority not by influence. It may have lacked the prestige of the royal army, but it was a sure career, well rewarded for those who were able to survive beyond the junior ranks. By 1772 the officer corps of the East India Company, with the Bombay and Madras army bringing the total up to some 1560, was already more than half the size of the 2800 then serving with the British army.[59]

The Bengal revenues also enabled the East India Company to construct a civil administration on a much more elaborate scale than was ever attempted in any colony in the Americas. This administration grew out of the commercial service of the Company. Numbers in the Bengal civil service increased rapidly, from some 70 in the 1750s to about 250 in 1773.[60] Expansion was again largely achieved by appointing very young men to work their way up. Formally they were nominated by the directors of the Company, but the directors were under intense

[56] Cited in J. Roach, 'The 39th Foot and the East India Company, 1754–7', *Bulletin of the John Rylands Library*, LXI (1958–9), 136.

[57] 9th Report Secret Committee, 1773, *Reports from Committees*, IV. 506, 592.

[58] P. J. Marshall, *East India Fortunes: The British in Bengal in the Eighteenth Century* (Oxford, 1976), 239–40.

[59] Houlding, *Fit for Service*, 99.

[60] Marshall, *East India Fortunes*, 15.

outside pressure. Sir George Colebrooke later wrote that, as chairman, 'I had been able to gratify a great many of the first people of the kingdom, and had received applications from more. The number of letters I received ... was equal to that of a prime minister. My house likewise was crowded with petitioners.'[61] His correspondence at the time confirms that he had been trying to oblige a number of great political figures and prominent men in the City.[62] The list of those who pressed for boys to go to India was not very different from the lists of those who applied for land in Florida.

The stampede for writerships was set off by stories about great fortunes being made in the Company's Bengal service. These had real substance. In the aftermath of the battle of Plassey, those lucky enough to survive violence and disease were exceptionally well placed to gather in shares of presents distributed by Indian claimants to office in Bengal, to extract profits from trading in certain commodities where prices could be regulated and from private commissions and perquisites arising from the Company's first involvement in direct administration of the revenues. Clive amassed a fortune in Britain of £400,000. A number of other men can be shown to have been worth well over £100,000.[63] During the 1770s the boom in private profiteering from administrative positions was to subside, but the scale of official salaries steadily increased. By 1783 average emoluments in the Bengal civil service were over £2250 a year.[64] The civil service in the East India Company had acquired the same characteristics as the East India Company's army. It offered far fewer openings and was much more difficult to get into than the army, but those whose families who had sufficient influence to win one of these much coveted posts could expect sure rewards for their offspring for the span of their working lives. India had begun the role that it was to play for so long as the provider of genteel careers.

An older historiography which saw expansion overseas as shaped by the policies of ministers in pursuit of such objectives as 'trade' or 'dominion' or a preference for one kind of colony rather than another has been replaced in recent years by analysis of the forces in eighteenth-century Britain that provided the dynamic for expansion. Stress is placed in particular on the 'advanced forms of commercial capitalism' that had evolved from the late seventeenth century[65] and on the capacity

[61] *Retrospection*, I. 196.

[62] Letter to Clive, rec'd 4 Sept. 1769, British Library, Oriental and India Office Collections, MS Eur. G. 37, box 58, p. 52.

[63] Marshall, *East India Fortunes*, 239–40.

[64] Ibid, 182.

[65] P. J. Cain and A. G. Hopkins, *British Imperialism: Innovation and Expansion 1688–1914* (1993), 85–6.

of the new British 'military-fiscal' state to 'create a world-wide overseas commercial and in the end territorial empire'.[66] Developments between 1763 and 1775 certainly demonstrate the expansive role of British capitalism and of the British state, but they also show their limitations outside the British Isles.

The North American, the West Indian and the East Indian trades all grew rapidly, if erratically, between 1763 and 1775. Yet there were also many commercial failures. Speculative and often under-funded projects turned out badly. The boom in East India stock that followed the *diwani* subsided after three years, when it became clear that there was to be no easy transfer of wealth from Bengal to Britain through the East India Company. A quick return could be obtained on purchases of lands in the Ceded Islands, but profits on American land could only be realised over a long period. Great world-wide speculators like Lauchlin Macleane and Sir George Colebrooke ended up as ruined men, dragging down their numerous creditors with them.

Victorious war did not produce any immediate diversification of British overseas trade. Attempts to develop new commodities in the Floridas were largely unsuccessful. British merchants replaced French ones in Quebec's fur and grain trade, but significant new resources could not be added to them. British capitalism showed that it could still only operate successfully overseas within certain clearly defined limits. Success was largely confined to those trades that met established patterns of demand, either supplying tropical produce to British consumers or British goods to colonial markets, and that were sustained by existing networks of credit.[67]

The market for tropical commodities in mid-eighteenth-century Britain was very buoyant. The Ceded Islands were therefore a valuable spoil of war. Very large sums could be raised to bring the new islands into cultivation. Those who developed them may have underestimated the cost of doing so and strained their credit to the utmost, but their ultimate objective was sound. British consumption of sugar doubled between 1750 and 1775 without any decline in price.[68] The demand for sugar was linked with the rising consumption of tea. Under a different fiscal regime in Britain, the East India Company's strategy of transferring its Bengal revenues to Canton to pay for greatly increased shipments of tea would also have been a sound one. In time the Company would be able to export large quantities of Bengal silk of a quality and at a

[66] Lawrence Stone, 'Introduction', *An Imperial State at War: Britain from 1689 to 1815*, ed Lawrence Stone (1994), 5.
[67] See J. M. Price, 'Credit in the Slave Trade and Plantation Economies', *Slavery and the Rise of the Atlantic System*, ed B. L. Solow (Cambridge, 1991), 293–339.
[68] D. Richardson, 'Slaves, Sugar and Growth 1748–76', *British Capitalism and Caribbean Slavery*, ed B. L. Solow and S. L. Engerman (Cambridge, 1988), 111–12.

price that could meet the British demand. Without an American Revolution, East Florida, as an adjunct to South Carolina, might eventually have become a considerable supplier of indigo for the British textile industry.

The success of the African, the plantation and East India trades together with increasing British exports across the Atlantic created opportunities for profit at many different levels of the British domestic economy. They also created gainful employment abroad for merchants, planters, factors, overseers and sea-faring people. But the agents of commercial capitalism were being matched by the servants of the state as the beneficiaries of empire after the Seven Years War.

By the end of the Seven Years War the British state had shown that it could mount expeditions all over the world with devastating effect. Yet the record of British policy overseas after the war was abject. Direct administration over Quebec was established with difficulty, while supervision of the western lands and their Indian peoples was a failure, as were, of course, attempts to maintain authority over the Thirteen Colonies. But inspite of an incapacity to devise or to implement policy, the extent of the British presence overseas still did much to ensure the consolidation of empire after 1763. Nowhere could the British state levy local resources adequate to finance its operations. Since governments would not disengage from commitments accepted after 1763, money was spent overseas in peacetime on a scale that was entirely new. The East India Company, which could impose taxes on its subjects, was at the same time creating a new British-Indian state and armed forces that involved even more lavish spending. Money spent by the British armed forces enabled American colonies to import British goods. Colebrooke was one of several wartime contractors for supplying or paying the forces of the crown who invested in empire after 1763. Businessmen on both sides of the Atlantic continued to be enriched as contractors, commissaries or paymasters to the army and navy overseas in peacetime. Supplying the forces of the East India Company was a powerful stimulus to private British and Indian business in Calcutta.

Very much more numerous, if individually less lucrative, were the large additions to military and civilian employment opening up under the crown and the Company in the Americas and India. More and more eager and talented young Scots, Irish Protestant gentry or younger sons of English landed families were serving abroad in the army, the navy or in administrative and professional positions in India or under colonial governments. The grip of such people on the good things of empire, provided for them by the British and the Indian tax payer, was to be an enduring legacy of the Seven Years War, lasting until far into the twentieth century.

THEGNS AND KNIGHTS IN ELEVENTH-CENTURY ENGLAND: WHO WAS THEN THE GENTLEMAN?

By John Gillingham

READ 24 SEPTEMBER 1994

I SHALL be considering England during the long eleventh century—from the 990s, the Battle of Maldon and Byrhtferth of Ramsey's 'Life of Oswald', to the 1130s, the world of Geoffrey Gaimar. I shall do so in the light of a situation where, on the one hand, historians of Anglo-Saxon England commonly refer to gentlemen and gentry in their period but do so casually, as though their presence there is something to be taken for granted, and, on the other, where scholars who regard themselves as historians of the gentry seem reluctant to admit that the phenomenon they study can have existed much before 1200, if then.[1] In the first part of this paper I shall argue that there was a gentry in eleventh-century England, that below the great lords there were many layers of society whose members shared the interests and pursuits of the great, i.e. we should accept the terminology of historians of Anglo-Saxon England from Sir Frank Stenton onwards.[2] I shall also argue that in all probability many vigorous members of the Anglo-Saxon gentry were knights, using the word 'knight' to mean the kind of person whom, in the late twelfth century, Richard FitzNigel described as an active knight (*strenuus miles*), i.e. someone whose characteristic and indispensable possessions were his body armour and the requisite horses.[3] Because from about 1200 the term 'knight' came to be used in an increasingly exclusive way, applied to increasingly restricted and

[1] For example in a book sub-titled 'The Gentry of Angevin Yorkshire, 1154–1216' Hugh M. Thomas refers to that period not only as 'the earliest period in which sufficient information survives for a detailed regional study of the gentry'—which it may well be—but also as 'a time when the gentry in some ways were first beginning to emerge as an independent force in English history', *Vassals, Heiresses, Crusaders and Thugs* (Philadelphia, 1993), 3. According to a recent article, 'Henry II was the gentry's midwife', Jean Scammell, 'The Formation of the English Social Structure: Freedom, Knights, and Gentry, 1066–1300' *Speculum* 68 (1993), 618.

[2] E.g. Sir Frank Stenton, *The First Century of English Feudalism 1066–1166* (Oxford, second edn. 1961), 23, 120.

[3] Richard Fitz Nigel, *Dialogus de Scaccario*, ed. and trans. C. Johnson, F. E. L. Carter and D. E. Greenway (Oxford, 1983), 111. I assume here that wealthy men owned expensive horses and that training for war was only one of the factors that made some horses more expensive than others.

elevated sections of the 'gentle' elite, historians have often written of the 'rise of the knight' and have suggested that this 'rise' should be seen in terms of the spiralling costs of knightly equipment. However I shall argue that in the eleventh century the active knight (in Richard FitzNigel's sense) rose (in the sense of becoming more numerous) as a consequence of the diminishing cost of military equipment. I shall argue this in the context of an England characterised by rapid economic growth and a powerful monarchy: 'Campbell's kingdom'. I shall also argue that in these respects the Norman Conquest made little difference. In the second part of this paper I shall focus on the 'honour of arms', the political and military values of the secular elite. Here, by contrast, I shall argue that '1066 and All That' led to important changes.

I begin with what John Blair has called the new landscape of late Anglo-Saxon England, the result, in his words, of 'drastic changes in the structure of local economy and society, the same changes which produced stable nucleated villages and common field-systems. Great estates broke up into small ones, of the same order of magnitude as a typical high medieval parish and village territory, which provided the economic base for a new extensive class of country gentry. Just as a great lord in the eighth century had his proprietary minster, so a modest local thegn in the late tenth had his manorial church'.[4] This same period saw the emergence of that other familiar feature of the English landscape: the market town. Recently Robin Fleming has emphasised the urban as well as the rural setting within which the landowners of Domesday England moved.[5] Presumably many of the four or five thousand secular English landlords whose existence in 1066 is indicated by Domesday Book, belonged to a category of 'middling landowners', even though identifying them with precision (e.g. distinguishing between separate individuals with common names) is notoriously difficult. This has not prevented local historians such as Alan Everitt from identifying regions (e.g. the Kentish Downland) in which lesser landowners were particularly numerous; nor others, such as John Blair, from using words like 'country gentry' on the basis of their own study of a particular locality.[6] Here then, both in town and country, there appears to be the economic base for a gentry—the sort of people who could 'live idly and without manual labour' and were thus able to 'bear the port, charge and countenance of a gentleman'.[7] One eleventh-

[4] John Blair, 'The Making of the English Parish', *Medieval History*, 2. 2, (1992), 15.

[5] Robin Fleming. 'Rural Elites and Urban Communities in Late-saxon England', *Past and Present*, 141 (1993), 3–37.

[6] Alan Everitt, *Continuity and Colonization: the evolution of Kentish settlement* (Leicester, 1986), pp 175–180; John Blair, *Early Medieval Surrey* (Stroud, 1991), 160–161.

[7] Sir Thomas Smith, *De Republica Anglorum: a discourse on the Commonwealth of England* ed. L. Alston (Cambridge, 1906), 39–40.

century Hampshire thegn able to bear such 'port, charge and countenance' was Alvric. When he had a church built at Milford, it was
stipulated that the 'priest should wait for Alvric before beginning the
service'.[8]

But most historians of the gentry would probably wish to argue that
more than an economic base is required before they would be willing
to concede the existence of a gentry. Three criteria widely regarded as
crucial are first, the participation by local landowners in local public
office; second, the existence of county solidarities; and third, the
participation by some local landowners in national assemblies.[9] It seems
to have been the perceived absence of this combination of criteria that
led many of the contributors to a volume on *Gentry and Lesser Nobility in
Late Medieval Europe* to decide that in 'their' countries they could see no
real equivalent of the English gentry.[10] But by precisely these criteria it
seems to me more probable than not, that the peculiarly English brand
of the lesser nobility existed before 1066 and, in some respects at least,
was re-created after it.

Recent trends portray Anglo-Saxon England as a much-administered
land. As James Campbell has put it, it was 'one in which the connections
between the central authority and the localities mattered very much
and one in which the number of men, below the level of sheriff, who
were in some sense agents of government, was very large'.[11] Between
village reeves and sheriffs there were the hundred reeves, responsible
for chairing meetings of the hundred courts every three or four weeks;
some of these reeves also managed royal manors, holding them at farm
from sheriffs. By the tenth century public concern about levels of crime
had led to a number of men in each hundred being made responsible
for policing, for keeping the peace and for managing the suretyship
system.[12] The evidence for this is nearly all in the form of legislation,
reasonable enough as evidence for concern but obviously a poor guide

[8] Also that the priest who was sent to Milford from Christchurch, should be fed at
Alvric's table whenever he was at Milford. P. H. Hase, 'The Mother Churches of
Hampshire' in *Minsters and Parish Churches. The Local Church in Transition 950–1200* ed. John
Blair (Oxford, 1988), 60.
[9] For the clearest exposition of this view of the gentry see Peter Coss, *Lordship,
knighthood and locality. A Study in English Society c. 1180–c. 1280* (Cambridge, 1991), 307–10. I
am also much indebted to Peter Coss's kindness in helping me to clarify my thoughts by
sending me an as yet unpublished discussion of these issues.
[10] Very much the consensus of the contributors to the volume on *Gentry and Lesser
Nobility in Late Medieval Europe*, ed M. Jones (Gloucester, 1986). For a particularly clear
statement of this see F.R.H. Du Boulay's contribution, 'Was There a German Gentry?',
119–132, esp 124.
[11] James Campbell, 'Some Agents and Agencies of the Late Anglo-Saxon State' in
Domesday Studies ed. J. C. Holt, (Woodbridge, 1987), 201–218, esp 205.
[12] For a convenient summary of the policing and pledging system see Helen M. Jewell,
English Local Administration in the Middle Ages (Newton Abbot, 1972), 159–68.

to practice. In two other spheres of government, however, the evidence is much better. First, the evidence of geld rolls and geld accounts demonstrates the presence of collectors working within an effective taxation system. Secondly, the evidence of surviving coins shows a considerable number of moneyers active in the localities and operating within a centrally controlled currency system. In the   light of the workings of late Anglo-Saxon public finance it seems reasonable to believe in the real existence of a law enforcement and peace-keeping system based upon the shire, the hundred and the vill. As Ann Williams has put it, 'However powerful the earls and king's thegns, or for that matter, the bishops and abbots might be, they were not allowed to slip through this net.'[13] As long ago as 1612 the first great historian of medieval England, Samuel Daniel, was led to observe that 'these links thus intermutually fastened, made so strong a chaine to hold the whole frame of the State together in peace and order, as all the most politique regiments upon earth, all the interleagued societies of men, cannot shew us a streighter forme of combination.' He then went on to wonder whether the existence of this strong chain might not answer the question of 'how so great a kingdome as England then was, could with one blow be subdued by so small a province as Normandy'. 'For', he suggested, 'this might make the Conqueror, coming upon a people thus law-bound hand and foot, to establish him so soone and easily as he did.'[14]

Like many of those who held local office later the agents of the late Anglo-Saxon state could be described as part-time and unpaid, though some of them evidently and sometimes legitimately found some of the profits of the system sticking to their hands.[15] That these men met together frequently at either hundred or shire level or both seems reasonably certain. That they met together often enough to form local solidarities articulated at the shire level is implied by the comment of the Anglo-Saxon Chronicle on the breakdown at the end of Aethelred's reign. 'In the end no shire would even help the next'[16] In J. R. Maddicott's opinion 'the county community, where the gentry found a voice, predated the Conquest'.[17] At this level numerous English land-owners must have survived the conquest and although many traditional solidarities must have been overthrown, the continued functioning of

    [13] Ann Wlliams, 'A Bell-house and a Burh-geat: Lordly Residences in England before the Norman Conquest' in ed. R. Harvey and C. Harper-Bill, *The Ideals and Practice of Medieval Knighthood IV* (Woodbridge, 1992), 240. I am deeply indebted to Ann Williams' kindness in reading a draft of this paper and suggesting many references.
    [14] Samuel Daniel, *The First Part of the Historie of England*, (1612), pp. 69, 128–30.
    [15] Campbell, 'Agents and Agencies', 208–9, 216.
    [16] ASC, 1010.
    [17] J. R. Maddicott, 'Magna Carta and the Local community 1215–59', *Past and Present* 102 (1984), 25.

shire and hundredal institutions would surely have led to the re-emergence of new local solidarities. Of course those who doubt the usefulness of the term 'county community' when applied to the four-teenth and fifteenth centuries will doubtless doubt that it should be applied to the eleventh century either. My concern here is merely to point to respects in which there is much similarity—though not a simple continuity—between these two periods.[18]

That some of these men also met regularly at national level is stated firmly for William I's reign by the author of the Anglo-Saxon Chronicle. In his words, the Easter, Whitsun and Christmas crown-wearings were attended by 'all the powerful men over all England, archbishops and bishops, abbots and earls, thegns and knights (*cnihtas*).'[19] Did men below the level of earl and thegn manage to make their opinions heard? As is well known Henry I's Coronation Charter shows that by 1100 it was well worth offering concessions to the *milites … per loricas*. Certainly contemporaries believed that on occasions the *milites gregarii* or the *milites pagenses* were able to give Henry significant support.[20] Such men were not always followers of fashion. According to William of Malmesbury, a fashion—albeit a shortlived one—for having short hair was started by a *miles provincialis*.[21] Consider the 'deep speech' which began four days after the Christmas festivities of 1085 and ended with the decision to launch the Domesday inquiry. I find it hard to believe that this was not discussed in an informal way over Christmas and that the cnihts who had turned up for the Christmas crown-wearing had not expressed their views, particularly no doubt on the subject of how they had suffered during the quartering of the great army on their estates.[22] Paucity of evidence makes parallels for the pre-conquest period harder to find—though we should certainly remember James Campbell's question: Whom was the Confessor seeking to please when he abandoned the *heregeld* in 1051?[23] In Byrhtferth's *Life of Oswald* there is an account of a stormy general assembly in which the forces of righteousness were hard put to it to win the day against pressure from the 'unworthy crowd' (*indignus vulgus*). At this meeting the last speech, by

[18] In Freeman's opinion the late medieval shire was 'ruled by an assembly not so very unlike what the gathering of the thegns of Herefordshire must have been in the days of Cnut', E. A. Freeman, *The History of the Norman Conquest* (Oxford, 1876), v, 445–50.

[19] ASC, 1087.

[20] Florence of Worcester, *Chronicon ex chronicis*, ed. B. Thorpe, 2 vols. (London, 1848–9), ii. 49. *The Ecclesiastical History of Orderic Vitalis*, ed. M. Chibnall, 6 vols. (Oxford, 1969–80) [hereafter *OV*], vi. 206; W. Stubbs, *Select Charters* 3rd edn. (Oxford, 1876), 101.

[21] William of Malmesbury, *De Gestis regum Anglorum*, ed. W. Stubbs, 2 vols. RS 1887–9. ii. 531.

[22] ASC 1085. The Worcester chronicler believed that, as well as barons and sheriffs, the *praepositi regis* were among those required to share the burden, FW ii. 18.

[23] James Campbell, *The Anglo-Saxons* (1982), 244.

Byrhtnoth, addressed *ad exercitum*, begins with the words: 'Listen to me, *seniores et juniores*'—for which I suggest we consider the translation 'thegns and cnihts'.[24]

In eleventh and early twelfth century England then we find a local elite, a broad land-owning class with urban connections, many of them holding public office in a part-time and unpaid fashion, exercising social control over the populace, attending meetings both locally and nationally. All this suggests that there is a strong prima facie case for believing that historians of Anglo-Saxon and Anglo-Norman England are justified in using the term 'gentry'. After all in a kingdom which enjoyed remarkable territorial stability from the tenth century onwards, in terms of its frontiers as well as its internal boundaries, the distances to be covered in moving between centre and locality differed hardly at all between the early and later middle ages; between these periods, even though horse-drawn transport may have improved, there was nothing approaching a communications revolution.[25]

Yet it is widely believed by historians of the gentry that there was no gentry in England until, at the earliest, the late twelfth century. How can this be? Partly, I think, because seduced by the proliferation of administrative records from the end of the twelfth century onwards they have not taken sufficient account of the power of the crown in earlier centuries, nor of the number of local offices involved in the policing and pledging system. And partly because they have tended to see early medieval society as a two-tier system with a huge gulf between the nobles and all the rest.[26] In consequence they have seen some of the non-nobles, the knights for instance, as rather more humble than they were. It is true that before 1200 the word *miles* was used in a less exclusive fashion than it was later. But it certainly does not follow that, as has recently been claimed, until the late twelfth century knights 'were not clearly distinguished from the cultivators from whom they were drawn'.[27] Indeed there can be no doubt whatever that by the

---

[24] *Historians of the Church of York*, ed. J. Raine, (RS, 1879), I, 444–6. Whitelock translated *seniores et juniores* as 'veterans and young men', *English Historical Documents*, 2nd edn. (1979) [hereafter *E.H.D.*], i. 914. However we translate *juniores* (bearing in mind the range of meanings of 'iuvenis'), it is clear that Byrhtferth saw the *vulgus* as well as the nobles as capable of political action, ib. 444. On this meeting see also the details in ed E. O. Blake, *Liber Eliensis* (Camden Soc., 3rd ser., XLII, 1962), 85.

[25] As Christine Carpenter has observed of the later medieval and early modern periods, 'fundamental conditions remain in outline to a large degree constant: a more or less centralised monarchy lacking a large bureaucracy, standing army or police force, and an absence of modern technology to transmit and enforce orders on the ground', in 'Who ruled the Midlands in the later Middle Ages' *Midland History, XIX (1994), 5*.

[26] For an eloquent protest against this view of Anglo-Saxon society see Campbell, *The Anglo-Saxons*, 244.

[27] Scammell, 'The Formation', 591, 597, 604. On p. 593 the argument that the same person could be at once cultivator and knight and in both capacities dependent, is

1130s, at the very latest, *chevaliers* were *gentil hommes* and in absolutely no danger of being confused with 'cultivators'. On this point the evidence of Geoffrey Gaimar's *Estoire* is decisive. Written for the wife— 'dame Custance la gentil'—of a Lincolnshire landowner it is a work of immense significance, the earliest extant history composed for the serious entertainment of the lesser nobility.[28] In Gaimar great nobles admired for their military skills such as Robert of Bellême or Gilbert Fitz Richard are referred to as *chevaliers*; so too are the 1,700 men attached to King William II's household. We are told that many a *gentil home* was dubbed (*adubat*) at Rufus's great feast which is the climax of Gaimar's courtly history. Hereward the Wake and his companions were both *chevaliers* and *gentil hommes*; their enemies were French *chevaliers*. In Gaimar's mind such men existed both before and after 1066. In the wars between Cnut and Edmund Ironside 'many a *gentil home*' lost his life. During Earl Siward's 1053 expedition against Macbeth among the English casualties was 'un des chevaliers le rei/E les huscherles qu'il menat.' When Godwin was put on trial for the murder of Alfred, a *chevalier* called Merleswein spoke, characterised just two lines later as 'riche barun'. Earlier King Edgar treated a *chevalier* as his most confidential advisor and when he spoke to him addressed him as 'brother'. Earlier still King Alfred summoned *chevaliers*, sergeants and archers to the siege of London.[29] Although Gaimar's history has been very little taken into account in the discussion of knighthood and the rise of the gentry, as evidence for the varying ways in which 'gentil hommes' and 'chevaliers' were perceived in the England of the 1130s it could not be bettered, composed as it was within and for a society of *chevaliers*, *gentil hommes* and gentle ladies, and in their language.

But how seriously can we take Gaimar's view of earlier generations, of the 'gentil hommes' of Domesday Book and beyond? It is at this point that Sir Frank Stenton's views have cast a long shadow. It was Stenton's contention that 'The ordinary knight of the eleventh century was a person of small means and insignificant condition'.[30] When Sally

---

supported by quoting from the early eleventh century text in which, allegedly, Hugh of Lusignan was told by his lord, William of Aquitaine. 'You must obey my will because you are mine. If I tell you to work as a peasant (*rusticus*), you must do it'. But this text (ed. J Martindale, 'Conventum inter Guillelmum Aquitanorum comes et Hugonem Chiliarchum', *EHR* 84 (1969), 542–48) is, of course, anything but a manner of fact statement of the rights of a lord. See Stephen D. White, 'Stratégie rhétorique dans la *Conventio* de Hugues de Lusignan' in *Mélanges offerts à Georges Duby*, (Publications de l'université de Provence: Aix en Provence, 1993), vol 2, 147–57.

[28] On the milieu in which Gaimar wrote see Ian Short, 'Gaimar's Epilogue and Geoffrey of Monmouth's *Liber Vetustissimus*', *Speculum* 69 (1994), 323–43.

[29] Geffrei Gaimar, *L'Estoire des Engleis*, ed. A. Bell, Anglo-Norman Text society (Oxford, 1960), II. 3359–60, 3627–31, 4232, 4930–32, 5051–2, 5462, 5568–71, 5835–7, 5882, 6076.

[30] Sir Frank Stenton, *Anglo-Saxon England* 3rd edn. (Oxford, 1971), 636.

Harvey, in a justly famous article, referred to Domesday *milites* as 'men of low social status' and as 'humble people no better off than prosperous peasants', she was retaining Stenton's tone and doing so on the back of statistical evidence showing that in terms of income from land some of them may indeed have been no better off than rich farmers (*villani*).[31] But this does not automatically mean that they were 'humble' or 'of low social status'. In whose eyes? To my eye even if some milites were not richer than farmers, they none the less lived in much closer association with their lords than did farmers, and they therefore belonged to a different social group.[32] Of course a great and snobbish aristocrat like Waleran of Meulan who saw himself as 'the flower of knighthood of all France and Normandy', looked at them with condescending eyes. According to Orderic, he dismissed even knights attached to the king's military household as 'country bumpkins' (*pagenses et gregarios*).[33] It may well be that in the eleventh and twelfth centuries many well armed and armoured men were of lower status than such men had been in earlier centuries, because all the evidence suggests that armour and weapons were being produced on a bigger scale than ever before, were becoming more widely available, and hence cheaper— just as the 'Great Re-Building' of c. 1050–c. 1150 (the age of the mass-produced church) meant that stone churches were becoming cheaper.[34] In earlier centuries, say the seventh to ninth centuries, the increasing availability of armour had been on a scale sufficient to create an aristocratic class of heavily armed warriors, and thus to create a gulf between them and the ordinary warrior equipped with spear and shield.[35] But by the eleventh century the further increase in manufacture, itself partly a result of an English government initiative, was such that now it was not only aristocrats who could afford decent armour. As James Campbell put it, 'A countryside whose economy was developing ... could support more gentlemen of the horse and hauberk owning kind than heretofore'.[36] This development may help to explain why it

---

[31] Sally Harvey, 'The Knight and the Knight's Fee in England' *Past and Present*, 49 (1970), 3–43. Careful reconsideration of her statistics still leaves room for the contention that 'many of the smallholdings assigned to Domesday *milites* were insufficient for the support of a heavy cavalryman', Donald Fleming, 'Landholding by *Milites* in Domesday Book: a Revision' in *Anglo-Norman Studies*, xiii, ed. M. Chibnall (Woodbridge, 1990), 97.

[32] J. Gillingham, 'The Early Middle Ages in ed. K. O. Morgan, *The Oxford Illustrated History of Britain* (Oxford, 1986), 158.

[33] OV, vi. 350–1. Not that Orderic alleges that Waleran called them peasants. In Orderic's eyes a *pagensis eques* was quite capable of finer feelings and of meeting the cost of transporting William I's abandoned corpse from Rouen to Caen. ib. iv. 104.

[34] Blair, *Minsters and Parish Churches*, 9–10.

[35] See, e.g. Josef Fleckenstein, 'Zur Frage der Abgrenzung von Bauer und Ritter in his *Ordnungen und formende Kräfte des Mittelalters* (Göttingen, 1989), 307–14.

[36] James Campbell, 'Was it Infancy in England? Some Questions of Comparison',

was that in Aethelred's reign ealdormen and king's thegns came to owe heriots higher than previously. For once high-quality wargear was more widely available, heriots at the traditional levels may no longer have seemed appropriate to men of the highest rank.[37] Indeed the very number of eleventh-century texts on status might be thought to indicate a new level of contemporary concern with social mobility. Hence the eleventh-century legal text which insisted that a ceorl remained a ceorl—a 'mere' freeman—even though 'he possesses a helmet and a coat of mail and a gold-plated sword'.[38]

But this free man with his helmet, sword and hauberk who was not a thegn, should he be thought of as a cultivator, a peasant, albeit a prosperous one? Or, given the emphasis on his military equipment, would it not seem more appropriate to think of him as a knight—even, to use a contemporary English term, as a *cniht*? And if he was a *cniht*, what would this tell us about his status? It has often been claimed to be significant that the English word 'knight' is derived from 'cniht'. Those who downgrade the *miles* similarly downgrade the *cniht*. According to Stenton, 'the Old English *cniht* was essentially the retainer of some greater man' and he noted that the word 'cnihtas' could be used, as in the Anglo-Saxon Chronicle entry for 1083, of 'any miscellaneous body of armed Frenchmen'. Stenton clearly found, as he himself acknowledged, the status of the cniht a difficult question and his discussion of it in *The First Century of English Feudalism* is uncharac-teristically opaque and ambiguous. Thus although he acknowledged that the Anglo-Saxon cniht was a retainer attached to the personal service of a nobleman, that his service might well require him to fight by his lord's side, mounted and otherwise equipped for war, and that his service might be so highly regarded that 'more than one man of this class acquired property which must have given him an important place among the landed gentry of his shire'—none the less, despite all this, Stenton gave no indication that a *cniht* might be a man of aristocratic or gentle birth. Indeed he refers to one group of *cnihts* as 'a group of hunt servants'.[39] This treatment of the *cniht* allowed Sally

---

England and her Neighbours, 1066–1453. Essays in honour of Pierre Chaplais, ed. M. Jones and M. Vale (1989), 12–14.

[37] This, of course, is not to deny that the defence needs of Aethelred's government also acted as a stimulus to change. On the whole subject see N. P. Brooks, 'Arms, Status and Warfare in Late Saxon England', *Ethelred the Unready*, ed. D. Hill (Oxford. 1978), 81–103.

[38] The *Northleoda laga* cited by Richard Abels, *Lordship and Military Obligation in Anglo-Saxon England* (1988), 165.

[39] Stenton, *First Century*, 132–36. Even in the third edition of his *Anglo-Saxon England* (Oxford, 1971), 527, he contented himself with the observation that 'the position of the Old English cniht is a difficult question' and a reference to these pages in his earlier work.

Harvey, explicitly referring back to Stenton, to describe the cniht as the 'unheralded serving retainer'. Similarly David Crouch, while pointing to the similarity between OE *cniht* and 'another French word for knight, *bacheler*,' chose to emphasise the word's 'servile' and 'grubby' associations.[40]

But Stenton's analysis of the Old English cniht is, I think, flawed and this is, in part at least, a consequence of his—equally flawed—belief in 1066 to 1166 being 'The First Century of English Feudalism'. This pushed him into believing that Anglo-Saxon cnihts could not be 'proper' knights, knights in what he called 'the technical sense of the word', because it was an article of faith for him that knights in the technical sense of the word could only exist after feudalism began, i.e. only after 1066. Indeed he suggested that after 1066 the word 'cniht' was sometimes—but only sometimes—used in what he called 'the Norman sense of the word' and as such referring to men of significantly higher status than when used in its old English sense. Thus, he claimed, even an Englishman like the author of the Anglo-Saxon Chronicle was using the word in its 'Norman' sense when he listed *cnihtas* as being among those 'powerful men' who attended the Conqueror's crown-wearings.[41] Clearly if only Stenton could have accepted that cniht in the 'Old English' sense carried the same range of meanings as in the allegedly new Norman sense then his analysis would have been much less tangled. He could have returned to Maitland's position, that the difference between the cniht of the tenth century and the knight of twelfth is one of military tactics.[42] Certainly the word cniht has strong overtones of service and this may have made the chronicler prefer to say 'ridere' rather than cniht when referring to the dubbing of a king's son in 1086. Even so, in preferring 'ridere', the chronicler was not choosing a word that clearly indicated a man of higher status than cniht.[43] The crucial point is that although the Old English cniht served, the service he characteristically rendered was noble service. Indeed the cniht was often a nobleman, a young noble in the service of another lord. The two cnihts (Wulfstan's son and Offa's kinsman) who figure in the *Battle of Maldon* both clearly belong to this category of cniht as young noblemen.[44]

[40] Harvey, 'The Knight and the Knight's Fee', 4; David Crouch, *The Image of Aristocracy in Britain 1000–1300 (1992)*, 130.

[41] Stenton, *First Century*, 132–33, esp. n. 3 for his assertion that post 1066 the word embraced both 'knights in the strict sense and sergeants'.

[42] F. W. Maitland, *Domesday Book and Beyond*, (Fontana edn., 1960), 363. As Abels pointed out Aelfric of Eynsham's choice of the word *cniht* to translate *miles* in the phrase *miles portat gladium* is very striking, *Lordship and Military Obligation*, 138.

[43] Thus in the chronicler's account of Rufus's 1092 campaign in Normandy we hear of one castle being garrisoned with cnihts and others with 'ridere'. ASC 1086, 1092.

[44] *Battle of Maldon* lines 9 and 153.

One noble landowner explicitly referred to as a cniht in an Anglo-Saxon charter was Osulf, a kinsman of Bishop Oswald, who was leased an estate in two manors and for several lives by the bishop of Worcester.[45] This brings me to Oswald's famous letter to King Edgar in which he set out the terms on which he had leased estates, beginning with the requirement that they should perform the *omnis lex equitandi ... quae ad equites pertinent* and continuing with payment of church dues, the obligation to provide horses, to be responsible for building work on bridges and the church, and for helping with the bishops's hunt by erecting hedges and providing spears. Attention has focused on the 'lex equitandi' ever since Maitland wrote, 'For a moment we are tempted to say the law of chivalry'. Although he rejected the temptation he did not unwrite it, and he concluded his discussion of the subject with the comment that 'the day for heavy cavalry and professional militancy was fast approaching when Oswald subjected his tenants to the lex equitandi.'[46]

However, against Maitland, Stenton showed that the law of riding more probably referred not to military service but to the duty of escorting the lord from place to place, and he summed up the services set out by Oswald as a 'very incoherent series of obligations. They range from hunting service to bridge-building and at many times resemble the miscellaneous duties of the 11th century geneat'. (In Stenton's view, the geneat 'was a peasant with some of the characteristics of a mounted retainer').[47] Stenton's dismissive tone may have influenced Christopher Dyer's comment on Oswald's memorandum. 'The services owed to the bishop were confined to escort duties, assistance with hunting, administrative work and so on. Had the bishops really given up hundreds of hides of land in the form of about seventy substantial holdings merely to obtain such relatively minor services?'[48] Escort duty, assistance with hunting and administrative work. Minor services! Of course if we assume that tenth century England was quintessentially a military society, and in consequence all that really mattered were military values and obligations, then all other services are by definition minor. My impression is that most historians of Anglo-Saxon England acknowledge the importance of escort and hunting services but take them for granted, and quickly pass on to discuss—and at some length—

[45] A. J. Robertson, *Anglo-Saxon Charters* (Cambridge, 1939), no. 46.
[46] Maitland, *Domesday Book and Beyond*, 358–63.
[47] Stenton, *First Century*, 125, 129–30. In a footnote, 127 n. 2, he acknowledged that 'the persons who received Oswald's leases form a somewhat aristocratic body'—though without then reconsidering his comparison of the services they owed with those owed by the geneat. For his assessment of the geneat's status, *Anglo- Saxon England*, 473.
[48] Christopher Dyer, *Lords and Peasants in a Changing Society. The Estates of the Bishopric of Worcester 680–1540* (Cambridge, 1980), 43.

the question of whether or not the memorandum deals with military service, and if so, in what form. Since most recent discussions of the memorandum and the lex equitandi have been in books on military obligation and organisation, this focus has been entirely justified. But intentionally or not, this approach has inevitably tended to reinforce the assumption that in Anglo-Saxon society all that really mattered was war. So in the hope of restoring a balance I shall spend a little time elaborating what has been taken for granted.

Richard Abels has already pointed out that the services owed by Bishop Oswald's tenants recall not only, as Stenton had observed, what the author of the eleventh-century treatise known as the *Rectitudines* had to say about the 'geneat's law', but also what he had to say about 'thegn's law'.[49] According to this author, a thegn's services included responsibility for the deer fence at the king's residence and for guarding his lord. According to another eleventh-century text on status, the 'promotion law', characteristic of the prospering thegn was that he rode in the king's household band on his *radstefn*—an unusual term meaning, according to Dorothy Whitelock, that as well as serving in the king's bodyguard he was expected to undertake important errands as a mounted messenger. According to the *Rectitudines* the geneat's obligations varied from estate to estate but characteristic were paying rent, riding and performing carrying services, entertaining his lord, reaping and mowing, cutting deer hedges and maintaining places from which deer may be shot, building and fencing the lord's house, bringing strangers to the village, acting as guard to his lord, taking care of the horses and carrying messages far and near wheresoever he was directed.[50] Clearly there is a core of services common to Oswald's memorandum and to the law of thegns and geneats: these are escort and bodyguard duties, messenger and hunting services. What they have in common is that they bring the person who performs them into close proximity to his lord, and it is this proximity, of course, which was the key to advancement. These, I suggest, were the sorts of services the cniht owed.[51] Who could not see the advantages of owing escort services, of having to be attached at least for a while, to a lord's riding household? Being at the bottom of this particular ladder of service, the geneat's obligations included the more menial ones of reaping and mowing, although whether the prospering geneat performed these services in person or whether he merely took responsibility for getting them done, while giving his personal attention to those duties which brought him

---

[49] Abels, *Lordship*, 153.
[50] EHD, i. 468; ii, 875.
[51] This point was made by Peter Coss, *The Knight in Medieval England 1000–1400* (Stroud, 1993). 12.

closer to his lord, is another matter.[52] The important point here is that some of the services he owed his lord were precisely the kinds of service which the highest in the land owed to the king. According to the Kent Domesday when the king came to Canterbury or Sandwich he was obliged to provide food and drink for the members of a bodyguard provided for him by Alnoth Cild and his like. Alnoth was one of the magnates of Kent, important enough to be taken to Normandy as a hostage in 1067.[53]

Since effective political and military action depended upon the rapid reception and distribution of accurate information, reliable envoys were absolutely vital. One of the scenes in the remarkable South German eleventh-century poem *Ruodlieb* describes this very well and makes it clear that the envoy when surrounded by a large and excited crowd, had to be sufficiently at ease to be able to address a king directly and deliver his message accurately.[54] This is the thegn acting as envoy, the thegn who, in the words of the promotion law, went on his lord's errand to the king.[55] In all manner of circumstances a lord needed men who could speak on his behalf. Thus one of the obligations laid upon Alvric's priest at Milford was that 'he should accompany Alvric to the Hundred whenever he went there.'[56] The geneat, on the bottom rung of this ladder, presumably carried only messages for lesser lords or just routine ones for greater lords.

The tendency for scholarly literature to concentrate on military matters can also be seen in the attention it has given to the Berkshire customs in Domesday Book—an almost exclusive focus on the so-called 5 hide system. But these customs contain other passages which suggest that hunting services were also amongst the characteristic duties of the Berkshire 'tainus vel miles regis dominicus'. His heriot, here referred to as 'relief', could include dogs and hawks as well as arms and horses. These customs also contain the provision that a man who failed to respond to the royal summons to assist at a hunt had to pay a 50

---

[52] As Abels, *Lordship*, 144, suggests some of the services owed by sokemen may have been performed by their dependents.

[53] *Domesday Book. Kent*, ed. P. Morgan (Chichester, 1983), 1b, a reference I owe to the kindness of Ann Williams.

[54] *Ruodlieb*, ed. F. P. Knapp, (Stuttgart, 1977) III, lines 31–70. This envoy is variously referred to in the poem as *missus, nuntius, iuuenis* and *legatus*. The king called him 'Friend' and rewarded him with 3 marks of gold. In terms of the useful distinction made by Mary C. Hill, *The King's Messengers 1199–1377* (London, 1961), pp. 6–7, between 'messengers' and 'envoys', he was clearly an envoy. See also the discussion of *legati regis* by Campbell, 'Some Agents', 212–14.

[55] EHD, i. 468; for an example of the importance of such men see the events of 1065 as described by both the DE version of the Anglo-Saxon Chronicle and the *Life of King Edward*, ed. F. Barlow (2nd edn. Oxford, 1992), 78–81.

[56] Hase, 'The Mother Churches of Hampshire', 60.

shilling fine.[57] We have here a package of duties, escort and bodyguard, messenger and hunting services; those who perform them are on the inside track. If we wish to see the 'lex equitandi' in operation in the eleventh century then we need do no more than look again at a very familiar image—the second scene of the Bayeux Tapestry: Harold in the company of his milites with his hawk and his hounds, and the legend 'Harold dux Anglorum et sui milites equitant ad Bosham'.

The people who perform these kinds of service are not peasants. The eleventh century tract on the reeve sets out in mind-boggling detail the work of villagers, but contains not a word about helping with the hunt.[58] Those who are involved with hunting are associated with their lords, and with the life-style of lords. Hunting was central to the gentle life-style. Thus Offa's kinsman on the eve of Maldon released his hawk only when battle was imminent.[59] Even at his most forlorn the noble travelled with his hunting dog.[60] When one eleventh century author, Andrew of Fleury, described a man as born into rustic ignobility but who rose to higher things and lived nobly to such effect that he was able to marry a wife from a noble family, then the attributes of the parvenu on which he dwelt were his stables, his kennels and his mews.[61] This story is located in Burgundy and told at Fleury, but it is hard not to think that in these respects England and the continent were alike. Living like an earl rather than a monk meant, in Eadmer of Canterbury's words, keeping horses and going hunting with hounds and hawks.[62] As Asser had observed, the 'ars venatoriae' was one of the skills appropriate to noblemen, and the whole art of hunting was, for a model king, second in importance only to the art of governing his realm.[63] The author of the *Life of King Edward*, of course, gives the impression that for Edward the Confessor it was hunting that took precedence. Moreover this author tells us that although in public Edward carried himself as a king and lord, in private and with his followers he behaved as one of them (*ut consocium*). And where if not out hunting—as was his wont, for in the woods and glades with his hawks and hounds were, we are told, his only worldly pleasures—can King Edward have been most

---

[57] *Domesday Book Berkshire*, ed. P. Morgan (Chichester, 1979), 56c.

[58] *Anglo-Saxon Prose*, ed. M. Swanton (1975). 25–27. However one of the reeve's many springtime duties might include seeing to the cutting of a deer-fence.

[59] *Battle of Maldon*, ll. 5–8; and see Gale R. Owen-Crocker, 'Hawks and Horse-trappings: the Insignia of Rank', in ed. Donald Scragg, *The Battle of Maldon AD 991* (Oxford, 1991), 220–37.

[60] *Ruodlieb*, I, lines 44–47.

[61] *Les Miracles de Saint Benoit*, ed E. De Certain (Paris, 1858), 218.

[62] *Memorials of St Dunstan*, ed. W. Stubbs (RS, 1874), 238.

[63] *Asser's Life of King Alfred*, ed. W. H. Stevenson (Oxford, 1959), chapters 75–6. On the centrality of hunting for the 9th century aristocracy see Janet L. Nelson, *Charles the Bald* (1992), 68–9.

typically in private?[64] At least in this respect the Confessor conformed to the conduct of the great king in *Ruodlieb*, who at feasts preferred to talk and joke with fellow huntsmen rather than with rich counts. Mastery of the special skills and language of the hunting field quite as much as great wealth or high birth could take you into the inner circle. This is how the young Ruodlieb won his access to the court of the great king, in a passage strikingly reminiscent of the way Gottfried von Strassburg's Tristan, incognito, won his entree into the court of King Mark.[65] To hunt with a lord was to serve and accompany him in his pleasures. But to share the pleasures of hunting was also to share the dangers. When he was out hunting a lord was at risk, whether from accidents, from the over-boisterous humour of young men at play, or from ambush—as Tristan ambushed and killed Duke Morgan of Brittany.[66] Those who went hunting with their lord had his life in their hands. As a 'iuvenis', Ruodlieb had, the poet claimed, served his lords supremely well, risking his life for them both in war and in the hunt.[67] Those who hunted with the king guarded the king and they were appropriately rewarded. According to the *Constitutio Domus Regis* of c. 1136 knight-huntsmen ('milites venatores') were paid 8d a day and other huntsmen (*catatores*) 5d a day, eight or five times as much as the sergeants who received 1d a day. Also attached to the hunting staff of the king's 'domus' were archers; those who carried the king's bow were paid 5d a day.[68] It was believed that Nigel d'Albini began his illustrious career by carrying the king's bow.[69] Hunting and shooting were central to the interests of the gentlemen of that time. Fishing too? Perhaps not yet, though Ruodlieb made a great impression—and more than once—by his knowledge of how to catch lots of fish and make a game of it.[70] Many centuries earlier Wilfrid had impressed the South Saxons by his fishing expertise, but had not—not at any rate to judge from Bede's earnest phrases—treated it as a sport.[71]

[64] *Life of King Edward*, 18, 62, 78.

[65] *Ruodlieb*, I, lines 92–141, II, lines 1–48. Gottfried von Strassburg, *Tristan*, trans. A. T. Hatto (Harmondsworth, 1960), 78ff.

[66] *Tristan*, pp. 114–16. Cf. Nelson, *Charles the Bald*, 68, 256.

[67] *Ruodlieb*, I, lines 9–10.

[68] *Dialogus*, 135. The best discussion of the hunting establishment of the Anglo-Norman kings is F. Barlow, *William Rufus* (1983), 122–129.

[69] J. O. Prestwich, 'The military household of the Norman kings', *EHR* 96 (1981), 24–5.

[70] *Ruodlieb*, fragments II and X, esp. II line 16 'Sic piscando sibi ludum fecitque sodali.' Perhaps Chrétien's Fisher King was playing a different game; none the less when Perceval encountered him he was fishing mid-stream with hook and line, *Chrétien de Troyes, Arthurian Romances* (Harmondsworth, 1991), 424. At Avignon, in Clement VI's bed-chamber, at Runkelstein and in the Louvre there are fourteenth and fifteenth century paintings showing angling as an aristocratic pursuit for both sexes. My knowledge of these scenes I owe to the kindness of Andrew and Jane Martindale.

[71] Bede, *Historia Ecclesiastica*, iv. 13.

More serious is the fact that hunting became a political issue in the eleventh century. Cnut's law—'It is my will that every man is to be entitled to his hunting in wood and field on his own land'—anodyne though it sounds, may none the less be evidence that hunting rights had become a cause for concern.[72] Were a disturbingly large number of people now joining in the exclusive game, e.g. by keeping staghounds or hawks, the sorts of animals a thegn might, as we know from one surviving will, bequeathe to a king?[73] Serious efforts were made, above all by William the Conqueror in England, to stop people hunting who wanted to do so. According to the Anglo-Saxon Chronicle, when Rufus was facing difficulties at the start of his reign, he tried to attract the English to his cause; he promised to forbid unjust taxes 'and granted people their woods and hunting rights'.[74] Loss of status was reflected in loss of hunting rights. If the numbers of English who survived the Conquest were to play a crucial role in ensuring the continuation of English government, there may none the less have been a period—a generation or two—when for some of them the loss of their hunting rights meant a loss of gentility.[75]

Below the great lords, the earls and king's thegns, there were many layers of society—lesser thegns and the thriving freemen, cnihts and geneats—who shared common interests and pursuits. In the context of a comment on cnihts and milites, Peter Coss has recently observed that English society on the eve of the Norman Conquest 'was very little different from that which prevailed in France.'[76] This I think is right. But at this point we have to add in the ingredient that was different— the institutions of a powerful royal government in England.[77] It is certainly arguable that for a generation or two after 1066 great landowners had more power over their major tenants than had been the case at the end of the Anglo-Saxon era, none the less in the continuing network of shires and hundreds we have an institutional framework which allows us to see the 'lesser nobility' as a gentry— both before and after 1066.[78]

I turn to the word 'gentleman' in the sense of someone who accepts a

[72] EHD, i. 467.

[73] D. Whitelock, *Anglo-Saxon Wills*, no. XI. Cf. above n. 56.

[74] ASC 1087, 1088; followed by William by Malmesbury, *Gesta Regum*, ii. 361.

[75] Although Oliver Rackham, *The History of the Countryside* (1986), 49, 223, believes that in England interest in deer husbandry began with that blessedly familiar landmark, 1066, there seems to be some evidence for both fallow-deer and deer parks before that date.

[76] Coss, *The Knight*, 18. It is worth noting that no eleventh-century French or Flemish author, whether writing in England or about England, appears to feel any need to comment on differences between continental and insular *milites*.

[77] Campbell, *The Anglo-Saxons*, 244.

[78] See John Hudson, *Land, Law, and Lordship in Anglo-Norman England* (Oxford, 1994), 4, 48–60, 227–9, 279, for the county court and tenants' rights after 1066.

code of honour. It was to this code that Edward duke of York appealed when he swore 'on my trouthe and as y am trewe gentilman' and in the light of it that Henry duke of Somerset was accused of lacking 'verray gentilness and the noble honoiur that oweth to be grounded in every gentilman.'[79] Given the common interests and pursuits of the upper reaches of Anglo-Saxon society we might reasonably expect to find them accepting a code of behaviour, if not yet a code of chivalry, none the less a code of the kind described by Karl Leyser:

> a brotherhood in arms which bound together men of high birth, great wealth and assured positions with much more modest warriors, often their vassals, with whom they shared certain fundamental values and rituals. A modern simile might be that of an officers' mess, where there is a common bond between all members, regardless of rank. It would indeed be unwise were the most junior second lieutenant to presume on this and occupy habitually his colonel's favourite armchair but the community of attitudes and status is there none the less.[80]

Obviously values like loyalty and courage and prowess—the values usually called 'heroic' or 'the traditional military values'—are explicitly articulated in many eleventh century sources, the Song of Maldon and the *Encomium Emmae* to name but two. Courage should not lead to rashness. Although it is certainly arguable that Byrhtnoth made a strategically defensible decision when he allowed the Vikings to cross the causeway, the poet clearly disapproved. 'Because of his pride the earl set about allowing the hateful race too much land'[81] In the Bayeux Tapestry William exhorts his milites to prepare themselves for battle *sapienter* as well as *viriliter*. In the *Battle of Maldon* those who stood and fought, of whatever rank, were said to be acting 'in a thegnly fashion'.[82] Kings too were expected to act in a thegnly fashion, displaying the prowess of the warrior as well as of the huntsman. As Karl Leyser pointed out, the Sallustian topos, the *officium militis et imperatoris*, was used by both the Worcester Chronicle and William of Malmesbury in order to praise Edmund Ironside and King Harold.[83] A king like Aethelred the Unready who consistently absented himself from cam-

---

[79] Cited by D. A. L. Morgan, 'The Individual Style of the English Gentleman' in ed. Jones, *Gentry and Lesser Nobility*, 17.

[80] Karl Leyser, 'Early Medieval Canon Law and the Beginning of Knighthood' in his *Communications and Power in Medieval Europe. The Carolingian and Ottonian Centuries*, ed. T. Reuter (1994), 51–2.

[81] *Battle of Maldon*, ll. 89–90. The author of the account of the battle contained in the *Liber Eliensis* (p. 135) also felt that Byrhtnoth set out to challenge the Vikings *nimia animositate*.

[82] *Battle of Maldon*, ll. 232, 294. In twelfth century French those who fought courageously, of whatever rank, were said to be acting like *chevaliers*, *Jordan of Fantosme's Chronicle* ed. R. C. Johnston (Oxford, 1981), ll. 865, 1233.

[83] Leyser, 'Early Medieval Canon Law', 54.

paigns was likely to find himself in serious political trouble.

How far down society were men expected to live up to these military values? Ann Williams has pointed out that each of the five men who utter words of encouragement in the *Battle of Maldon* belong to different ranks of society and has suggested that they speak not as individuals but on behalf of the social groups to which they belong: three for the aristocrats (the earls, king's thegns and median thegns) and two for the freemen, or at any rate for their upper ranks, the geneats and the thriving ceorls. All five share the same sentiments and all share the same fate, dying on the field of battle. Of course this is a poem, a poem with a message, that loyalty, fidelity of lord and man and of both to the king, is what upholds land and people, and if Ann Williams is right, it is a message which is suspiciously neatly arranged, a kind of propaganda.[84] On the other hand there is evidence to suggest that these values were felt as well as encouraged. The majority of the Englishmen mentioned in Domesday Book as having fought at Hastings were freemen.[85] According to the Anglo-Saxon Chronicle there were many from South Eastern England who willing to live and die with Godwin in 1052.[86] According to Orderic, at Bourgtheroulde in 1124 one of the aristocratic rebels observed: 'Odo Borleng and his men have dismounted. A mounted soldier who has dismounted with his men will not fly from the field. He will either die or conquer'. Here the men who had chosen to stand and fight were precisely those whom Waleran labelled 'the country bumpkins'.[87]

There were words for those who lived and fought close by their lords side. One such word was *commilitones*, to which Karl Leyser drew attention in the writings of Widukind.[88] According to Gilbert Crispin, Herluin was outstanding among the *domi ac militiae commilitones* of Count Gilbert.[89] Those who dismounted with Odo were his *commilitones*.[90] In the

[84] Ann Williams, 'The battle of Maldon and "The Battle of Maldon": History, poetry and propaganda', *Medieval History*, 2 (1992), 41–44.

[85] Abels, *Lordship*, 143–4. Doubtless, as Abels has emphasised, we should resist the old idea that Harold's army had been based on a general levy of all able-bodied freemen. The freemen named in Domesday Book would have been lords in their own right, gentleman farmers rather than peasants, and presumably owing honourable services to their own lords.

[86] ASC, CD; however the Worcester Latin version makes it sound as though it was the lithsmen rather than all the good men and true of the south-eastern counties who were willing to commit themselves to Godwin's cause. cf. *Life of King Edward*, 40.

[87] OV, vi. 3501-1.

[88] Leyser, 'Early medieval canon law', 54.

[89] *Vita Herluini*, ed. J. A. Robinson, in *Gilbert Crispin, Abbot of Westminster* (Cambridge, 1911), 87. Cf. Leyser, 'Early medieval canon law', 50.

[90] OV, vi. 350. Orderic emphasises how much Odo was loved by his men. Cf. Ralph of Caen's characterisation of the relationship between Tancred and his *commilitones*. 'Ita enim dicebat in corde suo: "Thesaurus meus sint milites mei"'. Ralph of Caen, *Gesta Tancredi in expeditione Hierosolymitana*, c. 51.

Life of Oswald's account of Maldon we hear of Byrhtnoth's *commilitones*.[91] According to the twelfth-century story—which there are reasons to believe may go back to a contemporary or near-contemporary version— as Byrhtnoth en route to challenge the Vikings

> approached the abbey of Ramsey and sought hospitality and pro-visions from Abbot Wulfsige for him and for his men, he was told that the place would not suffice for such a great multitude, but that provision could be made for him and seven of his men. To this he is said to have replied courteously (*eleganter*): 'The lord abbot knows that just as I have no desire to fight without them so I will not dine without them'.

At Ely he and his men received a better reception and in consequence the estates once destined for Ramsey were granted instead to Ely.[92] In any case whatever may have happened and whatever Byrhtnoth may— or may not have—said, the attitude the story enshrines was well known in Anglo-Saxon England, being attributed to Alexander the Great in both Old English and Latin versions of the apocryphal *Letter of Alexander to Aristotle*.[93] Another word for these men was *socii*. According to the Abingdon Chronicle, at Hastings Harold and his *socii* were killed.[94] The same term was applied by the Worcester chronicle to the men who came to England with Alfred in 1036, and with both Duke William and Count Eustace in 1051.[95] In the Anglo-Saxon Chronicle they are *geferan*.[96] In Gaimar's French, the word is *cumpaignon*. Where their lord went, his companions went too, in one case even remaining in the chamber with a king as he carried out an act of rape.[97]

But it seems to me that the model of conduct to be followed by nobles and their companions in eleventh century England did not involve only the 'heroic' virtues. The word 'thegnly' could also be applied to honourable behaviour at a meeting of the shire, as is clear from the account of a Herefordshire lawsuit in Cnut's time.[98] At such meetings, as well as on the eve of battle, eloquence was clearly regarded as an admirable quality. For example, one of the speakers at the great assembly described in Byrhtferth of Ramsey's 'Life of Oswald' is the *intrepidus miles Alfwoldus*, praised amongst other things as *affabilis eloquio*.

---

[91] *Vita Oswaldi*, p. 456. Translated as 'fellow-soldiers' by Whitelock (*EHD*, i. 917) and as 'personal retinue' by Lapidge in *The Battle of Maldon* ed. Scragg, 54.

[92] *Liber Eliensis*, ed. Blake, Bk II, Chap. 62.

[93] Alan Kennedy, 'Byrhtnoth's Obits and Twelfth-Century Accounts of the Battle of Maldon' in ed. Scragg, *Maldon*, 73.

[94] *Chronicon Monasterii de Abingdon*, ed. J. Stevenson (RS, 1858), i. 483.

[95] FW i. 191, 205, 207. and in these contexts *milites* was evidently a natural equivalent.

[96] *Two of the Saxon Chronicles Parallel* ed. C. Plummer and J. Earle, i. 158–9, 172–3, 176.

[97] Gaimar, *Estoire*, lines 1090, 1525, 1891, 2623–4, 3217, 3227, 5515, 5541, 5549.

[98] Robertson, *Anglo-Saxon Charters*, no. LXXXVIII.

Alfwold was brother of the powerful ealdorman Aethelwine, and son of Athelstan Half-King. Very strikingly, in a long passage which was a conscious digression from his main subject, Byrhtferth portrayed the sons of Athelstan as the model aristocratic family, and he explicitly picked out Aethelwine as the best of the brothers. He praised Aethelwine's urbane eloquence, his upright conduct and his fine appearance. But the quality which Byrhtferth praised above all others was Aethelwine's *mansuetudo*, his gentleness of spirit.[99]

It is worth recalling here what Stephen Jaeger writes on the subject of *mansuetudo* in his 'The Origins of Courtliness'. He calls it the 'civic virtue par excellence' and claims that its gradual filtering through the ranks of the lay nobility marks nothing less than the civilising of Europe. 'Mansuetudo is one of the dominant themes of medieval ethical writings: be slow to anger, tolerate wrongs for the sake of a more distant goal, do not seek revenge'. 'Its opposite vices, wrathfulness and vengefulness, entangle societies and social groups in destructive networks of conflict and make impossible the peace and tolerance necessary for civilized interaction'. Of course showing a calm benevolence to friends and enemies alike involves a degree of dissimulation and in analysing 'mansuetudo', Jaeger quotes Proust's contrast between 'the great gentleman' and the 'smart and wealthy man of the world of finance or big business'. 'Where one of the latter would have thought he was giving proof of his exclusiveness by adopting a sharp haughty tone in speaking to an inferior', the former, 'affable, pleasant, smiling' practised 'an affectation of humility and patience, a pretence of being just one of the audience, as a privilege of his good breeding'. Jaeger argues that this affectation of affability was immensely valuable in the inner circle of advisors and ministers to a king, a situation where a group of ambitious, talented and proud men was thrown together in direct competition with each other for favour.[100]

Byrhtferth of Ramsey was not exactly writing from within the world of the secular aristocracy. Indeed Jaeger—had he analysed any tenth and eleventh century authors writing in England—would probably have said that here was an ecclesiastical author seeking to educate lay society.[101] None the less Jaeger's view of court politics is, it seems to me, entirely applicable to English politics in the crises of 975–8, 1035–6, and 1051–2. As Campbell has pointed out, in the last two centuries of its existence, the nearest Anglo-Saxon England 'seems to have come to civil war was in the crisis of 1051–2; and in that crisis war was

[99] *Vita Oswaldi*, 428–9, 445–6, 465, 467.

[100] C. Stephen Jaeger, *The Origins of Courtliness, Civilizing Trends and the Formation of Courtly Ideals 939–1210* (Philadelphia, 1985), 36–8.

[101] Given his argument that this set of ideals was first developed in tenth-century Germany, he might also have pointed to Byrhtferth's interest in matters German.

avoided.' He emphasises the role of royal violence in maintaining that peace.[102] No doubt. But perhaps a code of aristocratic restraint also played a part in the avoidance of war. In the *Life of King Edward*, the family which dominated the last thirty years of Anglo-Saxon England was praised in terms strikingly similar to those used of Aethelwine by Byrhtferth of Ramsey. Godwin, we are told, was notable for

> his equable temperament ... with pleasing and ready courtesy, polite to all (*iocunda et promta affabilitate omnibus affabilis*) ... He did not discard the gentleness (*mansuetudo*) *he had learnt from boyhood but as though it was natural to him* (my italics), took infinite trouble to cultivate it in all his dealings with inferiors and among equals.[103]

Harold too 'walked in his father's ways, that is to say, in patience and mercy and with kindness to men of good will ... he was endowed with mildness of temper. He could bear contradiction well, not readily revealing or retaliating—never, I think, on a fellow-citizen or com-patriot.' Moreover both Harold and Tostig are described as having 'at times so cleverly disguised their intentions that one who did not know them was in doubt what to think.'[104] In the context of the praise for the courtly and gentle behaviour of Aethelwine and Godwin, it is interesting to note that in the crises in which they were involved, men could be killed and yet that violence was not allowed to escalate into civil war. In 978 King Edward the Martyr was murdered—'yet' in the words of the Anglo-Saxon Chronicle, 'his earthly kinsmen would not avenge him'.[105] Aethelwine's brother Alfwold had one of those trying to recover property from Peterborough Abbey put to death, and in consequence went to Winchester as a penitent. But Bishop Aethelwold ordered him to be given a magnificent reception and treated as a *miles Christi*.[106] Godwin's involvement in the murder of the atheling Alfred in 1036 may have incurred some ecclesiastical censure, but not until fifteen years later was it dragged up to threaten his career. Killing, it seems, was still an acceptable continuation of politics.[107] And yet, despite the

---

[102] Campbell, 'Was it infancy', 5–6. However there were elements of civil war in 1014–16.

[103] *Life of King Edward*, 8–9, especially 'quamque a puero addidicerat mentis man-suetudinem non exuit, verum hanc, ut naturaliter sibi inditam, erga subditos et inter pares eterna assiduitate excoluit'. See pp. 32 and 42 (also ASC 'E') for his restraint in 1052. In Cicero's, *De Officiis*, Ulysses is represented as a model of affability, tolerating insults in order to achieve his ultimate ends, Jaeger *Origins of Courtliness*, 36.

[104] *Life of King Edward*, 48–51, 78–80.

[105] ASC 978.

[106] *Vita Oswaldi*, 446; Blake, *Liber Eliensis*, xii–xiii.

[107] John Gillingham, '1066 and the introduction of chivalry into England' in *Law and Government in Medieval England and Normandy* ed. G. Garnett and J. Hudson, (Cambridge, 1994), 38–40.

killings, civil war was averted—at any rate until the trouble in Nor-
thumbria in 1065 with its consequences for the catastrophe of 1066.[108]
Of course it may also be that the relative peacefulness of England
meant that in 1066 its soldiers were relatively inexperienced in the
exercise and wiles of war when compared with their Norman enemies.
Despite the existence of Old English maxims such as 'a mounted troop
must ride in regular array', the author of the *Carmen de Hastingae Proelio*
clearly regarded the English as naive in military matters.[109]

This brings me to the recent and important paper by Matthew
Strickland in which he suggests that 1066 led to the introduction of
'differing conceptions and conventions of warfare'. He argues on the
basis of passages from William of Poitiers and Orderic that in mid-
eleventh century France there existed a convention of taking prisoners
for ransom in battle and that this operated as a mechanism offering
both financial gain and mutual protection to aristocratic opponents.
Where private war was endemic, where the dominance of the castle
led to protracted campaigns, war—he suggests—became such an integral part of the warrior's existence that such conventions were likely to
develop. Thus 'for the Norman knighthood of 1066, killing on the scale
habitually seen in Anglo-Scandinavian warfare had become a remote
phenomenon'. In Anglo-Saxon sources by contrast he found no
examples of warriors being spared in pitched battle. Vikings often took
prisoners, of course, but only during the course of raids; they did not
look to do so—as, he argues, the French did—in battle. In battle they
preferred to kill. Thus the English experience of war—raiding and
slaving on an occasional basis from a distant kingdom, rather than the
endemic local warfare of France—meant there was no call for such
chivalrous conventions. Paradoxically the very peacefulness of England
inhibited their development.[110]

Similarly I have argued that whereas in England before 1066
aristocrats who found themselves at the mercy of their enemies had to
reckon with the real possibility that they might suffer death or mutilation,
the influence of French conventions in the generations after the Norman
Conquest meant that similarly placed nobles could be increasingly
confident that life and limb would be spared.[111] As Henry of Huntingdon

---

[108] See the explicit comments on the avoidance of civil war in ASC 'D' for 1052 and
in the *Life of King Edward*, 80.

[109] Maxims I, from the Exeter Book, in S. A. J. Bradley, *Anglo-Saxon Poetry* (1982), 347;
The Carmen de Hastingae Proelio, ed. C. Morton and H. Muntz (Oxford 1972) where the
English 'Nescia gens belli solamina spernit equorum' (I.369) are contrasted with the
French, 'Artibus instructi, Franci, bellare periti' (I.423).

[110] Matthew Strickland, 'Slaughter, Slavery or Ransom: the Impact of the Conquest on
Conduct in Warfare' in *England in the Eleventh Century* ed. C. Hicks (Stamford, 1992), 41-
60.

[111] Gillingham, '1066 and the Introduction of Chivalry', 31-55.

put it, there was a sense in which the Norman Conquest had been less cruel than the Danish because—in stark contrast to the bloodbath among the English upper aristocracy which accompanied Cnut's victory in 1016–17—the Normans granted life to the defeated.[112] It is easy to write of 'traditional military values' as though they were timeless and unchanging. Doubtless some of them such as loyalty, courage and prowess were. But in other literally vital ways, matters of life and death, the honour of arms was changing. I have called this change the introduction of chivalry. Was it a change of which contemporaries were aware? Orderic thought so. According to him the matter was debated in 1088 when the rebels in Rochester castle were on the verge of surrender. On one side William II, urged on by his loyal English subjects, wanted to put the 'traitors' to death. On the other many of the great men in William's army argued that he should temper his royal rigour with mercy; having overcome them by his strength, he should spare them by his graciousness (*mansuetudine*).[113] Orderic is late evidence for attitudes in 1088. On the other hand if he is right that the difference between Norman and English law regarding traitors helps to explain the contrasting fates of Earls Roger and Waltheof in 1075–6, then it does seem probable that the difference would have been observed and debated at the time.[114] That such matters were indeed debated, if not in England, at any rate in the eleventh century, is clear from the *Ruodlieb*. Much of the early part of that remarkable work takes the form of an insistent argument against hanging high status prisoners of war. Ruodlieb told a count that he deserved to be hanged from a tree by the calves of his legs,—at which point everyone shouted 'Get on with it then!'—but instead the hero advocated mercy. 'Be a lion in battle but like a lamb when taking vengeance'. Mercy, he advises the king, is the best policy. 'You conquer with lamblike clemency and wisdom better than another could conquer by the sword'.[115]

If the eleventh and early twelfth centuries witnessed changes in the ways in which aristocrats treated each other, it saw also changes in the way they treated 'ordinary soldiers'. The demise of slavery meant that ordinary soldiers who could not afford ransoms were no longer a potential source of profit and in consequence, especially in the closing stages of a combat, were now more likely to be killed than captured. On the other hand once non-combatants were no longer the targets of the slave-raid, with all its attendant terrors and massacres—as they still had been, according to Wulfstan, at the time of Danish conquest—

---

[112] Henry of Huntingdon, *Historia Anglorum*, ed. T. Arnold (RS, 1879), 138.
[113] OV iv. 126–135.
[114] OV ii. 314, 318. Both William of Jumièges and William of Poitiers felt that English political mores were more bloodthirsty than Norman ones.
[115] Ruodlieb, III, lines 5–14; IV, lines 86–7.

then they were distinctly better placed than in earlier centuries. In this respect too the Norman Conquest marked, as Marjorie Chibnall observed, a real watershed in English history, 'the first conquest that did not lead to an increase in the number of slaves'.[116]

By way of conclusion I shall try to locate these developments within a much longer chronological perspective. In many respects the secular values of the late Anglo-Saxon period still seem to be those of the eighth century. Take Bede's story of the Northumbrian noble Imma who was knocked unconscious in a battle against the Mercians. The next day when he was taken prisoner he was afraid to admit that he was a *miles* and passed himself off as a poor peasant (*rusticus pauper*). In consequence he was thrown into chains but, much to his captor's astonishment, the fetters kept falling off. Eventually the Mercian lord whose prisoner he was, questioned him, promising not to harm him if he told the truth about his identity. Imma then confessed to being one of the king's thegns (*ministrum regis*). 'Then', said the Mercian, 'you ought to die because all my brothers and kinsmen were killed in the battle. But I shall not break my sworn promise and so I shall not kill you.' Instead Imma was taken to London, presumably to a slave-market, and sold to a Frisian. Naturally his new master had no better luck with manacles. Eventually the Frisian allowed Imma to go to the royal court of Kent in return for his promise to raise the money for his redemption or return to his master (*dominus*), if he couldn't. In fact he raised the money—apparently he had old connections at the Kentish court—and sent it as promised.[117] The assumptions behind this story are many and all of them, in this context, important. That a noble keeps his promises, even when given to a slave dealer and his owner, even when to do so conflicts with other obligations such as that to seek vengeance for the blood of kinsmen. It shows that battles could result in many high-status casualties. On the Northumbrian side a king was killed; on the Mercian, all the brothers and kinsmen of Imma's aristocratic captor. In consequence a high-status prisoner was likely to be put to death, while a commoner involved in supplying the 'milites' would be spared and sold into slavery.[118] So also in the late Anglo-Saxon period—in which, of course, Bede continued to be read, and in

---

[116] Marjorie Chibnall, *Anglo-Norman England* (Oxford, 1986), 187–8. For further development of this point, John Gillingham, 'Conquering the Barbarians: War and Chivalry in Twelfth-Century Britain', *The Haskins Society Journal* 4 (1992), 70–4.

[117] Bede, *HE*, iv. 22.

[118] In this context it is worth reading the scene in Beowulf where the Swedish king Ongentheow besieged his mortal enemies. All night long he repeatedly threatened them saying that in the morning he would dispatch them, some by the sword's edge, some on the gallows-trees, for the birds' entertainment. Although such threats were also made in the twelfth century they cannot have sent shivers down the spine of a besieged nobleman in quite the same way as they must have done earlier.

English as well as in Latin—we see a world in which men of high status still had reason to fear violent death, a world of slaving and of a sense of honour, the honour of vengeance and of keeping promises. On the other hand, although it was a world which accepted assassination, it had become one in which internal war was avoided remarkably successfully. I have suggested that the courtly and restrained aristocratic values espoused in the 'Vita Oswaldi' and the 'Vita Edwardi' may have had something to do with this—though Northumbrian society probably remained untouched by them. After 1066 the nobles and gentry of England were much more willing to take up arms and go to war against each other than they had been during the last century of Anglo-Saxon England. But after 1066 wars were no longer slave hunts nor did the victors slaughter their high-status enemies in battle, not at any rate until the battle of Evesham in 1265. Nor indeed did they put them to death after battle, not at any rate until after Boroughbridge in 1322. From then on, of course, in what Maitland called 'the ages of blood', we see, in essence, a reversion to pre-Conquest Anglo-Scandinavian practice, different only in that the influence of professional lawyers in the later period meant that when the fighting was over there was usually a rather more elaborate parade of judicial process before the killing began.[119] In these variations in the prevailing ethic of the secular elite over many centuries there is little room for the notion of a straightforward advance from bloodier to more peaceful or humane values.

[119] Gillingham, '1066 and the Introduction of Chivalry', 44–50. However, as Jane Martindale kindly pointed out, my discussion of *diffidatio* in this article clearly overestimates the extent of William of Malmesbury's originality as a consequence of my forgetting the use of the verb *defidavit* in Hugh of Lusignan's *conventum* (see above n. 26). Fortunately although this weakens the case for William's originality, it also strengthens the case for the influence of French political mores and vocabulary in post-conquest England. For further cogent discussion of *diffidatio* see David Carpenter, 'From King John to the first English duke: 1215–1337' in eds. R. Smith and J. S. Moore, *The House of Lords, a thousand years of British tradition* (1994), 28–38.

KNIGHTS, ESQUIRES AND THE ORIGINS OF SOCIAL GRADATION IN ENGLAND

By Peter Coss

READ 24 SEPTEMBER 1994

ONE of the abiding characteristics of the English gentry has been its system of social gradation. And yet the origins of this system have received relatively little attention from historians.[1] Of course, we are well used to describing a local society of knights and esquires in the fourteenth century and of accommodating the addition of gentlemen, albeit with some hesitancy, in the fifteenth. Historians have highlighted the sumptuary legislation of 1363, which points to the gentility of the esquire, and the Statute of Additions of 1413 which gives legal recognition to the mere gentleman. We may understand that neither piece of legislation is to be taken entirely at face value. Nevertheless they are recognised to be significant markers in the evolution of a graded gentry.

As to the highest gradation—that of the knight—we are now on relatively firm ground. We know that knighthood changed significantly in character during the early to mid thirteenth century and that the rise of chivalric knighthood had a profound effect upon the élite mentality of the emergent gentry. Precise numbers continue to elude us, but even here we have a clear trajectory. Numbers were much higher at the beginning of the thirteenth century than was once thought and, indeed, a recent study by Kathryn Faulkner points to the existence of at least four and a half to five thousand knights in the counties during the reign of King John.[2] Numbers were probably already falling by then, and they reached their nadir in the middle decades of the century. They would seem to have risen somewhat in the time of, and as a result of the activities of, Edward I. Nonetheless, both the so-called Parliamentary Roll of Arms and the summonses to the Great Council of 1324 suggest that Denholm-Young's estimate of 1,250 actual knights within the counties at this time was of the right order of magnitude. Knights had become a small élite.[3]

---

[1] The most important recent study has been Nigel Saul, *Knights and Esquires: The Gloucestershire Gentry in the Fourteenth Century* (Oxford, 1981), ch. i.

[2] K. Faulkner, 'The Transformation of Knighthood in Early Thirteenth-Century England', *English Historical Review* (forthcoming).

[3] For the present state of knowledge on the subject see P. R. Coss, *The Knight in Medieval England* (Stroud, 1993), pp. 70–1, 82–5.

The significance of chivalric knighthood would be difficult to over-estimate. Not only did it provide an element of cohesion between higher nobility and local society, but it also inculcated ways of thinking and behaving which penetrated steadily downwards as the English gentry took shape. What is much less understood, however, is the rise of the esquire as a gradation and it is this that I wish to explore in this paper. Our understanding of this important phenomenon tends to rest on one major assumption, *viz.* that esquire takes shape as a residual category to occupy the space left by the retreating knights—to satisfy, that is, the aspirations of those heads of families and collaterals whose forebears had abandoned knighthood. *A priori* this assumption has a lot going for it: it appears to be what happened in much of France; the English government under Edward I and Edward II recruited sub-knightly cavalry from landowners under terms such as *armiger*, often translated as esquire; the sheriffs' returns of men-at arms summoned to the Great Council of 1324 contain many heads of once-knightly families. In Warwickshire, for example, of the nineteen non-knights returned, four were subsequently knighted, six were men whose ancestors had been knights and another five shared the surnames of con-temporary knights.[4]

On closer examination, however, the matter is by no means so clear cut. We do not find in England men described in charters as N of X *armiger* (or variants), as we do in France, comparable to *dominus* N of X *miles*.[5] Does this simply reflect an insularity in diplomatic fashion, or was the esquire as a social grade late in developing in England? Let us begin by looking at the evidence arising out of Edward I's military concerns. The government of Edward I continued the policy of dis-training to knighthood adopted by his predecessor and there are some surviving returns. Over and above this, however, the government repeatedly sought military service from those with £20 or more in income from land and rent and required sheriffs to provide lists of landowners at and above specific income levels.[6] In May 1297 sheriffs were ordered to return the names of all those holding £20 land and rent. In his return the sheriff of Northamptonshire differentiated between categories of landowner. He gave a list of ninety seven knights (two of whom were in fact earls) and another of forty one *armigeri*, as well as

---

[4] *Ibid.*, p. 129.

[5] For a recent summary of the French evidence see David Crouch, *The Image of Aristocracy in Britain, 1000–1300* (London and New York, 1992), p. 169–70. As he points out, English society ceased to be international, except at its highest levels, and this may help to explain the differences.

[6] On this subject see, especially, Michael Prestwich, *War, Politics and Finance under Edward I* (1972), ch. 3.

ladies, clerics holding lay fees, and a list of abbots and priors.[7] The list of forty one *armigeri* comprises a broad range of men. In some ways it is reminiscent of the lists of knights we can put together from legal sources earlier in the century. Moreover, it produces similar problems. In some cases the men are obscure, that is to say they are not revealed by the manorial descents given in county histories nor by the national records revolving around the knight's fee. Nevertheless, the majority are readily identifiable. They include heads of families who have not, or who have not as yet, taken up knighthood. They include collaterals of families whose main line had traditionally furnished knights and who would themselves have provided additional knights in the past. They include heads of some families which had not been knightly, they include men holding by marriage or by succession and they include men who had risen through service. There is, however, one fundamental difference between the 1297 list of *armigeri* and the lists of knights of the grand assize. Inclusion here is founded upon income rather than status. There are likely to have been many men whose actual status in society was similar but who did not reach £20 per annum, or at least not according to the sheriff's returns.

Lists such as these provide a convenient entrée into county society, as Nigel Saul has shown particularly eloquently for contemporary Gloucestershire. But are we entitled to conclude that *armiger* or esquire was in actual use as a status term, as a courtesy title for a non- knight? In a similar writ of 14 January 1300 the government used different terminology, when it instructed sheriffs to summon knights, *scutiferi* and others holding land and rents amounting to £40 per annum to come with horses and arms to Carlisle, and to supply the names to the Wardrobe. This, of course, is not an insuperable problem. If we look for terminological exactitude in medieval sources we are likely, as often as not, to be disappointed. A word can be used in more than one sense, while different words can be used in the same sense.[8] Edward I recruited large numbers of non- knightly cavalry for his wars. One of the several words used to describe such a man was indeed *armiger*, which in origin meant armour-bearer, another was *scutifer* or shield-bearer. To be sure, *armiger* was the Latin word most often used to translate the French *écuyer* or *escuier*. In the present context, however, *armiger* and *scutifer* may mean nothing more than mounted man-at-arms. As the government endeavoured to draw upon a wider spectrum of landowners for its wars, it naturally called upon the sons of knights

---

[7] The sheriffs' returns are published in *Parliamentary Writs*, ed. F Palgrave, 2 vols. in 4 (1827–34), vol. ii, div. 2, pp. 288–90, drawing on BL MSS Harley 1192 fo. 8b and Cott. Claud. C.II fo. 56.

[8] Government departments, for example, differed from one another in their employment of terminology to describe men-at-arms (Saul, *Knights and Esquires*, p. 15).

who were not themselves knighted, upon members of cadet lines of established families and upon members of families which had shed knighthood during the thirteenth century. *Armiger*, with its military connotations, was perhaps a useful term to use for those laymen who came within the royal purview and were not knights. In all probability the king was not employing a social category as such but rather indicating that these men had exercised or could exercise arms as cavalrymen. When addressing people for other purposes in its writs to the localities, the government seems not to have used such terms, suggesting that their usage was as yet restricted. Below knights we hear rather of *probi homines, bones gentz*, even of free tenants.[9] When military service is required, however, it is sought from earls, barons, knights and other men-at-arms, and it is in this context that we find terms like *armigeri* and *scutiferi*.

Esquire, moreover, has other and humbler connotations. As is well known, esquire in origin denoted a knight's servant with particular responsibility for his horses and arms.[10] As the romances show, it was an ideal situation for a trainee or apprentice knight, but many esquires were never in this category; less so, it seems, the farther we go back in time. No doubt there was prestige in having an esquire of high social rank and of obvious breeding. Not all esquires, however, were of gentle stock, even in the thirteenth century. Nevertheless, the personal service involved in such a position could be prestigious and could bring material rewards. In the late twelfth century, for example, Gilbert Picot gave land in Coventry to Robert Calvin, his esquire (*armiger*). Robert was later to convey this property, amounting to three messuages, to Combe Abbey for the good of his soul.[11] One can imagine, moreover, that many men may have been more than content to have themselves described as the esquire of some important personage.

But, however prestigious it might be, esquire was nonetheless a service role. We see this clearly enough in the Statute of Arms of 1292, which attempted to regulate the role of esquires and other servants at tournaments.[12] They were allowed to play only a limited role in the fighting. Significantly, only those esquires who were accustomed to carve their lord's meat were to attend the festivities afterwards, and

[9] See, for example, *Parliamentary Writs*, i, pp. 53–4; ii. 2, pp. 408, 501, 738.

[10] See, in particular, Matthew Bennett, 'The Status of the Squire: the Northern Evidence', in *The Ideals and Practice of Medieval Knighthood*, i, ed. C. Harper-Bill and R. Harvey (Woodbridge, 1986), pp. 1–11.

[11] *The Early Records of Medieval Coventry*, ed. P. R. Coss, British Academy Records of Social and Economic History, n.s., 11 (Oxford, 1986), p. 355.

[12] See Juliet R. V. Barker, *The Tournament in England, 1100–1400* (Woodbridge, 1986), pp. 57–60.

this reminds us, too, that esquire had household connotations.[13]

A neglected source for the study of aristocratic society which reveals the position of the esquire is the forest eyre; in particular the evidence for lordly poaching or, to be technically precise, offences against the king's venison.[14] For example, Gerard de Furnivall was found guilty of poaching in Northamptonshire in August 1283 with William de la Hurst his *armiger*, Robert de Bradefeld and many others of his household (*familia*), while Robert de Beaumond and John de Cawynton, knights, had committed a similar offence with two of their *armigeri* in Sherwood Forest in 1329.[15] Equally significant is an offence committed in the Forest of Dean in 1275 and reported in 1282. Walter de Beauchamp, knight, was convicted of poaching with John de Sapy and others of his household. John, it is said, was at that time Walter's esquire, but is now a knight (*qui tunc fuit armiger eius et modo est miles*).[16] The idea of esquire as trainee knight was clearly very much alive at this date.

But this *cursus* was presumably not open to all esquires, many of whom were on a more menial plane. The role of the esquire as an attendant is revealed in some of the early indentures of retainer. The 1297 indenture between Aymer de Valence and Sir Thomas, lord Berkeley stipulates that Thomas will remain in his household (*mennage*) with his banner and five knights (i.e. himself plus four), receiving £50 yearly, both in peace and war, and robes for his knights. In addition to the fee and the robes, however, there will be food at Aymer's table for himself and the knights, for two esquires (*esquiers*) to serve him and for an esquire for each of the knights.[17] Similarly, in an indenture of the same date between the Earl Marshal and Sir John de Segrave, the latter agreed to serve with fifteen knights throughout the earl's life.

---

[13] For *armigeri* and *esquiers* in households see Kate Mertes, *The English Noble Household* (Oxford, 1988), p. 26 and *Household Accounts from Medieval England*, ed. C. M. Woolgar, British Academy Records of Social and Economic History, n.s., 17–18 (Oxford, 1992–3), part 2, no. 25. See also N. Denholm-Young, *Seignorial Administration in England* (Oxford, 1937), p. 25 and G. A. Holmes, *The Estates of the Higher Nobility in Fourteenth-Century England* (Cambridge, 1957), pp. 58–9. According to Mertes, however, the word most often employed for honourable service in the household from around 1300 was *generosus*, meaning noble or gentle man.

[14] For what follows I am indebted to Jean Birrell who is working on hunting and the royal forests. See, for example, 'Who Poached the King's Deer?', *Midland History*, vii (1982), pp. 9–25 and 'A Great Thirteenth-Century Hunter: John Giffard of Brimpsfield', *Medieval Prosopography* (1994), pp. 37–66.

[15] P.R.O. E32/76 m. 13 and E32/132 m. 16. Many such examples could be cited.

[16] P.R.O. E32/30 m. 14.

[17] *Private Indentures For Life Service In Peace And War 1278–1476*, ed. Michael Jones and Simon Walker, in Camden Society Miscellany xxxii, Camden Fifth Series volume 3 (Royal Historical Society, 1994), no. 4. The timely appearance of this volume, shortly after the presentation of the paper, has allowed me to be sparing in my citations. Unless otherwise indicated, the full text and references are to be found there.

When they were summoned to be with him, there would be *bouche à court* for Segrave and his knights, for the esquires, and wages for the grooms.[18] The position of esquires is once again indicated in the indenture between Aymer de Valence and Robert fitz Pain in 1303. Robert promised to serve at tournaments with two knights from Christmas 1303 to Easter 1305 for £100. He was to have *bouche* for himself and the knights, for his three valets and for two esquires for each of his knights.[19]

The relative position of valets and esquires is something to which we will need to return. Meanwhile, however, let us move forward to the more concentrated evidence from the 1320s. In October and December 1321, writs were sent to the sheriffs summoning knights and *armigeri*. On 7 February 1322 writs were issued enforcing the Statute of Winchester. These referred to knights, *armigeri* and other *homines equites* as well as *homines pedites*. On 20 June 1322 sheriffs were instructed to send all bannerets, knights, *armigeri* and other *homines ad arma equites*, who are not in retinues, to the muster at Newcastle.[20] Does this mean that by this date there was a clear distinction between *armigeri* and men-at-arms, that is to say that the esquire as a social category has actually arrived?

In this respect, the sheriffs' returns are in fact rather disappointing. They responded variously. Some gave a single list, others did not include all categories.[21] Some ran categories together. The three sheriffs of Bedfordshire and Buckinghamshire, Hertfordshire and Essex included all categories but returned the names of *armigeri* and men-at-arms in an undifferentiated list.[22] Of the surviving returns, only those from the sheriff of Oxfordshire and Berkshire listed *armigeri* and *homines ad arma* separately. It is worthwhile examining these closely.

In 1322 the sheriff of Oxfordshire and Berkshire returned the names of eighteen *armigeri* and nine men-at-arms in the former county, and of four *armigeri* and ten men-at-arms in the latter who were not already attached to retinues; that is to say, men who constituted an additional pool of potential cavalrymen which had not been tapped.[23] What was

---

[18] *Indentures For Life*, no. 5. The text is in Denholm-Young, *Seignorial Administration*, pp. 167–8.

[19] *Indentures For Life*, no. 11. For a recent discussion of the early indentures of retainer see also J. M. W. Bean, *From Lord to Patron: Lordship in Late Medieval England* (Manchester, 1989), ch.ii.

[20] *Parliamentary Writs*, ii. 2, pp. 540, 542, 545, 586.

[21] *Ibid.*, pp. 586–95. Original returns survive as PRO C47/1/9.

[22] This is readily understandable, for in a sense all these were men-at-arms. On 24 June 1322 the sheriff of Northants. received a writ ordering him to send the names of the men-at-arms in his county via William la Zouch of Harringworth. He duly returned an undifferentiated list (*Parliamentary Writs*, ii. 2, p. 596).

[23] *Parliamentary Writs*, ii. 2, p. 593.

it that distinguished the *armigeri* from their fellows? Were they the sons
of knights? Had they perhaps recently succeeded to their estates and
would in the course of time become knights, or were expected to
become knights? Or were they the heads of more established families,
of more illustrious ancestry, or more entrenched in the county? A host
of detailed family histories would be out of place here, but the plain
fact is that on all counts these men fail our test. As far as the *armigeri*
are concerned, their knightly credentials are variable and not all were
of ancient stock, and if some of the men-at-arms are newcomers on
the county scene, there were others who were of distinguished ancestry
and the sons of knights. If the *armigeri* tend on the whole to come from
more established families than the men-at-arms, there is nonetheless
considerable overlap. In Oxfordshire, for example, the men-at-arms
include Richard de Abberbury, who belonged to a rising administrative
family and ultimately of peasant stock;[24] but they also included Ralf
des Préaux whose family had held at Great Tew since it was bestowed
upon them by Earl Ranulf III of Chester in 1206 and which had been
settled upon him by his father Sir John des Préaux in 1304. On almost
any reckoning he should have been placed on the upper side of a
dividing line. As far as Berkshire is concerned, in each case against
some of the criteria, the men-at-arms Andrew de Hautot, Peter le
Botiler, Aimery Fettiplace and Richard de Coleshill[25] have a claim to
be considered socially as in as high a bracket as the *armigeri* Philip de
Englefield and Robert Punchardon,[26] let alone the less elevated William

[24] For the Abberburys see Simon Walker, 'Sir Richard Abberbury (c. 1330–99) and
His Kinsmen: the Rise and Fall of a Gentry Family', *Nottingham Medieval Studies*, 34 (1990),
pp. 113–40. For Ralph des Préaux and his ancestors see *VCH Oxfordshire*, xi, p. 229.

[25] Andrew de Hautot seems to have been the son of a knight. He was lord of West or
Great Shenford which had been acquired by Sir Richard de Hautot in 1274. Richard de
Coleshill, lord of Coleshill, was probably the grandson of a knight. The family had held
Coleshill at fee farm of the abbess of Winchester since the late twelfth century. They
were, in fact, something of a professional family, having produced sheriffs of several
counties over generations. Aimery Feteplace, of North Denchworth and Padworth, was
the son of a knight. Philip Feteplace had been MP in 1302. Peter le Botiler, of Basildon
and elsewhere, was the younger son of a knight who had succeeded his brother in 1318.
His brother, Thomas, had been MP for Gloucs. in 1305. Peter le Botiler himself was
returned as MP for Berks. in 1325 but *in loco militis*. Richard de Coleshill and Peter le
Botiler had recently succeeded to their estates and could have been considered as
candidates for knighthood as much as the *armigeri*, if this had been the criterion for the
higher status. For the family histories see *VCH Berkshire*, iii, pp. 415, 459; iv, pp. 239, 290;
519–20. See also the relevant entries in C. Moor, *Knights of Edward I*, i–iv (Harleian
Society, vols. 80–84, 1929–32).

[26] Philip's family had held at Englefield since the twelfth century. He had recently
succeeded Roger de Englefield, MP in 1307 and 1312, who had been living in 1316 (*VCH
Berkshire*, iii, pp. 405–6). Robert was the grandson of Sir Oliver Punchardon who had
married one of the two heiresses to Stanford Bingley and had died in 1282. Robert had
succeeded his father, another Oliver, only recently (*VCH Berkshire*, iv, pp. 111–2). Oliver

Pluckenet and Peter de la Huse.[27] Perhaps there were factors inhibiting full acceptance, the ultimate bourgeois origins of the Fettiplace family for example—Aimery was the grandson of the rich burgess Adam Fettiplace, mayor of Oxford. If the divide between *armigeri* and men-at-arms in these counties is a genuine social divide, which of course it may yet prove to be, then all one can say is that the basis of that divide is by no means clear to us.

However, we must countenance the possibility that separate categories of *armiger* and man-at-arms did not actually exist in the counties, i.e. that the sheriff of Oxfordshire and Berkshire responded in the way he did simply because this is what the writ asked him to do. In this respect, it may be indicative that most of the other sheriffs fudged the distinction. When in 1324 the same sheriff was asked, with the others, to send the names of knights and men-at-arms (*homines ad arma*) in his counties to meet with the prelates, earls, barons and *proceres* at the Great Council to be held at Westminster on 30 May, he responded, once again, precisely under the required headings. In fact, he submitted two lists, one of knights for the two counties and one of men-at-arms, again running the two counties together.[28] Three of the 1322 Berkshire *armigeri* figure among the men-at-arms in 1324, Peter de la Huse alone being missing. Interestingly enough, only two of the 1322 men-at-arms—Richard de Coleshill and Aimery Fettiplace—are now included. Were the others now considered too insignificant, given that these returns were associated with the Great Council? These two men were certainly among the wealthiest of the 1322 men-at-arms. Significantly, the sheriff's returns for Oxfordshire conform to the same pattern. In 1322 he sent the names of eighteen *armigeri* and nine men-at-arms. In 1324, thirteen of the eighteen *armigeri* figure among the men-at-arms, while only one of the nine erstwhile men-at-arms does so.

Does the distinction, then, mean anything? After all, as we have seen, in 1322 most of the sheriffs ran the categories together. Sheriffs often tended to obey writs as literally as possible. When in 1324, by

---

Punchardon, junior, and Roger de Englefield had been summoned to military service by Edward I on a property qualification, but then so had Richard de Coleshill senior and Thomas le Botiler. See *Parliamentary Writs*, i, pp. 485, 544, 583, 795.

[27] The Pluckenets had held at Chipping Lambourn since the twelfth century. William had succeeded his father in 1311 and had proved his age in 1319 (*VCH Berkshire*, iv, p. 253). They may have been related to the illustrious knight, Sir Alan Pluckenet, whose landholding stretched across seven counties. Peter de la Huse certainly had a wealthier relative, in Sir John de la Huse. He had land in Hampshire as well as at Finchampstead in Berkshire where Peter's father and John had married the two heiresses, daughters of William Banister, by 1299. Peter had succeeded his father back in 1306 (*VCH Berkshire*, iii, pp. 243–4). See also the relevant entries in Moor, *Knights of Edward I*.

[28] *Parliamentary Writs*, ii. 2, pp. 656–7, where they are given solely, but incorrectly under Berks.

contrast, they were asked for lists of men-at-arms they sent lists of men-at-arms, but these included a majority of men listed in 1322 as *armigeri*.[29] The sheriff of Warwickshire and Leicestershire, however, sent a list not of men-at-arms as in the writ but of *armigeri*. Did he consider that for all intents and purposes the terms were identical? The sheriff of Sussex, having listed the knights in his county, gives the names of other men-at-arms or *armigeri* (*nomina aliorum hominum ad arma vel armigerorum*). Was he aware of any distinction?[30]

Two more sheriffs acted distinctively. The sheriff of Lincolnshire returned a list of *armigeri* who exercise arms (*qui exercuerunt arma*) while the sheriff of Worcester returned, in addition to those who are knights, the names of those in his county who *had* exercised arms (*qui exercuerunt arma*). If we can extrapolate from this, it would seem that the sheriffs were returning not men who arguably ought to go to war, by reason of their social position, but in fact those among the most substantial landowners, below the level of knights, who were or who had been militarily active; in 1322 they had returned a somewhat broader group. But the designations were not significant. They seem not to have corresponded with any precise status divisions within the counties.

But, notwithstanding the way the sheriffs reacted, the government itself must have meant *something* by these categories. Moreover, a writ in French sent out in December 1324 ordered the selection of *chivalers, esquiers & autres gentz darmes* for service overseas in the spring of 1325.[31] At this time we hear a lot about hobelars, lightly armed horseman, e.g. *hobelours mountez a chivalx*.[32] These, however, were recruited on a different basis and it seems most unlikely that they are the men-at-arms referred to in the sources under discussion. Moreover, non-knightly cavalrymen drawn from county landowners can hardly have varied much in terms of the military equipment they brought or in terms of their military training. Perhaps the clue to what lay in the government's mind is contained within the 1322 writ itself. The sheriffs were asked to send the names of those who were not already serving in retinues.

Not all of the sheriffs, however, did as they were asked. The sheriff of Rutland gave information on twenty eight individual men, explaining their circumstances as he knew them and what action he had been able to take in pursuit of the writ.[33] He included men who were actually

---

[29] The writs and the sheriffs' returns are printed in *Parliamentary Writs*, ii. 2, pp.636–657. The originals survive as PRO C47/1/10.

[30] The sheriff of Norfolk and Suffolk, however, returned for both of his counties lists of *armigeri ad arma* and lists of other men-at-arms.

[31] *Parliamentary Writs*, ii. 2, p. 687.

[32] *Ibid.* p. 689. For the hobelars see Philip Morgan, *War and Society in Medieval Cheshire 1277–1403* (Manchester, 1987), pp. 38–48.

[33] *Parliamentary Writs*, ii. 2, pp. 594–5.

serving in retinues as well as those who were not. Of the twenty eight, ten are given as knights, one is given as a cleric and six are given as *armigeri*. Against the other eleven there is no designation.

As we have come to expect by now, the *armigeri* are of varying backgrounds, and there is no need to rehearse this. In the course of his comments, however, the sheriff of Rutland conveys some important facts. Two of the six *armigeri* were actually currently serving in retinues. John de Wittlebury was in the retinue of Ralph Basset of Drayton, while Robert de Helewell was in the retinue of William la Zouch of Harringworth.[34] Moreover, a third *armiger*, Robert de Sheldon, elderly now and ill, is said to hold his land of the gift of Ralph Basset, one of the lords of retinues already mentioned. Everything suggests that he was a life retainer. His 100s land at Exton is precisely of the right order in this context.[35] These six, however, are probably not the only *armigeri* in the sheriff's return. The return was presumably made on the basis of hundreds and all six are from Alstoe hundred.

The returns from the other hundreds are less punctilious over designations. In all, eleven men are without designation. They fall, however, into two categories. The first includes Ralph Basset and William la Zouch themselves, together with three other comparatively elevated figures.[36] Of the remaining six men, all but one are said to be currently in retinues. We are not told anything of their status. However, there are indications that some of them at least were not casually recruited men-at-arms. Brice le Daneys is said to be over seventy years old. It seems hardly likely that he would have been with John de Segrave on a casual basis.[37] He sounds like a long-standing retainer. Thomas de Greenham had latterly been in the wardship of Roger de Northburgh, bishop of Coventry and Lichfield, who had recently arranged his marriage.[38] His choice of retinue is thus readily explained.

---

[34] John was lord of Wittlebury while Robert held a manor at Whissendine (*VCH Rutland*, ii, pp. 158, 160).

[35] This, for example, was the sum Aymer de Valence contracted to provide for life for John Darcy from his manor of Gainsborough, Lincs., in their indenture of 1309. See below p. 165. The other three named *armigeri* were Richard de Harington of Whissendine, who is said to be infirm and unable to work, John de Bussy, lord of Thistleton, and Bernard son of John de Brus of Exton. Richard de Harington was the son of Sir John de Harington, lord of Glaston (*VCH Rutland*, ii, p. 183). Also included in the sheriff's return, he was said to be over eighty.

[36] They are Edmund de Passelewe, the royal justice who was lord of Empingham, and two barons of parliament, John la Ware, lord of Woodhead and Great Chasterton, and John de Crombwell, lord of Essendine. The latter, the sheriff tells us, was serving in the royal retinue. Ralph Basset, Edmund de Passelewe and John la Ware were all summoned to the Great Council from Rutland as knights in 1324 (*Parliamentary Writs*, ii. 2, p. 649).

[37] Brice held the manor of Tickencote (*VCH Rutland*, ii, p. 276).

[38] Thomas is said to hold around £10 land in Ketton. His father had died in 1316 and his wardship was eventually sold to Bishop Roger de Northburgh who married him to

It would seem that Thomas was in fact a member of the bishop's household. The young Richard Seintliz, who had just succeeded to his inheritance, may similarly have been in the Segrave household.[39]

A case can be made, then, for suggesting that the distinction in the 1322 writ (and in some of the sheriffs' returns) between *armiger* and man-at-arms took its meaning from the retinues. That is to say, *armigeri* were distinguished from other men-at-arms precisely because they were either regular members of households or they had been formally and individually retained. Could it be that the *armigeri* the government hoped to recruit via the sheriffs were men who had formerly participated in retinues or whose fathers had done so and who were therefore expected to follow suit? Did it mean by men-at-arms, in contrast, those who participated on a more ad hoc basis—for example, they were among those whom retainers brought with them to war?

The early indentures of retainer can be used to give support to this idea. There is, however, an immediate problem over terminology. The indentures are, for the most part, in French, and the word most commonly used for a sub-knightly retainer, is not esquire, the expected vernacular equivalent of *armiger*, but valet (*vadlet, vallet*).[40] In 1297, for example, Sir John Bluet retained William Martel, *seon vallet*, for life.[41] In addition to his fee, William was to receive two robes annually and to be provided with food and drink as a *gentil homme*, with two grooms. William undertook to serve John loyally as a valet in the current war between the kings of England and France and in any future war. Similarly in 1309 Aymer de Valence, earl of Pembroke retained John Darcy for life in peace and in war.[42] He was to receive his sustenance and suitable robes as do the earl's other *valletz*, together with his horse and armour in time of war. John was to receive 100s rent, but on taking up knighthood Aymer was to enfeoff him of thirteen and a half marks in land and rent when he will serve as one of the earl's

---

Alice, daughter of Roger de Sulgrave of Helpston, Northants. Thomas obtained seisin, in fact, in 1322 (*VCH Rutland*, ii, p. 256).

[39] Richard is said to have around £15 land in Seaton and to be in the retinue of Sir John de Segrave. He had succeeded his father William by the summer of 1321 (*VCH Rutland*, ii, p. 215). The others without designation were: Walter de Yarmouth, said to hold £10 land in Cottesmore and to be in the retinue of Bernard de Brus (lord of Exton); John Hacluyt, said to be in the royal retinue, who held the manors of Braunston and Leighfield in Oakham and was keeper of the forest of Rutland (*VCH Rutland*, i, p. 254, ii, pp. 16, 33); and John de Boyvill who held the manor of Ayston (*VCH Rutland*, ii, p. 59).

[40] The problem is compounded by the translation of valet as yeoman in calendars and the tendency for historians to follow suit.

[41] *Indentures For Life*, no.7.

[42] *Indentures For Life*, no. 15. See also no. 17.

bachelors.[43] In these examples then, valet has both household and military connotations, and a natural progression is indicated from valet to knight.

Valet was undoubtedly a term regularly employed by the magnates to denote retinue membership. Among the muniments of Earl Thomas of Lancaster noted after the battle of Boroughbridge was a list of the names of the *Contes, Barons, Chevalers* and *Valletz* of his retinue.[44] Indentures, moreover, sometimes specifically mention valets in the provision of service. In 1311, for example, Sir Nicholas Hastings contracted to stay in the service of Ralph, lord FitzWilliam 'for the term of their two lives'. He was to come with two valets and ten grooms when summoned in time of war, with the two valets and only four grooms in time of peace.[45] In 1318 Hugh Despenser the younger retained Hugh de Neville of Essex with two additional knights and seven *vadletz*.[46]

When we move back from the vernacular into Latin, even in documents which refer to the same milieu as the indentures, for example household accounts, we find ourselves back with *armiger*. The surviving household account of Thomas of Lancaster, for 1313-14, speaks of livery given to seventy knights and twenty eight *armigeri* as well as clerks, officials, grooms, archers, minstrels and carpenters.[47] Administrative officers often seem to have been called valets. Thomas of Lancaster gave a life-grant to William Galon, valet, in 1319. William was no less a person than the earl's receiver at Embleton who had custody of Dunstanburgh Castle.[48] Thus a valet can be called an *armiger* and it certainly looks as though this was the case in the sheriffs' returns of 1322.

What, then, was the relationship between the terms valet and esquire? The latter was occasionally used in place of valet in indentures of retainer. When Henry, earl of Lancaster, retained Philip of Castle Martin for life in 1333, he undertook to treat him *aussicom un autre des esquiers le dit counte*.[49] Similarly, when Ralph Basset of Drayton retained

[43] The Darcy situation does not appear to have been in any way unusual. Sir Bartholomew de Enfield who contracted with the earl of Hereford in 1307, had made a previous agreement with him before he became a knight and by which he received a life-interest in an estate. See Bean, *From Lord to Patron*, p. 67 note 14, citing *CPR 1292–1301*, p. 84.

[44] Printed in Holmes, *Estates of the Higher Nobility*, pp. 140-1.

[45] *Indentures For Life*, no. 19.

[46] *Indentures For Life*, no. 29.

[47] J. F. Baldwin, 'The Household Administration of Henry Lacy and Thomas of Lancaster', *EHR*, xlii (1927), pp. 198-9.

[48] Homes, *Estates of the Higher Nobility*, p.71; J. R. Maddicott, *Thomas of Lancaster 1307–22: A Study in the Reign of Edward II* (Oxford, 1970), pp. 14, 21.

[49] *Indentures For Life*, no.35.

Philip de Chetwynd for a year's service in 1319, he undertook to treat him as he did his other *esquiers*. However, should Philip take the order of chivalry within the year, i.e. become a knight, he would take service with Ralph before any other, but on renegotiated terms.[50] The words appear to be used synonymously when Hugh le Despenser the younger retained Sir Hugh de Neville in 1318. The two knights bachelor and seven *vadletz* with whom Neville undertook to serve are referred to as his *bachilliers et esquiers avantditz* in the subsequent clause giving *bouche à court*.[51]

Like esquire, valet had strong service connotations. It, too, could be employed on a relatively low level. The 1297 indenture between Aymer de Valence and Thomas of Berkeley refers, in addition to the latter's knights and their esquires, to three *vallez de meyster* who carry the packs (*males*) of Thomas and his knights.[52] And this example does not stand alone. In 1328 Henry lord Percy retained Ralph lord Neville with twenty men-at-arms, of whom five were to be knights.[53] He was to receive robes and saddles for himself and his knights. In time of war, he and his *gentiz gentz* would eat in hall with six *vallez de mester*. What is interesting here is that these *valets de mestier* seem to be below the level of gentility. We cannot expect uniformity in terminology and usage. Perhaps they would be called grooms (*garcons*) elsewhere. In preference, however, and especially where it was used without qualification, the word valet was employed to denote a man of some significance.

That significance was most often derived from a vertical association with a higher lord.[54] Its origin was the Latin *valletus*, meaning 'little vassal'.[55] This word is found in the mid-thirteenth century to denote non-knightly household retainers.[56] True enough, it was also used regularly by the Crown in the thirteenth century for those who ought to be knights or who were avoiding knightly status, and it was later used to describe members of parliament for the counties who were not knights and should, therefore, receive expenses at a lower rate.[57]

---

[50] *Indentures For Life*, no. 30. See also M. C. Prestwich, 'An Indenture between Ralph, lord Basset of Drayton, and Philip de Chetwynd, 4 March 1319', *Stafford Historical and Civic Society, Transactions* (1971–3), pp. 18–21. I am most grateful to Professor Prestwich for supplying me with a copy of this publication.

[51] *Indentures For Life*, no. 29.

[52] *Indentures For Life*, no. 4.

[53] *Indentures For Life*, no. 33.

[54] For a letter of receipt by Roger de Merdesfen, *valletus* of Aymer de Valence, dated 7 June 1303, see PRO E213/13. I owe this reference to the kindness of Mr Adrian Ailes.

[55] Crouch, *The Image of Aristocracy in Britain*, pp. 164–6.

[56] See, for example, E. F. Jacob, *Studies in the Period of Baronial Reform and Relellion, 1258–67*, Oxford Studies in Social and Legal History, viii (Oxford, 1925), pp. 127–8, citing *CPR 1266–72*, pp 146–7.

[57] *Crown Pleas of the Wiltshire Eyre*, ed. C. A. F. Meekings, Wiltshire Archaeological and

Although the terms were sometimes treated as synonymous, valet was often employed in preference to esquire to denote a man who enjoyed some social status, perhaps because the latter had more obvious, or more exclusive, service connotations. But equally, valet was employed as a term of convenience; it was not a title or a social rank.

By contrast, the term man-at-arms was employed more generally. In 1319, for example, William lord Latimer agreed to serve Earl Thomas of Lancaster for life with forty men-at-arms (hommes darmes).[58] Clearly the status of the men-at-arms would vary, and ten of those who were knights (the number is not stipulated) were to receive robes and saddles from the earl. In 1317 the same earl contracted with Sir Adam Swillington and Sir John Eure. In each case they were to come with ten men-at-arms in time of war. The ten had to include three knights, and these were to receive robes and saddles. All were entitled to bouche à court.[59] In 1327 Henry, earl of Lancaster made a similar agreement with Sir Philip Darcy who was to bring seven men-at-arms.[60] The indentures between magnates and the king for specific campaigns were also generally for service with a specified number of men-at-arms.[61] Men-at-arms then, in such documents, encompasses men who were knights, those who were otherwise known as or retained under the name of valet or occasionally esquire, and presumably men who were neither.

In short, the word armiger, traditionally translated as esquire, could equally be synonymous with valet. It certainly seems to be the case that the Latin term had a wide and by no means consistent usage; it was used as approximation, one might say, or as a catch-all. We cannot assume that when we meet armiger in our documents we are meeting the esquire as a social rank. Indeed, all the indications are that we are not. I am not suggesting by this that no social distinctions existed below the level of knight, but only that there is as yet no general rank of esquire.

Thus far, I have spent a good deal of time attempting to prove a negative. So when did the esquire emerge as a social gradation?. The inevitable bench mark is the sumptuary legislation passed by parliament in 1363, which attempted to regulate the apparel which the different

---

Natural History Society, xvi (Devizes, 1961), pp. 31, 38–9, Helen Cam, *Liberties and Communities in Medieval England* (Cambridge, 1944), p. 239.

[58] *Indentures For Life*, no. 31. The text is in Holmes, *Estates of the Higher Nobility*, pp. 122–3.

[59] *Indentures For Life*, nos. 24, 27.

[60] *Indentures For Life*, no. 32.

[61] See, for example, M. C. Prestwich, 'Cavalry Service in Early Fourteenth-Century England', in *War and Government in the Middle Ages: Essays in Honour of J. O. Prestwich*, ed. J. Gillingham and J. C. Holt (Bury St Edmunds, 1984), pp. 156–7.

social strata should be allowed to wear. We find two levels of esquire. There were those who were on the same level economically as knights and their immediate families, who were to be treated in broadly the same way, and there were other esquires and all manner of gentle men below the estate of knight (*esquiers & toutes maneres de gentils gentz desouth lestat de chivaler*). In other words the legislation was based upon status groupings but was forced to recognise that these cut across actual income levels. Esquire is now a social position.

There is other evidence about this time confirming the emergence of the esquires. The Scrope-Grosvenor case in the Court of Chivalry c. 1385 makes reference to Sir Robert Laton's lost roll of arms dating from c. 1370 which included esquires as well as knights. This was taken by Denholm-Young to signal the heraldic arrival of the esquires.[62] The evidence is fragile and the reality a good deal more complicated than this.[63] Some sub-knightly landowners were certainly employing heraldic devices on their seals well before this date. But clearly 1370 is another convenient *terminus ad quem* for the social emergence of the esquire.

The evidence of sepulchral monuments also points in this direction. At Lambourn in Berkshire, for example, there is a brass of two figures with an inscription identifying them as John Estbury, *armiger*, founder of St Mary's chantry, who died 25 October 1372 and Thomas his son [see plate]. The date of the latter's death is not filled in except that it is post 1400.[64] Once again, this evidence is from later than the date concerned; nevertheless, it was understood that John Estbury had enjoyed the status of esquire and that this was something to be celebrated.

Moving forward a few years, the poll tax of 1379, being a graded tax, naturally gives designations. The preamble distinguishes between three types of esquire, each to be taxed at different rates. The esquire who by estate ought to be a knight pays 20s, the esquire of lesser degree 6s 8d and, finally, the esquire not in possession of lands, rents or castles who is in service or has been armed 3s 4d. We are reminded that esquire still retains some of its service connotations even though it has also gone, so to speak, 'out of court'. To take one county as an example, the fragmentary returns for Warwickshire yield the names of nineteen esquires or *armigeri*.[65] One of them, Thomas de Bishopston, pays 20s.[66]

---

[62] N. Denholm-Young, *Country Gentry in the Fourteenth Century* (Oxford, 1969), p. 5.

[63] See Saul, *Knights and Esquires*, pp. 20–3.

[64] Thomas was living in 1408 and the date of the brass is thought to be c. 1410. See W. Lack, M. Stuchfield and Philip Whittemore, *The Monumental Brasses of Berkshire*, Monumental Brass Society (1993), p. 86. See also *VCH Berkshire*, iv, p. 235.

[65] PRO E179/192/23 & 24. I am most grateful to Professor R. H. Hilton for the loan of his transcript.

[66] For the Bishopstons see *VCH Warwicks.*, iii, 261; iv, 223, and v, 80. Heads of this family had enjoyed knighthood from the early thirteenth century through to the time of

Seven pay 3s 4d.[67] The majority, however, pay at the rate of 6s 8d.[68] These are the standard esquires as it were. A few of them are heads of families which were once knight-bearing: John de Langley of Ettington,[69] George de Castello of Withybrook,[70] John de Clopton[71] and Robert Turvill of Wolston.[72] Most of them, however, were not. Annabel Comyn was the widow of an esquire, John Comyn, the last of a sub-knightly family which had long held a small manor at Newbold Comyn.[73] Thomas de Merington of Little Lawford belonged to a family of mercantile origins,[74] while William de Catesby of Shuckburgh was of peasant stock.[75] Roger Harewell of Wooton Wawen was described as

Sir John, who was living in 1337. Whether Thomas himself became a knight is unclear. The line ended with Sir William who died in 1447.

[67] They are: Edmund Compton of Stratford, Philip de Aylesbury [D(a)lusb(ur)y] of Lapworth, John Fulwode of Tanworth, Richard Kynton of Compton Wynyates, Richard Gay of Halford, John Bretford of Rugby and Thomas de Clifton of Stretton under Fosse.

The preamble's statement that the esquires at this level were without land or rents should not be taken literally. Men who were presumably the forebears of Richard Gay and John Bretford contributed to the 1332 subsidy at Halford and Rugby respectively. The Fulwodes held a manor in Tanworth (see below), while Philip of Aylesbury was a member of the family who held a manor at Lapworth and may have been its head who bore that name (*VCH Warwicks.*, v, p. 110). The status of these men can hardly have been very different from that of the men who follow.

[68] The sum paid by Robert Turvill is lost, but it was most probably 6s 8d.

[69] This is almost certainly the man later known as John de Langley of Atherstone-upon-Stour. He was the grandson of Sir Edmund de Langley, and the head of a family no longer knight-producing and now in straightened circumstances. See P. R. Coss, *The Langley Family and its Cartulary: A Study in late medieval 'Gentry'*, Dugdale Society Occasional Papers, 22 (1974), pp. 19–20.

[70] His ancestor, William de Castello, had succeeded the knight Nicholas fitz Nicholas at Withybrook but had respite of knighthood himself in 1256 (P. R. Coss, *Lordship, Knighthood and Locality: A Study in English Society c. 1180–c. 1280* (Cambridge, 1991), p. 263; *VCH Warwicks.*, vi, pp. 265–6. A later Sir William de Chastel appears on the Parliamentary Roll of Arms bearing *goules a ii barres e un quarter en lun quarter un chastel de sable*.

[71] John de Clopton of Clopton in Stratford upon Avon was the son of Walter de Clopton, himself the son of Walter de Cockfield who had acquired the manor from the eponymous Cloptons. He may have been related to them, although the families bore different arms. Robert de Clopton had been a knight in the early 13th century, but the family (with a small manor) had ceased to be knight-bearing (*VCH Warwicks.*, iii, p. 262; Coss, *Lordship, Knighthood and Locality*, pp. 236, 258).

[72] This branch of the Turvill family, which had held at Wolston since 1240, was about to become extinct. Sir Richard de Turvill, who was described as of Wolston in 1309, may have been its only knight. In 1314 he was discharged of the office of coroner as infirm (*VCH Warwicks.*, vi, p. 275). According to the Parliamentary Roll of Arms he bore *goules a iii cheverons de veer*, while Sir Nicholas de Turvill of Pailton bore *goules a ii cheverons de veer*.

[73] *VCH Warwicks.*, vi, p. 158.

[74] Coss, *Early Records of Medieval Coventry*, pp. xl, xlii; R. A. Pelham, 'The Early Wool Trade in Warwickshire and the Rise of the Merchant Middle Class', *Transactions of the Birmingham Archaeological Society*, lxiii (1944), pp. 53–4; *VCH Warwicks.*, vi, pp. 188–9.

[75] His father was John de Hull of Flecknoe, two miles north of Catesby, which name

keeper of the estates of the Wootton Wawen Priory in 1373.[76] The others were Henry Standyche of Clifford[77] and Thomas Rich[78] and Henry Sidenhale, both of Tanworth in Arden. In short, the esquires of 1379 were of very mixed ancestry. However, some (probably rather loose) differences in degree and service connotations notwithstanding, their existence as a social rung is now open to view.

Once again, we can set this evidence against that from indentures of retainer. During the 1330s to 1350s esquire and valet continue to co-exist. In 1337 William son of John de Roddam of Northumberland agreed to serve Henry, lord Percy with 'a sufficient companion' when summoned in peace or in war. During the latter he and his companion were to receive robes like other valets.[79] Valet continued to be used of administrative officers in particular. The roll of the liveries of cloth and fur made in the household of lady Elizabeth de Burgh in 1343 includes ninety three esquires. One of these is John de Hertford, called elsewhere *notre cher vallet Johan de Hertford notre seneshal de Clare*.[80] As late as 1356 the Black Prince ordered £10 to be given yearly for life to his valet, William Greenway, his chamberlain of Chester, whom he had retained in peace and war.[81]

On the other hand, the word esquire was coming increasingly to the fore. In 1353 Sir John de Sully was retained by the Black Prince for life, to serve with an esquire, both of them enjoying *bouche à court*.[82] In 1365 the prince retained Sir Geoffrey de Warburton with two esquires for peace and war. Two years later, he retained Sir Baldwin de Bereford

---

he seems to have assumed. The family's rise was through the usual means of good marriage, legal training and administration. See J. B. Post, 'Courts, councils and arbitrators in the Ladbroke Manor dispute, 1382–1400', in *Medieval Legal Records*, ed. R. F. Hunnisett and J. B. Post (1978), pp. 290–1, and N. W. Alcock, 'The Catesbys in Coventry: A Medieval Estate and its Archives', *Midland History*, xv (1990), pp. 1–4. William acquired his manor at Shuckburgh in 1353 (*VCH Warwicks.*, vi, p. 217).

[76] He acquired property at Wootton Wawen through marriage, and was succeeded by his son whose effigy is in the church there. According to Dugdale, Roger was the brother of John Harewell, bishop of Bath and Wells (*VCH Warwicks.*, iii, p. 198; Sir William Dugdale, *The Antiquities of Warwickshire* (1656), rev. W. Thomas (1730), ii, p. 809).

[77] Clifford is Ruin Clifford near Stratford, but Henry's ancestry is obscure. He sealed heraldically in 1383 (Gregory Hood Deeds, Shakespeare Birthplace Trust, no. 479). His seal carried a saltire with a border engrailed.

[78] Occasionally, the tax returns lapse into the vernacular so that Thomas Rich is described not as *armiger* but as *squier*. Similarly we find Thomas *of* Bishopston and John *of* Clopton.

[79] *Indentures For Life*, no. 36.

[80] Holmes, *Estates of the Higher Nobility*, p. 58. See also *ibid.* pp. 68–70 for other examples from the Bohun estates.

[81] *Register of Edward the Black Prince*, ed. M. C. B. Davies, 4 vols. (1930–33) iii, pp. 475–6. See also Bean, *From Lord to Patron*, p. 60.

[82] *Indentures For Life*, no. 41. See also *Register of the Black Prince*, iv, p. 91, for Sir Edmund de Manchester who was similarly retained with an esquire two years before.

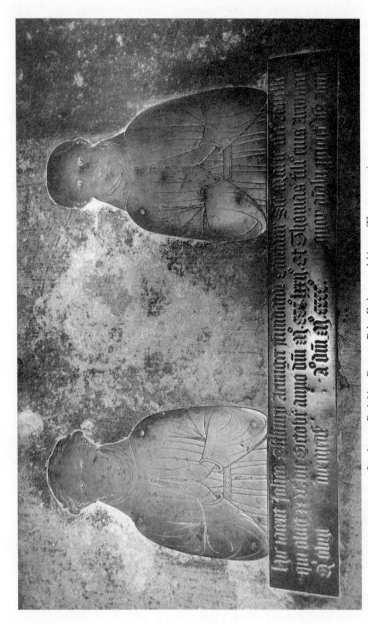

Lambourn, Berkshire: Brass to John Estbury and his son Thomas, esquires

who was to find two sufficient esquires in time of war.[83] In other words we are finding the word esquire where valet would once have been preferred. Esquire could now be used as a title, as when Humphrey de Bohun, earl of Hereford, retained William de Stapelton, *nostre bien ame esquier*, in 1370, or Thomas de Beauchamp, earl of Warwick, retained John Russell, esquire, in 1372.[84] From their beginning John of Gaunt's indentures were with esquires as well as knights.[85] The first of his esquires for whom an indenture survives is Nicholas Atherton. This dates from March 1370. There are three more from 1371 and no less than twenty three for 1372. Clearly, however, the status of men like Atherton extended beyond the household. They formed the nucleus of the army of knights and esquires which Gaunt contracted to provide for the king's wars.[86] Gaunt's Register also shows letters of protection being granted to men styled esquire as well as to knights who were going off to war overseas in the summer of 1372.[87] The word valet, found in an equivalent sense in the early indentures, seems to have gone out of fashion.[88] Perhaps this shift is coterminous with the emergence of the esquire as a social grade.

Everything seems to point then to the decades *immediately before* the sumptuary legislation of 1363 as the crucial stage. There is one further line of approach to the question, and that is through the use of heraldic seals. The social history of the seal is still in its infancy in England, but the work of Professor Paul Harvey and Mr Andrew McGuinness has already indicated the dividends it is going to pay in the study of this particular period, notwithstanding its methodological complexity.[89] The increasingly common borrowing of seals, for example, means that we can accept a seal as a grantor's only when it explicitly says so or where we can deduce this with certainty from additional documents. Nonetheless, some important general points can be made. It is not surprising that amongst the earliest examples of non-knightly heraldic sealing should be some from collaterals of knightly families. One example that has been noticed is Robert de Langley, lord of Wolfham-cote in Warwickshire and younger brother of Sir John de Langley. He

---

[83] *Indentures For Life*, nos. 49, 51.

[84] *Indentures For Life*, nos. 53, 62.

[85] See the list in Bean, *From Lord to Patron*, appendix iii.

[86] *John of Gaunt's Register*, 1372–6, 2 vols., Camden Society 3rd series, xx–xxi (1911), i, p. 35.

[87] *Ibid.* i, pp. 31–5.

[88] It was already travelling downwards, socially. See, for example, Saul, *Knights and Esquires*, pp. 16–20.

[89] P. D. A. Harvey, 'Personal Seals in Thirteenth-Century England', in *Church and Chronicle in the Middle Ages: Essays presented to John Taylor*, ed. Ian Wood and G. A. Loud (1991), pp. 117–127; P. D. A. Harvey and A. F. McGuinness, *A Guide To British Medieval Seals* (1995).

was not himself a knight but he sealed with the Langley arms in 1317.[90] Another example is that of James de Clinton of Baddesley Clinton. Around 1300 James sealed two documents with what the legend to one of them says was his own seal. It was a shield bearing *upon a chief two mullets pierced*.[91] He was, in fact, the fourth son of Sir Thomas de Clinton of Coleshill (d. 1277). The Parliamentary Roll of Arms of c. 1308 reveals clearly that James was sealing with one of several variants of the Clinton arms, or differenced to use the correct terminology. Sir John de Clinton of Maxstoke, that is the head of the eldest line, bore *argent od le chef de azure a ü molets de or*, while another Sir John, undoubtedly the second of Thomas's four sons, bore *argent od le chef de azure a ü flures de or*. A second type of individual who began to seal heraldically was the head of a knightly family who was not himself, or at least not yet, a knight. Before 1300, certainly, such men had sealed with what were in effect signets. However, this was to change. In 1342 John de Langley son of Sir Edmund used the family arms on his own seal although he was not, and did not become, a knight.[92] The chronology, however, remains unclear, and a great deal of work remains to be done on this particular issue. It is not an easy matter, for so many seals have been lost or defaced.

The most intriguing, and potentially rewarding category of all, however, is the family which has not been knightly but whose head will come to be called esquire in the fourteenth century. In order to be able to interpret seals in this context we need collections of original charters of sufficient size from sub-knightly families. One such collection is that of the Archers of Tanworth in Arden, Warwickshire. Tanworth is a large parish with a number of small manors held since the twelfth century by just such non-knightly tenants. In the king's hands in 1086, it came to Henry de Newburgh when he was made earl of Warwick. The Archers themselves originate with Robert the archer (*sagittarius*) who, according to Dugdale, received Umberslade in Tanworth from Henry de Vilers and Roger de Hulehale as a gift to himself and his wife during the reign of Henry II. Robert's son, William, received additional land from Earl Waleran (1184–1204). He was allowed a chapel here in 1234–5. His son, John, acted as a champion for Earl Thomas (1229–42) from whom he received extensive rights of hunting and hawking in the territories of Tanworth, except in the earl's park, in return for twelve broad arrowheads and two capons yearly.[93] It seems

[90] See Saul, *Knights and Esquires*, pp. 20–22.

[91] Calendar of Baddesley Clinton MSS, Shakespeare Birthplace Trust, nos. 11, 17. Two slightly later deeds, of 1318 and 1322, show him to have been lord of Baddesley Clinton. He died in 1323.

[92] Gregory Hood Deeds, Shakespeare Birthplace Trust, no. 342.

[93] For the Archers and for the history of the various manors in Tanworth see *VCH Warwicks.*, v, pp. 168–71 and Dugdale, *Antiquities of Warwickshire*, pp. 780–4.

almost certain, therefore, that the Archers were in the earl's service.

With the aid of the Archer pedigree we can examine the changes in their seal usage. The earliest example of heraldic sealing by a member of the family is in 1321 when John le Archer of Tanworth gave the manor, no doubt as the first step in creating a settlement, to Brother Thomas le Archer, prior of the hospital of St John of Jerusalem, who seems in fact to have been John's brother, and to Nicholas le Archer, another kinsman. The document carries two seals, undoubtedly those of John and Thomas. They used similar seals, *viz.* three arrows and three arrow heads respectively on a shield. The latter has the legend … L'ARCHER.[94] That it belonged to Thomas is clear from the identical device with which he sealed a quitclaim to his nephew John le Archer a few years later.[95] It corresponds with the family's later known arms: *azure three arrows or.*[96]

Extant thirteenth-century seals, by contrast, show no sign of heraldry. William Archer sealed with an eagle, John Archer with a device which appears to be an insect on his own seal c. 1225. Two late thirteenth-century deeds of John le Archer and John le Archer son of John le Archer are sealed with the owners' seals, respectively a stag passant and a bow and arrow being drawn.[97] Unfortunately, there are no deeds from the first two decades of the fourteenth century to pinpoint the change more precisely. It may be added that Robert de Hulehale of the same parish, who was of similar station to the Archers, sealed with

---

[94] Archer Deeds, Shakespeare Birthplace Trust, no. 416.

[95] Archer Deeds no. 455. It carries the legend: FRATER THOM-E ---CHER. The seal was Thomas's personal seal and not the seal of the order. On this point see E. J. King, *The Seals of the Knights of St John of Jerusalem* (1932), pp. 63, 99, 106–8 and plates xvii and xviii. For the confused state of the order during his time as prior see *The Knights Hospitallers in England, being the report of Prior Philip de Thame to the Grand Master Elyan de Villanova for A.D. 1338*, ed. L. B. Larking with an historical introduction by J. M. Kemble (Camden Society, Old Series no. 65, 1857), pp. lvii, 215. By 1328 he had ceased to be prior. He died 28 Aug. 1329. Two other Archers, John le Archer senior and John le Archer junior, were preceptors of the order in 1338 (*ibid.*, pp. 11, 65, 208). I am most grateful to Dr. Anthony Luttrell for his help on these points.

[96] These arms reappear in 1392 when Thomas le Archer granted his manors to four feoffees. The seal carries three arrows pointing downwards on a shield and bears the legend SIGILLUM TOME DE … CHER (Archer Deeds, no. 800). Meanwhile he, or an earlier Thomas, had sealed heraldically on four occasions between 1366 and 1385 but with borrowed arms (Archer Deeds, nos. 709, 734, 751, 772). However, another member of the family, Simon le Archer, who belonged to a collateral line, had sealed with a complex heraldic (or quasi-heraldic) device in 1328 and 1340: a lion rampant debruised by a shield with a martlet in chief, three scallops in fess and three arrowheads pointing down in base (Archer Deeds, nos. 462, 452). The seal was his own. John le Archer's widow, Margery le Tracy, had sealed in 1325 with three crosses on a fess between a bird and three arrowheads, the latter presumably reflecting her husband's arms (Archer Deeds, no. 452).

[97] Archer Deeds, nos. 42, 47, 251, 283.

his own seal bearing a sheaf of corn in 1282.[98] The Hulehales sold their manor of Monkspath (with property at Bedsworth) in Tanworth to John le Archer before the end of the thirteenth century. Clearly the Archers were growing in prosperity, and this may have influenced their early adoption of arms.

The deed collection, moreover, contains seals from the other sub-knightly families with manors in the parish. The family of Crewenhale, for example, of the manor of that name, also sealed heraldically. Their seal is in evidence in 1349 when Robert de Crewenhale seals with his own seal, *viz.* a shield *vairy upon a fess, three arrows pointing downwards.*[99] Robert, moreover, lent his seal to his neighbours. It was used in 1340, for example, when William de Sidenhale granted land in Tanworth to Henry de Sidenhale and his wife.[100] The Sidenhales held the manor of that name in the parish. By 1365 Henry de Sidenhale had his own heraldic seal: on a shield *a fess between two crescents.*[101] Henry de Sidenhale paid 6s 8d as an *armiger* in the 1379 poll tax.

The Fulwodes, again residents of the same parish, are also instructive, for John Fulwode was also given as an *armiger* in the same poll tax. The Fulwodes held the manor of Fulwood or Clay Hall.[102] John de Fulwode sealed non-heraldically in the 1360s, but heraldically in 1383 and 1399. We find a paschal lamb in 1366, a bird and a stag's head in 1368; there is nothing to indicate that these are personal seals, and the paschal lamb for example is commonly found in the collection.[103] By contrast the seal of 1399 is said on the legend to be his. It is a shield *crusily, three buckles on a bend.* The 1383 seal is also crusily with a bend.[104] Two other members of the Fulwode family appear to have sealed heraldically, however, as early as 1349, *viz. within a bordure a bend between six mullets.*[105]

[98] Archer Deeds, no. 268.

[99] Archer Deeds, no. 659.

[100] Archer Deeds, no. 557. The Crewenhale seal was also used by Robert de Bentforde of Tanworth in 1365 (Archer Deeds, no. 703).

[101] Archer Deeds, no.704. We find him using the device again in 1383 and 1395; in the former case the legend once again says the seal is his. In these last cases, however, there are three crescents not two (Archer Deeds, no. 765, 811). Thomas le Archer had on one occasion used the Sidenhale seal.

[102] According to Dugdale the Sidenhale manor passed to them by marriage in 1330, but this is clearly in error. John de Fulwode had license for a private oratory in 1395 and the family did well in the fifteenth and sixteenth centuries.

[103] Archer Deeds, nos. 706, 718, 720.

[104] Archer Deeds, nos. 764, 823. A crusily is a variety of field semé, that is powdered with charges; in this case with crosslets.

[105] One is an agreement between Robert de Fulwode, perpetual vicar of Tanworth and Simon son of Robert de Fulwode and his wife, while the other involves Ranulph son of Robert de Fulwode (Archer Deeds, nos. 635, 662). John's father, however, appears to have been William de Fulwode who had used a variety of non-heraldic devices during the 1340s, and possibly earlier (Archer Deeds, nos. 475, 516, 602, 603). The pedigree is unclear.

The limitations of the evidence from a single, though quite extensive, deed collection, are obvious. The lack of earlier deeds for some of these families makes proof difficult, but the evidence points clearly to the increasing adoption of heraldic seals by them during the middle decades of the fourteenth century. The Archers appear to lead the way, as early as 1321, and it may be significant that they had become more prosperous in recent times. However, the status of Brother Thomas, as prior of the Hospital of St John, must also have been a factor. The Archers were followed by Robert de Crewenhale who had an heraldic seal by 1340, and by Henry de Sidenhale and the Fulwodes thereafter. John Fulwode, Henry Sidenhale and Thomas le Archer all figure as esquires in the 1370s.[106] In the preceding decades they had become heraldic. None of the families were ex-knightly. It would seem then that by the 1320s heraldic seals were already being used sporadically by men of such station, and that this became commoner from the 1340s.

Despite its limitations, the evidence appears, cumulatively, to be reasonably clear. The appearance of esquire as a social rung can be dated to the middle third of the fourteenth century. Esquire as we perceive it more clearly in the 1360s and 1370s is a fairly inclusive category. This may help to explain the delay in its development. There is evidence from the early fourteenth century, if not before, of status consciousness below the level of the knight. We can discern it in the growing fashion for heraldic sealing and we seem to perceive it in the relatively restricted groups who were summoned to the Great Council in 1324. It would be very surprising had this not been the case within the localities. But, of course, there were no rites below knighthood to generalize any differentiation and there was a lack of clear social terminology. The emergence of a broad category of esquire may well represent something of a retreat from narrower and more exclusive feelings of social superiority.

What it represents, arguably, is the triumph of a territorial conception of status. It can hardly be coincidental that this development followed hard upon the emergence of the Commons as a significant political force and that it was concurrent with the maturation of the justice of the peace. In short, the development of the esquire is symptomatic of the formation of the English gentry.[107]

The rise of the esquire as a social category did not, of course, fix matters for all time. Although the category was a wide one, it did not include all those with a claim to gentility, as the sumptuary legislation

---

[106] According to Dugdale, Thomas was an esquire of the earl of Warwick at this time (*Antiquities of Warwickshire*, p. 780). He may well be the man who is called Thomas Rich in the 1379 poll tax returns.

[107] On this point and on the general question of territoriality see my recent essay, 'The Formation of the English Gentry', *Past and Present*, no. 147 (May, 1995).

of 1363 makes clear. Tension around this issue may well have increased towards the end of the century. One has only to think of Chaucer's Franklin.[108] By the first decade of the fifteenth century, moreover, the status of esquire was being explicitly celebrated in funeral monuments. In addition to the Lambourn brass already mentioned, there is the brass to John Mulsho, esquire, and his wife at Geddington, Northamptonshire, dated 1400, for example, and the brass to Thomas Seintleger, esquire, at Otterden, Kent, of 1408.[109] Among early stone effigies which make reference to the status is that to John Wyard at Meriden, Warwickshire, of around 1405.[110] Despite the Statute of Additions of 1413, the social acceptance of the mere gentleman took some time to achieve.[111] A spirit of social exclusion may help to explain the appearance of esquire as a designation in witness lists during the 1420s and 1430s.[112] One must be wary, though, of taking diplomatic fashion too much at face value. The status of esquire had been well recognised for some considerable time. When Thomas le Archer of Tanworth in Arden conveyed his manors to feoffees in 1392, the transaction was witnessed by Thomas Maureward, knight, and by Henry Sidenhale and John Fulwode. Although we know Henry and John to have been esquires from the 1379 poll-tax returns they are lacking here in any designation. By contrast, however, two of the feoffees are named, in the body of the text, as William Bracy of Warmington, esquire, and John Charnels, esquire.[113] Although the fifteenth century was to see much readjustment before social gradation reached full maturity, by the middle of the fourteenth century the process was well underway.

[108] See Coss, *The Knight in Medieval England*, pp. 153–8 and the essays cited there.

[109] See M. Norris, *Monumental Brasses: The Memorials*, 2 vols. (1977), i, pp. 55, 58 and ii, figure 67, and the same author's *Monumental Brasses: The Craft* (1978), figure 60.

[110] See Brian Kemp, 'English Church Monuments during the Period of the Hundred Years War', in *Arms, Armies and Fortifications in the Hundred Years War*, ed. Anne Curry and Michael Hughes (Woodbridge, 1994), p. 200 and plate xxxi. For the inscription see Dugdale, *Antiquities of Warwickshire*, p. 987. I am extremely grateful to Professor Kemp for his advice and for saving me from error in these matters.

[111] For recent confirmations of this, see Eric Acheson, *A Gentry Community: Leicestershire in the Fifteenth-Century c. 1422–c. 1485* (Cambridge, 1992), p. 34, and Christine Carpenter, *Lordship and Polity: A Study of Warwickshire Landed Society, 1401–1499* (Cambridge, 1992), p. 44.

[112] *Ibid.*, p. 48.

[113] Archer Deeds, no. 802.

FROM STENTON TO McFARLANE: MODELS OF SOCIETIES OF THE TWELFTH AND THIRTEENTH CENTURIES

By David Crouch

READ 24 SEPTEMBER 1994

THE growth of the study of medieval society is a process which falls well within living memory. Precisely how old it might be considered to be is a matter of definition. Taking social history to be the empirical reconstruction of past social and political systems, structures and their properties, then social history was a phenomenon of the inter-war period in Britain.[1] If one looks for a significant date to mark its full emergence (so far as we are considering *later medieval* society) then there is no date more significant than 1929, when Frank Merry Stenton delivered the Ford Lectures, which set in train the publication of *The First Century of English Feudalism*; a seminal event in the writing of social and medieval history in this country.

But there was something called 'social history' before Stenton, and although he stands at the beginning of my title, it is not his work that we will be considering first. Rather, we will start by looking at the historical context in which he worked. Stenton's stands strangely aloof from other work of his day, but it was that other work which produced ideas with which we still live, and which have much influenced our reconstructions of past societies. It is those reconstructions which are the principal business of this paper. We will be looking at Stenton's model of society, which remains still the most powerful influence on present historians of the society of post-Conquest England. We will also be looking at models which have evolved more recently, not least that of Bruce McFarlane, a historian of later medieval aristocracy, whose 'bastard feudalism' has of late begun heavily to influence historians of earlier society, not least myself.

But first to that period before Stenton, when it would hardly be fair to say that there was any coherent and holistic model of twelfth and thirteenth-century society. What there was, however, was a number of presuppositions, which are still with us. The first, and most pervasive,

[1] C. Lloyd, *Explanation in Social History* (Oxford, 1986) 14–17, for the novelty and definition of social history in Britain; but as a modernist he would date its appearance to the 1940s.

was a perception that medieval society was one of a hierarchy of social groups. This idea, as much else in the study of medieval society, is derived ultimately from the study of Domesday Book. One cannot underestimate the effect of the survival of Domesday Book on the study of medieval society.[2] It is to it that we owe the rich tradition of English scholarship on the subject of the manor and agrarian economy. By existing, Domesday Book has led social and economic historians to concentrate their efforts on manor, sake and soke, and the many orders of peasant. Maitland, Vinogradoff, Kosminsky, Latham and Lennard inspired a situation where, until perhaps the late 1960s, rather more emphasis had been placed in English scholarship on the peasant than on his lord!

But Domesday Book's rather less positive contribution to a comprehensive study of society lies in the way it was compiled. The guiding intelligence behind it was concerned to know the precise tenure of estates under the king. The eventual record scrupulously recorded the tenant *in capite*, but also, if there was one, the subordinate tenant or tenants of the same estate. Tenants of the third level—which must have existed—are never recorded.[3] It was as a result of this selective inquest and its returns that Maitland (for it was he) popularised the metaphor for English society in 1086 as a cone or pyramid.[4] It was all the easier to pursue this hierarchical image since pre-Conquest lawbooks and tracts do portray a society rigidly divided into status levels. You have therefore in England the quite unwarranted tradition of identifying a theoretical tenurial hierarchy with the idea of a social hierarchy supposed to underlie it. Stenton's senior contemporary, H. W. C. Davis in 1905 talked confidently of a 'complex hierarchy' presiding over post-Conquest England, and sketched in bold lines a ranked society, from baron to peasant.[5]

The same idea has passed all but unquestioned to the present day. I take several books which have been influential formers of undergraduate minds over the past two generations as examples. In 1948, Sayles's basic text, *The Medieval Foundations of England* portrayed a hierarchical social structure of king-earls-barons-knights-peasants.[6] Less slavish to Domesday Book, but still bearing the mark of hierarchical social

[2] P. Sawyer, 'Domesday Studies since 1886' in, *Domesday Book: a Reassessment* (1985), 1–4, amply demonstrates the great activity in the area of Domesday studies in the last century.

[3] C. P. Lewis, 'The Domesday Jurors', *Haskins Society Journal: Studies in Medieval History*, 5 (1993), 32–4.

[4] F. W. Maitland, *Domesday Book and Beyond* (repr. Cambridge, 1972), 170.

[5] H. W. C. Davis, *England under the Normans and Angevins* (1905), 186.

[6] G.O. Sayles, *The Medieval Foundations of England* (1948), 224–30.

thinking is Geoffrey Barrow's *Feudal Britain* (1956).[7] Barrow entitles a chapter section 'The Classes of Society' and portrays a society of (in order of importance) barons, knights, serjeants, townsmen and peasants. These were contemporary collective terms, but I would maintain that translating them into an ordered class hierarchy is not warranted in the twelfth century. The classic exposition of a Domesday hierarchy as applied to general society comes in 1969 in Allen Brown's *The Normans and the Norman Conquest*. Here we find a standard definition of the aristocracy as comprehending tenants-in-chief and sub-tenants, all within 'the social hierarchy of the upper classes'.[8]

It is a significant comment on Stenton's ability and originality as a historian that he was singularly and presciently cagy about ideas of social class and hierarchy as applied to post-Conquest society. He was clearly immune to the side-effects of the Domesday bug to which his contemporaries had succumbed. He noted how rigid status distinctions evaporated with the Norman Conquest. He particularly noted how the author of the *Leis Willelme* (a tract of the 1130s) was unable to formulate a comparison between pre-Conquest and post-Conquest social distinctions. He also noted the vagueness attached to the term 'vavassor' and he concluded most significantly that 'the term is vague because the structure of society was still indefinite'.[9] This pragmatically cautious attitude was followed by Lady Stenton in her influential and popular study, *English Society in the Early Middle Ages* (1951).

My own feeling is that Stenton was very right to be cautious about the model of hierarchical class when applied to post-Conquest society. When we read contemporary sources we get an idea that there was at the head of each kingdom or territory a tiny group of *optimates, magnates, nobiliores* or whatever. We also receive a clear impression that people perceived *rustici, villani, nativi*, or what have you, as the sump of society. But of any recognisable hierarchy of social groups in between, there is no trace. It is, of course, quite true that contemporaries were not merely alive to, but obsessed with, *individual* status. But nobody drew their place in society from being born into a social group. The formation of a hierarchy of social groups was a long and slow process which began in the late twelfth century and was hardly complete by 1400.[10]

To move from a social model which was nothing much to do with Stenton, I want now to move to one for which he was largely responsible. At this point it is necessary to say some things about

[7] G. W. S. Barrow, *Feudal Britain: the Completion of the Medieval Kingdom, 1066–1314* (1956), 34–97.

[8] R. A. Brown, *The Normans and the Norman Conquest* (London, 1969), 5, 23.

[9] F. M. Stenton, *The First Century of English Feudalism, 1066–1166* (Oxford, 1952) 5, 23.

[10] Ideas considered in, D. Crouch, *The Image of Aristocracy in Britain, 1000–1300* (1992), 5–38.

Stenton as a historian. He was unique amongst his contemporaries in his methodology. Not merely was he unique, he was also not well-known outside academic circles. To people of his own day interested in reading up on medieval society, it was not Frank Merry Stenton's name that would been linked to the subject, but that of George Gordon Coulton.[11] Coulton's was the sort of social history pioneered by Carlyle and Macaulay, and which had its last exponent of any distinction in G. M. Trevelyan.[12] It was what Eileen Power in 1933 tactfully called 'interpretative studies'; colourful evocations of medieval scenes and types. It was the sort of history decidedly not pursued at the London School of Economics in her day, where new ideological considerations were shaping the writing of history.[13] In Coulton's books you can read his gleanings from his vast reading about 'Popes and Prelates', 'Village Dance and Song', 'Nature and Superstition' and 'Chivalry', but what you will not find is anything resembling studies of power, class and social structure.[14]

Stenton was self-consciously the professional historian, and the heart of his precocity and uniqueness lay in the methodology by which he approached the study of post-Conquest society. He nowhere explains its origins, although we find some of his views in a lecture given during the Great War where he advocated a professionalism in historical writing which grew out of technical training and caution in judgment. He was against the 'great book' and in favour of the technical monograph, which was plainly what he regarded his *First Century* and *Anglo-Saxon England* as being.[15] It is possible to guess at some of the intellectual sources of his methodology. There is the *Quellenkritik* characteristic of Oxford after Stubbs, the admirer of Ranke.[16] There is

---

[11] Bishop Hensley Henson, for instance, himself once a history Fellow at All Souls, regarded Coulton as the leading exponent of his day, H.H. Henson, *Retrospect of an Unimportant Life* iii *1939–46* (Oxford, 1950), 99–100 (*s.a.* 1940), 341–2 (*s.a.* 1946). Coulton's trenchant anti-Catholicism was however, what chiefly intrigued and amused Henson, as it irritated Coulton's contemporaries in University departments, see H. S. Bennett, 'George Gordon Coulton', *Proceedings of the British Academy*, xxxiii (1947), 277–81.

[12] Coulton traced his own ultimate inspiration to Carlyle's remark that what people wanted from historians (but did not get) was answers to '... that great question: how men lived and had their being', G. G. Coulton 'Some Problems in Medieval Historiography', *Proceedings of the British Academy*, xviii (1932), 181, repeated in idem, *Medieval Panorama* (Cambridge, 1938), p. xiii.

[13] E. Power, 'On Medieval History as a Social Study', in, *The Study of Economic History*, ed. N. B. Harte (1971), 111–22 (her reprinted 1933 inaugural lecture). See on the significance of this, C. Parker, *The English Historical Tradition since 1850* (Edinburgh, 1990), 168–70.

[14] As in, Coulton, *Medieval Panorama, passim*.

[15] Parker, *English Historical Tradition*, 89–90.

[16] See, D. S. Goldstein, 'History at Oxford and Cambridge: Professionalization and the Influence of Ranke', *Leopold von Ranke and the Reshaping of the Historical Discipline*, ed. G. G. Igges and J. M. Powell (Syracuse, N.Y., 1990), 141–53. Stenton's Oxford pedigree is not

Stenton's own meticulous work on Anglo-Saxon diplomata, and his immersion in Domesday studies. But perhaps the greatest influence on him must have been the quirky genius of John Horace Round. Stenton shared with Round a hunger for reading and digesting twelfth-century charter material.[17] Round used charters to disentangle family history or knotty points of terminology; Stenton's greater genius was to use them as the basis for the reconstruction of a society. The maturity of Stenton's approach was well ahead of his time, and incomprehensible to some of his contemporaries. His were books for the professional and bright undergraduate, not the casual reader. About the only comparable contemporary figure in the English-speaking world was Charles Homer Haskins, to whom Stenton admitted a debt.[18] But Haskins was essentially a historian of cultures and institutions, not of societies.

One could look outside the Anglophone world and find other possible influences and comparisons. One was certainly Paul Guilhiermoz, another avid consumer of cartularies. Stenton heavily trawled Guilhiermoz's eccentric *essai* on aristocracy.[19] But Stenton had a surer touch with evidence than the Frenchman, whose talent was for sorting facts, rather than extrapolating from them. For all his greatness, Marc Bloch does not make for a good comparison with Stenton because Bloch did not go in for the empirical study of local societies; he was at the mercy of other's models and ambitious to consider all Christendom. France's equivalent of Stenton did not appear until Georges Duby produced his study of the Mâconnais in 1953.[20] In the German-speaking world, Otto Brunner was a historian of society in a similar mould, and in the same Rankean tradition (even though he might not have admitted it): his *Land und Herrschaft* (1939), with its meticulous reconstruction of the aristocratic superstructure of medieval Austria, bears some comparison with Stenton's work.[21] But they do not seem to have in any way influenced each other, even if they were known to each other.

Perhaps the most convincing explanation of the appearance of

---

entirely straightforward, but Sir Maurice Powicke at least believed he belonged in an Oxonian pantheon, F. M. Powicke, *Modern Historians and the Study of History* (1955), 170–1.

[17] For Round's appetite for charters, E. King 'John Horace Round and the *Calendar of Documents Preserved in France*', *Proceedings of the Battle Conference*, iv, ed. R. A. Brown (Woodbridge, 1982), 97–8. For Stenton's early debt to Round, who in 1902 found him work him with the Victoria County Histories which became his academic lifeline while working as a schoolmaster at Llandovery College 1904–8, see D. M. Stenton, 'Frank Merry Stenton' *Proceedings of the British Academy*, liv (1968), 350–60.

[18] Stenton, *First Century*, 12.

[19] P. Guilhiermoz, *Essai sur la noblesse du moyen âge* (Paris, 1902).

[20] G. Duby, *La société aux xie et xiie siècles dans la région mâconnaise* (Paris, 1953).

[21] O. Brunner, *Land und Herrschaft* (Vienna, 1939), now translated into English by H. Kaminsky and J. V. Melton as, *Land and Lordship: Structures of Governance in Medieval Austria* (Philadelphia, 1992).

Stenton and Haskins in the Anglo-Saxon world, Brunner in Austria, and of Guilhiermoz and Duby in France, is that something like them was bound to appear one day. For although there was little cross-connection between their work, they lived in a time of greater awareness in western scholarship of the variety of available sources for the study of social history, and their greater availability through the opening up of record offices and archives. They also lived in a time when a quasi-scientific method was being applied to historical studies, which encouraged systematic and comprehensive exploration of the sources.

So Stenton was a great original, and in his originality he produced his honorial model of post-Conquest society, the one we are now to consider. Stenton perceived the honor, the landed estate of the great magnate, as the basic unit of twelfth-century society. Behind this perception lay Stenton's view of English society at that time as fundamentally jurisdictional—or, to put it another way, a view of society as organised around landlordship, its rights and obligations. Such a view in Stenton was hardly to be wondered at since he examined and analysed charters and feodaries as his principal source. Anyone who becomes closely acquainted with such sources will soon fall into sympathy with Stenton's model. Myself, I have little doubt that the honor in England was at least a potential focus for power and patronage for several generations after the Conquest. The purpose of this paper is not to challenge the idea that honors were important in post-Conquest society.

But in going along with Stenton, it is possible to overlook the complications in his thesis. His honorial model of society is founded on a narrow evidential base. The private charters of the twelfth century are conveyances, or if not, are settlements, many of which arose out of honorial courts. If they become your chief source, they are bound to project a picture of English society in which the honor court dominates the foreground. To argue the importance of the honor, as Stenton did, from sources which derive from the honor, is to indulge in an argument of unsupported circularity. Feodaries likewise are honorial documents—whether generated from within the honor or by external inquisitions into internal obligations. This has to warn us to be cautious, very cautious, about *overemphasising* the place of the honor in the structure of local power. Stenton did not have such reservations initially, and in his first edition of *The First Century of English Feudalism* talked of the honor as 'a feudal kingdom in miniature': the later omission of this phrase may indicate that his enthusiasm for the idea was tempered on maturer reflection.[22]

Another criticism of the honorial model of English society lies in

---

[22] An observation I owe to Professor R. R. Davies.

Stenton's unwillingness to see the honor as anything other than an integral unit. There is some justification for the view that honors *might* form coherent aristocratic communities. Furthermore, *some* honors were very effective political units; notably, those ruled over by great and wealthy magnates and those in exposed frontier lands. The members of these honors perceived themselves as a group of *compares*; they took heraldry which flattered their lord's by imitation; there was an element of intermarrying between member families of an honor (encouraged by the institution of wardship), and they might, on rare occasions (like the tenants of Pontefract in the winter of 1135–6) take drastic, joint political action.[23] But even a large honor, when closely analysed, can show widespread fragmentation of loyalties amongst its members.

A notable example is the honor of Clare, as analysed by Richard Mortimer. Dr Mortimer makes the important point that the honor as a community has a certain artificiality. Again, this is a problem of evidence. The artificiality resides in looking at the honor 'from the top downwards', that is, regarding it as a coherent bundle of relationships— a hierarchy of tenure—and forgetting that the tenants of the honor were men with diverse ambitions and interests, which naturally led some of them outside the honor. Dr Mortimer describes an honor in which there was certainly a strong attachment among most of the tenants to the lord of Clare (expressed, for instance, in tenants' patronage of Clare religious foundations) but that did not prevent their having formed large interests outside the honor, and in many cases those complex alternative links of lordship went back before the time of the Domesday Survey. This was particularly true of the greater tenant families.[24] Behind the honor of Clare we can therefore glimpse a more complicated model of society which the honor did not comprehend, because the honor was only part of the framework of twelfth-century political society. It might be argued that the Clare honor was exceptional, but the particular concern flagged by Dr Mortimer had been noted over twenty years earlier by Sir James Holt. In *The Northerners* (1961) he noted how knights holding of several different lords in the north of England were more characteristic of Northern honors than those who held of one lord. He also noticed that such knights were likely to have been among the more significant social figures.[25] Other

[23] For Stenton's discussion of the significance of the appearance of *compares*, *First Century*, 60–1. For honorial heraldry in the earliest phase of heraldry's evolution see Crouch, *Image of Aristocracy*, 232–5; for the political assassination perpetrated by the tenants of Pontefract, W. E. Wightman, *The Lacy Family in England and Normandy, 1066–1194* (Oxford, 1966), 68–73.

[24] R. Mortimer, 'Land and Service: the Tenants of the Honour of Clare', *Anglo-Norman Studies*, viii, ed. R. A. Brown (Woodbridge, 1986), 177–97.

[25] J. C. Holt, *The Northerners* (Oxford, 1961), 36–7, 55–60, note particularly p. 60: 'The social and political independence which Mr McFarlane has seen these men [i.e. the

studies, relating to the single honor and region, have confirmed the widespread existence of multiple allegiance. It has been found to be common in the honors of Leicester, Holderness and Huntingdon.[26]

So, while accepting that the honor was one possible mechanism for power in the twelfth-century socio-political world, and although admitting that it was a reflection of magnate activity in the countryside, it cannot really be said—as Stenton's emphasis leads us to assume—that it lay at the core of the whole social structure of England. We glimpse another reality beyond it, a further set of circumstances to which twelfth-century tenants were responding. That it is a commonplace among historians that the honor deteriorated rapidly as a vehicle for expressing local power and lordship in the later twelfth and early thirteenth centuries, is itself an indicator that we should not overestimate the power of the structure which the honor represented. I would go further and say that in many cases it can never have amounted to much to begin with. To link its decline to Angevin legal reforms may be over much of a compliment to the strength of the honor court: I would suspect that the reforms of Henry II were filling a jurisdictional vacuum, rather than setting up a competing force of law. Milsom, perhaps unintentionally, has implied as much in seeing the reforms as initially intended to make the honor court more efficient.[27] This, despite his acquired view from Stenton that there had been a heyday of seigneurial justice in the localities in the twelfth century.[28] The *Leges Henrici Primi* and the evidence of Henry I's edict of 1108 show, however, that honor courts were not regarded as by any means sovereign or even effective at the beginning of the twelfth century.[29] As Peter Coss has said of this period: 'Notions of neighbourhood and district must have co-existed with the feudal, and it is here if anywhere that we should seek the primeval principle of social organisation.'[30]

Northern knights] enjoying in the fifteenth century, and Professor Treharne and Mr Denholm-Young in the middle years of the thirteenth century, was not new at these dates.'

[26] H. M. Thomas, *Vassals, Heiresses, Crusaders and Thugs: the Gentry of Angevin Yorkshire, 1154–1216* (Philadelphia, 1993), 19–32, reviews the evidence for a break down in the honorial structure of the North East. For Leicester, D. Crouch, *The Beaumont Twins: the Roots and Branches of Power in the Twelfth Century* (Cambridge, 1986), 115–31; for Holderness, B. English, *The Lords of Holderness, 1086–1260* (Oxford, 1979), 153–6; for Huntingdon, K. J. Stringer, *Earl David of Huntingdon: A Study in Anglo-Scottish History* (Edinburgh, 1985), 127–32.

[27] As in, S. F. C. Milsom, *The Legal Framework of English Feudalism* (Cambridge, 1976), 186.

[28] J. Hudson, 'Milsom's Legal Structure: Interpreting Twelfth Century Law', *The Legal History Review*, lix (1991), 64–5, pinpoints this attitude.

[29] See on this J. A. Green, *The Government of England under Henry I* (Cambridge, 1986), 110–11.

[30] P. R. Coss, *Lordship, Knighthood and Locality: A Study in English Society, c. 1180–c. 1280* (Cambridge, 1991), 8.

So this brings me to my third model of society, or rather, the first part of it—the locality, and, to begin with, the county as a social unit. The idea of England as a comprehensible and cosy collection of 'gentry' communities, all happily intermarrying, socialising and representing their interests at the centre of things, is the product of historians of the seventeenth century, and Alan Everitt in particular.[31] From Everitt the model was projected back to later medieval historians, who have produced a number of county studies, with conclusions generally unsatisfactory to the existence of such a social community.[32] That the model might be projected back even further, into the earlier middle ages has been the suggestion of John Maddicott. One throw-away observation he made has never had the exploration it deserves, that is, that 'the county community, where the gentry had a voice, predated the Conquest and had long given corporate expression to local opinion'.[33] Dr Maddicott's principal concern was the opposition to royal policy in the thirteenth century, and there was no opportunity for him to follow up that observation, but it is interesting to speculate on the logic behind it. The antiquity of county feeling is a subject we find in Maitland, who was the first historian to talk of 'the community of the county' noting the social significance of the institution of the county court as a forum for the greater freemen of a district.[34] The same theme surfaces in the work of Sayles, who observed that 'provincialism was always a strong force in the early middle ages for between the various parts of the country were barriers of geography, of dialects, of law, culture and traditions'.[35]

There is a certain warmth to the idea of breaking up England into

---

[31] On the Everitt school of thought see critiques in, C. Holmes, 'The County Community in Stuart Historiography', *Journal of British Studies*, xix (1980), 54–73; C. Hill, *People and Ideas in Seventeenth-Century England* (Brighton, 1986), 21–4. I profited much from discussions on this historiographical point with Dr Ian Archer and Dr Sarah Foot.

[32] C. Carpenter, 'Gentry and Community in Medieval England', *Journal of British Studies*, xxxiii (1994), 344–65, gives a forthright critique of recent late medieval county studies and finds the idea of county communities very woolly. Indeed she thinks that the whole idea of 'community' is misapplied by historians. Although I would agree that one should be cautious about the word, I use it here unashamedly, on the grounds that medieval people were fond of the word *communitas*, and clearly saw some point in using it. Woolliness and misapplication by modern historians does not invalidate a word with such a clear contemporary application, see further, S. Reynolds, *Kingdoms and Communities in Western Europe, 900–1300* (Oxford, 1984).

[33] J. R. Maddicott, 'The County Community and the Making of Public Opinion in Fourteenth-Century England', *ante*, 5th ser., xxviii (1978), 22–45; idem, 'Magna Carta and the Local Community', *Past and Present*, no. 102 (1984), 25–65, for the quotation, p. 25.

[34] F. Pollock and F. W. Maitland, *The History of English Law* (2 vols, Cambridge, 1911) i, 536.

[35] Sayles, *Medieval Foundations*, 230.

inward-looking natural communities which is very attractive. There is too sufficient evidence at the county level to put some body to the idea, if you wish it. Leaving aside the administrative dimension of the shire for the moment (we will come back to it) there is evidence for the sort of 'culture' described by Sayles. That one's language betrayed one's origins in the twelfth century is clear enough, not just from what linguists suggest, but from such distinctive out-county surnames as Kenteis or Deveneis.[36] Then there is the well-known story of Abbot Samson of Bury, a man of Norfolk, whose origins were instantly recognisable to the men of Suffolk, amongst whom he lived, from his manner of English speech.[37] You can find a number of examples of twelfth-century county patriotism. Jordan Fantosme ventured the opinion that Norfolk was 'a place that could not be bettered if you looked as far as Montpellier' (the proverbial end of the world for an Anglo-Norman).[38] The monk Lucian of Chester devoted a good part of a tract to the praise of his native county of Cheshire.[39] Perhaps the best evidence for provincial particularism is a late twelfth-century poem by a monk of Peterborough, whose sole purpose was to denigrate the *Norfolcienses*. It told of an unnamed Roman emperor who was supposed to have commissioned men to travel the globe and report back as to the nature of the lands they found. Back comes one: 'Hear me, lord', he says, 'I have crossed the seas and explored the confines of all lands, but no region is so truly awful as Norfolk.' The poet goes on for hundreds of lines to belittle the sense, morals, diet and habits of the men of Norfolk.[40] And what is even more interesting is that this splendid, malicious pamphlet provoked a reply, from another monk, John de St-Omer (despite his name, a native of Norfolk) in whom the barbs had sunk deep, as perhaps they were intended to do in the first

[36] For dialect diversity in Middle English, A. C. Baugh, *A History of the English Language* (2nd edn, 1951), 227–31, particularly noting how the English of Devon was regarded as archaic in the twelfth century, which would account for the county toponym *Deveneis*. Kentish English had a long history as a dialect; the obviously marked differences between Suffolk and Norfolk English within the East Midland dialect are interesting, both were sizable counties, however, and that might well have encouraged diversity. It is perhaps significant that county toponyms are all derived from physically large counties. A family called 'Kenteis' or 'Kentensis' was established in the borough of Warwick as early as the 1170s, R. Dace, 'Richard the Kentishman', *Warwickshire History*, viii (1991), 20–4; a family called 'Deveneis' or 'de Devonia' was established in mid thirteenth century Northamptonshire, *Luffield Priory Charters*, ed. G. R. Elvey (2 vols, Northamptonshire Record Society, xxii, xxvi, 1957–75) ii, 230–329, *passim*.

[37] *The Chronicle of Jocelin of Brakelond*, ed. H. E. Butler (1949), 12.

[38] *Jordan Fantosme's Chronicle*, ed. R. C. Johnston (Oxford, 1981), 68.

[39] *Liber Luciani de laude Cestrie*, ed. M. V. Taylor (Lancashire and Cheshire Record Society, lxiv, 1912), 52, 65.

[40] *Descriptio Norfolcensium*, in, *Early Mysteries and other Latin Poems of the Twelfth and Thirteenth Centuries*, ed. T. Wright (1838), 93–8.

place: 'Whoever once enters Norfolk', he says, 'will not wish to leave as long as he lives, for once he has seen so fine a land, he will declare it a minor Paradise'. And this he says he must declare for, 'I am of the race of the men of Norfolk, and it is proper that I defend my native land' (the word he uses is *patria*).[41]

Such exchanges are the seedy underpinnings of community, a sense of communal superiority. I have little difficulty in believing in twelfth-century *county feeling* after reading them. But whether such feelings can be translated into a socio-political structure based on the county is quite another matter. Feelings towards county can be matched in the sources by parallel feelings towards different communities. It is significant that both Jordan Fantosme and Lucian of Chester—while clearly convinced of the unique virtues of Norfolk and Cheshire—reserved their highest praises for towns. For Jordan it was London. Lucian's main purpose was to exalt Chester, only incidental to his purpose was to reflect on the virtues of Cheshire and the *Cestrenses*. Jordan was not the only writer to praise London inordinately in the twelfth century. As early as the 1140s a canon of St Pauls shamelessly attempted to appeal to the self-love of the citizens in a Life of St Erconwald, London's early patron.[42] The panegyric on London by William fitz Stephen, Becket's hagiographer, is so well-known as to need no quotation.[43] Men took their urban attachments and rivalries seriously in the twelfth century. After the sack of Worcester in 1139, John of Worcester took little heed of the fact that his city lay on the fault line between royalist and Angevin support in England. To him, the real reasons for the cataclysm were the bribes and envy of neighbouring Gloucester.[44] Group names in twelfth-century writings help define perceptions of communities. We find counties well-represented: *Norfolcenses*, *Suðfolcenses*, *Eboracenses* and *Hamtunenses*; but we also find urban identities defined in the existence of *Londonenses*, *Bristollenses*, and *Hastingenses*, and the *communitates burgensium* of many more places besides.[45]

[41] John de St-Omer, *Norfolchiae Descriptionis Impugnatio*, in *ibid.*, 99–106.

[42] *Vita sancti Erconwaldi*, in, W. Dugdale, *History of St Paul's*, ed. H. Ellis (1818), 291, in which the citizens of Erckenwald's time are depicted as claiming that only such a saint was a fitting patron for 'so glorious a city' with such martially accomplished inhabitants.

[43] *Descriptio Londoniae*, in, *Materials for a History of Thomas Becket*, iii, ed. J. C. Robertson (Rolls Series, 1878), translated, H. E. Butler in F. M. Stenton, *Norman London* (Historical Association, 1934), 26–32.

[44] *The Chronicle of John of Worcester, 1118–1140*, ed. J. R. H. Weaver (Oxford, 1908), 57.

[45] *De Expugnatione Lyxbonensi*, ed. C. W. David (New York, 1936), 54–6, 100, refers to *Norfolcenses et Suðfolcenses, Hamtunenses et Hastingenses*. For the *barones Eboracenses*, see Robert de Torigny, *Chronica*, in *Chronicles of the Reigns of Stephen, Henry II and Richard*, ed. R. Howlett (4 vols, Rolls Series, 1886–9) iv, 264. For the *Bristoenses*, see *Gesta Stephani*, ed. K. R. Potter and R. H. C. Davis (Oxford, 1976), 62–4, where the author (who had suffered from their

The idea of a plurality of communities and allegiances does not necessarily undermine the idea of twelfth-century county communities: it is perfectly possible to belong to, and be loyal to, more than one community at a time.[46] But a plurality of allegiances does somewhat erode any suggestion that a county community was central to perceptions of society of society at the time. A possible resolution of the argument would be a conclusive assessment of the precise local importance of the *comitatus*, the shire court. The difficulty here is that evidence is very scarce for the early twelfth century. For the early thirteenth century, Peter Coss has suggested that the shire court was poorly attended in its regular meetings, that knights tended to avoid sessions unless men of their status were particularly required, but might absent themselves even then.[47] Even in the early twelfth century there were mechanisms for greater men to default on their obligations to attend and send a steward or other officer to represent them.[48] This being so, we are on uncertain ground when we try to assess the importance of the county court in this early period despite the evident belief of some historians that there had been a 'golden age' of county politics somewhere vaguely back at the beginning of the twelfth century.

There are indeed arguments that the county court was of considerably more importance in 1100 than it had become by 1200, and one should not hastily dismiss them. After all, the Normans were so taken with the *comitatus* that they exported it: initially to Wales (to Glamorgan and Pembroke) and later to Ireland.[49] Indications of a greater readiness of local magnates to attend the court do exist for the earlier period. The *Leges Henrici Primi* and the writs of the Norman kings are agreed that

attentions) subjects them to a vicious assassination of character. A writer from south-east Wales a century later had a similarly low opinion of the *Bristollenses*, M. L. Colker, 'The "Margam Chronicle" in a Dublin Manuscript', *Haskins Society Journal*, 4 (1992), 137.

[46] Reynolds, *Kingdoms and Communities*, 2–3.

[47] P. R. Coss, 'Knighthood and the Early Thirteenth Century County Court', in, *Thirteenth-Century England*, ii ed. P. R. Coss and S. D. Lloyd (Woodbridge, 1988), 55–7.

[48] *Leges Henrici Primi*, ed. L. J. Downer (Oxford, 1972), c. 7.7–7a; an actual example of this of the time of Henry I has been pointed out to me by Dr Paul Brand, *Visitations and Memorials of Southwell Minster*, ed. A. F. Leach (Camden Society, new ser., xlviii, 1891), 196.

[49] For the *comitatus* of Glamorgan or Cardiff, see *Glamorgan County History*, iii, *The Middle Ages*, ed. T. B. Pugh (Cardiff, 1971), 16. For Pembroke, we hear of its sheriff and hundred courts in the time of Henry I, see Haverfordwest Record Office, PEM 1; *Pipe Roll of 31 Henry I*, 136 and its *comitatus* in 1233, *Royal and Other Letters Illustrative of the Reign of Henry III*, ed. W. W. Shirley (2 vols, Rolls Series, 1862–6) i, 426. We find the sheriff of Trim making his tourn in mid-thirteenth century Meath, *Calendar of the Gormanston Register*, ed. J. Mills and M. J. McEnery (Dublin, 1916), 177, and there is evidence for a sheriff of Dublin in the 1190s and sheriffs in Waterford and Meath early in the next century, see F. X. Marin, 'John, Lord of Ireland, 1185–1216', in, *A New History of Ireland*, ii, *Medieval Ireland*, ed. A. Cosgrove (Oxford, 1981), 143–4, although the existence of *vicecomites* does not automatically mean that there were also *comitatus*.

the earl of a shire—if there was one—was consulted in matters to do with it. The Wigmore Chronicle describes a session of the Herefordshire *comitatus* at Leominster between 1141 and 1143 and depicts as present there the bishop, the magnate, Hugh de Mortemer, and their retinues with them; the assembly also included many knights, other freemen, and clerks of the shire.[50] Similarly, a report of a joint *comitatus* of Norfolk and Suffolk at Norwich, held between 1148 and 1151, describes it as attended by a large contingent of significant landholders, although in this case royal justices were present in court, which may have had an effect on general attendance.[51] Judith Green's investigations of the careers of Anglo-Norman sheriffs has found that in Stephen's reign in particular, but occasionally in earlier reigns, sheriffs were also or had been stewards or followers of dominant local magnates.[52] Ralph Davis had already demonstrated from private charters how certain earls secured the office of sheriff as part of their range of patronage after 1138.[53] These findings would seem to me to indicate an interest amongst great magnates in harnessing the administrative structure of the shire to their own purposes. It may have taken exceptional circumstances for them to fulfil this ambition, but the existence of the ambition in itself argues for a desire amongst earls and barons to operate in and control the county court for their own ends.

By the thirteenth century there is not much evidence that magnates were in any way interested in the county at all. The occasional magnate might secure a shrievalty—such as the Marshal family's temporary holds on Gloucester and Sussex—but the magnate himself was in that case the sheriff and answerable at the exchequer as a royal officer. Also, such grants were rare events, unless, like the Salisbury family and Wiltshire, the earl had an ancestral claim on the office. Apart from magnates, at a local level one has also to ask whether knights were fully identified with particular counties. Even at a modest level the landed interests of a knight could span more than one shire. To take a thirteenth-century example from Warwickshire (which has become the English Mâconnais), that of the Bracebridge family. The Bracebridges came from Lincolnshire, where Bracebridge was a large manor in the honor of Bolingbroke. Around 1200, Peter of Bracebridge obtained the marriage of the heiress of the large manor of Kingsbury in Warwickshire,

---

[50] The occasion is called *une grand congregation ... pur hautes busoynes*, and the judicial function of that assembly leaves no doubt that it was a shire moot, *Monasticon Anglicanum*, ed. J. Caley and others (7 vols in 8, 1817–30) vi, 345.

[51] H. Cam, 'An East Anglian Shire Moot', *English Historical Review*, xxxix (1924), 569.

[52] J. A. Green, *English Sheriffs to 1154* (1990), 16; eadem, 'Financing Stephen's War', *Anglo-Norman Studies*, xiv, ed. M. Chibnall (Woodbridge, 1992), 95–8.

[53] R. H. C. Davis, *King Stephen* (3rd edn, 1990), 30–1, 125–41.

doubtless through the agency of his lord, Earl Ranulf of Chester.[54] To which county then did Peter belong? His Lincolnshire allegiance would have been clear previously; now it was divided. He was one of many in a similar position, and together they make up a fairly numerous group within local society.[55] It is well-represented among the knights of the Warwickshire grand assize juries of the mid-thirteenth century. Men like Sir Bardolf of Chesterton and Sir Guy fitz Robert, who were collectors of the aid for the county of Oxford in 1235, could be, and were, as active on Warwickshire juries as on Oxfordshire ones, for their estates spanned the county boundary. Guy, moreover, acquired a Devonshire estate in the course of his career.[56] Other Warwickshire knights appear on juries in Gloucestershire, Dorset, Staffordshire and Berkshire and elsewhere.[57] In the first half of the reign of Henry III six of the sixty or so knights who appear on Warwickshire and Leicestershire juries appear as frequently on Leicestershire as on Warwickshire juries. Their county, for these knights, was a matter of where they were on business.

The case for the early medieval county community remains not proven, so far as it can be examined at all. My belief is that there was a real feeling (even amongst clerics with French surnames) that one could belong to a shire and define oneself as a member of its community. I also incline to the view that the shire court may have been more of a real political focus for the county in the Norman period. Yorkshire can be found negotiating through its county court with the king for the remission of onerous dues as early as 1130, and this was only the first of many indications of a communal identity being forced on the shires by a central government eager for money and information.[58] But to say all that is to risk going further and overstating the case. By the thirteenth century the real importance of the shire court lay in its providing a theatre for touring royal justices, rather than as acting as a village hall to air local concerns and house local ambitions. As a community it was never an exclusive focus for its people's loyalties;

[54] For the Bracebridges, Coss, *Lordship, Knighthood and Locality*, 280–7.

[55] Carpenter, 'Gentry and Community', 348–9, makes this point independently for the later middle ages, my contention is that it is just as true for the earlier period.

[56] *Book of Fees* i, 445; ii, 820, 957, 958; iii, 827, 837, 1276; PRO JUST1/699 m. 17. For Guy, see in particular D. A. Carpenter, 'Was there a crisis in the knightly class in the thirteenth century? The Oxfordshire evidence', *English Historical Review*, xcv (1980), 733n.

[57] William of Luddington in Dorset, PRO JUST1/200, m. 2; Robert of Halford in Berkshire, PRO JUST1/273, m. 14, JUST1/342, m. 1d; Henry de St Maur in Staffordshire, PRO JUST1/802, m. 16 (not to mention also in Northamptonshire and Huntingdonshire, PRO JUST1/616, m. 4, JUST1/343, m. 1).

[58] *Pipe Roll of 31 Henry I*, 34. See on this, J.C. Holt, 'The Prehistory of Parliament', in, *The English Parliament in the Middle Ages*, ed. R. G. Davies and J. H. Denton (Manchester, 1981), 24–6.

there were other communities and other areas of ambition. Certainly by the thirteenth century its one political and judicial focus, the shire court, was undoubtedly in a poor way. It is a matter of personal belief whether you think it never amounted to much in the first place. There is one problematical exception to this pessimism about political county communities. After 1214 the views of shires were solicited by the king. For their part the shires combined to frame grievances against the centre. There are problems in assessing who it was who was articulating them, and for whom, but this area, that of the representation of local views at the centre, may be one area where the county may yet be found acting as a focus of local opinion.[59]

This brings us to a second dimension of the local model of power in society, the more restricted idea of the 'neighbourhood', the *visnetum* or *patria*. More restricted spatially, perhaps, but less restricted in that such a concept tends to have no fixed boundaries. Peter Coss has recently written on the subject in his study of the region surrounding Coventry. It might be argued that such studies are self-defining—choose your region and you will find means to make it coherent (one thinks of Hilton's study of the West Midlands in that regard). But Peter Coss is aware of that danger and quite as well acquainted with the broader setting of the Coventry area as he is with Coventry itself. What he portrays *is* a singularly local society. It had an early focus in its forming a coherent block of estates held by the earl of Chester, which was itself a descendant of the earlier holding of the Countess Godiva at the time of the Domesday Survey. The administrative and honorial infrastructure of the earldom might have given this area an initial coherence, and later the city of Coventry itself might have helped to form a feeling of locality; for every urban area needs a hinterland as market and source of food. Admitting the existence of a local community, as Coss does, does not necessarily admit that the members of it (particularly the greater members) had no interests elsewhere. But nonetheless endogamy, the pattern of landholding and economy, and the existence of lordship, did create a coherent *patria* in this corner of Warwickshire.[60]

Peter Coss provides us with one very skilful portrait of a functioning local community. I cannot think of any parallel to such a study, but neither can I think of any reason (other than a dearth of sources) why it might not be paralleled. The association of urban centre and hinterland is one that easily can produce a socio-economic community, and there are other forms of social organisation that could parallel it. I am thinking particularly of that represented by a great abbey. Towns and abbeys as focal points of communities will be long-lasting. Another,

[59] Maddicott, 'Magna Carta and the Local Community', 36–7, 46–7, 61–5.
[60] Coss, *Lordship, Knighthood and Locality*, 53–60.

such as that which depended on the momentary power of a great magnate, will be transitory, although perhaps more powerful in its day.

I have long been of the opinion that the most significant form of political organisation in England in the twelfth and thirteenth centuries had little to do with honors, counties and fees. It was a form of power focussed on a discrete region and a dominant personality who sought to control it. It was a form of control recognised by Bruce McFarlane and dubbed 'bastard feudalism', in a phrase drawn from Charles Plummer.[61] For us, to define it takes only one factor, a dominant personality seeking to establish control over a neighbourhood of his choice. Recent writings and debate have established with an unusual unanimity that we *can* apply such a model of local power to thirteenth-century society, long before the reign of Edward I, to which McFarlane considered it belonged in the first instance.[62] Whether the 'bastard feudal' model has any place before 1200 is another matter entirely. I think it has, but I can see some strong objections to such a point of view.

If we, however, cling to the idea of the core of 'bastard feudal' lordship as domination of a distinct area by an individual magnate *through a variety of means*, then the twelfth century can show a number of examples of such local lordship. One of the most significant examples I have found is in a letter of Bishop Nicholas of Llandaff to Theobald, archbishop of Canterbury. The bishop had been busy in support of Gloucester abbey's claims to the church of St Gwynllyw in Gwent. He had secured witnesses to assist the abbey and he adds that 'there are these men and others, men of the earl of Gloucester *and of other sort*, who avoid the truth fearing to incur the earl's ill will, but who could be forced to speak up if it was necessary for the abbot and if it suited the archbishop.'[63] Here we have a quite open statement, cleric to cleric, of the ways that injustice was promoted in the lay world. It was by

---

[61] For the original classic statement of this sort of political structure, K. B. McFarlane, 'Bastard Feudalism', reprinted in, *England in the Fifteenth Century*, ed. G. L. Harriss (1981), 23–44.

[62] For the literature on this shift in perceptions see, S. L. Waugh, 'From Tenure to Contract: Lordship and Clientage in Thirteenth-Century England', *English Historical Review*, ci (1986), 811–39; J. M. W. Bean, *From Lord to Patron: Lordship in Late Medieval England* (Manchester, 1989); D. Crouch, *William Marshal: Court, Career and Chivalry in the Angevin Empire* (1990), chapters 5–6; D. Crouch, D. A. Carpenter and P. R. Coss 'Debate: Bastard Feudalism Revised', *Past and Present*, no. 131 (1991), 165–203; D. A. Carpenter, 'Simon de Montfort: the First Leader of a Political Movement in English History', *History*, 76 (1991), 10–13; D. Crouch, 'A Norman *Conventio* and Bonds of Lordship in the Middle Ages', in, *Law and Government in Medieval England and Normandy: Essays in Honour of Sir James Holt*, ed. J. Hudson and G. Garnett (Cambridge, 1994), 299–324.

[63] *Llandaff Episcopal Acta, 1140–1287*, ed. D. Crouch (South Wales Record Society, 5, 1988), no. 14, my translation.

menace, and not only by misconceived loyalty of tenant to lord. The earl of Gloucester could extend himself to influence people in the geographical area in which his honorial power made him dominant, people quite other than those who held fees from him. This was in 1156 and the earl of Gloucester was William, to whose political standing and effectiveness historians have not been particularly respectful.[64]

A formula occasionally met with in mid-twelfth century charters puts the same situation with more delicacy. At a time between 1138 and 1147 Earl Ranulf II of Chester issued a charter to Calke priory and added at the end, 'I entreat (*precor*) my neighbours, and instruct (*precipio*) my men by the faith they owe me' that they maintain, protect and defend the canons.[65] A similar clause appears in an act of Earl William III of Warenne in favour of Nostell priory: he entreats his friends and instructs his ministers to keep safe the alms he had granted to the priory.[66] Both magnates know that they have a right to dispose of their men and ministers, but they also assume to themselves a right of politely guiding people who are not bound to them other than by good feeling. And what then if these friends and neighbours would not be guided? Then there might happen the circumstances described by Jordan Fantosme, who depicted Earl Robert III of Leicester boasting that in his part of the country there was hardly a knight whom he could not overthrow, if he refused the earl aid.[67] It may well be that Jordan put such boastful threats in the earl's mouth to make him appear ridiculous, or as material to condemn his disloyalty to the king, but there has to have been a reality behind such a characterisation to make it effective.

Some case studies serve to illustrate the point. Both come from Stephen's reign, when the opportunity to exert local lordship was there to be seized by anyone ambitious to do so. The first concerns John fitz Gilbert, the king's marshal. In 1135, when Henry I died, John held estates concentrated in the Kennett valley on Hamstead Marshall where John had a hall. From his friend, King Stephen, John obtained the great gift of the castles of Marlborough and Ludgershall. Using these, he was able after 1138 (the year he fell out with the king) to dominate the North Wiltshire Downs. In doing so, he extended his control to the lands of people who were not his tenants. The abbey of Abingdon, and a number of other churches, found him claiming lordship over lands within his sphere of interest, and levying dues on them. He secured the

---

[64] D. Crouch, 'William, earl of Gloucester and the end of the Anarchy: new evidence relating to the honor of Eudo Dapifer', *English Historical Review*, ciii (1988), 69–75.

[65] *Charters of the Anglo-Norman Earls of Chester, c. 1071–1237*, ed. G. Barraclough (Record Society of Lancashire and Cheshire, cxxvi, 1988) no. 45.

[66] *Early Yorkshire Charters* ed. W. Farrar and C. T. Clay (12 vols, Yorkshire Archeological Society Record Series, 1914–65) viii, 83.

[67] *Jordan Fantosme's Chronicle*, ed. R. C. Johnston (Oxford, 1981), 70.

estate of Newbury, whose lord was an absent French count, and built a castle there, so as to mark the eastern extent of his influence. John fitz Gilbert's logic was territorial. He defined an area for expansion and nailed it to the landscape with castles. Such was the state of England at the time that he could act the prince and use his military resources to levy taxation and extort acknowledgement of his lordship from estates to which he had no title other than its lying within his own self-defined protectorate. Unfortunately for him he was not alone in employing such local tactics. His southern neighbour, Earl Patrick of Salisbury, decided that the Marshal ought to accept *his* lordship. After a campaign John found Earl Patrick 'too strong a neighbour' (as his son's biographer put it) and so capitulated.[68] Such might be the volatility of territorial lordship; fortunes and spheres of domination shifted.

A second example is much more formidable, that of Earl Roger of Hereford. He inherited from his father a dominant position in the southern March and Herefordshire. To this he added the allegiance of a whole flock of lesser magnates of the region—the lords of Ewyas Harold, Monmouth, Clifford, Wigmore and Osbert's Castle. The result was a regional lordship of considerable power. Earl Roger continued to develop it through the last years of Stephen's reign, when he attempted to secure Worcestershire within his area of power. Parallel to this process of recruiting minor magnates was another process by which he formed treaties with surrounding magnates: the earls of Gloucester and Leicester and the lord of Buellt and Radnor. The last named treaty, with William de Briouze, provides a further insight into the process of regional domination. It is specifically directed against a third party, Gilbert de Lacy, a dispossessed local rival of the earl in Herefordshire. Again therefore we see a magnate extending his power by means which had little to do with the tenurial framework of the honor. As with John fitz Gilbert, a central component of the process *was* the honor inherited from his father. But the patrimonial lands provided only the opening stake in a formidable game of power.[69]

Both the Marshal and Hereford examples come from the reign of Stephen when social conditions were volatile and the royal curia was no longer attractive to the ambitious magnate seeking advancement. But, as with the examples of the earls of Gloucester in 1156 and Leicester in 1173, the binding force in regional lordship was fear of what an ambitious magnate might do, and this was clearly as much the case in the reign of Henry II as that of Stephen. King Henry was

---

[68] Crouch, *William Marshal*, 9–18.
[69] D. Crouch. 'The March and the Welsh Kings', in, *The Anarchy of King Stephen's Reign*, ed. E. King (Oxford, 1994), 281–6.

himself intimidated by magnates, for he proved reluctant to reverse the
gains several great regional magnates had made in Stephen's reign. An
abortive attempt to neutralise Earl Roger of Hereford in 1155 was
abandoned, and the earl remained in possession of the bulk of his gains
and alliances until death removed him from the king's agenda at the
end of the same year. Reginald, earl of Cornwall, and Robert II, earl
of Leicester, were able to survive unchallenged within their enhanced
lordships till 1176 and 1168 respectively. It was only when they died
that the king was able or willing to counteract their gains, knowing
perhaps that such influence and domination was personal to the
magnate who created it, and could not be inherited.

Supposedly dominant Angevin kingship did not inhibit the development of regional domination by particularly capable magnates. William
Marshal was able to construct a formidable sphere of influence for
himself in the south west of England, being particularly strong in
Gloucestershire and Wiltshire, exerting an attraction over minor magnates, like the Berkeleys, Earleys and Musards, and over county knights.
Again, at the core of his endeavours lay the lands of his father, John
fitz Gilbert, a relatively small honor but the same as that which had
earlier formed the basis of John's enterprises in Stephen's reign. Earl
William Marshal's power reached rather further than had John fitz
Gilbert's, but the location of the honor meant that father and son both
sought to extend themselves in the same region. In William's case,
however, closeness to the crown, an advantageous marriage, rents and
offices, and a general aura of power and influence, brought him much
wider local influence, without the necessity of adding military conquest
to his repertoire of power.[70]

I have now presented several models of society, and although only
the last—and the least explored by historians—seems satisfactory, there
is an element of validity in all of them. It would be unreasonable to
expect a Grand Unifying Theory of medieval social structures, although
historians seem to think it is expected of them (doubtless the influence
of Marx). With the idea of *local* lordship and *local* community we have—
it has to be admitted—reached the lowest reducible level of social
analysis. It has to be true, because it really is a fundamental point that
communities will form at a local and regional level before coalescing
into the national.[71] That a magnate will aspire to expand and maintain
his interests in areas where he already has a presence, if he is a man
of energy and determination, is not a truism of aristocratic behaviour
that is ever likely to be challenged. A case in point. The earl of Leicester

[70] Crouch, *William Marshal*, 62–4.
[71] S. R. Bassett, 'In Search of the Origins of Anglo-Saxon Kingdoms', in *The Origins of
Anglo-Saxon Kingdoms*, ed. S. R. Bassett (Leicester, 1989), 23–7.

came to control the south west of his shire in the reign of Henry I. Even before the reign of Stephen he had identified as local rivals the earl of Chester and the bishop of Lincoln. Slowly, decade by decade, by hook and by crook, the earl eroded the position of these rivals until by the reign of King John, the Chester and episcopal interests were broken and acquired.[72] Such examples might be multiplied.

Since I am now talking as a reductionist, without I hope becoming absurd, then we must address the question of how the honor and county fit into this picture of local and regional ambition. I have not denied that either might be a real potential community of interest in society. What I have questioned is the degree to which they were communities that might be animated. The metaphor is a good one; it was a matter of making dry bones live. Communities are less able to direct themselves to action and agendas than individuals: another truism. They were in some degree empty bodies with the potential to be galvanised and moved by a directing intelligence. The honor is particularly interesting in this regard. It was in essence no more than an accumulation of acts of patronage between a lord and those who had consented to become his men; frozen by custom and obligation. Initially it would be flexible and even lively, capable of growth while free lands were available for further distribution. Then in two, three or four generations that flexibility would in the end stiffen, and the honor would become a fossilised shell of a community of interest long departed. Only the largest of them or those (like the small honors of the March) bonded closer by external pressures, would I think have a chance of any extended life. In that light, honors were a variation on other forms of local lordship. And as we have seen with the Marshal family and the earls of Hereford and Gloucester, they were only one mechanism amongst several by which a greater or lesser magnate could exert himself. The county too might be a vehicle for a magnate's activities, if only through a magnate's ambition—rarely satisfied—to control its rudimentary administrative structure.

Finally, while talking at the local level, we have to consider where the lesser landowner fitted into this pattern. I have perhaps depicted them as the poor bloody infantry of magnate activity in the localities, but that would be less than just to them. Local landowners, knights, squires and freemen had each their own agenda. It might be that self-improvement through service to a greater man was top of that agenda but there were other items. There were areas of England, notably Worcestershire and Gloucestershire, where magnates were thin on the ground, and where houses of religion were the dominant landowners.

---

[72] D. Crouch 'Earls and Bishops in Twelfth-Century Leicestershire', *Nottingham Medieval Studies*, xxxvi (1993), 19–20.

In such places small landowners would necessarily be more independent, and perhaps themselves become predatory.[73] But even where there were magnates with local ambitions to court, the local knight would not necessarily see his allegiance as guaranteed to his chief lord. By the later twelfth century, a number of the greater tenants of the honor of Clare had expanded their interests outside their principal magnate allegiance, and when they did so it was often to acquire estates from other lords with lands neighbouring Clare.[74] This was no more that the magnate did, although at an even more local level. By doing this, of course, the honor as community was necessarily compromised, but then the honor could not be allowed to be the only arbiter of social behaviour.

Local society was a teeming mass of ambitions and personalities; an image Peter Coss captures very well in his study of the Coventry hinterland. If we were to look at the broader picture of Warwickshire society we would soon get lost in its complexities. This is of course why we invent labels like 'gentry' or 'magnate interests', it seems to help make sense of the whole business by introducing categorisations and trends to analyse. There were gentry and there were magnates and they did interact with each other. But where categorisation falls flat is that in the twelfth and thirteenth centuries the historian is dealing with a period when the idea of social categories was hardly in the forefront of the conscious contemporary mind. This means that society was fluid, infuriatingly so for a twentieth-century mind. It is best to take an example, and mine is from Warwickshire and consists of a family called Montfort: not a family in any way exceptional in wealth or connections. The heads of the family principally held their lands from the earls of Warwick, their distant cousins.[75] The family's lands were located in two blocks, a substantial and concentrated one in Rutland, and a centre at Beaudesert just outside Henley-in-Arden, Warws.[76] Montforts can be found loyally attesting Warwick acts from the 1090s through to the 1180s.[77] It was in that decade that the tenurial link lost its force (after

---

[73] A good example in Worcestershire is the family of le Seneschal of Evesham, which seems to have been more than a match for the abbey it once served in an hereditary stewardship, see *Chronicon abbatiae de Evesham ad annum 1418*, ed. W. Dunn Macray (Rolls Series, 1863), 289–91; *Monasticon Anglicanum*, ii, 18–19; Cartulary of Evesham, Brit. Libr., ms Harley 3763, fos. 68r, 92r-v; PRO, E159/2, m. 14; JUST1/56, m. 32.

[74] Mortimer, 'Land and Service', 194–5.

[75] For the cousinship, G. E. Cockayne and others, *The Complete Peerage*, (13 vols in 14, 1910–59) viii, 120 and n.

[76] For the Montfort soke of Preston, Rutl., *Pipe Roll of 31 Henry I*, 134; *Rotuli Hundredorum*, ii, 49; PRO, KB26/146, m. 1d. For Beaudesert as their early Warwickshire centre, *Regesta Regum Anglo-Normannorum*, ed. H. W. C. Davis and others (4 vols, Oxford, 1913–69) iii, no. 597.

[77] The last Montfort known to have attested a Warwick act was Henry, who died c. 1199, and who attested acts of Waleran of Warwick, who had become earl in 1183.

three generations of apparent loyalty). After the 1180s the Montforts of Beaudesert and the earls of Warwick were connected only by the customary dues inherent in knight service. The Montforts held ten and a quarter fees of the earls, and were not therefore simple knights, but neither were they magnates.[78] For that matter, they were never simple Warwick followers. In pursuit of their own agenda in western Warwickshire, they obtained fees from other local magnates. Henley-in-Arden belonged to the lords of Stafford, and it is unsurprising to discover that in 1166 Thurstin de Montfort held a fee of Stafford at Henley. He had also picked up several western Warwickshire fees from the straggling estates of the Mowbray family.[79] We do not know how they got these fees: grant or purchase or even inheritance, but there is a clear territorial logic to them at least. The Montforts had not done with magnates. They were closely involved with the Cantilupes in the reign of John, and in the mid-thirteenth century (probably due to Cantilupe influence) Peter de Montfort came into the orbit of Earl Simon de Montfort (no relation), who at the time attained some local eminence in the central Midlands.[80] After the cataclysm of 1265 the family gravitated into independent royal favour, and formed a longstanding minor magnate connection in the Midlands.[81] But it had long had such a penumbra of lesser connections in western Warwickshire, through marriage and small grants of land. So what were the Montforts of Beaudesert? Were they gentry, or were the gentry the smaller families who battened on them? Were they magnates in waiting? We are trapped now in hierarchical thinking. I would suggest that in the twelfth and thirteenth centuries people did not think in those terms, and in conclusion, I would venture the opinion that we should not either.

[78] For the fees held of Warwick, *Red Book of the Exchequer*, ed. H. Hall (3 vols, Rolls Series, 1896), i, 325.

[79] For the Stafford and Mowbray fees, *Red Book*, i 268; *Charters of the Honour of Mowbray*, ed. D. E. Greenway (British Academy, 1972), 264.

[80] The Cantilupe connection derived from the wardship by William de Cantilupe of Thurstin (III) de Montfort early in John's reign, which led to a marriage with a Cantilupe daughter, *Complete Peerage*, vii, 123n. In 1236, Thurstin's son, Peter, called William de Cantilupe the younger, 'his lord', *Calendar of the Patent Rolls, 1232–47*, 140.

[81] For the later Mountforts of Coleshill, derived from an illegitimate son of Peter (II) de Montfort, see W. Dugdale, *The Antiquities of Warwickshire*, ed. W. Thomas (1702) ii, 1009.

MILES IN ARMIS STRENUUS: THE KNIGHT AT WAR

By Michael Prestwich

READ 24 SEPTEMBER 1994

WAR was more important to medieval knights than to many of their historians. They have been more concerned to debate shifts in the social status and numbers of knights, than to examine their military role. Varied scenarios of knights rising in social status, gaining a more powerful political voice as they became wealthier, and of declining knights, increasingly aggrieved at their failure to maintain their position in society, have vied one with another. Military obligation has, of course, proved to be a battlefield on paper for many historians, but debate on this has not always been informed by awareness of the muddy realities of war. It would be reasonable to suppose that major transformations in the social position of English knights were a response to, or at least a reflection of, changes in their military functions. Yet the only link that is commonly made is the assumption that changes in the social position of English knights were in some measure the result of the rising costs of the military equipment they needed to possess.

In the eleventh century mounted troops were all termed *milites*, or knights. Post Conquest knights ranged from men of high standing to the comparatively lowly, even, it has been argued, including men of unfree status.[1] By 1400 a very small proportion of the mounted troops was knighted, and those who were formed a notable élite. Differentiation within the cavalry began to appear in the second half of the twelfth century. The 1166 return into service owed from the FitzAlan lands in Shropshire reveals the existence of 'mounted semi-knightly' soldiers. These were perhaps the product of the peculiarities of border warfare, but mounted archers fought alongside knights in Ireland in Henry II's reign, and in England there are clear references to mounted sergeants,

---

[1] R. A. Brown, 'The Status of the Norman Knight', *War and Government in the Middle Ages*, ed. J. Gillingham and J. C. Holt (Woodbridge, 1984), 18–32; J. Scammell, 'The formation of the English Social Structure: Freedom, Knights and Gentry, 1066–1300', *Speculum* 68 (1993), 598–9. D. Fleming, 'Landholding by *Milites* in Domesday Book: a Revision', *Anglo-Norman Studies*, 13 (1990), 83–98, points out that the *milites* of the late eleventh century might include not only heavy cavalry, but also light horsemen and infantry. My thanks are due to Clifford J. Rogers for his valuable comments on an earlier version of this paper.

notably during the rebellion of 1173–4. In 1193 the garrison of the Tower of London numbered twenty knights along with twelve mounted sergeants with hauberks, and six without.[2] There is also French evidence for the widespread use of such mounted sergeants; Philip Augustus's surviving account roll details 174 such men in pay in August 1202.[3] By the second half of the thirteenth century the proportions had changed; in 1267 William de Leyburn took a force of eight knights and thirty sergeants to Nottingham, where the garrison consisted of two knights, their squires, and twenty sergeants, along with archers, crossbowmen and others.[4] The terminology used for those heavy cavalry who were not knights changed in the course of time; under Edward I, there were still sergeants in the royal household, but most non-knightly cavalrymen were termed squires (*scutiferi*) or valets (*valetti*), terms which might be synonymous.[5] Later, all might simply be called men-at-arms (*armigeri*).

In Edward I's reign, between 20% and 30% of the cavalry were of knightly standing. On the Caerlaverock campaign in 1300 about 22% of the cavalry in royal pay were knights. The proportion of knights had decreased most sharply among those performing feudal service, falling to just below 10% in 1300 and standing at about 8% in 1310. The overall level remained similar until the 1370s. On the ill-fated 1322 expedition to Scotland 24% of the cavalry were knights. For Salisbury's troop in Scotland in 1337 the figure was lower, at 18%. In Brittany in 1343 22% of Henry of Lancaster's retinue were knights, though Walter Mauny's contained only 16%. Perhaps, as a foreigner, he found it harder to recruit men of status to his service. In the Black Prince's massive contingent in the 1359 campaign, the proportion stood at 24%.[6] After the reopening of the Hundred Years War in 1369 there was a dramatic fall in the level of knightly participation. John of Gaunt's retinue in 1369 showed no change from earlier patterns, for 27% of the cavalry troops were of knightly rank. However, for his great chevauchée of 1373 the figure was very different, at no more than 13%, and for the 1375 Brittany expedition it fell to under 5%. In 1380 it stood at 6.5%. An indenture with the earl of Salisbury in 1372 suggests some alarm at what was happening, for it laid down that twenty of his 120 men-at-

[2] F. C. Suppe, *Military Institutions on the Welsh Marches, Shropshire, 1066–1300* (Woodbridge, 1994), 63–87; *Expugnatio Hibernica: the Conquest of Ireland, by Giraldus Cambrensis,* ed. A. B. Scott and F. X. Martin (Dublin, 1978), 185; *Pipe Roll 20 Henry II* (Pipe Roll Soc., 1896), 67, 94, 132, 139; *Pipe Roll 5 Richard I,* ed. D. M. Stenton (Pipe Roll Soc., 1927), 132.

[3] *La France de Philippe Auguste,* ed. R-H. Bautier (Paris, 1982), 583.

[4] Public Record Office [hereafter PRO], E 101/3/10.

[5] *Liber Quotidianus Contrarotulatoris Garderobiae,* ed. J. Topham *et al.* (1787), 232.

[6] J. E. Morris, *The Welsh Wars of Edward I* (Oxford, 1901), 159, 163; *Liber Quotidianus Contrarotulatoris Garderobiae,* 195 ff; *Parliamentary Writs,* ed. F. Palgrave (1827–34), II, 1. 401–8; British Library [hereafter BL] MS Stowe 553, f. 56. ff; PRO, E 101/20/25; PRO, E 36/204, ff. 102v, 103; PRO, E 101/393/11, f. 79.

arms were to be knights. Sherborne demonstrated that between 1369
and 1380 only eight knights of county gentry origin served as captains
of retinues in France, and of those, six were king's knights at the time.
He was disinclined to see this as evidence of the declining overall
contribution of the knightly class to the war, but taken in conjunction
with the indications of the sudden fall in the proportion of knights in
the armies of this time, it points firmly in that direction.[7] The decline
continued. In the Agincourt army, the proportion of knights, at about
8%, was exceptionally high.[8] The figure fell as enthusiasm for the
French war declined. In 1337 those of knightly and higher status formed
3.5% of the army. In the Duke of York's force of 1441 the level was
2.4%. When in 1443 Somerset took some 600 cavalry to France,
approximately 1.3% of the force were of knightly rank or above. He
noted, not surprisingly, a 'lakke of barons, bannerets and knights'
prepared to accompany him.[9]

The number of knights who fought was therefore very different from
the total number of cavalry. Nor are such numbers easy to calculate.
Record evidence is not available prior to the thirteenth century, but
some chronicle estimates have a degree of plausibility. Orderic Vitalis
claimed that Rufus had 1,700 knights on campaign in 1098, but he put
the number of those who fought for Henry I at Brémule at no more
than 500.[10] Gerald of Wales, whose evidence on numbers appears more
trustworthy than that of most chroniclers, thought that Henry II took
a force of about 500 knights, with many archers both mounted and on
foot, to Ireland in 1171. Record evidence suggests that John's Irish
expedition of 1210 was larger; the roll of prests shows that there were
at least 800 knights present in the army.[11] That level was not maintained.
Muster lists from the mid 1220s imply that royal household knights and
their followers amounted to two hundred men or more. Troops provided
by the magnates would have added many more to the total. Feudal
service by the early thirteenth century could not provide numbers

<hr/>

[7] J. W. Sherborne, 'Indentured Retinues and English Expeditions to France, 1369–
1380', *EHR* 79 (1964), 722, 729–30, 732, 738; PRO E 101/32/30. The problem Gaunt
faced in recruiting bannerets and knights is noted by S. K. Walker, *The Lancastrian Affinity
1361–1399* (Oxford, 1990), 52.

[8] Figures calculated from N. H. Nicolas, *The History of the Battle of Agincourt* (1827), 333–89.

[9] A. Curry, 'English Armies in the Fifteenth Century', *Arms, Armies and Fortifications in
the Hundred Years War*, ed. A. Curry and M. Hughes (Woodbridge, 1994), 47; M. Jones,
'John Beaufort, duke of Somerset and the French expedition of 1443', *Patronage, The Crown
and The Provinces*, ed. R. A. Griffiths (Gloucester, 1981), 92, 100.

[10] J. O. Prestwich, 'The Military Household of the Norman Kings', in *Anglo-Norman
Warfare*, ed. M. Strickland (Woodbridge, 1992), 103.

[11] *Expugnatio Hibernica*, 92–3; *Rotuli de Liberate ac de Misis et Praestitis*, ed. T. D. Hardy
(1844), 172–253.

approaching the traditional quotas of some 5,500 knights: the summons of 1223 yielded a force of 387 knights and 145 sergeants. In 1228 an estimated 545 knights took part in the Welsh campaign.[12] Under Edward I, it is likely that when the king mounted his major Scottish expeditions, such as those of 1298 and 1300, his armies contained at least 500 knights. In 1322 about 325 knights took part in Edward II's disastrous expedition to Scotland.[13] Edward III was able to call on rather larger number of knights. The 1335 army in Scotland contained over 500 men of knightly rank and above. In the army that promised so much and achieved so little in France in 1359 there were some 950 knights, of whom probably 900 were English. Numbers of knights began to decline rapidly with the reopening of the French war in 1369. In 1373 John of Gaunt's chevauchée included a mere 266 knights, and two years later the Brittany expedition contained only 95 men of knightly rank. The fall in the number of fighting knights appears to have been far more rapid than can be explained by the overall decline in knightly numbers.[14]

The periods of major change appear, therefore, to have been the later twelfth century, when knights and mounted sergeants became clearly differentiated, and the late fourteenth century when knightly numbers declined dramatically. Does the evidence for the changing numbers and proportions of knights coincide with changes in the way they fought? A central issue is whether they fought on horseback, or on foot, and here there was a contrast between the twelfth and thirteenth centuries. Hastings was certainly won by mounted knights, but in the battles in Normandy in the early twelfth century, success went to knights fighting for Henry I on foot, probably with archers in support. Stephen and many of those in his army fought on foot at the battle on Lincoln in 1141.[15] Yet thirteenth century knights fought on horseback, even, it seems, in the unsuitable circumstances of fighting within the city of Lincoln in 1217. At Lewes and Evesham mounted knights played a prime role, and Edward I's knights fought on horseback. The contraction in knightly numbers therefore roughly coincided with a change in battle tactics, but it would not be easy to demonstrate a causal connection.

[12] R. F. Walker, 'Hubert de Burgh and Wales, 1218–1232', *EHR*, 87 (1972), 475, 480.
[13] BL MS Stowe 553, f. 56 ff.
[14] A. E. Prince, 'The Strength of English Armies in the Reign of Edward III', *EHR* 46 (1931), 357, 368; Sherborne, 'Indentured Retinues and English Expeditions to France, 1369–1380', 729–30; A. Ayton, 'English Armies in the Fourteenth Century', *Arms, Armies and Fortifications in the Hundred Years War*, 29–30.
[15] The most recent discussion of the battle tactics of the Norman period is S. Morillo, *Warfare under the Anglo-Norman Kings 1066–1135* (Woodbridge, 1994), 169–74. See also J. Bradbury, *The Medieval Archer* (Woodbridge, 1985), 41–57.

Significant change in the opposite direction took place in the fourteenth century, as knights once again fought on foot. At Boroughbridge in 1322 both sides were dismounted, Harcla's men in defensive Scottish style formation, and the baronial troops under the earl of Hereford in order to cross the narrow bridge.[16] Destriers, the great warhorses, were not thought necessary in 1327; swift horses were needed to pursue the Scots, but battle (which did not take place) would be on foot.[17] The series of great victories from Dupplin Moor and Halidon Hill to Crécy, Poitiers and Agincourt owed much to knights and men-at-arms fighting in a melée on foot. Changes in fighting techniques do not therefore coincide with the dramatic fall in the numbers of knights in the late fourteenth century. It would be dangerous to conclude too much from the fact that the mounted knight appeared rarely on the battlefield, for this is to neglect the amount of skirmishing that took place, the smallscale encounters between scouting troops, the swift raids into enemy territory, and the large scale destruction of farms, villages and crops, for all of which mounted knights were needed. The knight, even if he could be persuaded to dismount for battle, remained throughout first and foremost a mounted warrior, and it was the problems of how to fight on horseback that dominated the development of knightly equipment.

Study of the cavalry of a much later period, the nineteenth century, suggests that there were immense problems in fighting from horseback with sword and lance. The lance, over nine feet in length, was not capable of tackling the shields, armour, or even padded clothes of the Sikhs, and experiments with light, longer, bamboo lances were a failure. Captain Nolan, who achieved undesirable fame at Balaclava, pointed out that the lance was virtually useless once a rider pulled up, for it depended on the momentum of the horse. The use of swords from horseback also proved problematical. When thrust, swords often bent and proved useless. If a successful thrust was made, the sword was hard to withdraw. Used as a cutting weapon, it was certainly possible to cleave a man's head in two, yet even cotton clothing could resist a sword cut surprisingly effectively. The long stirrups of the nineteenthcentury English cavalrymen meant that they could not rise up from their horses to engage in effective swordplay, in contrast to the Sikhs with a more effective riding style. The charge was rarely successful, so hard was it to co-ordinate large numbers of horsemen. Wellington had written that 'Our horse, although I believe it the best in the world,

---

[16] *Vita Edwardi Secundi*, ed. N. Denholm-Young (1957), 124. It is worth noting that the references to mounted knights, *ibid*, 122, are not warranted by the Latin.

[17] *Rotuli Scotiae*, ed. D. Macpherson, J. Caley, W. Illingworth and T. H. Horne (1814), i. 208.

becomes unmanageable in proportion as his rate of going is increased'. Regulations permitted the 'charge' to be sounded no more than forty yards from the enemy lines.[18] More than that, and horses would scatter, so that the charge would lose its shock effect.

Medieval knights must have faced similar difficulties to the cavalrymen of the nineteenth century, though their weapons were probably better than those of Nolan's day. The knightly riding style looks to have been as awkward as that criticised by Nolan. The saddle, with high cantles and pommels, locked the rider in place. The long stirrups which appear in many contemporary illustrations, placed inconveniently far forward, dictated a straight-legged style.[19] This aided balance when wearing armour, but there was no way that a knight thus equipped could have risen in his stirrups to engage in swordplay. Armour, not matter how well fitted, must have hampered movement, while a helmet with visor lowered would have limited vision and communication. It must have been extremely difficult to organise an advance, much less a charge. It is not surprising that the helmet was the last item of equipment to be put on, as is demonstrated by the celebrated case of the earl Marshal at the battle of Lincoln in 1217, when a squire reminded the veteran warrior at the last minute that he had not yet donned it.[20] The medieval lance was certainly effective in skilled hands: the Marshal killed the future Richard I's horse with a single thrust in one celebrated encounter.[21] Lances were easily broken, however, and were of little value in a melée.[22] The fight before the walls of Le Mans in 1189 was marked by much breaking of lances; William the Marshal even lost his horse when it trod on one of the broken pieces which littered the ground. The lance could be adapted for fighting on foot, by being substantially cut down: at Nogent in 1359 Eustace d'Aubrichecourt ordered his men to shorten their lances to five feet.[23] Medieval swords were probably much more effective than those of the nineteenth century cavalry; for one thing, they were not kept in metal scabbards which blunted them. Their value was demonstrated at the battle of Lincoln in 1141, when the earl of Gloucester's men disdained from engaging in the initial encounters with lances, but charged from

[18] H. Strachan, *From Waterloo to Balaclava* (Cambridge, 1985), 55 91.

[19] A. Hyland, *The Medieval Warhorse from Byzantium to the Crusades* (Stroud, 1994), 7–8. Gerald of Wales commented on the awkwardness of the high, curved saddle, which made swift mounting and dismounting impossible: *Expungnatio Hibernica*, 246.

[20] *L'Histoire de Guillaume le Maréchal*, ed. P. Meyer (Société de l'histoire de France, 1891–1901), ii. lines. 16597–604.

[21] *L'Histoire de Guillaume le Maréchal*, i. lines. 8845–9.

[22] 'I never spoke with an English lancer who had been engaged in the late Sikh wars that did not declare the lance to be a useless tool, and a great incumbrance in close conflict.' L. E. Nolan, *Cavalry; its History and Tactics* (1853), 127.

[23] *Chroniques de J. Froissart*, ed. S. Luce (Paris, 1869–1975), v. 168.

the first with drawn swords, so succeeding in breaking through the lines
of King Stephen's men. Gerald of Wales noted how John de Courcy,
fighting in Ireland, 'lopped off now a head from someone's shoulders,
or again arms or hands from their body', so effective were the blows
from his sword.[24]

The argument that the rising costs of armour, arms, and horses
dissuaded men from taking up knighthood is a familiar one. Denholm-
Young suggested that in the twelfth century a knight might equip
himself for £5, but that in the thirteenth century the cost rose between
five and ten-fold. Complete armour for man and mount, the latter
costing from £20 to £100, the equivalent, he suggested, of a light tank
in 1939, made knighthood a heavy financial burden.[25] For Professor
Coss, 'the cost of increasingly elaborate equipment (especially horses
and armour), and the cost of the ceremony of becoming a knight'
provide the key to the decline in numbers of knights in the hundred
years from 1180. In contrast, Professor Crouch has argued that the
costs of knighthood in peacetime were far more significant than those
of wartime equipment[26] The view that knighthood was becoming more
expensive has some contemporary warrant. According to the author of
the *Histoire* of William Marshal, when his hero was young a king's son
might ride out with no more equipment than his cloak rolled up; by
the time he wrote, in the second quarter of the thirteenth century,
there was scarcely a squire who did not demand a packhorse for
his possessions.[27] Royal grants to men taking up knighthood certainly indicate that honour was not without price. John de Castellione
received £15 for this purpose in 1255, and John fitzBernard £10, for
equipment for the knighting of himself and a companion. William
Bigod was promised £5 in 1255, as were four knights in the following
year.[28]

The chronology of the development of armour is well-known. There
was relatively little change for a century and more after the conquest.
In the late twelfth century the pot helm, fully covering the head,
appeared. Shields were becoming steadily smaller and more manoeuvr-
able. Mail had the merits of great flexibility, and resistance to cutting
blows. But it was vulnerable to steel-tipped arrows, and could not resist
crushing blows. It is usually assumed that it was not until the late

[24] *The Historia Novella by William of Malesmesbury*, ed. K. R. Potter (1955), 49; *Expugnatio
Hibernica*, 176–7.
[25] N. Denholm-Young, *History and Heraldry* (Oxford, 1965), 19–20.
[26] P. R. Coss, *Lordship, Knighthood and Locality. A study in English Society c.1180–c.1280*
(Cambridge, 1991), 253–4; D. Crouch, *The Image of Aristocracy in Britain 1000–1300* (1992),
147.
[27] *L'Histoire de Guillaume le Maréchal*, i. lines 763–768.
[28] *Calendar of Liberate Rolls, 1251–1260*, 212, 230, 259, 266.

thirteenth century that pieces of plate armour began to be worn in
addition to the mail hauberk. As early as 1224, however, there is a
reference to a hauberk and a pair of iron greaves being placed in
pledge for 6s. 8d. An inventory of goods stolen from a chest in 1289
included not only two hauberks, but also iron greaves, two 'pairs of
plates', which were probably body armour, quisses, or thigh pieces,
iron gauntlets and a plate gorget, or neck piece.[29] Inventories of goods
forfeited after Boroughbridge in 1322 suggest that by that date a knight
would be expected to have as his helmet a bacinet, with some form of
protection for the neck, a mail hauberk, plate armour for thighs and
shins, with iron gauntlets and shoes.[30] Yet Jean le Bel recalled how, on
the 1327 campaign, English armour was very old fashioned. The
English, he wrote, had no plate armour, but wore antiquated hauberks,
topped not with up-to-date bacinets, but with great helms of iron or
hardened leather.[31] The period of rapid change came thereafter, when
there was a swift transition from mail to plate armour. In the fifteenth
century 'white armour', undisguised by any fabric coverings, emerged
to display the armourer's skill to the full. Plate armour clearly lacked
the flexibility of mail, but its rigidity had obvious advantages in resisting
blows.

Much work was involved in making mail. Each individual ring was
separately riveted together, and the whole had to be shaped with skill
and care.[32] Plate armour demanded a different technology which was
not widely available until the fourteenth century, but it is not immediately evident that it was more expensive or difficult to make than mail.
The quality could vary considerably, with different methods being used
to case-harden or temper the steel.[33] It is apparent that rapid change
in the technology of armour did not coincide with the periods when
the numbers and proportions of knights in English armies were altering
markedly.

Information on the cost of arms and armour is somewhat scanty,
especially before the widespread adoption of plate. Royal accounts
provide the best evidence of the costs of armour, but the equipment
provided for kings is likely to have been of the highest quality, and
proportionately costly. Under John on one occasion a hauberk cost £1,
and a haubergel 13s. 4d. Two hauberks, four haubergels and six helmets

[29] Select Cases of Procedure without Writ under Henry III, ed. H. G. Richardson and G. O.
Sayles (Seldon Soc., 60, 1941), 56; Select Cases in the Court of King's Bench, Edward I, iii, ed.
G. O. Sayles (Seldon Soc., 58, 1939), p. cv, n. 5.
[30] Calendar of Inquisitions Miscellaneous, 1307–49, nos. 527, 797.
[31] Chronique de Jean le Bel, ed. J. Viard and E. Déprez (Paris 1904), 156.
[32] Brown, 'The Status of the Norman Knight', 28, where it is suggested that to make
a hauberk with butted, not rivetted, rings would take 140 hours.
[33] M. Pfaffenbichler, Armourers (1992), 62–6, describes the technicalities.

cost £7 8s.[34] Two surcoats, two corslets, presumably of mail, and two pairs of iron boots were bought in London for Henry III for £10 13s. 4d.[35] Seven haketons bought for Edward II early in 1312 cost ten shillings each; repair of the royal sword came to 9s. 4d.[36] In 1321 the king bought a new haubergeon and two new swords, and had a range of equipment repaired, for a total cost of £10 5s. 8d. The king could afford the best; an account presented by one of Edward III's armourers, Hugh de Bungay, indicates the costs of what was no doubt good quality equipment. A pair of plate gauntlets cost 6s. 8d. A pair of greaves with poleyns (covering shins and knees), with burnished fittings, came to 26s. 8d. A war helmet cost £2, and a painted crest for it cost a further 5s. Two bacinets, much simpler helmets, cost 13s. 6d. Surprisingly, the most expensive single piece of equipment was the cotton and fustian trapper worn by the royal charger, to protect him from being rubbed by his iron armour. This cost £2 12s. 8d.[37] The costs borne by normal knights would not have been of this order. An inventory of goods stolen in 1324 from John de Swynnerton shows that a haubergeon with mail fittings (aventail, pisan and collaret), was worth ten marks. Bacinets were valued at ten shillings each, and, surprisingly, war swords at a mere 3s. 4d., half the price of longbows. A set of leg armour (jainbers, cuissans and poleyns) came to 15s. Two tents, necessary for campaigning, were valued at six marks.[38] Such evidence does not suggest the costs of armour were excessive. A knight might, of course possess a substantial quantity of armour; Fulk de Pembridge, who died in 1326, left three of his sons a full set of armour each, with the fourth receiving two hauberks.[39] If it was normal to buy on that scale, it becomes difficult to accept arguments that the cost of armour was an excessive burden.

The life of the Marshal makes it very clear that possession of a good horse was vital, and that such animals were hard to come by. A tale about the theft of a good horse left unguarded was worth many lines, not merely because the Marshal chivalrously limited his retaliation against the thief to bashing his head so hard that one of his eyes was driven out of his skull.[40] Much attention was undoubtedly paid to the breeding of horses, and to the import of prized animals from abroad, though the sources do not reveal how far the quality of war horses was

---

[34] *Pipe Roll 2 John*, ed. D. M. Stenton (Pipe Roll Soc. 1934), 209; *Pipe Roll 9 John*, ed. M. A. Kirkus (Pipe Roll Soc., ns. 22, 1944), 31.

[35] *Calendar of Liberate Rolls, 1251–1260*, 380.

[36] BL Cotton MS., Nero C. VIII, f. 57.

[37] PRO, E 101/16/5.

[38] *Calendar of Inquisitions Miscellaneous, 1307–1349*, no. 797.

[39] N. Saul, *Knights and Esquires: the Gloucestershire Gentry in the Fourteenth Century* (Oxford, 1981), 24.

[40] *L'Histoire de Guillaume le Maréchal*, i., lines 1368–1372, 4343–4414.

improved as a result.[41] Size was not all that significant; Captain Nolan noted that he had seen 'a Persian horse fourteen hands three inches carrying a man of our regiment of gigantic proportions, and weighing in marching order twenty-two and a half stone'. He also recorded that an English officer in India laid a bet that he would ride his Arab charger of little more than fourteen hands four hundred miles in five consecutive days, a task that the horse survived with ease, unlike its rider who died shortly afterwards.[42] The medieval warhorse was probably not especially large; neither long-legged animals of modern type bred for high speed, nor heavy shire horses, would have been suitable for military use. Horses were very vulnerable in battle. The Conqueror lost three at Hastings; in 1098 Rufus lost over 700 horses to French archery in the Vexin. At Crécy in 1346 the English archers had a devastating effect on the enemy horses, forcing some to halt in their tracks, others to buck and bolt, and many to fall on each other helplessly. Horses might also die as a result of the tough conditions on campaign; many were lost through starvation when Edward I wintered in Scotland in 1301–2.[43]

The prices of individual warhorses might vary very considerably, and overall trends are hard to determine. The fact that the crown found it necessary to promise to repay men the price of horses lost in war shows how significant an investment a good horse was. Under Henry II a standard price appears to have been £2, though one animal was bought for £6 13s. 4d. From Richard I's reign there is evidence of war horses costing a mere 10 marks for two; towards the end of John's reign figures for purchase of horses show that the price could vary from 50 li Ang. to as little as 14 li Ang. Two Lombard horses cost £38 13s. 4d., but five Spanish horses were bought for £40 from a crossbowman called Gilot.[44] The ample early thirteenth century Pipe Roll evidence of warhorses and palfreys owed to the crown in part payment of fines demonstrates that they were highly prized. Brian de Lisle once offered two horses to be quit of a debt of £100, but the normal level was 30 marks, though how far this notional value related to the market price cannot be determined.[45] There is much later evidence to show that military

[41] R. H. C. Davis, *The Medieval Warhorse* (1989), 78–97, discusses the breeding of warhorses in medieval England.
[42] Nolan, *Cavalry; its History and Tactics*, 334.
[43] *The Ecclesiastical History of Orderic Vitalis*, ed. M. Chibnall (Oxford, 1969–80), iv. 218; *Chronique de Jean le Bel*, ii (1905), 103; *Willelmi Rishanger Chronica et Annales*, ed. H. T. Riley (Rolls ser., 1865), 210.
[44] Davis, *Medieval Warhorse*, 82; *Rotuli Litterarum Clausarum*, ed. T. Duffus Hardy (1833–4), i. 171b; *Documents Illustrative of English History in the Thirteenth and Fourteenth Centuries*, ed. H. Cole (1844), 238, 251. The *livre* of Anjou was worth about a quarter of the pound sterling.
[45] *Pipe Roll 12 John*, ed. C. F. Slade (Pipe Roll soc., 1951), 9, 200–1; *Pipe Roll 11 John*, ed.

chargers might be extremely costly. The evidence for the most expensive
horses suggests a substantial rise in price by the fourteenth century. A
horse bought for Edward III in 1338 cost £168; two years later the
king purchased one for his friend the earl of Salisbury, for £150. Such
prices were exceptional; chargers were bought on the same campaign
for about £50, and coursers and ordinary horses for half as much.
Even so, these were substantial sums.[46]

Very full evidence of horse prices is available from the valuations
drawn up so that compensation could be paid for animals lost in war.
These have been the subject of careful study by Dr Andrew Ayton,
who has shown that the mean values of knights' horses varied from
£14 to £33 between 1282 and 1343, with substantial variations from
one campaign to another.[47] As a rule knights had horses which were
valued at roughly twice as much as those of other cavalrymen, but it
is not evident how accurately these assessments mirrored true market
prices. It may be that the valuations reflected the rank of the owner at
least as much as the quality of the horseflesh. In Ralph Neville's
contingent in Scotland in 1335 his horse was assessed at £20, those of
his knights at 20 marks each, with the horses of his men-at-arms priced
at £10 and under; these figures look to have been determined more by
convention than by accurate assessment of the animals themselves.[48]
Changes in valuation levels from one campaign to another may reflect
decisions made by participants as to what type of horse to take on
campaign—cheaper for Scotland, more expensive for France—or the
relative generosity of the horse valuers on different occasions. Irrespective of their accuracy, however, the valuations do demonstrate that
the horse represented a very major investment for a knight, perhaps in
many cases equivalent to a year's income.

Nor, of course, did a knight have to provide himself with just one
horse: expectations as to how many were needed rose in the course of
time. The treaty between Henry I and the count of Flanders in 1101
provided that each man should have three mounts.[49] Details of the
costs of transport across the Channel in the initial phase of the Hundred
Years War show that by that period it was normal for a banneret to
have five horses, a knight four, and a squire three. Salisbury, with 117

D. M. Stenton (Pipe Roll soc., 1949), 198; *Pipe Roll 13 John*, ed. D. M. Stenton (Pipe Roll
soc., 1953), 200; *Pipe Roll 16 John*, ed. P. M. Barnes (Pipe Roll soc., 1962), 155.
[46] *The Wardrobe Book of William de Norwell, 12 July 1338 to 27 May 1340*, ed. M. Lyon, B.
Lyon, H. S. Lucas, J. de Sturler (Brussels, 1983), 216, 230–1.
[47] A. Ayton, *Knights and Warhorses. Military Service and the English Aristocracy under Edward
III* (Woodbridge, 1994), 194–251.
[48] BL. MS. Cotton Nero C. VIII, f. 281v.
[49] *Diplomatic Documents preserved in the Public Record Office*, i., *1101–1272*, ed. P. Chaplais
(Oxford, 1964), 1–4.

212   TRANSACTIONS OF THE ROYAL HISTORICAL SOCIETY

men in his retinue, took 387 horses to Flanders.[50] By Henry V's reign
it was assumed that a duke would have fifty horses, an earl twenty-
four, a baron sixteen, a man-at-arms four and a mounted archer one.
The earl of Suffolk in 1417 claimed to have twenty-four horses for each
of his five knights, six horses each for his twenty-four other men-at-
arms, and four horses for each mounted archer.[51]

The cost of horses was the most significant item in the knightly
budget; rises in the price of other equipment are not likely to have
been of equivalent importance, especially since men-at-arms would
have been expected to have similar arms and armour to those of
knights. Inflationary pressures were high in the late twelfth and early
thirteenth centuries, and changes in the costs involved in fighting as a
knight are likely to have been an important element in the differentiation
of the cavalry into knights and sergeants. It is much less easy to argue
that change in the cost of equipment and horses was a major factor in
subsequent periods; indeed, Dr Ayton's calculations point to a down-
ward trend in horse prices in the second half of the fourteenth century,
which suggests that high prices should not form part of the explanation
of the collapse in knightly numbers from the 1370s.[52]

Knightly skills were first and foremost individual. Roger Wendover
provides a fine description of the personal ability of the mounted knight
in his treatment of the rebellion of Richard Marshal. At Monmouth in
1233 the Marshal with a small force was attacked by Baldwin de Gynes
with a much larger one. During the conflict, Baldwin with a dozen
well-armed companions attempted to capture the Marshal. Swinging
his sword to left and right, the latter was able to keep his assailants off.
Eventually his horse was slain by lance thrusts, but the Marshal,
practiced in tournaments, unhorsed one of Baldwin's knights by pulling
at his leg. He then jumped into the saddle—no mean feat in full
armour—and continued his resistance. Baldwin, infuriated by the turn
of events, rode up and seized the Marshal's helmet, heaving at it so
hard that the blood poured from his mouth and nose. In his last fight,
which took place in Ireland when he was captured, the Marshal again
put up a magnificent display. Richard de Burgh attempted to grapple
with him and pull his helmet off, but as he tried to do so the Marshal
with one sword blow cut off his hands. Another knight wishing to
avenge Richard was struck a fearsome blow, which split his body in
two down to the navel. Not surprisingly, few dared to approach the
Marshal at close quarters, until the end of the battle when common
soldiers surrounded him and savagely attacked his mount. Fallen to the

[50] *The Wardrobe Book of William de Norwell*, cv, 230–1, 310–2.
[51] R. A. Newhall, *The English Conquest of Normandy* (Yale, 1924), 191, 194n.
[52] Ayton, *Knights and Warhorses*, 229.

ground, the exhausted Marshal was not so formidable an enemy, and he was mortally wounded by blows from behind. The emphasis in the account is not on the effectiveness of cavalry charging as a body, but typically on individual strength and stamina. No doubt there was skill too, but the techniques employed by the Marshal can hardly be described as subtle. The sword emerges as a much more important weapon than the lance, while hand-to-hand wrestling to seize a man's helmet appears to have been a favoured technique. That this was not unusual is shown by Edward I's conflict with the count of Chalons in 1273, which culminated in a similar physical struggle on horseback.[53]

There can be no doubt that knights might have great individual expertise. William Marshal, according to the *Histoire*, had the technical ability to suggest a way of bridling a horse with what sounds a very savage bit, so as to tame it.[54] It is not hard to imagine how skills were acquired. Orderic Vitalis tells the story of Hugh, son of Giroie, who was amusing himself with some friends by throwing lances, when one carelessly hurled by his squire wounded him mortally. This was not formal training, but skill was learned during such exercise of youthful high spirits. William FitzStephen's celebrated description of twelfth century London likewise tells of the pleasure taken by the young, many of them members of noble households, in practising martial skills. These skills were primarily individual, rather than collective.[55]

The tournament is, of course, commonly regarded with some justification as an effective form of military training, where the techniques of cavalry warfare might be learned. Richard I's decision to allow tournaments in England was on the grounds that this would improve the fighting quality of English knights. The tournaments of the twelfth and thirteenth centuries, characterised by the melée rather than the joust, must indeed have been valuable practice for war. Yet for Edward I, gallant tourneyer in his youth as he was, the tournament was not to be encouraged. In the *Statuta Armorum* of 1292 an attempt was made to control the sport. Control was followed by prohibition. Tournaments might provide a more attractive alternative to the rigours of campaigning in Scotland, and it was not argued that they provided valuable training. As tournaments and the equipment needed to compete in them became increasingly specialised in the fourteenth century, so their value in providing practical training for war must have diminished.[56]

[53] *Chronici Rogeri de Wendover*, ed. H. Hewlett, iii (Rolls ser., 1889), 62, 85–6; *The Chronicle of Walter of Guisborough*, ed. H. Rothwell (Camden soc., lxxxix, 1957), 211.
[54] *L'Histoire de Guillaume le Maréchal*, i. lines 1287–1302.
[55] *Materials for the History of Thomas Becket*, ed. J. C. Robertson, iii (Rolls ser., 1877), 9–10; *The Ecclesiastical History of Orderic Vitalis*, ed. Chibnall, ii, 31.
[56] J. R. V. Barker, *The Tournament in England, 1100–1400* (Woodbridge, 1986), 17, 58–61; Ayton, *Knights and Warhorses*, 35–6.

Although their skills were primarily individual, knights were organised in coherent groups, and were undoubtedly capable on occasion of sophisticated tactical manoeuvring. The prime example, of course, is the feigned retreat at Hastings, though it may be significant that such a complex tactic seems later to have vanished from the armoury of medieval commanders. A highly exceptional chronicler's glimpse of military training of a unit of men is provided by Gerald of Wales, describing the way in which Raymond le Gros' young followers in Ireland practiced their skills in a somewhat provocative demonstration before the royal representative, William FitzAldelin.[57] Good order in a cavalry troop was to be praised. The author of the life of William Marshal commented on several occasions on troops arrayed in their proper ranks, *seréement & sans desrei*.[58] In the thirteenth century Simon de Montfort exclaimed with typical arrogance when he saw Edward's troops advancing on him at Evesham that it was from him that they had learned how to keep such good order.[59] Yet good order was certainly not always maintained. The behaviour of Edward's cavalry at Lewes, when it proved impossible to control their headlong dash after a fleeing enemy, demonstrated this, as did the earl of Gloucester's ill-fated charge into the Scottish ranks at Bannockburn. The earl cannot have intended a solo exploit; but most of his men, notably Bartholomew Badlesmere, failed to follow him.[60] It is not surprising that there is so little evidence to suggest that knights and squires were trained to fight in units. It is unlikely that knights were better organised and drilled by the fourteenth century than they had been in the eleventh; indeed, the reverse was very possibly the case. There is surprisingly little evidence on the way in which armies were organised in the field; command structures were primitive, and it is only in the case of the infantry that a clear and logical structure of hundreds and twenties, commanded by constables and vintenars, can be observed.

At an individual level, each knight needed support, and in the twelfth century presumably operated in the way envisaged in the Templar Rule. When they formed up for battle, each knight would have two squires, one in front carrying his lance, one behind leading the spare horses. In battle, one squire would ride the reserve war-horse in support of his master; the other would take the rest of the horses and equipment to comparative security in the rear.[61] In the fourteenth century, the

[57] *Expugnatio Hibernica*, 168–9.

[58] *L'Histoire de Guillaume le Maréchal*, i. lines 1308, 1419–20, 2497–8.

[59] *The Chronicle of William of Rishanger of the Barons' Wars*, ed. J. O. Halliwell (Camden Soc, 1840), 45.

[60] M. C. Prestwich, *Edward I* (1988), 45; *Vita Edwardi Secundi*, ed. Denholm-Young, 52–3.

[61] Matthew Bennett, '*La Règle du Temple* as a military manual, *or* How to Deliver a

organisation favoured by the great English condottiere, John Hawkwood, was the three-man 'lance', in which two knights or men-at-arms were accompanied and served by a single page. This method was designed for fighting on foot; the men-at-arms would stand back to back in a melée, while the page would bring up the horses at the end of the encounter.[62] Froissart's account of James Audley's exploits at Poitiers in 1356 shows how one notable knight fought with the close support of four squires, the five men operating as a single unit.[63] In 1359 many knights were recorded in the pay book as coming with one, two or three squires and a handful of archers, presumably forming small fighting units.[64] The English authorities, however, did not try to structure their élite forces around the 'lance' as a unit, in the way that the French were to do from 1445.[65]

More important than such individual arrangements was the division of the knights and cavalry into groups. In pre-Conquest Normandy, according to Dr Chibnall, 'Mounted knights were trained as far as possible in small groups of five or ten, combined in larger units under their *magistri militum.*' She argued 'That knights would tend to become organised in groups of five or ten was, in the long run, inevitable: it was a fact of military tactics.'[66] No evidence, however, from military practice was cited in support of this assumption. J. H. Round long ago adduced more powerful arguments, arguing that the feudal organisation of Anglo-Norman England was based on *constabularia* of ten knights. The service men owed was assessed in fives and tens, and his very reasonable assumption was that tenurial arrangements reflected the reality of military practice.[67] It has been argued that in reality, military service was performed by men producing not necessarily their precise quotas, but 'a reasonable turn-out acceptable to the King and his Marshal',[68] and it is tempting to dismiss the constabulary as an ingenious academic construct that had no basis in the reality of the battlefield.

Cavalry Charge', *Studies in Medieval History presented to R. Allen Brown*, ed. C. Harper-Bill, C. Holdsworth, J. L. Nelson (Woodbridge, 1989), 7–19; C. Marshall, *Warfare in the Latin East, 1192–1291* (Cambridge, 1992), 159.

[62] M. Mallett, *Mercenaries and their Masters* (1974), 148.

[63] *Chroniques de J. Froissart*, v (1874), 46.

[64] PRO, E 101/393/11, ff. 79–81, 84v.

[65] P. Contamine, *Guerre, état et société à la fin du moyen âge* (Paris, 1972), 278.

[66] M. Chibnall, 'Military Service in Normandy before 1066', *Anglo-Norman Warfare*, ed. Strickland, 35–6.

[67] J. H. Round, *Feudal England* (1895), 206–8; A. L. Poole, *Obligations of Society in the XII and XIII Centuries* (Oxford, 1946), argued unconvincingly against Round's case, by confusing constabularies of infantry troops with cavalry units, and suggesting that it was only the former that existed.

[68] J. C. Holt, 'The Introduction of Knight Service in England', *Anglo-Norman Warfare*, ed. Strickland, 56.

Yet a list of knights serving John in 1215, most of them foreign mercenaries, shows them grouped into constabularies, each of about twenty-five. Perhaps more significantly, a document dating from late in Edward I's reign shows the cavalry forces of the royal household organised into *constabularia* in a decimal pattern. Thus John of Brittany, Arnold de Caupenne and John Russel together provided thirty knights, who are noted as forming three *constabularia*.[69] The *conroi* is a term used in the fourteenth century; at the siege of Romorantin in 1356, for example, Froissart says that the marshal of the Black Prince's army had the trumpets sounded for all to arm; they were then 'ordered and put in *conroys* ready for the assault'. In the same year the failure of Geoffrey of Harcourt's men to maintain their *conrois* contributed to their defeat.[70]

The bulk of the records, however, suggests that the retinue, not the constabulary or *conroi*, was the important cavalry unit. The more substantial retinues were those led by bannerets, though of course many were headed by simple knights. The *Histoire* of William Marshal suggests, when describing the household of the Young King, that since he had fifteen bannerets, he must have had at least two hundred knights at his disposal.[71] This implies about thirteen knights to every banneret. The average size of the banneret's retinue in the English army in Scotland under Edward I, to judge by the horse valuation lists and pay records, was between thirteen and fifteen. Such averages, however, conceal considerable variations. In 1300 Robert Clifford had a retinue of four knights and eighteen squires, John de la Mare one of two knights and eight squires, while Arnald de Gavaston had a mere four squires. By 1322 the average size of a banneret's retinue had risen to twenty, the largest being that led by John Darcy consisting of forty men. In Scotland in 1341–2 the average was higher still, at thirty. The upward trend continued, and by 1359 the average size of a banneret's following was sixty. The Black Prince commanded a retinue of seven bannerets, 136 knights and 444 squires. Retinues headed by bannerets became larger still after the renewal of the French war in 1369, averaging almost 200. These huge retinues were of course subdivided into smaller retinues headed by knights and squires, while some small retinues were not incorporated into larger ones. A further significant change was that mounted archers were also included in the retinue groupings in the Hundred Years War; they presumably marched together with the knights and men-at-arms, even if they were drawn up separately for battle.[72]

[69] S. Church, 'The Earliest English Muster Roll, 18/19 December 1215', *Historical Research*, 67 (1994), 8–16; PRO, E 101/13/35, no. 16.

[70] *Chroniques de Jean Froissart*, v, 10, 76–7.

[71] *L'Histoire de Guillaume le Maréchal*, i. lines. 4771–6.

[72] M. C. Prestwich, *War, Politics and Finance under Edward I* (1972), 66; *Liber Quotidianus*

Unfortunately, evidence is largely lacking as to how retinues were recruited and composed in the twelfth century. The bulk of surviving information about the performance of military service relates to castle-guard duties, which were a very different matter from service in the field. It may be, as Professor Crouch has argued, that obligatory service by feudal tenants 'was so much a matter of course that contemporaries did not bother to mention it, unless sharp practice or unusual circumstances brought it to the surface.'[73] It is more likely, however, that in the twelfth century, as in later periods, men tried to recruit competent and skilled men to serve them, irrespective of whose tenants they might be. Analyses of retinues from that of William Marshal in the early thirteenth century to that of John Talbot in the fifteenth all point to similar conclusions, and suggest that apart from a small core, there was surprisingly little continuity of membership from year to year, and that lords did not rely extensively on recruiting among their tenants. Certainly men might well retain members of their own family, or their own tenants; but for the most part the evidence suggests that there was a floating population of men willing to take service with whoever offered them the best terms. It was only an exceptionally charismatic figure, such as Robert Clifford in the early fourteenth century, who was served by the same men year after year. His following was strongly regional in character, featuring such north-western names as Vipont, Wigton, Leyburn and Lowther.[74]

There was, of course, no such thing as the typical career of a *miles strenuus*. The opportunities and the challenges were very different in different periods; there was far more place for chivalric glories while fighting for Edward III in France than there had been for English knights in the thirteenth century in Wales or Scotland. Yet patterns and concepts of a true knightly career did not alter as much as might be expected between the twelfth and fourteenth centuries.

How long might the career of a fighting knight be? The legal convention for the populace at large was that all men between the ages of fifteen and sixty were supposed to bear arms. It is clear that many of the knightly class continued to take an active part in war long after they would have been encouraged to take early retirement in more

---

Contrarotulatoris Garderobiae, 195, 197, 200; BL MS Stowe 553, ff. 56–62; PRO, E 36/204, ff. 99–100; E 101/393/11, ff. 79–81, 84v; J.W. Sherborne, 'Indentured Retinues and English Expeditions to France, 1369–1380', *EHR*, 79 (1964), 738. The inclusion of mounted archers in retinues is discussed by Ayton, *Knights and Warhorses*, 15–18.

[73] D. Crouch, *The Beaumont Twins. The Roots and Branches of Power in the Twelfth Century* (Cambridge, 1986), 134.

[74] D. Crouch, *William Marshal. Court, Career and Chivalry in the Angevin Empire 1147–1219* (1990), 138; A.J. Pollard, *John Talbot and the War in France 1427–1453* (1983), 83–101; PRO, C 81/1722/74; C 67/16.

recent times. There is a mass of evidence provided by the elaborate hearings in the chivalric dispute between Richard Scrope and Robert Grosvenor in Richard II's reign, but unfortunately some of it is rendered less than reliable because many of the witnesses had no accurate idea of their own age. John de Sully claimed to be 105, and had memories of battles from Halidon Hill in 1333 until Najera in 1367. He would, if his age is accepted, have been eighty-seven at the latter battle; it is more realistic to accept that he had a long military career lasting over thirty years. The most implausible example is that of John de Thirwell and his father. John was fifty-four, his father, 'the oldest squire in the north', had died at the age of 145, having borne arms for sixty-nine years. A more typical entry is Walter Urswick's. He was, he said, sixty years old, and had borne his coat of arms forty years and more. Despite his age, he went on the Scottish expedition in 1385. Some men claimed to have first borne arms in their teenage years: John de Loudham, aged thirty-four, had done so at fourteen, and Simon Moigne at sixteen.[75] Other evidence backs up the picture provided by the Scrope-Grosvenor hearings. Hugh Calveley can be shown to have campaigned as early as 1344, and as late as 1385, a career of over forty years. His companion Robert Knollys, who died in his nineties, was in arms for almost as long. Nor was it solely during the Hundred Years War that men had long military careers. William Marshal was knighted in 1167, aged twenty, and rode into battle for the last time at Lincoln in 1217, at seventy. John Botetourt first campaigned in Wales as a squire of the household in 1282, and last as a banneret in 1322. War was not an occupation solely for the young, and the *miles strenuus* might be a grizzled greybeard.

The picture of aristocratic youth, ill-furnished with landed wealth, seeking fame and fortune in tournament and war, has become one of the stereotypes of the twelfth century. Ralph the Red was one such under Henry I, and the early career of William Marshal fits the pattern well. Yet later parallels can be found. One of the most noted knights in early fourteenth century England was Giles of Argentine. His record under Edward I was patchy; he was in trouble in 1302 for deserting the army in Scotland in order to fight in a tournament in Surrey, and his arrest for 'various contempts' was ordered in 1303. He fought strenuously at the siege of Stirling in 1304, and in consideration of his efforts two of his yeomen were pardoned various offences they had committed in London and in Essex. In 1306 he repeated his offence of 1302, and deserted the Scottish campaign in favour of a tournament, this time overseas. His prowess in jousting was proven in 1309, when he was crowned 'King of the Greenwood' in a great tournament held

[75] *The Scrope and Grosvenor Controversy*, ed. N. H. Nicolas (n.d.) i, 51, 53, 57, 74, 181–2.

at Stepney. He went, as a good knight should, to fight in the East, though he was unfortunate enough to be captured en route to Rhodes, and to be held prisoner at Salonica. At Edward II's insistence he was released, to die in suitably heroic if foolhardy fashion at Bannockburn. For Barbour, he was the third best knight in Christendom.[76] Giles did not play a large part in county society or local administration; he was above all a fighting knight, a man skilled in the use of sword and lance. Such a man would fit in well with conventional notions of twelfth-century knighthood.

There were hard, professional knights in the twelfth century as well as young men given to knight errantry. Odo Borleng, who commanded the troops of the royal household at Bourgthéroulde, was one such. He does not seem to have been lavishly rewarded with lands, though he probably held Bray (Berks.) for 32s. a year.[77] The career of John Ward, captain of Edward III's household archers in the 1330s, provides a later parallel example of a professional fighting knight. He served as a sergeant in the royal household until promoted to knighthood in or soon after 1343. He fought at Crécy with a small retinue of three squires and two archers. In 1347 he was granted 2s. a day to maintain himself as a knight; his landed resources were inadequate for the purpose. Royal favour enabled him to maintain his small estate at Sproston in Cheshire safe against the legal challenges of a neighbour, Sir Hugh Venables, but that was all. John Ward was not an important member of the county community. Nor, as a fighting knight, was he exceptional in this.[78]

Examination of the knight at war suggests a rather different pattern of development to that which has emerged from other types of evidence. The later twelfth century appears as a period of significant change, when the previously undifferentiated cavalry were divided between knights and mounted sergeants. The numbers of fighting knights did not change dramatically thereafter until the late fourteenth century, when a striking decline took place. This picture does not coincide with the accepted pattern of development. In particular, to see military needs as driving the fortunes of the knightly class in the thirteenth century, with families dropping out of the social élite because they

---

[76] *Calendar of Patent Rolls, 1301–07*, 121, 242; *Calendar of Close Rolls, 1302–07*, 66; *Calendar of Close Rolls, 1313–18*, 71; H. Johnstone, *Edward of Caernarvon, 1284–1307* (Manchester, 1946), 116–17; *Chronicles of the Reigns of Edward I and II*, ed. W. Stubbs (Rolls ser, 1882), i. 157, 267; G. W. S. Barrow, *Robert Bruce and the Community of the Realm of Scotland* (1965), 295–6. Giles' death features in the *Vita Edwardi Secundi*, 53; it is interesting that he had been involved along with the putative author, John Walwayn, in an attack on a manor in Suffolk in 1302; *Calendar of Patent Rolls, 1301–7*, 86.

[77] M. Chibnall, 'Mercenaries and the *Familia Regis* under Henry I', *Anglo-Norman Warfare*, ed. Strickland, 87–8.

[78] P. Morgan, *War and Society in Medieval Cheshire* (Manchester, 1987), 52–3, 168–9.

could not afford the costs of horses and arms, is unconvincing. Nor does the evidence for the way in which knights were organised in the field clearly demonstrate a shift from a reliance upon landed tenants to a dependence on indentured retainers. It is possible that there was no strong link between social and military change, and that it is wrong to see social development as driven by, or even related to, the military situation. That is unlikely, for change in the late twelfth and early thirteenth century fits an economic explanation well: this was a period of serious inflation, which saw lesser landlords who were dependent on fixed rents suffer in comparison with large landowners who were able to switch to direct management of their estates. Jocelin of Brakelond's account of the abbacy of Samson at Bury St Edmunds is usually read from the perspective of successful monastic management, but the other side of the coin is that of local knights suffering at the hands of rapacious monks.[79] The decline in knightly numbers in the late fourteenth century should also be seen against an economic background, that of the aftermath of the Black Death, but many other factors need to be taken into account. The rise in social status of squires saw them come to occupy the place earlier held by knights. Nor should disenchantment with the French war be discounted as an element. The evidence of the armies in the field, and of the way that men fought, strongly suggests that there is a need to reconsider and reassess the chronology and nature of the development of knighthood and gentry in medieval England.

[79] *The Chronicle of Jocelin of Brakelond*, ed. H. E. Butler (1949), pp. 32–3.

INSTITUTIONS AND ECONOMIC DEVELOPMENT IN EARLY MODERN CENTRAL EUROPE

By Sheilagh C. Ogilvie

READ 9 DECEMBER 1994

I. Introduction

Institutions and economies underwent profound changes between 1500 and 1800 in most parts of Europe.[1] Differences among societies decreased in some ways, but markedly increased in others. Do these changes and these variations tell us anything about the relationship between social organisation and economic well-being? This is a very wide question, and even the qualified 'yes' with which I will answer it, though based on the detailed empirical research of some hundreds of local studies undertaken in the past few decades, is far from definitive. Many of these studies were inspired by an influential set of hypotheses, known as the 'theory of proto-industrialisation'. While this theory has been enormously fruitful, its conclusions about European economic and social development are no longer tenable. This paper offers an alternative interpretation of the evidence now available about proto-industrialisation in different European societies, and explores its implications by investigating one region of Central Europe between 1580 and about 1800.

'Proto-industrialisation' is the term used to describe the rise and growth of export-oriented domestic industries, which took place all over Europe during the early modern period. Long before the first factories, Europe had ceased to be a homogeneous 'less developed economy', producing largely for subsistence and trading only in luxuries. Instead, it had become a differentiated patchwork of interdependent regions, specialising in a wide array of agricultural and industrial activities, and trading in mass commodities through a network of towns and cities. This is something of which specialists have long been aware.[2] But in

[1] I should like to thank Jeremy Edwards, Emma Rothschild, Paul Seabright, Keith Wrightson and Tony Wrigley, who were so kind as to read and comment upon the manuscript of this paper; and André Carus, who read several drafts and made a large number of very stimulating suggestions.

[2] J. de Vries, *The economy of Europe in an age of crisis, 1600–1750* (Cambridge, 1976) [hereafter de Vries, *Economy*], esp. 32–47. The growth of cottage industries in the early modern period had received special attention from the German Historical School of Political Economy in the late nineteenth and early twentieth centuries, e.g. in W. Stieda, *Litteratur, heutige Zustände und Entstehung der deutschen Hausindustrie* (Leipzig, 1889).

the 1970s a series of publications appeared which focussed on the *industrial* aspect of regional specialisation, christened it 'proto-industrialisation', and claimed that this was the cause of industrialisation. Proto-industries, it was argued, caused population growth, commercialisation of agriculture, capital accumulation, labour surplus, proletarianisation, and the replacement of traditional social institutions by markets—all the prerequisites, in short, for capitalism and industrialisation.[3]

The ensuing explosion of case studies on early modern export industries showed wide acceptance of these views, but also gradually generated important criticisms.[4] Local and regional studies have revealed that proto-industrialisation was neither necessary nor sufficient for demographic change: in some proto-industrial regions marriage- and birth-rates increased, in others they decreased, and the same was true of agrarian regions.[5] The link with agriculture also varied hugely:

[3] The first published use of the term was in C. Tilly and R. Tilly, 'Agenda for European economic history in the 1970s', *Journal of economic history* 31 (1971), 184–98, citing the doctoral thesis of F. F. Mendels, 'Industrialization and population pressure in eighteenth century Flanders' (Ph.D. dissertation, University of Wisconsin, 1970), subsequently published as F. F. Mendels, *Industrialization and population pressure in eighteenth-century Flanders* (New York, 1981) [hereafter Mendels, *Industrialization*]. The concept was first extensively discussed in a now-classic article, F. F. Mendels, 'Proto-industrialization: the first phase of the industrialization process', *Journal of economic history* 32 (1972), 241–61 [hereafter Mendels, 'Proto-industrialization']. Over the ensuing five years the concept was extended in different directions by J. Mokyr, 'Growing-up and the industrial revolution in Europe', *Explorations in economic history*, 31 (1976), 371–96 [hereafter Mokyr, 'Growing-up'], who was sceptical about capital accumulation, but agreed tht proto-industry led to population growth and labour surplus; P. Kriedte, H. Medick and J. Schlumbohm, *Industrialisierung vor der Industrialisierung. Gewerbliche Warenproduktion auf dem Land in der Formationsperiode des kapitalismus* (Göttingen, 1977), English translation P. Kriedte, H. Medick and J. Schlumbohm, *Industrialization before industrialization: Rural industry in the genesis of capitalism* (Cambridge, 1981) [hereafter Kriedte, Medick and Schlumbohm, *Industrialization*]; and D. Levine, *Family formation in an age of nascent capitalism* (London, 1977) [hereafter Levine, *Family formation*].

[4] Thus the tenets of the theory were accepted by the vast majority of the 46 case-studies prepared for the Eighth International Economic History Congress in Budapest in 1982, collected in *VIII Congrès Internationale d'Histoire Economique, Budapest 16–22 août 1982, Section A2: La protoindustrialisation: Théorie et réalité, Rapports* 2 vols. eds. P. Deyon and F. Mendels (ms., Université des Arts, Lettres et Sciences Humaines, Lille, 1982) [hereafter *VIII Congrès*, eds. Deyon & Mendels]. However, important criticisms were already emerging: in particular, D. C. Coleman, 'Proto-industrialization: A concept too many?', *Economic history review*, (2nd series) 36 (1983) 435–48 [hereafter Coleman, 'Proto-industrialization']; and R. A. Houston and K. D. M. Snell, 'Proto-industrialization? Cottage industry, social change, and industrial revolution', *Historical journal* 1984, 473–92 [hereafter Houston and Snell, 'Proto-industrialization?'].

[5] This is pointed out by Houston and Snell, 'Proto-industrialization?', 480–8. P. Kriedte, H. Medick and J. Schlumbohm, 'Proto-industrialization revisited: Demography, social structure, and modern domestic industry', *Continuity and change* 8 (1993), 182–217, recently acknowledged that 'In sum, the empirical studies show that it is impossible

proto-industries were associated not just with commercial farming, but also with peasant smallholdings, cottager systems, subsistence cultivation, and even feudal domains worked with serf labour.[6] Furthermore, proto-industries were neither the exclusive nor even the chief sources of capital, entrepreneurship, or labour for later factory industries.[7] Nor did proto-industry always lead to falling living standards, growing landlessness, or proletarianisation, while these could often be found in purely agrarian regions.[8] Finally, proto-industrialisation was neither necessary nor sufficient for factory industrialisation: some proto-industrial regions developed factories, others remained proto-industrial, and still others returned to agriculture, while factory industries arose in many regions which never had any proto-industries.[9]

Important differences have thus emerged among proto-industries in different parts of Europe. While not encouraging for the original theories of proto-industrialisation, these findings do open new perspectives on what may be a more promising approach to explaining European economic development. This is to ask what might have caused such enormous economic variation across societies in the same continent. While not altogether new, such variation became much more pronounced in the early modern period, and its legacy—particularly the gap between eastern and western Europe—is evident to this day. Perhaps the greatest service performed by the concept of proto-industrialisation is to have generated so many studies of the same economic sector in such a wide variety of contexts, enabling more fruitful comparisons across societies. On the basis of such comparisons,

---

to establish a single behaviour pattern for all proto-industrial populations, and that we must take into account a whole array of differentiating factors' (225).

[6] Houston and Snell, 'Proto-industrialization?' 477–8; further shortcomings of theories about proto-industrialization as they relate to agriculture are discussed in G. L. Gullickson, 'Agriculture and cottage industry: Redefining the causes of proto-industrialization', *Journal of economic history*, 43 (1983), 832–50.

[7] As pointed out in Mokyr, 'Growing-up', 377–9; Houston and Snell, 'Proto-industrialization?', 488–92; and P. Hudson, 'Proto-industrialisation', *ReFresh* 10 (1990), 1–4 [hereafter Hudson, 'Proto-industrialisation'].

[8] Houston and Snell, 'Proto-industrialization?' 478–9; Hudson, 'Proto-industrialisation', 3. Recent surveys confirm this for particular countries: P. Deyon, 'Proto-industrialization in France', in *Proto-industrialization in Europe: An introductory handbook*, eds. S. C. Ogilvie and M. Cerman (Cambridge, 1995) [hereafter *Proto-industrialization in Europe*, eds. Ogilvie and M. Cerman], 38–48, concludes that 'the impoverishment of households has not been proved for all the very diverse models and all the successive phases of proto-industrialization'; the same conclusion emerges from U. Pfister, 'Proto-industrialization in Switzerland', in *ibid.*, 137–154 [hereafter Pfister, 'Proto-industrialization in Switzerland']; and C. Vandenbroeke, 'Proto-industry in Flanders: A critical review', in *ibid.*, 102–117.

[9] Coleman, 'Proto-industrialization', 442–3; Houston and Snell, 'Proto-industrialization?', 490–2; Hudson, 'Proto-industrialisation', 3. De-industrialisation was already recognised as a possible outcome of proto-industrialisation in Mendels, 'Proto-industrialization'; and in Kriedte, Medick and Schlumbohm, *Industrialization*, 145–54.

I will suggest that a major cause of the variation among economies in early modern Europe was the—widening—variation in their *social institutions*.[10]

A very clear story about social institutions is told by the original theorists. Before proto-industrialisation, they argue, Europe was a 'peasant' society in the sense used by Alexander Chayanov. Production, consumption and reproduction were strictly controlled by the strong peasant family. Families in turn were rooted in self-subsistent and highly-regulated communities. Taxation and regulation by landlords and princes were the only outside contacts. Markets were largely irrelevant. In towns, life was strictly regulated by strong patriarchal craft and merchant families. Urban privileges, craft guilds and merchant companies controlled every aspect of industry and commerce. Both the peasant economy and the guild economy were governed by non-market mentalities.[11]

Proto-industries, they say, changed all this. Family controls broke down: men lost control over women and parents over children. Village communities ceased to regulate settlement, marriage, inheritance, work, credit, and land. Landlords, too, lost their powers, as proto-industrialisation helped to break down feudalism. Urban domination over the countryside, and guild control over industry and commerce, broke down under cheap rural competition. The early modern state was largely irrelevant. It simply guaranteed market transactions, and occasionally helped merchants coerce proto-industrial producers. Soon production, consumption, and reproduction 'came to be entirely determined by the market'.[12] In short, wherever and whenever proto-

---

[10] The economic divergence among European regions during the early modern period is explored by J. Topolski, *Narodziny kapitalzmu w Europeie XIV–XVII wieku* (Warsaw, 1965); the economic and institutional divergence is discussed in de Vries, *Economy*, 47–83, and in S. C. Ogilvie, 'Germany and the seventeenth-century crisis', *Historical journal* 35 (1992), 417–441, here esp. 420, 432–4.

[11] These views are summarized in F. Mendels, 'Proto-industrialization: Theory and reality. General report', in *Eighth International Economic History Congress, Budapest 1982, 'A' Themes* (Budapest, 1982), 69–107 [hereafter Mendels, 'General report'], here esp. 80; Mendels, *Industrialization*, here esp. 16, 22–3, 26, 47–8, 210, 239–43, 245–7, 270; Kriedte, Medick and Schlumbohm, *Industrialization*, here esp. 12–13, 22, 38–9, 40–1, 51–2; Mokyr, 'Growing-up', 374. For Chayanov's original model of peasant society, see A. Chayanov, *The theory of peasant economy*, ed. D. Thorner, B. Kerblay and R. E. F. Smith (Homewood (Illinois), 1966). The reliance of proto-industrialization theories on the theories of Chayanov is explicit: Mendels, *Industrialization*, 239–41; Kriedte, Medick, and Schlumbohm, *Industrialization*, 43–4.

[12] See Mendels, 'General report', 80 (on the breakdown of village and landlord controls); Mendels, *Industrialization*, 16, 26 (on the breakdown of urban privileges and guild controls); Kriedte, Medick and Schlumbohm, *Industrialization*, 38–73 (on the breakdown of traditional family controls); 8, 16–17, 40 (on the breakdown of village and landlord controls); 13, 22, 51–2, 128 (on the breakdown of urban privileges and guild controls); 128–9 (on the

industries arose, so too did markets, displacing and destroying older social institutions. Proto-industry diminished social variations, which therefore played little role in subsequent economic development.

This story sounds so plausible that it has entered the historian's working vocabulary; it has almost become part of common sense. The facts, however, tell a very different tale. Trying to make sense of this tale can help us to explain why different European proto-industries developed in such divergent ways.

II. The worsted industry of the Württemberg Black Forest

What first alerted me to shortcomings in the prevailing story about social institutions and proto-industry was a particular empirical example. Later I discovered many parallels elsewhere in Europe, but their significance can best be shown by beginning where I did, in one small region of southwest Germany.

In the 1560s, the inhabitants of the Swabian Black Forest, a hilly and wooded region of the Duchy of Württemberg, found a new way of making a living. They began to weave light worsted cloths, and sell them to markets throughout central and southern Europe.[13] Swiftly this new industry became the most important single livelihood in many villages and small towns in the region, surpassing the older weaving of heavy woollens for local and regional consumption. For the next 240 years, the production of light, low-quality worsted cloths for export would remain one of the two most important industries in Württemberg, and the economic mainstay of a region of 1,000 square kilometres, one-ninth of the total land area of the duchy.[14] The history of this industry is not an economic success-story. Although it endured for more than nine generations, it stagnated after the first remarkable expansion, and its workers' struggle for survival became very grim. Yet it was probably the most important German worsted industry until about 1700 and, despite the rise of competitors, retained a significant presence on south German, Swiss and Italian markets until the late 1790s.[15]

The Württemberg worsted industry was identified as a proto-industry by the original theorists.[16] It produced mainly for export, selling tens

---

role of the state); 40 (on the market; quoted passage); and Mokyr, 'Growing-up', 374 (on the breakdown of urban privileges and guild controls).

[13] A distinguished early study of this industry, although based wholly on merchant and state documents, is W. Troeltsch, *Die Calwer Zeughandlungskompagnie und ihre Arbeiter: Studien zur Gewerbe- und Sozialgeschichte Altwürttembergs* (Jena, 1897) [hereafter Troeltsch, *Zeughandlungskompagnie*]; for a different perspective, based on community and guild documentation as well, see S. C. Ogilvie, *State corporation and proto-industry: The Württemberg Black Forest, 1580–1797* (Cambridge, 1995) [hereafter Ogilvie, *Württemberg*].

[14] Troeltsch, *Zeughandlungskompagnie*, 81.

[15] Troeltsch, *Zeughandlungskompagnie*, esp. 172–3, 177, 181–2, 186, 194–9.

[16] Kriedte, Medick and Schlumbohm, *Industrialization*, 2, 5, 49, 50, 54.

of thousands of worsteds every year to markets in Italy, Poland, Silesia, Switzerland, Austria, Bavaria, and the southern Empire.[17] It was dense, concentrated into six small administrative districts in the Black Forest, and employing up to half the families in some communities. It was rural, practised in villages and very small agrarian towns of 1,500–2,000 inhabitants.[18] It was carried out alongside farming: in 1736, 80 per cent of village weavers in the most important industrial district still lived partly from their own land.[19] It thus satisfies all the conditions for a classic proto-industry. But closer scrutiny reveals a number of features which throw doubt on basic assumptions about European proto-industrialisation.

III. Landholding institutions

One basic assumption is that proto-industry both resulted from and furthered a breakdown in the feudal powers of landlords.[20] But in Württemberg, the powers of landlords had all but disappeared long before proto-industries arose in the sixteenth century. Landlords began to abandon demesne cultivation and lease land out to peasants shortly after 1300. By 1450 at latest, most peasants enjoyed secure tenures and the right to sell, sub-divide and bequeathe their holdings. Restrictions on settlement, marriage and mobility disappeared or were commuted to small cash payments. In 1519, the nobility of the region declared themselves to be Free Imperial Knights, leaving the prince, the state church, and various public foundations as the only remaining landlords in the Duchy of Württemberg. These collected a rent of about ten per cent of output, and some minor cash payments in lieu of other former feudal dues, but exercised almost no control over peasant decisions.[21] The few vestigial powers of Württemberg landlords show no relationship

---

[17] Troeltsch, *Zeughandlungskompagnie*, esp. 172–3, 177, 181–2, 186, 194–9.

[18] For numbers of practising weavers and their distribution across communities, see Troeltsch, *Zeughandlungkompagnie*, 107 (table), 10, 17, 22, 40–1, 78, 103–5, 107–8, 176, 183, 209–10, 253–5, 282, 293–4, 298, 306, 310, 314, 334, 336–8, 383, 387, 392; and Ogilvie, *Württemberg*, chapter 7.

[19] Württembergische Hauptstaatsarchiv Stuttgart [hereafter WHSA] A573 Bü 6967 Seelentabelle 1736 ('soul-table' of the ten communities of the district of Wildberg in 1736).

[20] Mendels, 'General report', 80; Kriedte, Medick and Schlumbohm, *Industrialization*, 8, 16–17, 40.

[21] W. von Hippel, *Die Bauernbefreiung im Königreich Württemberg*, 2 vols. (Boppard am Rhein, 1977), vol. 1, 76ff, 94–105, 120–4; W. A. Boelcke, *Wirtschaftsgeschichte Baden-Württembergs von den Römern bis heute* (Stuttgart, 1987), 64–5, 113; D. W. Sabean, *Property, production and family in Neckarhausen, 1700–1870* (Cambridge, 1990), [hereafter Sabean, *Property*] 43–4; J. A. Vann, *The making of a state: Württemberg, 1593–1793* (Ithaca/London, 1984), [hereafter Vann, *Württemberg*, 41, 45–51; W. Grube, 'Württembergische Verfassungskämpfe im Zeitalter Herzog Ulrichs', in *Neue Beiträge zu südwestdeutschen Landesgeschichte* Festschrift M. Miller (Stuttgart, 1962), 144–60.

with either the timing or the location of proto-industry in the region.[22] But was Württemberg simply an exception? Not at all. In most areas of England, the Low Countries, and in parts of Switzerland and the Rhineland, the institutional powers of landlords had already disappeared long before proto-industries arose. The causes of this breakdown are a matter of debate, but proto-industrialisation cannot have been essential, since landlords had also lost their institutional powers in many agrarian regions.[23]

[22] Even the relationship between rural industry and partible inheritance (which in some European regions reflected weak landlord control, but also depended on an array of other factors including physical geography, local agrarian practice (e.g. viticulture), community institutions, legislation, and state policy) is still disputed. Thus H. Hoffmann, *Landwirtschaft and Industrie in Württemberg, insbesondere im Industriegebiet der Schwäbischen Alb* (Berlin, 1935), for instance, argues that rural industry was more successful in the Duchy of Württemberg than in neighbouring Free Imperial territories because its rulers permitted partible inheritance, see esp. 19–44. On the other hand, R. Flik, *Die Textilindustrie in Calw und in Heidenheim 1705–1870. Eine regional vergleichende Untersuchung zur Geschichte der Frühindustrialisierung und Industriepolitik in Württemberg* (Stuttgart, 1990), 55–61, contends that *within* Württemberg the Heidenheim linen proto-industry in eastern Württemberg was more successful than the Calw worsted proto-industry in the Black Forest region partly because of the unusual *strength* of local tenurial restrictions on land fragmentation in the district of Heidenheim. In turn, the empirical basis for Flik's argument is disputed in P. Kriedte, H. Medick & J. Schlumbohm, 'Sozialgeschichte in der Erweiterung—Proto-Industrialisierung in der Verengung? Demographie, Sozialstruktur, moderne Hausindustrie: eine Zwischenbilanz der Proto-Industrialisierungs-Forschung (Teil I u. II)', *Geschichte und Gesellschaft* 18 (1992), 70–87, 231–255, here footnote 12.

[23] On England, see K. Wrightson, *English society 1580–1680* (New York/London, 1982) [hereafter Wrightson, *English society*], 24–5, 47–9, 130–3; J. A. Sharpe, *Early modern England: A social history, 1550–1760* (London, 1987) [hereafter Sharpe, *Early modern England*], 127–36; de Vries, *Economy*, 75–82; Levine, *Family formation*, 4–6. On the Netherlands, see J. de Vries, *The Dutch rural economy in the golden age, 1500–1700* (Berkeley, 1974) [hereafter de Vries, *Dutch rural economy*], 25–8, 35–41; de Vries, *Economy*, 69–75. On the Rhineland, see H. Kisch, 'From monopoly to laissez-faire: The early growth of the Wupper Valley textile trades', *Journal of European economic history* 1:2 (1972) 298–407 [hereafter Kisch, 'Monopoly'], here 301, 303, 304; H. Kisch, 'Preußischer Merkantilismus und der Aufstieg des Krefelder Seidengewerbes: Variationen über ein Thema des 18. Jahrhunderts', in *Die Hausindustriellen Textilegewerbe am Niederrhein vor der Industriellen Revolution: Von der ursprünglichen zur kapitalistischen Akkumulation* ed. H. Kisch (Göttingen, 1981) [hereafter Kisch, 'Merkantilismus'], 94, 96; P. Kriedte, 'Proto-Industrialisierung und großes Kapital. Das Seidengewerbe in Krefeld und seinem Umland bis zum Ende des Ancien Regime', *Archiv für Sozialgeschichte* 23 (1983) [hereafter Kriedte, 'Großes Kapital'], 219–266, here 225. On Switzerland, see R. Braun, 'Early industrialization and demographic change in the Canton of Zürich', in *Historical studies of changing fertility* ed. C. Tilly (Princeton, 1978), 289–334 [hereafter Braun, 'Early industrialization'], here 299, 307; A. Tanner, *Spulen—Weben—Sticken: Die Industrialisierung in Appenzell Ausserrhoden* (Zürich, 1982), esp. 418–19; A. Tanner, 'Arbeit, Haushalt und Familie in Appenzell-Außerrhoden. Veränderungen in einem ländlichen Industriegebiet im 18. und 19. Jahrhundert', in *Familienstruktur und Arbeitsorganisation in ländlichen Gesellschaften* eds. J. Ehmer & M. Mitterauer (Vienna etc., 1986), 449–494 [hereafter Tanner, 'Arbeit'], here 451; A. Mirabdolbaghi, 'Population and landownership in the *Baillage Commun* of Grandson in the early eighteenth century' (Ph.D. dissertation, London School of Economics, 1994) [hereafter Mirabdolbaghi, 'Population'].

Moreover, there were many parts of central, eastern and southern Europe where landlords remained very strong despite widespread proto-industry. Originally, it was claimed that such 'feudal proto-industries' arose only in areas where feudalism had begun to weaken, and that they furthered this breakdown.[24] But Rudolph's research has shown that proto-industries arose throughout Russia in areas of classic feudal production on large estates, and neither caused nor required the abolition of labour services or their commutation to cash.[25] Similarly, proto-industries expanded rapidly in Bohemia, Moravia and Silesia after 1650, precisely when the 'second serfdom' began to strengthen landlords' powers. Landlords positively encouraged peasants to engage in proto-industry, for this increased their revenues from feudal dues on weavers and looms, concession fees for monopolies to yarn factors and merchants, and raw material sales from the demesne. Landlords forcibly reduced proto-industrial costs through 'forced wage labour', forced sales at fixed prices, restricting peasants' alternative options, and even sometimes using or selling peasants' labour services for proto-industrial tasks.[26] Strong feudal landlords also encouraged proto-industry by creating guild-free enclaves, a pattern also observed in parts of northern Italy.[27] Elsewhere, as in the Bulgarian province of Eastern Rumelia, landlords and graziers used their far-reaching institutional powers to restrict access to farmland, which pushed the population into proto-industry as the next-best option.[28] In eighteenth-century Lombardy, powerful sharecropping landlords used their institutional powers to benefit from the silk proto-industry, worsening the terms of lease contracts, restricting the options of the rural population, and themselves

[24] Kriedte, Medick and Schlumbohm, *Industrialization*, 18–19, 77, 98, 111.

[25] R. L. Rudolph, 'Agricultural structure and proto-industrialization in Russia: Economic development with unfree labour', *Journal of economic history* 45 (1985), 47–69, here 48, 54, 57–61, 63; R. L. Rudolph, 'Family structure and proto-industrialization in Russia', *Journal of economic history* 40 (1980), 111–118, here 111.

[26] A. Klíma, 'English merchant capital in Bohemia in the eighteenth century,' *Economic history review* 2nd ser., 12 (1959), 34–48 [hereafter Klíma, 'English merchant capital'], here 35, 38; A. Klíma, 'The role of rural domestic industry in Bohemia in the eighteenth century', *Economic history review* 2nd ser., 27 (1974), 48–56, here 51, 53; M. Myška, 'Pre-industrial iron-making in the Czech lands: The labour force and production relations circa 1350—circa 1840,' *Past and present* 82 (1979), 44–72, here 59–63; M. Myška, 'Proto-industrialization in Bohemia, Moravia and Silesia', in *Proto-industrialization in Europe* eds. Ogilvie & Cerman, 188–207 [hereafter Myška, 'Proto-industrialization'].

[27] Klíma, 'English merchant capital', 34–5; Myška, 'Proto-industrialization'; A. Klíma, 'The industrial development in Bohemia 1648–1781,' *Past and present* 11 (1957), here 89; C. M. Belfanti, 'Rural manufactures and rural proto-industries in the "Italy of the Cities" from the sixteenth through the eighteenth century', *Continuity and change* 8 (1993), 253–80 [hereafter Belfanti, 'Rural manufactures'], 259.

[28] M. R. Palairet, 'Woollen textile manufacturing in the Balkans 1850–1911: A study of protoindustrial failure', in *VIIIe Congrès* eds. Deyon & Mendels, contribution no. 34 [hereafter Palairet, 'Woollen textile manufacture'], here 1–3, 8–11.

operating proto-industrial enterprises.[29] In many European regions, therefore, powerful landlords not only survived but positively profited from proto-industry, which they therefore encouraged. There is no evidence that proto-industry broke down feudalism in eastern and southern Europe: this was ultimately accomplished, in agrarian and proto-industrial regions alike, only after centuries of bitter social and political struggle.

The relationship between proto-industry and the powers of landlords must therefore be different from that proposed by the original theory. What mattered for proto-industry was not the 'strength' or 'weakness' of landlords, but the precise effects of their institutional powers on industrial costs in the particular local context. Very *strong* landlords could encourage proto-industry, if their institutional powers enabled them to weaken guilds, prevent peasants from earning a living in agriculture, extort raw materials and labour inputs at low or zero cost, or dictate low output prices. This is what happened in proto-industries in Russia, Bohemia, Moravia, Silesia, Bulgaria, and parts of northern Italy. Very *weak* landlords could *also* encourage proto-industry, if they were so weak that they could not intervene in markets. This is what happened in England, the Low Countries, Switzerland, the Rhineland, and Württemberg. Low costs enabled a proto-industry to arise and endure, but the precise social institutions which created these low costs made an enormous difference to whether this proto-industry prospered, and what effect it had on people's well-being—as is shown by the divergent economic development of eastern and southern Europe, where low costs resulted from landlord strength, compared to western and northern Europe, where low costs resulted from landlord weakness. Institutional privileges for landlords were not incompatible with proto-industry (any more than with commercial agriculture); but they were incompatible with sustained economic growth.

IV. Communities

The same pattern emerges when we look at a second important social institution, the local community. Proto-industrialisation is supposed to have required, and furthered, the breakdown of community controls over economic, social and demographic behaviour.[30] In Württemberg, however, every local study confirms the extensive powers of local communities well into the nineteenth century. My own study of the

[29] C. M. Belfanti, 'The proto-industrial heritage: Forms of rural proto-industry in northern Italy in the eighteenth and nineteenth centuries', in *Proto-industrialization in Europe* eds. Ogilvie & Cerman, 155–170.
[30] Mendels, 'General report', 80; Kriedte, Medick and Schlumbohm, *Industrialization*, 8, 16–17, 40.

Black Forest district of Wildberg found that community regulation permeated every aspect of local life—including proto-industry. Communities permitted settlement, marriage and work only to citizens and their children; outside applicants were generally rejected, and the few non-citizen residents were restricted to the poorest occupations. Community officials, who made up as many as one-fifth of all male householders, closely supervised the three-field crop rotation, controlled the use of common lands, inspected the output and prices of every craft and service, and regulated markets in foodstuffs and raw materials. Every loan and land transaction had to be approved by the community court. Communities enforced the regulations of rural guilds, and penalised independent work by journeymen and unmarried women. Familial, marital and inheritance conflicts were resolved in a church court manned by the pastor and community officials. Poor relief was the responsibility of the community more than the family, and to prevent behaviour which might burden the poor-rate, communities closely regulated work, schooling, religion, sexuality, and even games and celebrations.[31]

This pervasive communal regulation showed no signs of breaking down, either during the initial proto-industrial boom of the 1580s, or at any point over the next two centuries, as the district of Wildberg developed into the largest and densest centre of worsted production in the Black Forest. It is hard to imagine that agrarian communities can have been any stronger than these proto-industrial communities. Available studies suggest that communities were strong everywhere in Württemberg until long past 1800, sustained by their symbiotic relationship with the state, which relied on them for tax-gathering and conscription, and in turn enforced their internal regulations.[32]

---

[31] These conclusions are based on detailed local research on the small town and 10–15 villages of the *Amt* (administrative district) of Wildberg, one of the ca. 60 *Ämter* of the duchy of Württemberg, between the late sixteenth and the late eighteenth century, whose results are presented in Ogilvie, *Württemberg*, here esp. chapter 4; S. C. Ogilvie, 'Coming of age in a corporate society: Capitalism, Pietism and family authority in rural Württemberg 1590–1740', *Continuity and change* 1 (1986), 279–331 [hereafter Ogilvie, 'Coming of age'], here 282–4, 286–91; S. C. Ogilvie, 'Women and proto-industrialisation in a corporate society: Württemberg woollen weaving 1590–1760', in *Women's work and the family economy in historical perspective* eds. P. Hudson & W. R. Lee (Manchester, 1990), 76–103 [hereafter Ogilvie, 'Women and proto-industrialization']; S. C. Ogilvie, 'Women's work in a developing economy: A German industrial countryside, 1580–1740 (MA diss., University of Chicago, 1993).

[32] On the powers of Württemberg communities, see also Vann, *Making of a state*, 38–43, 46–7, 51–2, 65, 99–109, 180–4, 187–8, 225, 237–44, 247–50, 278–9, 287–8; D. W. Sabean, *Power in the blood: Popular culture and village discourse in early modern Germany* (Cambridge, 1984), 1–36; Sabean, *Property*, 26–27, 38–57; H. Medick, 'Village spinning bees, sexual culture and free time among rural youth in early modern Germany', *Interest and emotion: Essays on the study of family and kinship* eds. H. Medick and D. Sabean (Cambridge/Paris,

But was Württemberg, with its important proto-industries and its strong communities simply an exception? By no means. It is certainly true that in Flanders, England, and parts of the Rhineland and Switzerland, many communities were very weak, while others were still quite strong, and proto-industry gravitated toward the weaker ones. Given heterogeneity in community strength, this was understandable: fewer community restrictions could indeed mean lower costs for proto-industries, and greater flexibility. However, it had not been proto-industry which dissolved these restrictions: in these societies communities had already become weak before proto-industry, and in regions which were purely agrarian.[33]

Moreover, there were many parts of Europe where, as in Württemberg, proto-industries co-existed with strong communities. In some, this was because other factors outweighed the disadvantages of strong communities. In Scotland, for instance, proto-industries arose in arable regions where communities were strong, rather than in pastoral regions where they were weak. This was because in arable areas another institutional feature, the 'cottar system', created a source of cheap proto-industrial labour: farmers sublet small plots to 'cottars' in return for part-time farm-work, and many cottars turned to proto-industry to supplement their earnings. In Scottish pastoral areas, by contrast, joint-ownership property rights created disincentives for landowners to permit a proto-industrial workforce to settle.[34] Similarly, in the Württemberg Black Forest other factors—weak seigneurial restrictions, an early start, favourable location—outweighed the disadvantages of community restrictions until at least 1700. Even then, the segmentation of early modern European worsted markets by transactions costs and warfare permitted the Württemberg worsted industry to survive for a century

---

1984); V. Trugenberger, *Zwischen Schloss und Vorstadt: Sozialgeschichte der Stadt Leonberg im 16. Jahrhundert* (Vaihingen/Enz, 1984); J. Mantel, *Wildberg: Eine Studie zur wirtschaftlichen und sozialen Entwicklung der Stadt von der Mitte des sechzehnten bis zur mitte des achtzehnten Jahrhunderts* (Stuttgart, 1974).

[33] On England, see Wrightson, *English society*, 40–60, 155–72; Sharpe, *Early modern England*, 90–98; de Vries, *Economy*, 75–82; A. Macfarlane, *The origins of English individualism: The family, property and social transition* (Oxford, 1978), 4–5, 68–9, 78–9, 119, 162–3; Levine, *Family formation*, 4–6. On the Netherlands, see J. de Vries, *The Dutch rural economy in the golden age, 1500–1700* (Berkeley, 1974) [hereafter de Vries, *Dutch rural economy*], 26–35, 49–67; de Vries, *Economy*, 53–67; H. A. Enno van Gelder, 'Nederlandse dorpen in de 16e eeuw' *Verhandelingen der Koninklijke nederlandse Akademie van Wetenschappen, Afdeling Letterkunde*, 59 (1953), 40–41, 110. On the Rhineland, see Kisch, 'Monopoly', 301–4; Kisch, 'Merkantilismus', 94–6; Kriedte, 'Großes kapital', 225. On Switzerland, see Braun, 'Early industrialization', 299, 307; Tanner, 'Arbeit', 451; Mirabdolbaghi, 'Population'.

[34] I. D. Whyte, 'Proto-industrialization in Scotland,' *Regions and industries: A perspective on the industrial revolution in Britain* ed. P. Hudson (Cambridge, 1989), 228–251, here 231, 237–8, 243–5.

longer, despite the visible costs imposed by its communities.[35]

And again, the precise impact of institutions on production costs determined the outcome in each case; particular community rules in particular circumstances could actually *lower* proto-industrial costs. Thus in Twente, in the Netherlands, the communal *marken* system restricted access to common land (essential for farming) to a group of established peasant families, excluding the rest of the population, which therefore turned to proto-industry.[36] In Cento, in northern Italy, the communal *partecipanza* system distributed land according to family size. Rather than emigrating (which involved losing land rights), people stayed in the community but turned to proto-industry to supplement earnings from an insufficient land-share.[37] Just as with landlords, so too with communities, it was not 'strength' or 'weakness' that mattered, but the precise effects of institutional arrangements on costs.

What this shows, as with landlord powers, is not that community restrictions had no relationship with proto-industry, but that this relationship must be different and more complex than originally proposed. In Württemberg, as we have seen, local communities regulated almost every aspect of behaviour. By controlling settlement, they limited population growth and expansion of the workforce, reduced labour mobility, maintained high marriage ages and small families, and prevented young men without land or guild licenses from setting up households, thereby compelling them to emigrate or take military service. The large numbers of women who therefore never married were prohibited from working in mainstream occupations, often through active harassment by male citizens in the community courts. Excluded from alternative options, these women became a cheap source of spinning labour for the worsted industry. By registering servants, compelling unmarried women to live in households headed by parents or employers, monitoring popular recreations, and severely prosecuting sexual offences, Black Forest communities all but stamped out illegitimacy, and reduced the incidence of early marriages caused by premarital sexual activity. By appointing guild foremen and cloth inspectors, supervising the keeping of guild accounts, and prosecuting offenders against guild regulations, communities played a vital role in enforcing guild privileges—not just in traditional crafts, but also (as we will see shortly) in proto-industry. Through their thoroughgoing regulation of markets in land, labour, capital, foodstuffs, and industrial products, Württemberg communities affected the cost of almost every decision

---

[35] Troeltsch, *Zeughandlungskompagnie*, esp. 172–3, 177, 181–2, 186, 194–9.

[36] F. M. M. Hendrickx, 'From weavers to workers: Demographic implications of an economic transformation in Twente (the Netherlands) in the nineteenth century', *Continuity and change* 8:2 (1993), 321–55, here 330–1.

[37] Belfanti, 'Rural manufactures', 265–6.

anyone made.[38] Indeed, communities still had so much economic influence in the nineteenth century that, according to Tipton, they clearly retarded industrialisation, not only in Württemberg but throughout the German south.[39]

V. Guilds and companies

A further set of social institutions important for the early modern economy were craft guilds and merchant companies. According to the original theories, proto-industries arose in the countryside precisely to avoid guilds and companies, which then collapsed because of rural competition.[40] For the historians of England and the Low Countries who carried out the first proto-industrial case studies, and those who focussed on the period after about 1750, this seemed self-evident. But Württemberg shows the dangers of generalising the English and Flemish experience, and that of the nineteenth century, to the bulk of early modern Europe.

No sooner did worsted-weaving arise in the Württemberg Black Forest than the weavers began to lobby for guild privileges from the state. Between 1589 and 1611, each Black Forest district obtained its own guild. Anyone weaving worsteds, in either town or countryside, had to gain admission to the district guild and submit to its regulation. These exclusive guild privileges over this proto-industry endured until 1864.[41]

It is sometimes argued that guilds were ineffectual, that their negative impact is exaggerated, or even that they were positively beneficial.[42] So it is important to find out what they actually did. A priceless documentary discovery, the yearly account-books of the worsted weavers' guild of the district of Wildberg, which survive from 1598 to 1760, made it possible for me to do this. This guild, I discovered, strictly regulated entry to the worsted industry in both town and villages: incoming and outgoing apprentices, as well as new masters, paid fees and were

[38] The detailed research results behind these conclusions are presented in Ogilvie, 'Coming of age'; Ogilvie, 'Women and proto-industrialisation'; Ogilvie, Württemberg, chapters 4, 7, 8 and 9; and Ogilvie, 'Women's work in a developing economy'.

[39] F. B. Tipton, Regional variations in the economic development of Germany during the nineteenth century (Middletown (Connecticut), 1976) [hereafter Tipton, Regional variations], 23, 46, 52–3, 58–9, 68, 71.

[40] Mendels, Industrialization, 16, 26; Mokyr, 'Growing-up', 374; Kriedte, Medick and Schlumbohm, Industrialization, 7, 13, 22, 106, 115, 128.

[41] Troeltsch, Zeughandlungskompagnie, 10–14; Ogilvie, 'Coming of age', 281–2, 284–5; Ogilvie, Württemberg, chapter 5.

[42] This is argued specifically for proto-industry by M. Cerman, 'Proto-industrialization in an urban environment: Vienna, 1750–1857', Continuity and change 8:2 (1993), 281–320, here 282. For a more general argument to the effect that guilds were beneficial, see C. R. Hickson & E. A. Thompson, 'A new theory of guilds and European economic development', Explorations in economic history 28 (1991), 127–68.

registered by name, community of origin, and whether they were masters' sons; practising masters and widows paid quarterly dues, and were listed each year in a new register; unlicensed practitioners were reported and penalised. Admission rates declined over time, non-citizens and non-weavers' sons were excluded, and master numbers reached a plateau in most communities by about 1740. The record of fines and officers' activities show an unremitting and thoroughgoing effort to monitor output volume, loom numbers, employment of journeymen and apprentices, women's work, piece-rates and outside employment for spinners, technology, cloth quality, permissable worsted varieties, output prices, and even certain forms of social behaviour; offenders were fined by the guild and often again by the civil authorities. A mass gathering of the guild was held at least once a year; attendance was compulsory, and ranged between 90 and 100 per cent. From 1666 on, all practising masters paid guild dues equivalent to a day's wages each year. The guild's revenues amounted to the value of a modest house annually, and were expended largely on an unremitting lobbying campaign to secure and maintain the guild's privileges.[43]

Not only did the producers form guilds, but so too did the merchants. In 1650, a group of merchants and dyers in the small town of Calw a few miles from Wildberg set up a guild-like company, which secured extensive privileges from the state. For the next century and a half, all weavers in the Württemberg Black Forest were compelled to sell all their cloths to the company, at prices and quantities fixed by law; the company had the exclusive right to dye and export them, and in return was obliged to buy a fixed quota from each weaver. Like a guild, this merchant company restricted entry almost exclusively to sons of existing members. Cloth prices, wool prices, and output quotas were set through collective bargaining between company and guilds: the district bureaucrats supervised the negotiations and enforced the outcome. To protect its monopoly, the company inspected workshops, kept lists of licensed masters, collated its purchase registers every month with guild sealing registers, and confiscated smuggled cloths. Like the guilds, the company invested vast resources in lobbying the state to enforce and extend its privileges. It was not until 1797, when the costs of its obligation to buy cloths from the weavers began to outweigh its monopoly profits from selling them, that the company dissolved itself, against the resistance of the Württemberg state.[44]

[43] The activities of the worsted weavers' guild of the district of Wildberg between 1598 and 1760 are examined in detail in Ogilvie, *Württemberg*, chapters 5–12.

[44] A detailed account of this company is provided in Troeltsch, *Zeughandlungskompagnie*; further analysis of its activities and effects on the Württemberg Black Forest worsted industry is provided in Flik, *Textilindustrie*, 220–254; see also Ogilvie, *Württemberg*, chapters 5 and 8.

But were the guilds and merchant company of the Württemberg Black Forest simply an interesting local exception? Quite the contrary. It is true that in England, the Low Countries, and a few other institutional enclaves (parts of the Rhineland, parts of Saxony), the powers of guilds and companies did decline in the sixteenth century. But proto-industry was not necessary for this decline, since in these societies guilds and companies weakened even within the city walls, and even in traditional crafts.[45] Proto-industry was certainly not sufficient for this decline, since almost everywhere else in Europe proto-industries themselves were regulated by merchant companies, urban guilds, and often also rural guilds, long into the eighteenth century.

Merchant guilds and merchant companies were the rule, not the exception, in European proto-industries. Proto-industrial merchants wholly lacked institutional privileges only in England, the Low Countries, and Krefeld in the Rhineland (and there only until the 1730s).[46] Merchants enjoyed legal monopolies and other state privileges, but did not form companies, in the Swedish iron industry at Eskilstuna, the Westphalian linen proto-industries of Ravensberg and Osnabrück, the Silesian linen industry, the Bohemian woollen and linen industries, the Barcelona calico-printing industry, and the Krefeld linen industry (after about 1730).[47] Everywhere else, proto-industrial merchants were

[45] On England, see P. Clark & P. Slack, *English towns in transition 1500–1700* (Oxford, 1976), 97–110; J. R. Kellett, 'The breakdown of gild and corporation control of the handicraft and retail trades in London', *Economic history review* (1958) 381–94, here 381–82; P. Hudson, 'Proto-industrialization in England', in *Proto-industrialization* eds. Ogilvie and Cerman, 49–66; D. C. Coleman, *The economy of England 1450–1750* (Oxford, 1977), 73–5. On the Low Countries, see de Vries, *Dutch rural economy*, 48–49; K. Glamann, 'European trade, 1500–1750', in *The Fontana economic history of Europe* vol. II *The sixteenth and seventeenth centuries* ed. C. M. Cipolla, 519; H. Kellenbenz, 'The organization of industrial production', in *The Cambridge economic history of Europe* vol. V *The economic organization of early modern Europe* eds. E. E. Rich & C. H. Wilson (Cambridge, 1977), 462–547, here 566; H. Schmal, 'Patterns of de-urbanization in the Netherlands between 1650 and 1850', in *The rise and decline of urban industries* ed. H. Van der Wee (Leuven, 1988); H. Van der Wee, 'Industrial dynamics and the process of urbanization and de-urbanization in the Low Countries from the Late Middle Ages to the eighteenth century', in *Ibid*. On the Rhineland, see Kisch, 'Merkantilismus', 100–3, 116, 130–1, 140; Kriedte, 'Großes Kapital', 221, 225, 241, 246, 249, 258. On Saxony, see K. H. Wolff, 'Guildmaster into millhand: The industrialization of linen and cotton in Germany to 1850', *Textile history* 10 (1979), 7–74, here 33–5; K. Blaschke, 'Grundzüge der sächsischen Stadtgeschichte im 17. und 18. Jahrhundert', *Die Städte Mitteleuropas im 17. und 18. Jahrhundert* (Linz/Donau, 1981), 173–80, here 177.

[46] Hudson, 'Proto-industrialization in England', 52–3; de Vries, *Dutch rural economy*, 48–9; Kisch, 'Merkantilismus', 100–3, 116, 130–1, 140; Kriedte, 'Großes Kapital', 221, 225, 241, 246, 249, 258.

[47] On Eskilstuna, in Sweden, where a small number of putters-out enjoyed privileges over the producers as late as 1822, see L. Magnusson & M. Isacson, 'Proto-industrialization in Sweden: Smithcraft in Eskilstuna and southern Dalecarlia', *Scandinavian economic history review* 30:1 (1982), 73–99, here 78, 80–1. On Westphalia, see J. Schlumbohm, 'Agrarische

formally organised into guilds or companies: in the Bologna silk industry, the Igualada woollen industry in Catalonia, the Lyon silk industry, the Clermont-de-Lodève woollen industry, the Nîmes silk industry, the Rouen linen and cotton industries, the textile industries of the Cambrésis and the Valenciennois, the Saint-Quentin fine linen industry, the linen and cotton industries of Zürich, St Gallen and many other Swiss cantons, the linen, cotton, and stocking-knitting industries of Linz, Schwechat, Poneggen and other centres in Austria, the Vogtland woollen and cotton industries and the Upper Lusatian linen industry in Saxony, the Wupper Valley linen proto-industry in the Rhineland, and the linen proto-industries of Urach, Heidenheim and Blaubeuren in eastern Württemberg—to mention only those that have been closely studied by historians.[48]

Besitzklassen und gewerbliche Produktionsverhältnisse: Großbauern, Kleinbesitzer und Landlose als Leinenproduzenten im Umland von Osnabrück und Bielefeld während des frühen 19. Jahrhunderts', *Mentalitäten und Lebensverhältnisse. Rudolf Vierhaus zum 60. Geburtstag Festschrift R. Vierhaus* (Göttingen, 1982), 315–34, here 331; W. Mager, 'Die Rolle des Staates bei der gewerblichen Entwicklung Ravensbergs in vorindustrieller Zeit', in *Rheinland-Westfalen im Industriezeitalter*, vol. I: *Von der Entstehung der Provinzen bis zur Reichsgründung* eds. K. Düwell and W. Köllmann, (Wuppertal, 1983), 61–72, here 67. On Silesia, see H. Kisch, 'The textile industries of Silesia and the Rhineland: A comparative study of industrialization,' *Journal of economic history* 19 (1959), 186. On Bohemia, see Myška, 'Proto-industrialization'; Klíma, 'English merchant capital', passim. On Barcelona in Catalonia, see J. K. J. Thomson, 'State intervention in the Catalan calico-printing industry in the eighteenth century', in *Markets and manufacture in early industrial Europe* ed. M. Berg (Cambridge, 1991), 79–82. On Krefeld, see Kisch, 'Merkantilismus', 100–3, 116, 130–1, 140; Kriedte, 'Großes Kapital', 221, 225, 241, 246, 249, 258.

[48] On the Bologna silk industry, see C. Poni, 'A proto-industrial city: Bologna: XVI–XVIII century', in *VIIIème Congrès* eds. Deyon and Mendels [hereafter Poni, 'Proto-industrial city'], 5, 7–9, 17. On the Igualada woollen industry in Catalonia, see J. Torras, 'From masters to *fabricants*. Guild organization and economic growth in eighteenth-century Catalonia: A case-study', *European University Institute colloquium papers* 30 (1986) [= papers presented to conference on 'Work and family in pre-industrial Europe', Badia Fiesolana, 11–13 February 1986] [hereafter Torras, 'From masters to *fabricants*']; J. Torras, 'The old and the new. Marketing networks and textile growth in eighteenth-century Spain', in *Markets and manufacture in early industrial Europe* ed. M. Berg (Cambridge, 1991), 93–113 [hereafter Torras, 'The old and the new']. On the Lyon silk industry, see C. Poni, 'Proto- industrialization, rural and urban', *Review* 9 (1985) [hereafter Poni, 'Rural and urban'], here 313. On the Nîmes silk industry in the Bas-Languedoc, see G. Lewis, *The advent of modern capitalism in France, 1770–1840: The contribution of Pierre-François Tubeuf* (Oxford, 1993) [hereafter Lewis, *Modern capitalism*]. On the Clermont-de-Lodève woollen industry in the Languedoc, see J. K. J. Thomson, *Clermont-de-Lodève 1633–1789: Fluctuations in the prosperity of a Languedocian cloth-making town* (Cambridge, 1982) [hereafter Thomson, *Clermont-de-Lodève*]; C. H. Johnson, 'De-industrialization: The case of the Languedoc woollens industry', in *VIIIème Congrès* eds. Deyon & Mendels [hereafter Johnson, 'De-industrialization']. On the Rouen linen and cotton industries in Normandy, see G. L. Gullickson, *Spinners and weavers of Auffay. Rural industry and the sexual division of labor in a French village, 1750–1850* (Cambridge, 1986); J. Bottin, 'Structures and mutations of a proto-industrial space: Rouen and its region at the end of the sixteenth century', *Annales ESC* 43:4 (1988), 975–995. On the textile industries of the Cambrésis and the Valenciennois,

Guilds, too, were widespread in proto-industries. It is often forgotten that in almost all textile proto-industries, the finishing stages were carried out in towns; in many silk proto-industries, almost all stages were urban.[49] In most European towns, guilds retained power to a much later date than in England and the Low Countries: in Scotland and Switzerland, guilds weakened only in the late seventeenth century, in France and parts of Saxony only in the early eighteenth century, and in most other parts of Europe not until the later eighteenth or even the early nineteenth century.[50] An effective guild in an *urban* stage

---

see P. Guignet, 'Adaptations, mutations et survivances proto-industrielles dans le textile du Cambrésis et du Valenciennois du XVIIIe au début du XXe siècle', *Revue du Nord* 61 (1979), 27–59 [hereafter Guignet, 'Adaptions']. On the Saint-Quentin fine linen industry in northern France, see D. Terrier, 'Mulquiniers et gaziers: les deux phases de la proto-industrie textile dans la région de Saint-Quentin, 1730–1850', *Revue du Nord* 65 (1983), see 535–53. On the linen and cotton proto-industries of Zürich, St. Gallen and other Swiss cantons, see Braun, 'Early industrialization'; and Pfister, 'Proto-industrialization'. On the linen, cotton, and stocking-knitting proto-industries of Linz, Schwechat, Poneggen and other centres in Austria, see Cerman, 'Proto-industrialization in Vienna', 289; H. Freudenberger, 'Three mercantilist protofactories', *Business history review* 40 (1966), 167–189; H. Freudenberger, 'Zur Linzer Wollzeugfabrik,' in H. Knittler (ed.), *Wirtschafts- und sozialhistorische Beiträge. Festschrift für Alfred Hoffmann zum 75. Geburtstag* (Wien, 1979), 220–235; V. Hofmann, 'Beiträge zur neueren Wirtschaftsgeschichte. Die Wollenzeugfabrik zu Linz an der Donau', *Archiv für österreichische Geschichte* 108 (1920); G. Grüll, 'The Poneggen hosiery enterprise, 1763–1818: A study of Austrian mercantilism', *Textile history* 5 (1974), 38–79. On the Vogtland woollen and cotton industries and the Upper Lusatian linen industry in Saxony, see Wolff, 'Guildmaster', 38. On the Wuppertal linen proto-industry in the Rhineland, see Kisch, 'From monopoly to laissez-faire'. On the linen proto-industries of Urach, Heidenheim and Blaubeuren in eastern Württemberg, see Flik, *Textilindustrie*; Troeltsch, *Zeughandlungskompagnie*; H. Medick, ' "Freihandel für die Zunft": Ein Kapitel aus der Geschichte der Preiskämpfe im württembergischen Leinengewerbe des 18. Jahrhunderts', in *Mentalitäten und Lebensverhältnisse: Rudolph Vierhaus zum 60. Geburtstag* Festschrift R. Vierhaus (Göttingen, 1983); H. Medick, 'Privilegiertes Handelskapital und "kleine Industrie". Produktion und Produktionsverhältnisse im Leinengewerbe des alt-württembergischen Oberamts Urach im 18. Jahrhundert', *Archiv für Sozialgeschichte*, 23 (1983), 267–310.

[49] Cerman, 'Proto-industrialization in Vienna', 290–91; Poni, 'Proto-industrial city', 16–17; Poni, 'Proto-industrialization, rural and urban', 312–13; P. Kriedte, 'Die Stadt im Prozeß der europäischen Proto-industrialisierung', *Die alte Stadt* 9 (1982), 19–51, here 48; Lewis, *Modern capitalism*, 63–4.

[50] On Scotland, see Whyte, 'Proto-industrialization in Scotland', here esp. 233–4 on the 'considerable control over rural manufacturing' exercised by the craft guilds of the royal burghs until 1672, and the urban orientation of Scottish proto-industry well into the eighteenth century. On Switzerland, see Pfister, 'Proto-industrialization in Switzerland'; Braun, 'Early industrialization', 296. On France, see Guignet, 'Adaptions', 29–30; Lewis, *Modern capitalism*, 10, 63–4; G. Gayot, 'La longue insolence des tondeurs de draps dans la manufacture de Sedan au XVIIIème siècle', *Revue du Nord* 63 (1981), 105–34, here 108, 116, 122; Poni, 'Rural and urban'; Kriedte, 'Stadt', 48; Johnson, 'De-industrialization', 5–6. On Saxony, see Wolff, 'Guildmaster'. On societies in which guilds survived into the late eighteenth or early nineteenth century, see on Austria: Cerman, 'Proto-industrialization in Vienna', 290–1; Cerman, 'Proto-industrial development in Austria' in *Proto-industrialization in Europe* eds. Ogilvie & Cerman, 171–187; Freudenberger, 'Proto-factories',

of a proto-industry inevitably affected the costs faced by merchants and rural workers, since guilds invariably sought to keep down the prices their members paid to suppliers and keep up the prices they could charge to customers.

Rural proto-industrial producers were also organised into guilds. Rural guilds were particularly widespread in German territories, but were also found in Bohemia, Austria, Spain, and central and northern Italy. Thus new proto-industrial guilds, which included rural workers, were set up not only in the Black Forest worsted industry, but also in the linen industries of the East-Swabian micro-states, the trimmings and lace industry of the Erzgebirge-Vogtland in Saxony, the small iron goods industry of Berg, the scythe-industry of Remscheid in the Rhineland, the linen industry of the Wupper Valley in the Rhineland, the linen industries of Urach, Heidenheim and Blaubeuren in eastern Württemberg, the woollen and linen industries of the Württemberg possession of Mömpelgard in present-day Alsace, the linen-weaving, cotton-production, scythe-making, and iron-processing in various regions of Austria, the woollen and linen industries of northern and northeastern Bohemia, the textile industries of Castile, the gun-barrel industry of the north Italian valleys of Brescia, and the Prato woollen industry in Tuscany—again, to name only those which have been closely studied by historians. New rural guilds continued to be formed in proto-industries well into the eighteenth century, often to defend against privileged merchant companies, and often with the explicit support of the state.[51]

184; H. Freudenberger, 'An industrial momentum achieved in the Habsburg monarchy,' *Journal of European economic history* 12 (1983), 339–50, here 342–3; on Spain: Thomson, 'Proto-industrialization in Spain'; on Catalonia in particular: Torras, 'From masters to *fabricants*', 3, 6–9; Torras, 'The old and the new', 99, 105–6, 108, 113 notes 56–7; on Italy: Belfanti, 'Rural manufactures', 262, 266–7; Poni, 'Proto-industrial city', 16–17; on Scandinavia: M. Isacson & L. Magnusson, *Proto-industrialization in Scandinavia. Craft skills in the industrial revolution* (Leamington Spa/Hamburg/New York, 1987), 35, 37, 93; L. Magnusson, 'Markets in context: Artisans, putting out and social drinking in Eskiltuna, Sweden 1800–50', in *Markets and manufacture in early industrial Europe* ed. M. Berg (London, 1991), 292–320, here 304; on the survival of guild privileges in proto-industries in Bohemia and Moravia, despite countervailing privileges from feudal landlords, see H. Freudenberger, 'The woollen-goods industry of the Habsburg monarchy in the eighteenth century,' *Journal of economic history* 20 (1960), 383–406, here 385–8, 400; H. Freudenberger, 'Industrialization in Bohemia and Moravia in the eighteenth century,' *Journal of Central European affairs* 19 (1960), 347–56, here 351; Freudenberger, 'Proto-factories', 184; Klíma, 'English merchant capital', 34–5, 40; Klíma, 'Industrial development', 89; A. Klíma, 'The role of rural domestic industry in Bohemia in the eighteenth century', *Economic history review* 2nd ser., 27 (1974), 48–56, here 52.

[51] On Heidenheim, see Flik, *Textilindustrie*. On Urach, see Medick, 'Freihandel für die Zunft'. On Mömpelgard, see J.-P. Dormois, 'L'expérience protoindustrielle dans la principauté de Montbéliard 1740–1820: Aux origines de la révolution industrielle', (Mémoire de D. E. A., University of Paris-Sorbonne, 1984), here esp. 16–18, 24–5, 39;

Guilds and companies neither precluded proto-industry, nor were broken down by it. But they clearly affected how it developed. It is sometimes claimed that guilds actually often admitted outsiders, and thus did not exercise effective monopolies; but in the Württemberg Black Forest, both guilds and company effectively limited the number

---

further detail on these guilds is provided in C. Faivre, 'Les chonffes de la principauté de Montbéliard' (Thèse de droit, University of Paris, 1949); for an exploration of the demographic and social-structural ramifications of proto-industry in Mömpelgard, see J. P. Dormois, 'Entwicklungsmuster der Protoindustrialisierung im Mömpelgarder Lande während des 18. Jahrhunderts', *Zeitschrift für württembergische Landesgeschichte* 53 (1994), 179–204. On the East Swabian micro-states, see R. Kiessling, 'Entwicklungstendenzen im ostschwäbischen Textilrevier während der Frühen Neuzeit', in *Gewerbe und Handel vor der Industrialisierung. Regionale und überregionale Verflechtungen im 17. und 18. Jahrhundert* eds. J. Jahn & W. Hartung (Sigmaringendorf, 1991), 27–48, here 44–5. On Berg see A. Thun, *Die Industrie am Niederrhein und ihre Arbeiter* (2 parts, Leipzig, 1897), here Part 2, *Die Industrie des Bergischen Landes*; also Mager, 'Proto-industrialization and proto-industry', 188. On the Erzgebirge-Vogtland, see B. Schöne, 'Kultur und Lebensweise Lausitzer und erzgebirgischer Textilproduzenten sowie von Keramikproduzenten im Manufakturkapitalismus und in der Periode der Industriellen Revolution', in *Die Konstituierung der deutschen Arbeiterklasse von den dreißiger bis zu den siebziger Jahren des 19. Jahrhunderts* ed. H. Zwahr (Berlin, 1981), 446–67; B. Schöne, 'Posamentierer—Strumpfwirker—Spitzenklöpplerinnen. Zu Kultur und Lebensweise von Textilproduzenten im Erzgebirge und im Vogtland während der Periode des Übergangs vom Feudalismus zum Kapitalismus (1750–1850)', in *Volksleben zwischen Zunft und Fabrik. Studien zu Kultur und Lebensweise werktätiger Klassen und Schichten während des Übergangs vom Feudalismus zum Kapitalismus* ed. R. Weibhold (Berlin/DDR, 1982), 107–164; Mager, 'Proto-industrialization and proto-industry', 188. On Remscheid, see Kriedte, Medick and Schlumbohm, *Industrialization*, 115. On the Wuppertal, see Kisch, 'From monopoly to laissez-faire', 351–2, 400, 403–4, 406; the guild was granted a state charter in 1738, in an attempt by local bureaucrats to introduce a new player into their corporate rivalry against the merchant company for control of local politics. On Austria, for linen-weaving see A. Hoffmann, *Wirtschaftsgeschichte des Landes Oberösterreich*, (Salzburg, 1952) vol. I, 103ff; C. Halmdienst, *Die Entwicklung der Leinenindustrie in Oberösterreich (unter besonderer Berücksichtigung des Mühlviertels)* (Linz, 1993), 30–40; for cotton-production see L. K. Berkner, 'Family, social structure and rural industry: A comparative study of the Waldviertel and the Pays de Caux in the eighteenth century' (Ph.D. thesis, Harvard University, 1973), 123ff; A. Komlosy, *An den Rand gedrängt. Wirtschafts- und Sozialgeschichte des oberen Waldviertels* (Vienna, 1988); A. Komlosy, 'Stube und Websaal. Waldviertler Textilindustrie im Spannungsfeld verschiedener Verlagswesen Heim- und Fabriksarbeit', in *Spinnen—Spulen—Weben* ed. A. Komlosy (Krems/Horn, 1991), 119–138; H. Matis, 'Protoindustrialisierung und "Industrielle Revolution" am Beispiel der Baumwollindustrie Niederösterreichs', in *ibid.*, 15–48; for scythe-making, see F. Fischer, *Die blauen Sensen: Sozial- und Wirtschaftsgeschichte der Sensenschmiedezunft zu Kirchdorf-Micheldorf bis zur Mitte des 18. Jahrhunderts* (Graz, 1966), esp. xv–xvi, 19ff, 86–9, 93, 101–3; on iron-processing, see H. Hassinger, 'Die althabsburgischen Länder und Salzburg 1350–1650,' in *Handbuch der europäischen Wirtschafts- und Sozialgeschichte*, (Stuttgart, 1986) vol. 3, 927–967, here 950. On northern and northeastern Bohemia, see Klíma, 'English merchant capital', 37, 39–40. On Castile, see A.-G. Enciso, 'Economic structure of Cameros' dispersed industry: A case study in eighteenth century Castilian textile industry', in *VIIIème Congrès* eds. Deyon & Mendels, 1–3; J. K. J. Thomson, 'Proto-industrialization in Spain', in *Proto-industrialization in Europe* eds. Ogilvie and Cerman, 85–101. On the valleys of Brescia, see Belfanti, 'Rural manufactures and rural proto-industries', 262. On Prato, see *ibid.*, 266.

of people allowed to practise the industry, how many employees they could keep, and how much they could produce. After the late seventeenth century, sons of non-masters or non-citizens were almost completely excluded by the weavers' guild, and even masters could apprentice only one of their sons.[52] The merchant company was even more exclusive: in 147 years, it never exceeded forty members and admitted only one outsider. Output quotas far below the desired and technically feasible level of production were fixed and enforced by both guilds and company.[53] Widows of masters could produce at half quota and without employees; other women were forbidden any industrial task but spinning, which was paid at below-market rates set by the guild.[54] The demographic incentives these restrictions created can be observed in the later marriage ages of weaving couples, their smaller family and household size, and the enormous excess of unmarried women.[55] In 1736, three-quarters of these women lived wholly or partly from spinning, and almost all the rest from poor relief or begging.[56] Even the occasional desperate attempts by spinners and poorer weavers to evade guild and company restrictions confronted such enormous risks and penalties that they hardly amounted to an 'informal' or 'black-market' sector, let alone to the emergence of a 'market society'.[57]

[52] See the quantitative results presented in Ogilvie, *Württemberg*, chapter 7.

[53] The setting and enforcement of output quotas, and evidence of compliance with them, is discussed in detail in Ogilvie, *Württemberg*, chapter 8.

[54] The position of widows (and other women) in the Black Forest worsted industry is investigated in detail in Ogilvie, 'Women's work'; for an overview of the issues, see Ogilvie, 'Women and proto-industrialisation'.

[55] See the detailed demographic results presented in Ogilvie, *Württemberg*, chapter 9; for a preliminary overview of some of these, see Ogilvie, 'Coming of age'; Ogilvie, 'Women and proto-industrialisation'.

[56] Piece-rate ceilings for the spinners were set in all the worsted weavers' ordinances and much ancillary legislation from 1589 onward: 'Engelsatt-Weberordnung, vfgericht in Ao 1589', reprinted in Troeltsch, *Zeughandlungskompagnie*, 431–4, here 433; 'Engel-sattweberordunung in A. 1608 [actually 1611] vfgerichtet', reprinted in Troeltsch, *Zeughandlungskompagnie*, 435–53, here 446; 'Engelsattweberordunung in A. 1608 [actually 1611] vfgerichtet', emendations of 1654, reprinted in Troeltsch, *Zeughandlungskompagnie*, 435–53, here 446 footnote 2; 'Zeugmacher-Ordnung von 24 März 1686', in *Vollständige, historisch und kritisch bearbeitete Sammlung der württembergische Gesetze* 19 vols. (Stuttgart, 1828–51) ed. A. L. Reyscher [hereafter *Sammlung*, ed. Reyscher], vol. 13, 615–40, here 626; 'Rescript in Betreff des Zeugmachergewerbs' (8 Sep 1736), in *ibid.*, vol. 14, 178ff.

[57] Economists studying modern less developed societies draw a distinction between 'formal' (or 'regulated') markets, in which transactions are open, legal and enforceable by the state or other social institutions; and 'informal' (or 'black') markets, in which transactions do take place, but are secret, illegal and unenforceable because they are not endorsed (or are explicitly prohibited) by the legitimate institutions of the society. As many studies of less developed economies show, the development potential of the 'informal sector' derives from its ability to evade costly formal-sector regulations. However, the 'informal sector' is ultimately constricted by high transactions costs, high information costs, high risks, low worker protection, and high costs of capital (resulting in sub-optimal

It is also sometimes claimed that guilds were beneficial because they overcame capital market imperfections, maintained quality standards, or defended intellectual property rights. However, the only capital provided by the Wildberg weavers' guild was a lobbying fund and two funeral palls; raw wool, looms, stretching-frames, and fulling-mills were all provided privately.[58] The guilds and the company certainly justified their privileges partly in terms of quality control and protecting technical mysteries, but in reality the local worsteds were poor and primitive, never remotely approached the quality normal in the Low Countries or England, and lost ground even to German competitors as time passed.[59]

In fact, efforts to improve quality, variety, technology and the organisation of production repeatedly foundered on the rock of corporate privilege. After about 1600, rigid guild demarcations prohibited worsted- and woollen-weaving in tandem, despite technical complementarities and lower market risks.[60] In 1619–21, an Italian expert, brought in by a local dyer to introduce new techniques from the Low Countries and France, and supported by the ducal government, encountered such vehement opposition from a cartel of Calw merchants and from the weavers' guilds that he departed and refused all invitations to return.[61] From 1650 on, the merchants were obliged to supply raw wool to the weavers and the weavers to supply cloths to the company, at prices fixed by law; unable to adjust prices upwards, both merchants and weavers adjusted quality downwards, and Württemberg worsteds remained coarse and poor.[62] From 1665 on, the guilds prohibited

---

levels of investment), all of which result from its lack of legitimacy and its inability to enforce contracts. On this, see, for instance, M. P. Todaro, *Economic development in the Third World* (Harlow, 1989), 270–1.

[58] The worsted-weavers' guild was joint-owner (with the woollen-weavers' guild) of a fulling-mill in the town of Wildberg in the early seventeenth century; on this, see WHSA A573 Bü 219–948 1612–44 (account-books of the woollen-weavers' guild of the district of Wildberg). That capital-market imperfections governed the fulling sector is questionable, given that both previously and subsequently this mill was owned by professional fullers, and that in 1736 the Wildberg fulling mill was being operated by a woman (on this, see WHSA A573 Bü 6967 Seelentabelle 1736 ('soul table' for the town and villages of the district of Wildberg); and the discussion in Ogilvie, 'Women's work and economic development', 37).

[59] It was widely recognized, even by contemporaries, that Württemberg worsteds were low in quality and were failing to adapt to international improvements in technology and variety; see Troeltsch, *Zeughandlungskompagnie*, 163–5.

[60] Troeltsch, *Zeughandlungskompagnie*, 12–13, 110.

[61] See the discussion in Troeltsch, *Zeughandlungskompagnie*, 35–8.

[62] Troeltsch, *Zeughandlungkompagnie*, 101, 125–31; the effects of the rigid negotiations of the 'Moderation' (the regime of prices and quotas for raw wool and cloths periodically re-negotiated between company and guilds, under the supervision of the district-level ducal bureaucrats, and subsequently enforced by law) are discussed in detail in Ogilvie, *Württemberg*, chapter 8.

specialised wool-combers, although this reduced costs.[63] Spinning piece-rates were so low that spinners lacked the capital and the incentive to adopt the technically superior spool-spinning. Even for finer spinning, it was forbidden to pay higher rates; so the spinners simply would not produce the finer yarn required for better cloths. Higher and more differentiated spinning rates were repeatedly recommended by technical observers and state commissions, but were bitterly and successfully opposed by the guild to the end of the eighteenth century.[64] The introduction of new cloth varieties was always delayed by the merchant company until it could extend its state privileges to cover them: this took place in the 1660s, the 1690s, the 1720s, the 1750s, and the 1770s. Even then, the new company privileges generally involved such risks, and such threats to existing prices and quotas, that the weavers refused to produce the new varieties of cloth.[65] To the very end of the eighteenth century, both company and guilds opposed state concessions for any other textile manufactory in the area, successfully excluding new enterprises, new techniques, and new practices.[66] In this proto-industry, therefore, corporate privileges had economic effects which were not only real, but ruinous.

But was Württemberg just an isolated and unfortunate case? Without this sort of detailed analysis of more proto-industries, it is hard to say. There was certainly nothing atypical about the privileges, aims or visible activities of the guilds or the company in the Black Forest

[63] Troeltsch, Zeughandlungskompagnie, 8, 72, 110; the restriction was introduced in Rezesse of 1665 and 1674, and incorporated into the ordinance for the industry in 1686: 'Recess zwischen denen Färbern vnd Knappen zu Callw de dato 17. Augusti 1665', reprinted in Troeltsch, Zeughandlungskompagnie, 465–71; 'Recess Zwischen der Färbern Compagnie und Knappschaft d. Stuttgart d. 23.ten Apr. A. 1674', reprinted in Troeltsch, Zeughandlungskompagnie, 471–8; 'Zeugmacher-Ordnung' (24 Mar 1686), in Sammlung, ed. Reyscher, vol. 13, 615ff.

[64] For a detailed discussion of the spinning regulations, the failure to improve piece-rates, and the effects of this on the quality of spun yarn and of finished worsteds, see Troeltsch, Zeughandlungkompagnie, 125–30, 171; Ogilvie, 'Women's work', 62–4; Ogilvie, Württemberg, chapter 9.

[65] For a detailed discussion of this pattern of behaviour on the part of company and guilds, see Troeltsch, Zeughandlungskompagnie, 119, 161–9; Ogilvie, Württemberg, chapter 9. For an example of guild opposition to the introduction of new cloth varieties, see WHSA A573 Bü 851, account-book of the worsted weavers' guild of the district of Wildberg, Jan. 1698–Jan. 1699, fol 25v, where the guild undertakes a lobbying campaign against 'etlicher Compagnie Verwannten zu Callw, alß welche Neüe Sorten von Schlickh Cadiß anfangen Zumachen, und zuweben geben, dessen Sie aber nicht befuegt gewesen' ('several Company members in Calw, who have begun to make, and put-out for weaving, new sorts of Schlick Cadis, which however they are not entitled to do'); Cadis was a narrow variety of worsted.

[66] For an example from 1709, see WHSA A573 Bü 862, account-book of the worsted weavers' guild of the district of Wildberg for the year Apr. 1709–Apr. 1710, fol 26r–26v; for an example from the 1770s, see Troeltsch, Zeughandlungskompagnie, 130–1.

industry. Costly lobbying activities and violent socio-political struggles surrounded guild and company privileges in almost every European proto-industry.[67] Since people do not invest resources to defend or attack valueless privileges, we may presume that most proto-industrial guilds and companies secured real economic benefits for their members, and inflicted real economic costs on others. Furthermore, the abolition of guild and company privileges was often followed by an industrial boom, as with the dissolution of the Prato rural weavers' guild in northern Italy in 1770, that of the Schwechat company in Austria in 1762, or that of the Catalonian guilds in the 1830s.[68] These booms

---

[67] For examples of such corporate struggles in proto-industries throughout Europe: on Catalonia, see Thomson, 'Proto-industrialization in Spain'; on Igualada in Catalonia in particular, see Torras, 'The old and the new', 105–6, 108, 113 notes 56–57; Torras, 'From masters to *fabricants*', 9; on Sedan in northern France, see Gayot, 'Tondeurs', 108; on the Nîmes region in France, see Lewis, *Modern capitalism*, 63–4; on the Lodève region in Languedoc, see Johnson, 'De-industrialization', 5ff; Thomson, *Clermont-de-Lodève*, 12; on Vienna in Austria, see Cerman, 'Proto-industrialization in Vienna', 290–1; on Kirchdorf-Micheldorf in Austria, see Fischer, *Blauen Sensen*, 86–9, 93, 101–3; on the Wupper Valley in the Rhineland, see Kisch, 'From Monopoly to laissez-faire', 309, 351, 400, 403–4, 406; on the Vogtland in Saxony, see Wolff, 'Guildmaster', 39–41.

[68] On Prato, see Belfanti, 'Rural manufactures', 266; on Schwechat, see Cerman, 'Proto-industrialization in Vienna', 289; on Catalonia, see Thomson, 'Proto-industrialization in Spain'. Additional examples abound. Thomson, 'Proto-industrialization in Spain', ascribes the early decline of many Castilian proto-industries to guilds which 'created structures opposed to innovation in cloth types and to cutting costs'. Belfanti, 'Rural manufactures', 267, argues that the rural privileges the Florence guild retained after 1739 helped to retard the growth of proto-industry in Tuscany. Poni, 'Proto-industrial city', 5, 7–9, 16–8, shows how the inflexible corporate structure in which the Bologna silk industry became fixed prevented its adapting to changing market conditions, and led to a loss of international competitiveness. Poni, 'Proto-industrialization, rural or urban', 312–3, and Kriedte, 'Stadt', 48, both emphasize how the Lyon silk-merchants' guild 'strongly restricted the industry's room for manoeuvre'. Deyon, 'Roubaix', 64, argues that the corporate regulations governing relations between the privileged urban merchants and their proto-industrial workforce in the Roubaix region near Lille constituted a serious obstacle to nineteenth-century industrialization. Kriedte, medick and Schlumbohm, *Industrialization*, 15, mention that the scythe-smiths' guild in Remscheid in the Rhineland successfully resisted the introduction of water-driven scythe-hammers. Kisch, 'From monopoly to laissez-faire', 400–1, recounts how the Wupper Valley linen weavers' guild, in unusual alliance with the merchant company, successfully opposed the introduction of English spinning machines in the 1780s; see also 308–9, 325, 352, and 392, where he describes the 'exclusive rights', entry restrictions, output and price regulation, and monopsony power exercised by the merchant company. Gutkas, 'Österreichs Städte', recounts how the Linzer Wollfabrik in Austria enjoyed a monopoly over production and markets, and legislation giving it first claim on raw materials. Wolff, 'Guildmaster', 39, describes how the merchant guilds of the Vogtland in Saxony were able to limit admission, levy license fees, and restrict internal competition. According to the evidence presented in Schlumbohm, 'Besitzklassen', 330–1, and Mager, 'Rolle', 67, it seems unlikely that the merchants would have taken the trouble to enforce the 'Legge-Zwang' (compulsory delivery to the urban staple) from the 1770s on, and to resist its abolition in the early nineteenth century, had it not enabled them to secure important economic advantages.

strongly suggest that these guilds and companies had been constraining growth.[69]

VI. The state

Why were they able to do this? Why did guilds, companies, communities and landlords retain economic power in so many parts of Europe, while in a few they broke down much earlier? The case of Württemberg and, when one looks more deeply, many other European proto-industries, suggests that part of the answer may lie in a hitherto neglected factor, the role of the state. Theories about proto-industrialisation have restricted the economic role of the state to guaranteeing market transactions, and occasionally helping the 'capitalists' coerce the 'workers'.[70] Closer examination of many European proto-industries suggests that this is partly an unjustified generalisation of the English and Flemish pattern to the rest of Europe, and partly a projection of nineteenth-century developments back onto the very different experience of the early modern period.

In Württemberg, until 1800 at least, the economic role of the state was not to create a framework for voluntary market transactions between individuals, but rather to provide legal enforcement for the monopolies and privileges of corporate groups. Far from seeking to dissolve guilds and companies, the Württemberg state continued to confirm and enforce their privileges, and to benefit from the bribes, concession fees, loans, fiscal assistance, and economic regulation they rendered in return.[71] When, in the 1790s, the three main proto-industrial

---

[69] According to Tipton, *Regional variations*, 26–7, 30, 52–3, 59, 71, 72–6, they continued to constrain growth in many parts of nineteenth-century Germany during industrialization.

[70] Kriedte, Medick and Schlumbohm, *Industrialization*, 128–9.

[71] The importance of fiscal and regulatory assistance from corporate groups to the Württemberg state is stressed by Flik, *Textilindustrie*, 91, and illustrated on the basis of the merchant company with privileges over the linen proto-industry of the district of Heidenheim in the eighteenth century on 94. The intimate relationship between guilds and the state in Württemberg, which continued into the late eighteenth century, emerges from L. Hoffmann, *Das Württembergische Zunftwesen und die Politik der herzoglichen Regierung gegenüber den Zünften im 18. Jahrhundert* (Tübingen, 1905) [hereafter Hoffman, *Zunftwesen*], and G. Raiser, *Die Zünfte in Württemberg: Entstehung und Definition, interne Organisation und deren Entwicklung, dargestellt anhand der Zunftartikel und der übrigen Normativbestimmungen seit dem Jahre 1489* (Tübingen, 1978). An overview over the enormous number of state concessions to 'manufactories' and associated merchant companies, which were granted in almost every sector of the Württemberg economy from the mid-eighteenth to the early nineteenth century, is provided in J. Gysin, *'Fabriken und Manufakturen' in Württemberg während des ersten Drittels des 19. Jahrhunderts* (St. Katharinen, 1989), esp. 30, 43–7, 76–83, 125–6, 130, 139–140, 164–5, 170–1, 223, 225, 227. The ubiquity of state privileges in the Württemberg economy was remarked upon in 1793 by the Göttingen professor Christoph Meiners in the following terms: in Württemberg 'external trade ... is constantly made more difficult by the form which it has taken for a long time. Trade and manufactures are for the most

merchant companies in Württemberg sought to dissolve themselves because their legal obligations to the weavers' guilds outweighed their monopoly profits, they encountered enormous state opposition.[72] The proto-industrial guilds endured long into the nineteenth century. Nor did the state only support merchants against producers. Both the merchant companies and the weavers' guilds invested enormous resources in lobbying against each other's privileges. Had the state not granted the weavers some support, the guilds would surely have ceased to invest, and the companies to lobby against them.[73]

Even if the Württemberg *state* had wanted to create a framework for free market transactions, the power of local *communities* were too entrenched. Although the Württemberg princes maintained a paid bureaucracy on the district level, these officials were not numerous and they had no say in the appointment of community councils and community officials. It was this local office-holding *Ehrbarkeit*, or 'notability', which allocated and collected taxes, and determined and implemented community regulation of markets in land, labour, credit, foodstuffs, raw materials, and industrial products.[74] Communal arrangements were supported by powerful allies in the parliament and the bureaucracy, both of which were recruited from the same local 'notability' as the community officials in the district towns.[75] When the

part in the hands of closed and for the most part privileged associations' (C. Meiners, 'Bemerkungen auf einer Herbstreise nach Schwaben. Geschrieben im November 1793', in *Kleinere Länder- und Reisebeschreibungen* ed. C. Meiners, (Berlin, 1794) vol. 2, 235–380, here 292; cited in Medick, 'Privilegiertes Handelskpaital', 271).

[72] On the Calwer Zeughandlungskompagnie, see Troeltsch, *Zeughandlungskompagnie*, 326–30; on the Uracher Leinwandhandlungskompagnie, see *Ibid.*, 326, and Medick, 'Privilegiertes Handelskapital', 271, 275; on the Heidenheimer Leinwandhandlungskompagnie, see Flik, *Die Textilindustrie in Calw und in Heidenheim*, 100–7, esp. 106.

[73] For a detailed analysis of the lobbying campaigns of the worsted weavers' guild of the district of Wildberg against the Calw merchant company, and their outcomes, see Ogilvie, *Württemberg*, chapter 12. The same conclusion emerges from detailed study of the other main proto-industry in Württemberg, the linen industry of Urach, which was also monopolized by guilds and a merchant company with very similar privileges to those of the Black Forest worsted industry: according to Medick, 'Privilegiertes Handelskapital', 276, in the 'monopoly privileges of the Uracher Leinwandhandlungskompagnie, which were repeatedly renewed in the course of the seventeenth and eighteenth centuries, almost always a middle way was followed'.

[74] As is argued above in Section IV; see also Vann, *Making of a state*, 41, 52, 180–4, 187–8; W. Grube, *Vogteien, Ämter, Landkreise in der Geschichte Südwestdeutschlands* 2nd ed. (Stuttgart, 1960), 19–20; F. Wintterlin, *Geschichte der Behördenorganisation in Württemberg* (Stuttgart, 1902), vol. I, 3–10.

[75] On the Württemberg *Ehrbarkeit*, see H. Decker-Hauff, 'Die Entstehung der altwürttembergischen Ehrbarkeit, 1250–1534' (Ph.D. dissertation, University of Erlangen, 1946); Vann, *Making of a state*, 38–9, 41–6, 53, 56, 98–100, 103–7, 121–3, 178–82, 187–8, 245, 256, 278, 280, 284–5, 288–91; K. Marcus, 'A question of privilege: Elites and central government in Württemberg, 1495–1593' (Ph.D. dissertation, University of Cambridge, 1991).

central state did encroach on the economic prerogatives of communities, it was not by opening markets but by issuing countervailing privileges to its own concession-holders; even then, many such undertakings foundered against entrenched community resistance.[76] Both state and communities could generally derive more benefit from cooperation than from confrontation, and this gave rise to a tacit arrangement by which, as James Allen Vann puts it, in Württemberg 'the central government stopped at the gates of the towns'.[77]

This pattern was not unique to Württemberg. In every European proto-industry in which landlords, communities, guilds, or companies retained power—and, as we have seen, these were the majority—they did so because their privileges were legitimised and enforced, however reluctantly, by the state. Sometimes the state was simply not strong enough to break them down, but in many cases it actively opted to sustain them, in return for their indispensible fiscal and political support.

The powers of landlords increasingly depended on state enforcement, as emerges from many proto-industrial case studies. The establishment and control of proto-industries by feudal landlords in Russia, Bohemia, Moravia and Silesia was only possible because the state and the landlords supported one another, and indeed on the local level were effectively identical. In Silesia, the Hohenzollern state went so far as to prohibit linen mechanisation after 1780, to protect the profits of feudal landlords from serf weaving.[78] In the Bulgarian province of Eastern Rumelia, fiscal and political considerations led the Ottoman state to support the powers of landowners to restrict land access, pushing the population into proto-industry.[79] In the French Bas-Languedoc in the

[76] For examples of state concessions, and the often successful local resistance they evoked, see W. Söll, 'Die staatliche Wirtschaftspolitik in Württemberg im 17. und 18. Jahrhundert' (Ph.D. diss., University of Tübingen, 1934), 97–100; H. Liebel-Weckowicz, 'The politics of poverty and reform: Modernization and reform in eighteenth-century Württemberg', *The Consortium on Revolutionary Europe Proceedings* (Athens, Ga., 1981); S. Stern, *Jud Süss: ein Beitrag zur deutschen und zur jüdischen Geschichte* (Berlin, 1929); O. Linckh, 'Das Tabakmonopolie in Württemberg', *Württembergische Jahrbuch* (1893); A. Schott, 'Merkantilpolitisches aus Württembergs herzogszeit', *Württembergische Jahrbuch* (1900); W. Boelcke, 'Ein Herzoglich-Württembergischer Regiebetrieb des ausgehenden 18. Jahrhunderts', *Jahrbücher für Nationalökonomie und Statistik* 175 (1963); K.-G. Krauter, 'Die Manufakturen im Herzogtum Württemberg und ihre Förderung durch die württembergische Regierung in der zweiten Hälfte des 18. Jahrhunderts' (Ph.D. diss., University of Tübingen, 1951); K. Weidner, *Die Anfänge einer staatlichen Wirtschaftspolitik in Württemberg* (Stuttgart, 1931), 112–21; P. Wiedenmann, 'Zur Geschichte der gewerblichen Bierbrauerei in Altwürttemberg', *Württembergische Jahrbuch* (1934/5), 47–58; Vann, *Making of a state*, 108–9; Grube, *Stuttgarter Landtag*, 323–4. See also the long and ultimately successful resistance of the Württemberg guilds to attempts to increase state control, in Hoffmann, *Zunftwesen*, 38–43.

[77] Vann, *Making of a state*, 295.

[78] Kisch, 'The textile industries in Silesia and the Rhineland', 185.

[79] Palairet, 'Woollen textile manufacturing', 2–3.

1780s, the political influence of local seigneurs compelled the state to withdraw support from its own concession-holders when they tried to mechanise proto-industrial coal extraction.[80]

Community institutions, too, depended on state support. In the Netherlands province of Twente, the communal *marken* system which, by excluding part of the population from essential access to common lands, had generated a cheap proto-industrial labour force, was enforced by the state until the nineteenth century, and broke down only through state action around 1810 and 1830.[81] In the Prussian territory of Ravensberg, the linen proto-industry was not sufficient to break down the communal 'Acker-Marken-Wirtschaft'; only Hohenzollern state legislation enabled its gradual dissolution after about 1710 and its abolition in 1780. In the neighbouring prince-bishopric of Osnabrück, the state sustained the 'Acker-Marken-Wirtschaft' until 1810. Thus it was state action, not proto-industry, which led to the divergent development of communal institutions in Ravensberg and Osnabrück, and this in turn had enormous repercussions on proto-industry in both regions.[82]

State support was also crucial for guilds and companies. In the Wupper Valley, for instance, the proto-industrial merchant company only maintained its privileges through constant appeals to the government; the establishment of the rural weavers' guild in 1738 was positively encouraged by local government officials, and its abolition in 1783 was only accomplished by sending in the army.[83] The merchant company of Clermont-de-Lodève in Languedoc, and the various guilds which monopolised the different stages of woollen production, relied on state inspectors to help enforce their privileges; the company invested hugely in Paris connections to maintain its monopoly.[84] Indeed, it is rare to find a guild or a merchant company anywhere in Europe which effectively regulated markets without state enforcement.[85]

[80] Lewis, *Modern capitalism*, 1, 21, 54, 79–80, 89–91, 97.

[81] Hendrickx, 'From weavers to workers', 330–1.

[82] W. Mager, 'Protoindustrialisierung und agrarisch-heimgewerbliche Verflechtung in Ravensberg während der Frühen Neuzeit. Studien zu einer Gesellschaftsformation im Übergang', *Geschichte und Gesellschaft* 8 (1982), 435–74, here 443–4, 466–7; W. Mager, 'Gesellschaftsformation im Übergang: Agrarisch-heimgewerbliche Verflechtung und ökonomisch-Soziale Dynamik in Ravensberg während der Frühen Neuzeit und im Vormärz (16. Jahrhundert bis Mitte 19. Jahrhundert)', in *VIIIème Congrès* eds. Deyon & Mendels, here 6, 15–16, 20–1, 26; J. Schlumbohm, 'From peasant society to class society: Some aspects of family and class in a northwest German proto-industrial parish, 17th–19th centuries', *Journal of family history* 17:2 (1992), 183–99, here 187, 197; Schlumbohm, 'Besitzklassen', 334.

[83] Kisch, 'From monopoly to laissez-faire', 307–8, 316, 323, 345, 355, 372, 386.

[84] Johnson, 'De-industrialization', 5ff; Thomson, *Clermont-de-Lodève*, 3–13, 37, 91, 146–7, 233–5, 247–8, 322–31, 336–50, 353–60, 364–84, 389, 423, 427–30, 448, 459.

[85] State support for corporate groups in proto-industries was ubiquitous; for a selection of particularly explicit examples, see, for instance, in Switzerland: Pfister, 'Proto-

Not until the later eighteenth century did most European states became powerful enough to begin to dispense with support from landlords, communities, guilds and merchant companies. Even then, they did not necessarily replace them with markets, but rather created countervailing state privileges. Thus in the Habsburg lands it was the 'growth of central state power' which made possible the 'Theresian reforms' after about 1750, whereby the state gradually withdrew support for proto-industrial regulation by guilds and landlords; it did so by granting guild-free 'Fabrik' privileges to associations of merchants, and by increasing state regulations and subsidies for favoured industries.[86] The same pattern can be observed in proto-industries in Spain, France, Sweden, Italy, Bohemia, and the vast majority of German territories.[87] In more cases than not, industrial producers merely exchanged the privileges and regulations of traditional institutions for a different set of non-market institutions, operated in favour of new interest-groups, and enjoying even more effective enforcement from the political authorities.[88]

VII. Conclusion

To what extent does the Black Forest of Württemberg, and the many other industrial regions of early modern Europe, help us trace the links between social institutions and economic well-being?

The men and women of the Württemberg Black Forest worked hard,

industrialization in Switzerland', 150–2; Braun, 'Early industrialization', 296; in France: Gayot, 'Tondeurs', 116; Johnson, 'De-industrialization', 7; in Austria: Freudenberger, 'Bohemia and Moravia', 351; Freudenberger, 'Industrial momentum', 32–3; Freudenberger, 'Woolen-goods industry', 384, 386–7; Fischer, *Blauen Sensen* xv–xvi, 101–3; Cerman, 'Proto-industrial development in Austria'; in the Wupper Valley, see Kisch, 'From monopoly to laissez-faire', 398, 406; in the Vogtland in Saxony, see Wolff, 'Guildmaster', 38–9; in Ravensberg and Osnabrück in Westphalia, see Schlumbohm, 'Besitzklassen', 330–1; Mager, 'Rolle', 67.
[86] Cerman, 'Proto-industrial development in Austria'.
[87] On Spain: Thomson, 'Catalan calico- printing', 74; Torras, 'The old and the new', 99; Torras, 'From masters to *fabricants*', 7–9. On France: Johnson, 'De-industrialization', 5ff; Gayot, 'Tondeurs', 122. On Sweden: Isacson & Magnusson, *Proto-industrialization in Scandinavia*, 93; Magnusson, 'Proto-industrialization in Sweden', 210, 220–3. On Italy: Poni, 'Proto-industrial city', 16–17. On Bohemia and Moravia, where the feudal lords, as local authorities, replaced guild privileges with concessions from themselves: Klíma, 'English merchant capital', 34–5; Klíma, 'Industrial development', 86; Klíma, 'Role of rural domestic industry', 52; Myška, 'Proto-industrialization in Bohemia'. On the conflict between guild privileges and state attempts at abolishing them in Germany, which continued in most territories into the nineteenth century, see Tipton, *Regional variations*, 26–7, 30, 52–3, 59, 71, 72–6.
[88] As is shown, for example, in Tipton, *Regional variations*, 30, 59, 69, 71, which shows how ubiquitous and characteristic a feature of German industrialization in the nineteenth century were state monopolies and privileges issued to favoured interest groups.

and made the best living they could given the constraints of their society. But these constraints limited economic growth. Output levels and producer numbers stopped growing by about 1750, quality failed to improve, new techniques were rejected, new enterprises were excluded, competitors' products were not even copied, and markets were lost. Even the forty company merchants, despite their monopoly profits, achieved only modest prosperity. The hundreds of weavers lived frugally, married late, and struggled bitterly to retain some monopoly profits of their own; they did not become the entrepreneurs (or even the workers) of successful factory industries. Thousands of young men, lacking land and denied guild licenses, left for America or the swollen armies of Central Europe. Thousands of young women, unable to marry and forbidden many kinds of work, had the choice of begging, or spinning at rates the weavers set. By 1800, even proto-industry was languishing, and emigration had reached epidemic proportions; factory industrialisation was late and slow. This industry was no economic success-story.

But in early modern Europe successful economies were the exception, not the rule.[89] Württemberg was no anomaly. Although the precise institutions might vary, the underlying pattern recurred throughout Europe: in proto-industry, as in other sectors, overall economic well-being was constrained by the institutional privileges of corporate groups. Markets did not emerge in every proto-industry; they emerged in a few proto-industries in societies where they were already emerging in agriculture: in England and Flanders; in parts of Switzerland, Saxony and the Rhineland, and a few other institutional enclaves. Everywhere else, resources continued to be allocated not through markets, but according to the corporate institutional privileges of landlords, communities, guilds and merchant companies. These did not wither away under the onslaught of proto-industrialisation; they co-opted it, turning proto-industry into yet another source of monopoly profits for powerful social groups.

Corporate privileges gave their beneficiaries the incentive—and the power—to resist change. New practices which promised to increase wealth also threatened to alter its distribution. This made adjustment to change (whether opportunity or threat) very difficult. An initial opportunity was usually the source of proto-industrial growth, but few proto-industries could sustain this growth: the institutional framework in which they arose did not permit the initial distribution of its benefits to be altered without a prohibitively slow and expensive process of inter-group bargaining and state action. This institutional rigidity made it impossible for most proto-industries to adjust flexibly to changes in

---

[89] As is remarked by de Vries, *Economy*, 25–6.

the economic environment. For economic growth was caused not by proto-industry itself, but by the ability of producers—in whatever sector—to keep costs low, learn by doing, and respond to change in an uncertain world.

The crucial variable that determined whether producers could do this, and thus whether a given industry grew or stagnated, was the structure of its social institutions. In some European societies, institutions were so restrictive that proto-industry could never arise. This was quite rare: proto-industries arose almost everywhere in early modern Europe.

In other societies, no social groups obtained institutional privileges over input and product markets: costs were low because of genuine efficiencies, producers could respond flexibly to changing circumstances, and economic growth could be sustained. Sadly, this too was rare. By far the commonest pattern was for social institutions to permit proto-industry but constrain its growth, keeping some costs low by force, protecting other high-cost practices by excluding competitors, and creating a network of interlocking privileges and obligations inimical to change.

Why a 'corporate society' failed to develop in England, the Low Countries, and a few other fortunate enclaves of early modern Europe is a fundamental but still unresolved question. One way of addressing it, though, may be to look at why corporate societies *did* develop in the rest of Europe. The role of politics in this development cannot be under-estimated. Corporate privileges—whether of landlords, communities, guilds or merchant companies—could only be maintained with state support. Most of the states of early modern Europe grew much faster than the economies that sustained them, creating a mutual military menace so serious that they were willing to issue almost any institutional privileges to corporate groups, in order to obtain the resources and cooperation needed for survival. The resulting military entanglements and ruinous indebtedness kept most European states in thrall to these groups and institutions until the late eighteenth century, if not beyond. And what replaced these traditional institutions was often not markets, but new non-market institutions that continued to impose deadweight costs and distort economic activity in favour of privileged groups. The resulting costs, long borne by many European societies, are to be measured not just in economic terms—grinding poverty and foregone growth—but above all in terms of the deep resentments and bitter conflicts among social groups caused by allocating resources by institutional privilege and political force.

THE ROYAL HISTORICAL SOCIETY

REPORT OF COUNCIL, SESSION 1994-1995

THE Council of the Royal Historical Society has the honour to present the following report to the Anniversary Meeting.

1. Developments within the Society

  i. The Society's publications, with the exception of *Studies in History*, have been issued by the Cambridge University Press since January 1995. The Society has established a good working relationship with the Press and looks forward to successful co-operation with it.

  ii. The Council has agreed a new editorial structure for *Studies in History* as from 1 January 1996. The series will be brought directly under the aegis of the Publications Committee of the Society. The day-to-day running of the series will be undertaken by a small editorial board. Council wishes to place on record its gratitude to the *Studies in History* Editorial Board for its services and in particular to Professor Martin Daunton who has served as the Board's Acting Chairman since the death of Sir Geoffrey Elton.

  iii. In accordance with the decisions of the Anniversary Meeting 1994, the Society introduced the new category of Member of the Society and a new framework of subscriptions for Fellows from November 1994. To date 15 Members have been admitted to the Society.

  iv. Corresponding Fellows:
  Following the Society's Review, Council has agreed to increase the number of Corresponding Fellows from the current limit of 40. The principal criteria for election remains academic distinction, but in order to reflect more realistically interests within the Society and the growth of historical studies world-wide, numbers will be increased up to 100 over the next few years. This will allow for a much fairer geographical and chronological representation by Corresponding Fellows. Council is also pursuing ways of involving Corresponding Fellows more actively in the Society's affairs.

2. The Elton bequest

Sir Geoffrey Elton, President of the Society 1972–1976, died 4 December 1994.

Sir Geoffrey gave great service to the Society – both as President and through the *Annual Bibliography* and *Studies in History*, of both of which he was the founder. He left two most generous benefactions to the Society under the terms of his will. The first was the income from the royalties on his books and other publications, which will be used by Council to further those of the Society's activities which were close to Sir Geoffrey's heart. The second was a reversionary bequest in his Library to the Society from June 1995. After appropriate negotiations, and mindful of Sir Geoffrey's expressed wishes, Council agreed to place the bulk of the library intact (other than a few books selected to reinforce the Society's own collection) on permanent loan to the Borthwick Institute of Historical Research at the University of York. The Society wishes to record its indebtedness to Lady Elton and the Honorary Librarian for all their help in making the appropriate arrangements.

3. Issues of concern to historians

At a time of rapid change and far-reaching developments in British universities, the Society has played an increasingly active role in promoting and defending the interests of historical study in this country.

- In January 1995 a successful one-day conference was held at the Institute of Historical Research, attended by a hundred participants, to discuss the future of postgraduate studies in Britain. It is hoped to arrange a successor colloquium on some of the issues raised at the conference during the coming session.
- Fruitful exploratory discussions were held with the Officers of the Public Record Office and the British Library on issues of common interest to both bodies and to the Society.
- The President and Council made representations and gave evidence to various bodies on a range of issues during the course of the session – including the Research Assessment Exercise 1996 and the Review of Postgraduate Education.

4. Bibliographies

The Society continues to support two major bibliographies which are being prepared under its aegis.

a) The *Annual Bibliography of British and Irish History*. This bibliography was edited until 30 June 1995 by Professor Barbara English and Dr.

John Palmer of the University of Hull. Council wishes to record its gratitude to them and to their team for their services. Council also wishes to extend its thanks to Professor Ralph Griffiths (Vice-President) and the Honorary Librarian for taking overall charge of the enterprise from 1 July 1995.

b) The *British History Bibliographies* project which is being prepared under the general editorship of Dr. John Morrill (Vice-President) with its headquarters at the University of Cambridge. This major project is due to end in its present form in September 1996.

5. Other activities

a) The Society continues its close involvement with the British National Committee of the International Congress of Historical Sciences. The Committee gave subventions this session to conferences held at St. Andrews and Edinburgh. It also provided financial support for 32 scholars from Britain to attend the Quinquennial Congress at Montreal, 27 August – 3 September 1995.

b) The Society has renewed its funding for a Research Fellowship at the Institute of Historical Research, and continues to fund the Bursaries to assist holders of Overseas Research Students awards. During the session it also assisted from its Research Support Fund 28 individual research projects, provided 10 training bursaries, and made grants to the organisers of 8 colloquia and workshops.

c) The Society has continued to contribute to the Young Historian Scheme of the Historical Association, and provide prizes for outstanding A-level students.

6. Meetings of the Society

The Society held two Council meetings and paper readings outside London, at the University of Leicester and the University of Bristol; both events were well attended and were followed by receptions which enabled Council to meet members of the audience. As in previous years, the success of these meetings owed much to the excellent hospitality provided by locally-based Fellows of the Society. The Society has arranged to meet at Edinburgh, Swansea and Leeds during the 1995–96 session.

The annual one-day conference in September was held at the Institute of Historical Research, London. A two-day conference was held in Cambridge in March 1995. Arrangements are in hand to hold two further two-day conferences in London in September 1995 and March 1996.

A well-attended evening party was held for members and guests in the Upper Hall at University College London on Wednesday, 6 July 1994.

7. Prizes

(i) The Whitfield Prize for 1994 was awarded to Dr. V.A.C. Gatrell for his book *The Hanging Tree: Execution and the English People, 1770–1868* (Oxford University Press). Dr. D.M. Feldman was declared *proxime accessit* for his book *Englishmen and Jews: Social Relations and Political Culture, 1840–1914* (Yale University Press). The assessors commented on the high quality of the entries received.

(ii) The Alexander Prize for 1995 was awarded to Rachel Gibbons, BA, from the University of Reading, for her essay *'Isabeau of Bavaria, Queen of France: the creation of an historical villainess'*, which was read to the Society on 28 April 1995.

8. Publications

Transactions, Sixth Series, Volume 5; The Derby Diaries, ed. J. Vincent (Camden, Fifth Series, Volume 4); *The Austen Chamberlain Diary Letters, 1916–1937*, ed. R.C. Self (Camden, Fifth Series, Volume 5) and *Household Accounts and Disbursement Books of Robert Dudley, Earl of Leicester, 1558–1561*, ed. S. Adams (Camden, Fifth Series, Volume 6) went to press during the session and are due to be published in 1995.

The Society's *Annual Bibliography of British and Irish History, Publications of 1993*, was published by Oxford University Press.

Further volumes in the *Studies in History* series went to press during the session: Vivienne Larminie, *Wealth, Kinship and Culture: the Newdigates of Arbury* (Volume 72); Richard Stewart, *The English Ordnance Office, 1585–1615: a case study in bureaucracy* (Volume 73) and Lorna Lloyd, *Peace through Law* (Volume 74).

9. Papers read

At the ordinary meetings of the Society the following papers were read:

'Empire and Opportunity in later eighteenth-century Britain' by Professor Peter Marshall (6 July 1994: Prothero lecture).
'History through fiction: British lives in the novels of Raymond Williams', by Professor David B. Smith (14 October 1994: at the University of Leicester).
'Institutions and development in Early Modern Central Europe: Bohemia, 1650–1800', by Dr. Sheilagh Ogilvie (9 December 1994).
'The making of Angelcynn: English identity in the Early Middle Ages', by Dr. Sarah Foot (20 January 1995).

'The Soviet Political Compound, 1917–1991: Solvents and Stabilisers', by Profesor Robert Service (3 March 1994).
'Church and Chapel in Medieval England: history, literature and pictures', by Professor Nicholas Orme (26 May 1995 at the University of Bristol).

At the Anniversary meeting on 18 November 1994, the President, Professor R.R. Davies, delivered an address on 'The Peoples of Britain and Ireland, 1100–1400: II. Names, Boundaries and Regnal Solidarities'.
At the one-day conference entitled 'From Knighthood to Country Gentry, 1050–1400?' held at the Institute of Historical Research, London, on 24 September 1994, the following papers were read:

'Thegns and Knights in the Eleventh Century: where was then the gentleman?' by Mr. John Gillingham
'From Stenton to McFarlane: Models of Society in Twelfth and Thirteenth-Century England' by Professor David Crouch
'Knights, Esquires and the Formation of the English Gentry, 1200–1350' by Professor Peter Coss
'*Miles in armis strenuus*: the Knight at War' by Professor Michael Prestwich

At the two-day conference entitled 'Honour and Reputation in Early Modern England' held at Selwyn College, Cambridge, on 24 and 25 March 1995, the following papers were read:

' "To Pluck Bright Honour from the Pale-faced Moon": Gender and Honour in the Castlehaven Story' by Professor Cynthia Herrup
'Public Reputation in Country and Court: the Case of the Hoby Family' by Dr. Felicity Heal
'Honour in Life, Death and in the Memory: Funeral Monuments in Early Modern England' by Dr. Nigel Llewellyn
'The Construction of Honour, Reputation and Status in Late Seventeenth and Early Eighteenth-Century England' by Mr. Faramerz Dabhoiwala
'Male Honour, Social Control and Wife Beating in Late Stuart England' by Ms Elizabeth Foyster
'Women and the Popular Culture of Dishonour in Early Seventeenth-Century England' by Dr. Laura Gowing
'Boundaries of Female Honour: Community, Hierarchy and Reputation in Early Modern England' by Dr. Garthine Walker
'Purging Infected Blood: Anxiety for the Lineal Family in Jacobean Drama' by Professor Lisa Jardine.

10. Finance

The Society's finances returned to surplus this year, following two years of slight deficit. This was as forecast and the outcome of our decision to delay raising subscription rates pending completion of the Review of the Society's activities and the transfer of the bulk of our publishing activities to Cambridge University Press. These have now been completed. A subscription for Fellows of £28 was agreed at the 1994 Anniversary meeting and the new category of Member was introduced, with a subscription of £10 per annum. We are also happy to report an increase in our investment income. We are particularly appreciative of the bequest to the Society by Sir Geoffrey Elton of the income from royalties on his books.

Council records with gratitude the benefactions made to the Society by:

Mr. L.C. Alexander
The Reverend David Berry
Professor Andrew Browning
Professor C.D. Chandaman
Professor G. Donaldson
Professor Sir Geoffrey Elton
Mrs. W.M. Frampton
Mr. A.E.J. Hollaender
Mr. E.L.C. Mullins
Sir George Prothero
Professor T.F. Reddaway
Miss E.M. Robinson
Professor A.S. Whitfield

11. Membership

Council records with regret the deaths of 28 Fellows and 1 Associate. They included Honorary Vice-President and ex-President, Professor Sir Geoffrey Elton, and among Fellows—Dr. A.D. Macintyre and Dr. H. Wallis.

The resignations of 13 Fellows and 2 Associates were received. 65 Fellows, 15 Members and 1 Corresponding Fellow were elected. 59 Fellows transferred to the category of Retired Fellow. The membership of the Society on 30 June 1995 numbered 2163 (including 36 Life, 346 Retired, 39 Corresponding Fellows, and 136 Associates). The Society exchanged publications with 15 Societies, British and foreign.

12. Officers and Council

At the Anniversary Meeting on 18 November 1994, Dr. D.S. Eastwood was elected to succeed Dr. J.A. Ramsden as Literary Director. The remaining Officers of the Society were re-elected. The Vice-Presidents retiring under By-law XVII were Professor J. Gooch and Professor C.J. Holdsworth. Professor P. Collinson and Dr. R.D. McKitterick were elected to replace them. The members of Council retiring under By-law XX were Professor E.P. Hennock, Dr. R.D. McKitterick, Dr. R.C. Mettam and Professor A.G.R. Smith. Following a ballot of Fellows, Professor R.C. Bridges, Dr. P.J. Corfield, Professor J.L. Nelson and Dr. P.A. Stafford were elected in their place.

Council was delighted to note that Professor R.R. Davies, President, was awarded the C.B.E. in the New Year Honours List.

Professor P.J. Marshall has accepted Council's invitation to succeed Professor R.R. Davies as President of the Society from 1 December 1996.

Messrs. Davies Watson were appointed auditors for the year 1994–1995 under By-law XXXIX.

13. Representatives of the Society

The representation of the Society upon various bodies was as follows:
Mr. M. Roper, Professor P.H. Sawyer and Mr. C.P. Wormald on the Joint Committee of the Society and the British Academy established to prepare an edition of Anglo-Saxon charters;
Professor H.R. Loyn on a committee to promote the publication of photographic records of the more significant collections of British Coins;
Professor G.H. Martin on the Council of the British Records Association;
Emeritus Professor M.R.D. Foot on the Committee to advise the publishers of *The Annual Register*;
Dr. G.W. Bernard on the History at the Universities Defence Group;
Professor C.J. Holdsworth on the Court of the University of Exeter;
Professor A.G. Watson on the Anthony Panizzi Foundation;
Professor M.C. Cross on the Council of the British Association for Local History; and on the British Sub-Commission of the Commission International d'Histoire Ecclesiastique Comparée;
Professor J. Sayers on the National Council on Archives;
Miss V. Cromwell on the Advisory Board of the Computers in Teaching Initiative Centre for History; and on the Advisory Committee of the TLTP History Courseware Consortium;
Dr. A.M.S. Prochaska on the Advisory Council of the reviewing committee on the Export of Works of Art;
Professor R.A. Griffiths on the Court of Governors of the University of Wales Swansea;
Professor A.L. Brown on the University of Stirling Conference;
Professor W. Davies on the Court of the University of Birmingham;
Dr. R.D. McKitterick on a committee to regulate British co-operation in the preparation of a new repertory of medieval sources to replace Potthast's *Bibliotheca Historica Medii Aevi*; and

Professor P.K. O'Brien on the ESRC Working Group on *Quality and Data Collection.*

Council received reports from its representatives.

20 October 1995

THE ROYAL HISTORICAL SOCIETY

BALANCE SHEET AS AT 30TH JUNE 1995

	Note	£	1995 £	£	1994 £
FIXED ASSETS					
Tangible assets	2		1,628		1,503
Investments	3		1,753,227		1,649,119
			1,754,855		1,650,622
CURRENT ASSETS					
Stocks	1(c)	6,619		1,483	
Debtors	4	12,626		14,731	
Cash at bank and in hand	5	16,377		16,530	
		35,622		32,744	
LESS: CREDITORS					
Amount falling due within one year	6	37,164		88,190	
NET CURRENT (LIABILITIES)			(1,542)		(55,446)
NET TOTAL ASSETS			1,753,313		1,595,176
REPRESENTED BY:					
General Fund			1,654,586		1,501,906
Miss E.M. Robinson Bequest			66,107		60,558
A.S. Whitfield Prize Fund			34,790		31,935
Studies in History			(2,170)		777
			1,753,313		1,595,176

THE ROYAL HISTORICAL SOCIETY

Income and Expenditure Account for the Year Ended 30th June 1995

GENERAL FUND

	Note	1995 £	1995 £	1994 £	1994 £
INCOME					
Subscriptions	7		57,942		59,385
Investment Income			80,698		64,640
Royalties and reproduction fees			7,160		5,466
Donations and sundry income			2,594		1,084
G.R. Elton Bequest			4,718		—
Sales of library volumes			20,575		—
			173,687		130,575
EXPENDITURE					
SECRETARIAL AND ADMINISTRATIVE					
Salaries, pensions and social security		25,213		24,012	
Computer consumables, printing and stationery		5,901		5,550	
Postage and telephone		1,906		1,968	
Bank charges		2,006		1,968	
Audit and accountancy		2,681		3,290	
Insurance		773		601	
Meetings and travel		13,148		11,324	
Conference net costs		1,910		4,839	
Repairs and renewals		320		577	
Depreciation	1(b)	1,389		1,121	
			55,247		55,250
PUBLICATIONS					
Publishing costs	8(a)	9,448		(3,863)	
Provision for publications in progress	8(b)	20,350		72,450	
Other publication costs	8(c)	11,411		5,826	
			41,209		74,413
LIBRARY AND ARCHIVES	1(d)				
Purchase of books and publications		2,363		1,128	
Binding		5,822		2,553	
			8,185		3,681
			104,641		133,344
OTHER CHARGES					
Centenary fellowship		5,775		5,650	
Alexander prize		340		499	
Prothero lecture		250		254	
Grants		900		175	
Research support grants		13,605		12,015	
Donations and sundry expenses		263		653	
A-level prizes		900		900	
Young Historian Scheme		2,000		1,994	
British Bibliographies		—		2,000	
			24,033		24,140
			128,674		157,484
Surplus/(deficit) for the year			45,013		(26,909)
Realised surplus on sale of investments			76,679		108,268
Transfer to revaluation reserve			30,988		(90,268)
			152,680		(8,909)
Balance brought forward at 1.7.94			1,501,906		1,510,815
Balance carried forward at 30.6.95			1,654,586		1,501,906

THE ROYAL HISTORICAL SOCIETY

Income and Expenditure Account for the Year Ended 30th June 1995

SPECIAL FUNDS

	1995 £	£	1994 £	£
MISS E.M. ROBINSON BEQUEST				
INCOME				
Investment income		2,743		2,279
EXPENDITURE				
Grant to Dulwich Picture Gallery	2,000		2,000	
Other expenses	—		149	
		(2,000)		(2,149)
Surplus for the year		743		130
Realised surplus on disposal of investments		6,111		24,762
Transfer from revaluation reserve		(1,305)		(24,586)
		5,549		306
Balance brought forward at 1.7.94		60,558		60,252
Balance carried forward at 30.6.95		66,107		60,558
A.S. WHITFIELD PRIZE FUND				
INCOME				
Investment income		1,383		1,173
EXPENDITURE				
Prize awarded	1,000		1,000	
Other expenses	20		77	
		1,020		1,077
Surplus for the year		363		96
Realised surplus on disposal of investments		3,634		—
Transfer from revaluation reserve		(1,142)		935
		2,855		1,031
Balance brought forward at 1.7.94		31,935		30,904
Balance carried forward at 30.6.95		34,790		31,935
STUDIES IN HISTORY				
INCOME				
Royalties		1,125		2,080
Investment income		426		429
		1,551		2,509
EXPENDITURE				
Honorarium	3,500		3,500	
Editor's expenses	960		981	
Ex gratia royalties and sundry expenses	38		136	
		(4,498)		(4,617)
(Deficit) for the year		(2,947)		(2,108)
Balance brought forward		777		2,885
Balance carried forward		(2,170)		777

THE ROYAL HISTORICAL SOCIETY

NOTES TO THE ACCOUNTS FOR THE YEAR ENDED 30TH JUNE 1995

1. ACCOUNTING POLICIES
    (a) *Basis of accounting*
        The accounts have been prepared under the historical cost convention as modified by the revaluation of quoted investments to market value.
    (b) *Depreciation*
        Depreciation is calculated by reference to the cost of fixed assets using a straight line basis at rates considered appropriate having regard to the expected lives of the fixed assets.
        The annual rates of depreciation in use are:
        Furniture and equipment   10%
        Computer equipment   25%
        Prior to 1st July 1987 the full cost of fixed assets was written off to General Fund in the year of purchase.
    (c) *Stocks*
        Stock is valued at the lower of cost and net realisable value.
    (d) *Library and archives*
        The cost of additions to the library and archives is written off in the year of purchase.

2. TANGIBLE FIXED ASSETS

	Computer Equipment	Furniture and Equipment	Total
	£	£	£
Cost			
At 1st July 1994	9,254	620	9,874
Additions during year	961	553	1,514
At 30th June 1995	10,215	1,173	11,388
Depreciation			
At 1st July 1994	7,937	434	8,371
Charge for the year	1,271	118	1,389
At 30th June 1995	9,208	552	9,760
Net book value			
At 30th June 1995	1,007	621	1,628
At 30th June 1994	1,317	186	1,503

Prior to 1st July 1987 the cost of furniture and equipment was written off in the year of purchase. Items acquired before that date are not reflected in the above figures.

3. INVESTMENTS

	1995	1994
	£	£
Quoted Securities, at cost	1,027,035	950,614
Surplus on revaluation	661,358	632,817
Quoted Securities at market value	1,688,393	1,583,431
Money invested at call	64,834	65,688
	1,753,227	1,649,119

Quoted Investments are stated at market value in the Balance Sheet as at 30th June 1995.
The surplus arising on re-valuation plus profits (less losses) realised on disposals of investments is credited to Income and Expenditure Account in the case of investments held on General Fund and to the relevant fund accounts where investments are held for specific funds.
Movements in quoted investments during year were:

	£
Cost at beginning of year	950,614
Additions during year	288,816
Disposals during year	(212,395)
Cost at end of year	1,027,035

262

ROYAL HISTORICAL SOCIETY
THE DAVID BERRY ESSAY TRUST

Balance Sheet as at 30th June 1995

	1995 £	£	1994 £	£
Fixed Assets				
1117.63 units in the Charities Official Investment Fund (Market Value £7,483:1994 £7,298)		1,530		1,530
Current Assets				
Bank Deposit Account	10,500		9,957	
Less: Creditors				
Amounts falling due within one year	4,127		4,076	
Net Current Assets		6,374		5,881
Total Assets Less Liabilities		7,904		7,411
Represented by:				
Capital Fund		1,000		1,000
Accumulated Income Account		6,904		6,411
		7,904		7,411

Income and Expenditure Account for the Year Ended 30th June 1995

	1995 £	£	1994 £	£
Income				
Dividends		263		338
Bank Interest Receivable		280		215
		543		553
Expenditure				
Adjudicator's Fee		50		—
Excess of income over expenditure for the year . .		493		553
Balance brought forward		6,411		5,858
Balance carried forward		6,904		6,411

265

1. ACCOUNTING POLICIES
Basis of accounting. The accounts have been prepared under the historical cost convention.

The late David Berry, by his Will dated 23rd April 1926, left £1,000 to provide in every three years a gold medal and prize money for the best essay on the Earl of Bothwell or, at the discretion of the Trustees, on Scottish History of the James Stuarts I to VI, in memory of his father the late Rev. David Berry.

The Trust is regulated by a scheme sanctioned by the Chancery Division of the High Court of Justice dated 23rd January 1930, and made in action 1927 A 1233 David Anderson Berry deceased, Hunter and Another v Robertson and Another and since modified by an order of the Charity Commissioners made on 11 January 1978 removing the necessity to provide a medal.

The Royal Historical Society is now the Trustee. The investment consists of 1117.63 Charities Official Investment Fund Income units. The Trustee will in every second year of the three year period advertise inviting essays.

REPORT OF THE AUDITORS TO THE TRUSTEES OF THE DAVID BERRY ESSAY TRUST

We have audited the accounts on page 15 which have been prepared under the historical cost convention and the accounting policies set out on page 16.

Respective responsibilities of the Council and Auditors
The Trustees are required to prepare accounts for each financial year which give a true and fair view of the state of affairs of the Trust and of the profit or loss for that period.

In preparing those accounts, the Trustees are required to:
—select suitable accounting policies and then apply them consistently;
—make judgements and estimates that are reasonable and prudent;
—prepare the accounts on the going concern basis unless it is inappropriate to presume that the Trust will continue in business.

The Trustees are responsible for keeping proper accounting records which disclose with reasonable accuracy any time the financial position of the Trust. They are also responsible for safeguarding the assets of the Trust and hence for taking reasonable steps for the prevention and detection of fraud and other irregularities.

As described above the Trustees are responsible for the preparation of accounts. It is our responsibility to form an independent opinion, based on our audit, on those accounts and to report our opinion to you.

Basis of opinion
We conducted our audit in accordance with Auditing Standards issued by the Auditing Practices Board. An audit includes examination, on a test basis, of evidence relevant to the amounts and disclosures in the accounts. It also includes an assessment of the significant estimates and judgements made by the Trustees in the preparation of the accounts, and of whether the accounting policies are appropriate to the Trust's circumstances, consistently applied and adequately disclosed.

We planned and performed our audit so as to obtain all the information and explanations which we consider necessary in order to provide us with sufficient evidence to give reasonable assurance that the accounts are free from material misstatement, whether caused by fraud or other irregularity or error. In forming our opinion we also evaluated the overall adequacy of the presentation of information in the accounts.

Opinion
In our opinion the accounts give a true and fair view of the state of the Trust's affairs as at 30th June 1995 and of its surplus for the year then ended.

118 SOUTH STREET, DORKING

DAVIES WATSON & CO
Chartered Accountants
Registered Auditors

266

ALEXANDER PRIZE

The Alexander Prize was established in 1897 by L.C. Alexander, F.R.Hist.S. The prize is warded annually for an essay on a historical subject, which has been previously approved by the Literary Director. The essay must be a genuine work of original research, not hitherto published, and not previously awarded any other prize. It must not exceed 8,000 words, including footnotes, and must be sent in by 1 November. Further details may be obtained from the Executive Secretary. Candidates must *either* be under the age of 35 *or* be registered for a higher degree *or* have been registered for a higher degree within the last three years. The winner of the prize is awarded £250.

1995 PRIZE WINNER

Rachel Gibbons, BA
'Isabeau of Bavaria, Queen of France:
the creation of an historical villainess'

DAVID BERRY PRIZE

The David Berry Prize was established in 1929 by David Anderson-Berry in memory of his father, the Reverend David Berry. The prize is awarded every three years for an essay on Scottish history, within the reigns of James I to James VI inclusive. The subject of each essay must be submitted in advance and approved by the Council of The Royal Historical Society. The essay must be a genuine work of research based on original material. The essay should be between 6,000 and 10,000 words excluding footnotes and appendices. Further details may be obtained from the Executive Secretary.

1994 PRIZE

No award was made this year.

WHITFIELD PRIZE

The Whitfield Prize was established by Council in 1976 out of the bequest of the late Professor Archibald Stenton Whitfield. The prize is currently awarded to the best work on a subject of British history published in the United Kingdom during the calendar year. It must be the first solely authored history book published by the candidate and an original and scholarly work of research. Authors or publishers should send three copies (non-returnable) of a book eligible for the competition to the Executive Secretary before the end of the year in which the book is published. The award will be made by Council and announced at the Society's annual reception in the following July. The current value of the prize is £1,000.

1994 PRIZE WINNER

V.A.C. Gatrell, BA, MA, PhD
'The Hanging Tree:
Execution and the English people, 1770–1868'

Between 1770 and 1830, well over 7,000 people were publicly hanged in England, most choking to death painfully and lengthily. Until the abolition of public execution in 1868, this spectacle shaped attitudes to 'justice', death, and suffering at all social levels – among watching crowds, among polite witnesses and newspaper readers, and among the judges, home secretary, and king who decided who should hang and who should be reprieved. The justice delivered on the gallows and what people felt about it are the subjects of this book. Drawing on letters, diaries, ballads, broadsides, and images, as well as on the condemneds' poignant petitions for mercy, *The hanging tree* demonstrates that the long retreat from public hanging owed less to the growth of a humane sensibility than it did to new methods of punishment and law-enforcement, and to polite classes' deepening squeamishness and fear of the scaffold crowd.

269

STANDING COMMITTEES 1995

Finance Committee

PROFESSOR O. ANDERSON
PROFESSOR H.T. DICKINSON
P.J.C. FIRTH, MA
PROFESSOR R.A. GRIFFITHS
DR. P. MATHIAS, CBE, MA, DLitt, FBA
DR. J.R. STUDD
And the Officers

Publications Committee

PROFESSOR J.M. BLACK
PROFESSOR P.R. COSS
PROFESSOR C.R. ELRINGTON, MA, FSA
PROFESSOR H.C.G. MATTHEW
DR. R.D. MCKITTERICK
DR. J.S. MORRILL
PROFESSOR P.A. STAFFORD
And the Officers

Research Support Committee

MISS V. CROMWELL (Chairman)
PROFESSOR K. BURK
PROFESSOR P.A. CLARK
PROFESSOR P.J. CORFIELD
PROFESSOR J. GOOCH
DR. A.M.S. PROCHASKA
And the Officers

Membership Committee

PROFESSOR O. ANDERSON
DR. G.W. BERNARD
PROFESSOR R.C. BRIDGES
PROFESSOR L. JORDANOVA
PROFESSOR J.L. NELSON
PROFESSOR D.M. PALLISER
And the Officers

General Purposes Committee

PROFESSOR P. COLLINSON
PROFESSOR A.J. FLETCHER
DR. F. HEAL
PROFESSOR F. O'GORMAN
And the Officers

Studies in History Editorial Board

PROFESSOR M.J. DAUNTON, PhD
PROFESSOR R.J. EVANS, MA, DPhil
PROFESSOR J. GOOCH
PROFESSOR M.C.E. JONES

Dr. R.D. McKitterick
Professor A.N. Porter, MA, PhD
Professor P. M. Thane
Mrs C. Linehan